Fundamentals of

SOCIAL WORK RESEARCH

To Sandy, Yael, and Meir
– Ray Engel

To Beth and Julia
– Russ Schutt

Fundamentals of

SOCIAL WORK RESEARCH

Rafael J. Engel
University of Pittsburgh

Russell K. Schutt
University of Massachusetts, Boston

Los Angeles | London | New Delhi
Singapore | Washington DC

For information:

SAGE Publications, Inc.
2455 Teller Road
Thousand Oaks, California 91320
E-mail: order@sagepub.com

SAGE Publications Ltd.
1 Oliver's Yard
55 City Road
London EC1Y 1SP
United Kingdom

SAGE Publications India Pvt. Ltd.
B 1/I 1 Mohan Cooperative Industrial Area
Mathura Road, New Delhi 110 044
India

SAGE Publications Asia-Pacific Pte. Ltd.
33 Pekin Street #02-01
Far East Square
Singapore 048763

Printed in the United States of America

Library of Congress Cataloging-in-Publication Data

Engel, Rafael J.
Fundamentals of social work research/Rafael J. Engel, Russell K. Schutt.
    p. cm.
Rev. ed. of: The practice of research in social work. 2nd ed. ©2009.
Includes bibliographical references and index.
ISBN 978-1-4129-5416-7 (pbk.)

  1. Social service—Research. I. Schutt, Russell K. II. Engel, Rafael J. Practice of research in social work.
III. Title.

HV11.E57 2010
361.3072—dc22   2009015331

This book is printed on acid-free paper.

09 10 11 12 13 10 9 8 7 6 5 4 3 2 1

Acquisitions Editor:	Jerry Westby
Associate Editor:	Leah Mori
Editorial Assistant:	Eve Oettinger
Production Editor:	Astrid Virding
Copy Editor:	Jovey Stewart
Typesetter:	C&M Digitals (P) Ltd.
Proofreader:	Scott Oney
Indexer:	William Ragsdale
Cover Designer:	Gail Buschman
Marketing Manager:	Stephanie Adams

Brief Contents

Preface   xiii

Acknowledgments   xv

1. Science, Society, and Social Work Research   1
2. The Process and Problems of Social Work Research   23
3. Conceptualization and Measurement   50
4. Sampling   81
5. Group Experimental Designs   109
6. Single-Subject Design   139
7. Survey Research   176
8. Qualitative Methods: Observing, Participating, Listening   212
9. Qualitative Data Analysis   240
10. Evaluation Research   264
11. Quantitative Data Analysis   287
12. Reporting Research   322

> **Web Site:**

Reviewing Inferential Statistics

http://www.sagepub.com/fswrstudy/pdf/Reviewing_Inferential_ Statistics.pdf

Appendix A: Finding Information and Conducting Literature Reviews   340

Appendix B: Questions to Ask About a Research Article   353

Appendix C: How to Read a Research Article   356

References   363

Glossary/Index   375

About the Authors   396

Detailed Contents

Preface   xiii

Acknowledgments   xv

1. Science, Society, and Social Work Research   1

Reasoning About the Social World   2
Overgeneralization   3
Selective or Inaccurate Observation   3
Illogical Reasoning   4
Resistance to Change   5
Adherence to Authority   5
The Scientific Approach Is Different   6
Why Research Is Important for Social Work   6
Evidence-Based Practice and Social Work Research   7
Social Work Research in Practice   8
Descriptive Research: Who Are the Homeless?   9
Exploratory Research: What Is It Like to Live in a Homeless Shelter?   9
Explanatory Research: Why Do People Become Homeless?   10
Evaluation Research: What Services Help the Homeless?   11
Quantitative and Qualitative Methods   12

Strengths and Limitations of Social Work Research   13
The Validity of Research Findings   14
Measurement Validity   15
Generalizability   15
Causal Validity   17
Social Work Research in a Diverse Society   18
Conclusion   20
Key Terms   20
Highlights   21
Discussion Questions   21
Critiquing Research   21
Making Research Ethical   22
Developing a Research Proposal   22
Web Exercises   22

2. The Process and Problems of Social Work Research   23

Developing Social Work Research Questions   24
Examining Research Literature   25
Finding Literature for Evidence-Based Practice   26
Campbell Collaboration   26
Government-Supported Resources   27
Considering Social Diversity   27
Theory and Social Work Research   28

Alternative Research Strategies   30
  Deductive Research   31
  Inductive Research   34
  Descriptive Research   35
  Research Paradigms   35
The Time Element   36
  Cross-Sectional Designs   36
  Longitudinal Designs   36
    Trend Studies   37
    Panel Studies   38
    Cohort Studies   38
Guidelines for Social Work
  Research   39
  Scientific Guidelines   39
  Ethical Guidelines   40
  Honesty and Openness   41
  The Uses of Science   41
  Research on People   42
Conclusion   45
Key Terms   46
Highlights   46
Discussion Questions   47
Critiquing Research   47
Making Research Ethical   48
Developing a Research
  Proposal   48
Web Exercises   49

3. **Conceptualization and
Measurement**   50
Defining Concepts   51
  Concepts and Variables   52
  Operationalization   53
    Scales   55
    Treatment as a Variable   56
    Combining Measurement
      Operations   58
Characteristics of Variables   58
  *Nominal Level of
    Measurement*   59

*Ordinal Level of
  Measurement*   60
*Interval Level of
  Measurement*   61
*Ratio Level of
  Measurement*   64
The Case of Dichotomies   64
Mathematical Comparisons   64
Measurement Error   65
Assessing Measurement
  Accuracy   67
  Measurement Reliability   67
    Test-Retest Reliability   67
    Internal Consistency   68
    Alternate-Forms
      Reliability   68
    Interrater Reliability   69
    Intrarater Reliability   69
  Measurement Validity   69
    Face Validity   69
    Content Validity   69
    Criterion Validity   70
    Construct Validity   70
  *Reliability and Validity of Existing
    Measures*   71
Using Scales to Describe a Clinical
  Status   72
Measurement in a Diverse
  Society   74
Measurement Implications for
  Evidence-Based Practice   75
Conclusion   76
Key Terms   77
Highlights   77
Discussion Questions   78
Critiquing Research   79
Making Research Ethical   79
Developing a
  Research Proposal   79
Web Exercises   80

4. **Sampling** 81

   Why Sample? 81

   Preparing to Sample 82

     Evaluate Generalizability 84

     Assess the Homogeneity of the
       Population 85

   Sampling Methods 86

     Probability Sampling
       Methods 87

       Simple Random
         Sampling 89

       Systematic Random
         Sampling 89

       Stratified Random
         Sampling 91

       Cluster Sampling 93

     Nonprobability Sampling
       Methods 93

       Availability Sampling 94

       Quota Sampling 94

       Purposive Sampling 96

       Snowball Sampling 96

   The Sampling Distribution 97

   Unit of Analysis 99

   Enhancing Participation of Diverse
     Populations 101

   Implications for Evidence-Based
     Practice 103

   Conclusion 104

   Key Terms 104

   Highlights 105

   Discussion Questions 106

   Critiquing Research 107

   Making Research Ethical 107

   Developing a
     Research Proposal 107

   Web Exercises 108

5. **Group Experimental Designs** 109

   Causal Explanation 110

     Association 111

     Time Order 112

     Nonspuriousness 112

     Mechanism 112

     Context 113

   True Experimental Designs 113

     Types of True Experimental
       Designs 117

     "Difficulties" in True Experiments
       in Agency-Based Research 120

   Quasi-experimental
     Designs 121

     Nonequivalent Control Group
       Designs 121

     Time Series Designs 122

   Designs to Monitor
     Programs 123

     Types of Nonexperimental
       Designs 123

   Threats to the Validity of
     Group Designs 125

     Threats to Internal Validity 125

       Noncomparable Groups 126

       Endogenous Change 127

       External Events 127

       Contamination 128

       Treatment
         Misidentification 128

     Generalizability 129

       Sample Generalizability 129

       External Validity 129

       Reactivity 130

   Implications for Evidence-Based
     Practice 130

   Diversity, Group Design, and
     Evidence-Based Practice 131

   Ethical Issues Unique to
     Experimental Research 132

     Deception 133

     Selective Distribution
       of Benefits 133

Conclusion   134
Key Terms   135
Highlights   135
Discussion Questions   136
Critiquing Research   137
Making Research Ethical   137
Developing a Research
   Proposal   138
Web Exercises   138

6. Single-Subject Design   139
Features of Single-Subject
   Design   140
   Repeated Measurement   141
   Baseline Phase   141
     Internal Validity   143
   Treatment Phase   146
   Graphing   146
Measuring the Targets of
   Intervention   146
Analyzing and Interpreting
   Results   148
   Interpreting Visual
     Patterns   152
Types of Single-Subject
   Designs   158
   Basic Design (A-B)   158
   Withdrawal Designs   159
     A-B-A Design   161
     A-B-A-B Design   161
   Multiple Baseline Designs   161
   Multiple Treatment Designs   164
   Monitoring Designs   167
Implications for Evidence-Based
   Practice   167
Single-Subject Design in a Diverse
   Society   170
Ethical Issues in Single-Subject
   Design   170
Conclusion   172
Key Terms   172

Highlights   172
Discussion Questions   173
Critiquing Research   174
Making Research Ethical   174
Developing a
   Research Proposal   174
Web Exercises   175

7. Survey Research   176
Why Is Survey Research So
   Popular?   177
Errors in Survey Research   178
Questionnaire Design   180
   Maintain Consistent Focus   180
   Build on Existing
     Instruments   180
   Order the Questions   181
Writing Questions   181
   Write Clear Questions   181
     Avoid Confusing
       Phrasing   182
     Avoid Vagueness   182
     Provide a Frame
       of Reference   182
     Avoid Vague Words   183
     Avoid Negative Words and
       Double Negatives   183
     Avoid Double-Barreled
       Questions   183
     Avoid Jargon   183
     Reduce the Risk of Bias   184
     Memory Questions   184
   Closed-Ended and Open-Ended
     Questions   185
   Closed-Ended Questions and
     Response Categories   186
     Avoid Making Agreement
       Agreeable   186
     Social Desirability   187
     Minimize Fence-Sitting and
       Floating   187

Filter Questions   187
Utilize Likert-Type Response
    Categories   188
Matrix Questions   188
Scales   189
Sensitive Questions   189
Pretest!   190
Survey Design Alternatives   191
Mail Surveys   192
Group-Administered
    Surveys   194
Telephone Surveys   195
    Maximizing Response to Phone
        Surveys   195
In-Person Interviews   197
    Maximizing Response to
        Interviews   198
Web Surveys   198
Mixed-Mode Surveys   199
A Comparison of
    Survey Designs   199
Secondary Data   201
Survey Research Design in a Diverse
    Society   203
Translating Instruments   204
Interviewer-Respondent
    Characteristics   205
Implications for Evidence-Based
    Practice   205
Ethical Issues in
    Survey Research   206
Conclusion   207
Key Terms   208
Highlights   208
Discussion Questions   209
Critiquing Research   210
Making Research Ethical   210
Developing a Research
    Proposal   210
Web Exercises   211

8. **Qualitative Methods: Observing,**
    Participating, Listening   212
What Are Qualitative
    Methods?   213
Case Study: Making
    Gray Gold   214
Participant Observation   216
Choosing a Role   216
    Complete Observation   216
    Participation and
        Observation   218
    Covert Participation   219
Entering the Field   219
Developing and Maintaining
    Relationships   220
Sampling People
    and Events   221
Taking Notes   222
Managing the Personal
    Dimensions   224
Systematic Observation   226
Intensive Interviewing   226
Establishing and Maintaining a
    Partnership   227
Asking Questions and Recording
    Answers   227
Focus Groups   229
Photovoice   230
Qualitative Research in a Diverse
    Society   231
Implications for Evidence-Based
    Practice   232
Ethical Issues in Qualitative
    Research   233
Conclusion   235
Key Terms   236
Highlights   236
Discussion Questions   237
Critiquing Research   237
Making Research Ethical   238

Developing a
Research Proposal   238
Web Exercises   239

9. **Qualitative Data Analysis**   240
Features of Qualitative Data
Analysis   241
*Qualitative Data Analysis
as an Art*   242
*Qualitative Compared With
Quantitative Data Analysis*   243
Techniques of Qualitative Data
Analysis   244
Documentation   245
*Conceptualization, Coding, and
Categorizing*   245
*Examining Relationships and
Displaying Data*   246
Authenticating Conclusions   247
Reflexivity   249
Alternatives in Qualitative Data
Analysis   250
Ethnography   250
*Qualitative Comparative
Analysis*   251
Narrative Analysis   253
Grounded Theory   254
Computer-Assisted Qualitative Data
Analysis   254
Content Analysis   257
Ethics in Qualitative Data
Analysis   259
Conclusion   260
Key Terms   261
Highlights   261
Discussion Questions   261
Critiquing Research   262
Making Research Ethical   262
Developing a Research Proposal   262
Web Exercises   263

10. **Evaluation Research**   264
Evaluation Basics   265
Describing the Program: The Logic
Model   266
Questions for Evaluation
Research   270
Needs Assessment   270
Process Evaluation   271
Outcome Evaluation   272
Efficiency Analysis   273
Design Considerations   274
*Black Box or
Program Theory?*   274
*Researcher or Stakeholder
Orientation?*   275
*Quantitative or Qualitative
Methods?*   277
Simple or Complex Outcomes?   278
Implications for Evidence-Based
Practice   279
C2-SPECTR   280
Evaluation Research in a Diverse
Society   281
Ethical Considerations   282
Conclusion   283
Key Terms   284
Highlights   285
Discussion Questions   285
Critiquing Research   286
Making Research Ethical   286
Developing a Research
Proposal   286
Web Exercises   286

11. **Quantitative Data Analysis**   287
Preparing Data for Analysis   288
Displaying Univariate
Distributions   292
Graphs   292
Frequency Distributions   294

Summarizing Univariate
  Distributions   299
  Measures of
    Central Tendency   299
    Mode   299
    Median   300
    Mean   300
    Median or Mean?   301
  Measures of Variation   303
    Range   304
    Interquartile Range   305
    Variance   305
    Standard Deviation   305
Describing Relations Among
  Variables   307
  Graphing Association   309
  Describing Association   310
  Evaluating Association   311
Implications for Evidence-Based
  Practice   313
  Statistical Significance   313
  Choosing a Statistical Test   316
Ethical Issues: Avoiding Misleading
  Findings   316
Conclusion   318
Key Terms   319
Highlights   319
Discussion Questions   320

Critiquing Research   320
Making Research Ethical   320
Developing a Research
  Proposal   321
Web Exercises   321

12. **Reporting Research**   322
Beginning With a Research
  Proposal   323
Reporting Results   326
  Writing Can Be Frustrating!   326
  Writing for Journals   327
  Applied Research Reports   328
Empirically Summarizing Reports:
  Meta-Analysis   330
Implications for Evidence-Based
  Practice   333
Social Work Research in a Diverse
  Society   334
Ethical Considerations   335
Conclusion   336
Key Terms   337
Highlights   337
Discussion Questions   338
Critiquing Research   338
Making Research Ethical   338
Developing a Research Proposal   339
Web Exercises   339

WEB EXERCISES

Reviewing Inferential Statistics
http://www.sagepub.com/fswrstudy Reviewing_Inferential_Statistics.pdf

Appendix A: Finding Information and Conducting Literature Reviews   **340**

Appendix B: Questions to Ask About a Research Article   **353**

Appendix C: How to Read a Research Article   **356**

References   **363**

Glossary/Index   **375**

About the Authors   **396**

Preface

During the last 15 years, there has been tremendous progress by social work professionals and educators in building the profession's research infrastructure. There are now national research centers, federal and foundation research initiatives, institutional support, and dissemination efforts by organizations such as the Council on Social Work Education and the Society for Social Work Research. These accomplishments provide new opportunities for our graduates and make their research training even more critical.

The purpose of this book is to introduce students to the study of research in social work. Throughout this book, we demonstrate how research contributes both to understanding the causes and nature of social conditions and to testing effective interventions to ameliorate these conditions. We use different examples such as domestic violence, poverty, child welfare, and aging that cut across the domains of social work practice.

By the end of this book, students should have the skills necessary to critically evaluate the research articles they read in their other courses. Our students will learn that it is not enough that findings be accepted simply because they appear in print; rather, they must ask many questions before concluding that research-based conclusions are appropriate. What did the researchers set out to investigate? How were people selected for study? What information was collected, and how was it analyzed? Can the findings be applied to populations not part of the study? To different settings? Communities? Throughout this book, students will learn what questions to ask when critiquing a research study and how to evaluate the answers.

Another goal of this book is to prepare students to actually evaluate social work practice—their own and that of others. The various examples demonstrate the methods used by social work researchers to discover the efficacy of interventions, to identify needs, and to test the impact of social policies.

ORGANIZATION OF THE BOOK

The organization of the book reflects our belief in making research methods interesting and relevant by connecting research to social work practice; therefore, each chapter includes a section linking the content to evidence-based practice. We believe that content on ethics and diversity should be infused throughout the book, and there are sections in virtually every chapter dealing with these areas.

The first two chapters introduce the why and how of research in general. Chapter 1 shows how research has helped us understand homelessness and its consequences. The chapter introduces "evidence-based practice" to the student and the importance of understanding research in our diverse society. Chapter 2 illustrates the basic steps in formulating researchable questions. Chapter 3 demonstrates how broad concepts such as substance abuse and poverty are translated into measures. Chapter 4 reviews principles of sampling and lessons about sampling quality.

Chapters 5, 6, 7, and 8 present the four most important methods of data collection: experiments, single-subject design, surveys, and qualitative methods (including participant observation, intensive interviews, and focus groups). The substantive studies in these chapters show how social work researchers have used these methods to improve our understanding of the effectiveness of different treatment modalities, such as cognitive-behavioral therapy with different population subgroups, as well as our understanding of social work issues with different age-groups, including youth and the elderly. Chapter 9 then reviews major analysis techniques that are used by researchers to identify and understand data collected in qualitative research investigations. Reading Chapters 8 and 9 together will provide a firm foundation for further use of qualitative methods.

Evaluation research is the focus of Chapter 10. We illustrate how these primary methods may be used to learn about the effects of social programs and the need for others. We emphasize the importance of using a logic model to describe a program and to develop evaluation questions.

Chapter 11 provides a basic grounding in preparing quantitative data for analysis and using descriptive statistics. While we introduce inferential statistics, we encourage students to read more about inferential statistics on the text's Web site (http://www.sagepub.com/fswrstudy). Finally, Chapter 12 finishes with an overview of the process of and techniques for reporting research results, a second examination of the development of research proposals, and an introduction to meta-analysis.

🔲 DISTINCTIVE FEATURES

This book, more than other social work texts, integrates into each chapter substantive examples from real social work–related research. Examples from the literature are not simply dropped here and there to keep students' attention. Rather, each chapter presents a particular research method using real examples drawn from the many fields of social work practice. The following points are additional strengths of this text:

1. *Infusion of content on diverse populations.* Every step in the research process has different implications for different population groups. We identify concerns and strategies to make research culturally relevant throughout the book.

2. *Implications for evidence-based practice.* Each chapter has a special section detailing the implications of the chapter material for evidence-based practice.

3. *Ethical concerns and exercises on ethics.* Every step in the research process raises ethical concerns, so ethics should be treated in tandem with the study of specific methods. You will find ethics introduced in Chapter 2 and reviewed in the context of each method of data collection, data analysis, and reporting. Practice exercises on ethics appear at the end of each chapter.

4. *Thorough and up-to-date coverage of qualitative methods.* In our chapters on qualitative research design and data analysis, you will find an engaging presentation of qualitative methods appropriate to the field of social work. We include a section on Photovoice, which is increasingly being seen as a research method to enable participants a greater role in the research process.

5. *Examples of research in the real-world settings of social work practice.* We focus on interesting studies of homelessness, domestic violence, child welfare, welfare reform, aging, and other pressing social concerns.

6. *Emphasis on doing research.* Many different exercises and activities are included to prepare students to conduct research and evaluation.

We hope that readers of this text will enjoy learning about research and apply the skills and knowledge taught in a research course to their field of practice. Social workers are in a unique position to discover what interventions work, under what circumstances, and with what populations. In so doing, we benefit our clients and broader society.

ANCILLARY MATERIALS

To enhance the use of this book, a number of high-quality, useful ancillaries have been prepared, including (1) an open-access student study site and (2) a password-protected instructor resources site. Both sites can be accessed at www.sagepub.com/fswrstudy.

ACKNOWLEDGMENTS

Our thanks to Jerry Westby, executive editor, whose enthusiasm and support for this project has been crucial. Jerry is an exceptionally talented editor with a clear vision about how best to serve students and enhance their learning. We are also deeply indebted to Eve Oettinger, Astrid Virding, Jovey Stewart, and the other members of the Sage Publications staff, who made this text into something more than just words in a word processing file.

We are indebted to the talented group of social work professors whose feedback helped shape what the book is, including Diane Etzel-Wise, University of Kansas; Roenia DeLoach, Savannah State University; Kim Kotrla, Baylor University; Muammer Cetingok, University of Tennessee–Knoxville; Yoshie Sano, Washington State University–Vancouver; Michael

Wolf-Branigin, George Mason University; Julia W. Buckey, University of Central Florida–Daytona Beach; Eileen Mazur Abel, University of Central Florida; Donald Pierson, Idaho State University; DeAnn Gruber, Tulane University; Janet Ford, University of Kentucky; and Karen Fein, Bridgewater State College.

Our efforts have been enhanced by our colleagues, coauthors, and friends Ronet Bachman, Daniel Chambliss, Joseph Check, and Paul Nestor who have openly exchanged ideas about what works and what does not work in teaching students about the research process. Elizabeth Schneider, MLS (University of Pittsburgh), contributed the fine appendix on finding information, which provides students with the background needed to access information from a variety of media. We are grateful to all of them for sharing their talents with us.

We both thank our spouses, Sandy Budd and Elizabeth Schneider, for their love and support (and patience!), and our children, Yael, Meir, and Julia, for the inspiration they provide and the joy they bring to our lives.

CHAPTER 1

Science, Society, and Social Work Research

Reasoning About the Social World
Overgeneralization
Selective or Inaccurate Observation
Illogical Reasoning
Resistance to Change
Adherence to Authority

The Scientific Approach Is Different

Why Research Is Important for Social Work
Evidence-Based Practice and Social Work Research

Social Work Research in Practice
Descriptive Research: Who Are the Homeless?
Exploratory Research: What Is It Like to Live in a Homeless Shelter?
Explanatory Research: Why Do People Become Homeless?
Evaluation Research: What Services Help the Homeless?

Quantitative and Qualitative Methods

Strengths and Limitations of Social Work Research

The Validity of Research Findings
Measurement Validity
Generalizability
Causal Validity

Social Work Research in a Diverse Society

Conclusion

Key Terms

Highlights

Discussion Questions

Critiquing Research

Making Research Ethical

Developing a Research Proposal

Web Exercises

Burt had worked as a welder when he was younger, but alcoholism and related physical and mental health problems interfered with his career plans. By the time he was 60, Burt had spent many years on the streets. Fortunately, he obtained an apartment in 2008 through a housing program for homeless persons. Although the *Boston Globe* reporter who interviewed him reported that "the lure of booze and friends from the street was [still] strong," Burt had finally made the transition back to a more settled life (Abel, 2008, p. A14).

It is a sad story with an all-too-uncommon happy—although uncertain—ending. Together with one other such story and comments by several service staff, the newspaper article provides a persuasive rationale for the new housing program. Does Burt's story sound familiar? Such newspaper stories proliferate when the holiday season approaches, but what do they really tell us about homelessness? How typical is "Burt's" story? Why do people live on the streets? What helps them to regain housing?

In the rest of this chapter, you will learn how the methods of social science research go beyond stories in the popular media to help us answer questions like these. We describe the important role research plays in evidence-based practice. We explain the motivations for research using homelessness as an example. By the chapter's end you should know what is scientific in social science and appreciate how the methods of science can help us understand the problems of a diverse society.

▣ REASONING ABOUT THE SOCIAL WORLD

The story of just one homeless person raises many questions. How did Burt become homeless? Did Burt have any family? Was Burt working? But we can also ask broader questions about Burt and homelessness: Was Burt typical of the homeless population? What is it like to be homeless? Why do people become homeless? How do homeless individuals adjust to housing? What programs are effective in helping homeless people? Are social policies effective in reducing the number of homeless people?

We cannot avoid asking questions about the social world, which is a complex place. We all try to make sense of the social world and our position in it. In fact, the more that you begin to think like a potential social work researcher, the more questions will come to mind. But why does each question have so many possible answers? Surely, our perspective plays a role. One person may see a homeless individual as a victim of circumstances, another person may see the homeless as the failure of our society to provide sufficient affordable and adequate housing, while a third person may see the same individual as a lazy bum. People's different orientations will result in different answers to the questions prompted by the same individual or event.

People give different answers to questions about the social world for yet another reason: It is simply too easy to make errors in logic, particularly when we are analyzing the social world in which we are conscious participants. We can call some of these *everyday errors* because they occur so frequently in the nonscientific, unreflective discourse about the social world that we hear on a daily basis. These errors include overgeneralization, selective and inaccurate observation, illogical reasoning, resistance to change, and adherence to authority.

You do not have to be a researcher or use sophisticated research techniques to avoid these errors in reasoning. If you recognize these errors for what they are and make a conscious effort to avoid them, you can improve your own reasoning. In the process, you will also be implementing the admonishments of your parents (or minister, teacher, or other adviser) to not stereotype people, to avoid jumping to conclusions, and to look at the big picture. These are the same errors that the methods of social science are designed to help us avoid.

Overgeneralization

Overgeneralization occurs when we conclude that what we have observed or what we know to be true for *some* cases is true for *all* cases. We are always drawing conclusions about people and social processes from our own interactions with them, but we sometimes forget that our experiences are limited. The social (and natural) world is, after all, a complex place. We have the ability (and inclination) to interact with just a small fraction of the individuals who inhabit the social world, especially in a limited span of time. If we had taken facts about Burt, such as his alcohol abuse, and concluded that these problems are typical of the homeless, we have committed the error of overgeneralization.

Selective or Inaccurate Observation

We also have to avoid **selective observation**—choosing to look only at things that are in line with our preferences or beliefs. When we are inclined to criticize individuals or institutions, it is all too easy to notice their every failing. For example, if we are convinced in advance that all homeless persons are substance abusers, we can find many confirming instances. But what about homeless people like Debbie Allen, who ran away from a home she shared with an alcoholic father and psychotic mother; Charlotte Gentile, a teacher with a bachelor's degree living with two daughters in a shelter after losing her job; and Faith Brinton, who walked out of her rented home with her two daughters to escape an alcoholic and physically abusive husband and ended up in a shelter after her husband stopped paying child support? If we acknowledge only the instances that confirm our predispositions, we are victims of our own selective observation. Exhibit 1.1 depicts the difference between selective observation and overgeneralization.

Our observations can also be inaccurate. If a woman says she is *hungry* and we think she said she is *hunted,* we have made an **inaccurate observation.** If we think five people are standing on a street corner when seven actually are, we have made an inaccurate observation. Or our observations can be incomplete. If we see Burt sitting alone and drinking from a beer bottle, we would be wrong to conclude that he does not have any friends or that he likes to drink alone.

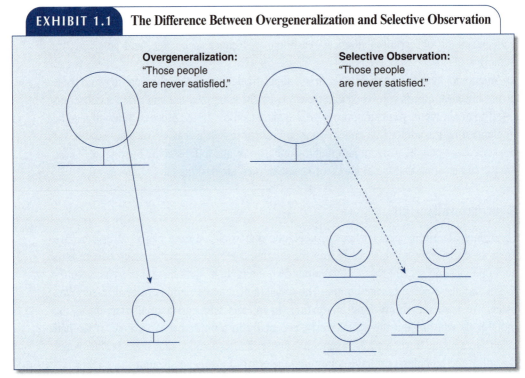

EXHIBIT 1.1   **The Difference Between Overgeneralization and Selective Observation**

Overgeneralization:
"Those people
are never satisfied."

Selective Observation:
"Those people
are never satisfied."

Source: Schutt (2005).

Such errors often occur in casual conversation and in everyday observation of the world around us. In fact, our perceptions do not provide a direct window onto the world around us, because what we think we have sensed is not necessarily what we have seen (or heard, smelled, felt, or tasted). Even when our senses are functioning fully, our minds have to interpret what we have sensed (Humphrey, 1992). The optical illusion in Exhibit 1.2, which can be viewed as either two faces or a vase, should help you realize that perceptions involve interpretations. Different observers may perceive the same situation differently because they interpret it differently.

Illogical Reasoning

When we prematurely jump to conclusions or argue on the basis of invalid assumptions, we are using **illogical reasoning.** For example, it is not reasonable to propose that homeless individuals do not want to work if evidence indicates that the reason many are unemployed is the difficulty in finding jobs for those who have mental or physical disabilities. However, an unquestioned assumption that everyone who can work will work is also likely to be misplaced. Logic that seems impeccable to one person can seem twisted to another; the problem usually is reasoning from different assumptions rather than just failing to "think straight."

EXHIBIT 1.2	An Optical Illusion

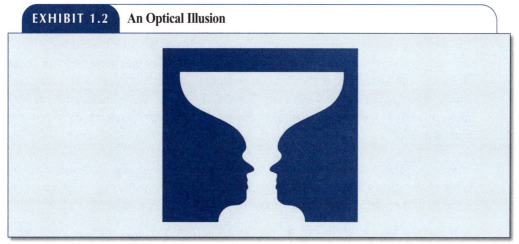

Source: Schutt (2005).

Resistance to Change

Resistance to change, the reluctance to change our ideas in light of new information, is a common problem. Our own egos can get in the way of observable reality. We know how tempting it is to make statements about the social world that conform to our own needs, rather than to the observable facts, and it is often difficult to admit that we were wrong once we have staked out a position on an issue. We also know that some degree of devotion to tradition is necessary for the predictable functioning of society, but too much devotion to tradition can stifle adaptation to changing circumstances.

Adherence to Authority

Sometimes it is difficult to change our ideas because someone in a position of authority has told us what is correct. **Adherence to authority** is given because we believe that the authority (the person making the claim) does have the knowledge. Too often we do not critically evaluate the ideas of those in positions of authority, whether they are parents, professors, or supervisors, or even the published word. We once had a student in a social welfare history and policy class who came back from Thanksgiving break saying, "You're wrong [about the impact of structural issues on economic well-being]; my parents told me that anyone can get ahead if they want to." In her eyes, her parents were right despite any evidence to the contrary. Students are right to question the "authority" of the professor if there is indeed no evidence to support the professor's assertions. One of the failings of social work professional literature is that there are many claims about practice effectiveness, but there is no evidence to support the claims (Gambrill, 2001).

▣ THE SCIENTIFIC APPROACH IS DIFFERENT

The **social science** approach to answering questions about the social world is designed to greatly reduce these potential sources of error in everyday reasoning. **Science** relies on logical and systematic methods to answer questions, and it does so in a way that allows others to inspect and evaluate its methods. Social scientists develop, refine, apply, and report their understanding of the social world more systematically than the general public:

• Social science research methods can reduce the likelihood of overgeneralization by using systematic procedures for selecting individuals or groups to study who are representative of the individuals or groups about whom we wish to generalize.

• Social science methods can reduce the risk of selective, inaccurate, or incomplete observation by requiring that we measure and sample phenomena systematically.

• To avoid illogical reasoning, social work researchers use explicit criteria to identify causes and to determine whether these criteria are met in a particular instance.

• Scientific methods lessen the tendency to develop answers about the social world from ego-based commitments, excessive devotion to tradition, or unquestioning respect for authority because they require that we base our beliefs on evidence that can be examined and critiqued by others.

▣ WHY RESEARCH IS IMPORTANT FOR SOCIAL WORK

The methods of social science research are invaluable tools for social work practitioners at any level of practice. The nature of our social world is the starting point for our profession, because much of what we do is in response to social, political, and economic conditions. Social policies and programs and interventions provided by human service agencies are based on assumptions about the cause of a social condition (Martin & Kettner, 1996). Is homelessness due to individual behavior? Individual pathology? Local housing-market conditions? Insufficient wages? The responses to these questions shape social policy about homelessness and the types of programs offered by human service providers.

Our profession works with people from diverse backgrounds and promotes the social and economic participation of groups who lack access to full participation. Through research we can challenge perceptions and popular sentiment of those who are in need. Burt reflects common stereotypes about the homeless, namely that they are male and that they are substance abusers. Yet we now know, thanks to the work of many researchers, that increasing numbers of homeless people are women with children or people diagnosed with HIV; they have different kinds of needs than Burt, and they require different types of services and interventions in the kinds of housing options offered.

Social science research provides methods to address these questions. Through systematic investigation, we begin to uncover the various dimensions of the social condition, the accuracy of our assumptions about what causes the social condition, the characteristics of people with a particular social status or social problem, and the effectiveness of our policies and programs to ameliorate the social problem.

Evidence-Based Practice and Social Work Research

Evidence-based practice (EBP) has emerged in the last several years as a popular model for social work practice. EBP, with its roots in medicine, is described by Eileen Gambrill (2006) as an evolving "philosophy and process designed to forward effective use of professional judgment in integrating information regarding each client's unique characteristics, circumstances, preferences, and actions and external research findings" (p. 339). EBP's emergence is, in part, a reaction to an overreliance on professional claims, that is, authority on the effectiveness of social work practice.

EBP requires that the choice of an intervention should be based on the best current research evidence to achieve a particular outcome, client values, client circumstances, and clinical expertise (Straus, Richardson, Glasziou, & Haynes, 2005). Empirical evidence is necessary but not sufficient; rather, social workers should utilize an intervention that fits the client's expectations and circumstances (Starin, 2006). What do each of these terms mean?

- *Best current research evidence.* Practitioners should utilize knowledge derived from research studies that provide evidence that has been obtained through systematic tests of its accuracy (Gambrill, 1999); that is, reliable and valid. Although there is debate about what kinds of research constitute "evidence," you will learn that it includes "any systematically collected information relevant to practice" (Pollio, 2006, p. 225). Therefore, quantitative studies (e.g., randomized clinical trials), qualitative methods (e.g., case studies and focus groups), and practitioner-collected information (e.g., single-subject design) all provide evidence. Such studies provide information that can test the accuracy of assessment tools or the effectiveness of different interventions.

- *Client values.* Clients bring their own preferences, concerns, and expectations for service and treatment (Haynes, Devereaux, & Guyatt, 2002; Straus et al., 2005). Such preferences may influence the type of intervention used. Clients may prefer individual interventions as opposed to group interventions, or they may prefer in-home services or interventions rather than going to a congregate site or an agency for services. This is not limited to individual clients but may include larger client systems. Community interventions require knowledge about what is acceptable within a particular community, just as organizational interventions require an understanding of what is acceptable given the culture of the organization.

- *Client circumstances.* You can imagine the variety of circumstances that bring clients to seek social services. Some clients may be facing a crisis while other clients confront a long-standing problem; they may be voluntary clients, or they may be court-ordered clients; they may live in rural areas, the suburbs, or urban communities. These are just some of the circumstances or situations that might be weighed in determining appropriate interventions.

• *Clinical expertise.* Clinical expertise involves using both past experiences with clients and clinical skills to assess and integrate the information learned from research studies, client values, and client circumstances (Haynes et al., 2002; Straus et al., 2005). A skilled social worker knows how to find the relevant research literature, evaluate its accuracy, and determine its usefulness to a particular client or client system (Gambrill, 2001). One key skill is having the knowledge to weigh and assess research findings to evaluate the evidence. A skilled social worker will have the communication skills needed to solicit client values and preferences and, in turn, communicate to clients their options. A social worker should be able to provide different interventions (or refer to appropriate providers) given a client's particular circumstances.

Another component of evidence-based practice is that social workers should provide clients with the information necessary to make decisions about services, including the effectiveness of the intervention, the client's role in the intervention, expectations of the client, and length of the intervention (Starin, 2006). Clients should be informed about the evidence, or lack of evidence, supporting a particular intervention. If there is no empirical evidence, social workers should provide the theoretical justification for the choice of service. Clients should also be told about alternative interventions and their relative effectiveness. With all of this information, clients can make informed decisions.

Although this may sound daunting, these themes are consistent with ethical obligations expected of social work practitioners as described in the National Association of Social Workers (1999) *Code of Ethics*: Enabling clients to make informed decisions is consistent with obtaining informed consent (1.03[a]). Social workers should keep up-to-date with relevant knowledge (4.01[b]), utilize interventions with an empirical basis (4.01[c]), and include evaluation and research evidence as part of professional practice (5.02[c]).

We hope you are beginning to see the critical role that understanding the research process plays in providing services to client systems. You will need the skill to find relevant research literature and the ability to evaluate studies critically so that you can determine the usefulness of the findings to your practice and to your clients. Therefore, as you read this book, you will learn about research issues such as measurement, sampling, and research design; how to find research literature; and how to understand statistics. In each chapter, you will read about the implications of the specific topic for EBP.

▣ SOCIAL WORK RESEARCH IN PRACTICE

Although social work researchers study different phenomena, social conditions, effects of different programs, and intervention methods, the purpose of these studies can be classified into four categories: description, exploration, explanation, and evaluation.

Descriptive Research: Who Are the Homeless?

Defining and describing social conditions is a part of almost any research investigation, but descriptive research is often the primary focus of the initial research about some issue. **Descriptive research** typically involves the gathering of facts. Some of the central questions asked in research on homelessness have been these: Who is homeless? What are the needs of homeless people? How many people are homeless?

In 1995, Martha Burt and her colleagues at the Urban Institute (a research and policy institute located in Washington, DC), in collaboration with 12 federal agencies, designed and implemented the *1996 National Survey of Homeless Assistance Providers and Clients* to address these questions (Burt et al., 1999). The study was designed to provide a nationally representative sample of programs assisting homeless persons as well as a representative sample of their homeless clients. The sample included the 28 largest metropolitan statistical areas across the country, 24 randomly drawn smaller metropolitan statistical areas, and 24 randomly selected rural Community Action Agency catchment areas. After choosing the locations, all agencies serving homeless people were identified and contacted. To interview clients, agencies were randomly selected and within each of the agencies, clients using the homeless program were randomly selected. Because the researchers were interested in providers and clients, the researchers had to be very careful in defining *homeless assistance program* and *homeless status.*

The design of the survey reinforces the importance of social scientific methods. Clear definitions were necessary, and the selection method had to ensure that the findings would be generalizable beyond the selected settings. Yet the characterizations of the homeless clients were limited to those people who were using assistance programs; otherwise, in places where there were fewer or virtually no programs for the homeless, many people might be missed. The lack of programs in rural areas may have biased the descriptions of the homeless in rural areas; agency policies about who is served may also have biased these descriptions (Burt et al., 1999).

This study revealed the diversity among the homeless population. About 34% of the homeless were members of homeless families, about 70% were men, 53% were non-White, and 38% had less than a high school diploma. In addition, fewer than 10% were currently married and 23% were veterans. Health problems were common, yet nearly one-quarter reported that, though they needed medical attention, they could not get it. Nearly two-thirds of the clients had an alcohol, drug, or mental health problem in the month previous to the interview.

Exploratory Research: What Is It Like to Live in a Homeless Shelter?

Exploratory research seeks to learn how people get along in the setting in question, what meanings they give to their actions, and what issues concern them. The goal is to learn "what is going on here" and to investigate social phenomena without expectations. This purpose is associated with the use of methods that capture large amounts of relatively unstructured information.

Among researchers interested in homelessness, an early goal was to learn what it was like to be homeless and how homeless people made sense of their situation. Alice Johnson (1999) wanted to learn about the events that led women with children to seek emergency shelter and what it was like for them to live in an emergency shelter. To answer these questions, Johnson conducted an exploratory study using the personal narratives of women who were ex-residents of an emergency shelter in Connecticut. She interviewed 25 women with children who, when they came to the shelter, were not recipients of Aid to Families with Dependent Children. The interviews typically took place in the women's current residences and lasted between 1 and 2 hours.

Johnson (1999) found that reactions to living in the emergency shelter changed over time. Initially, the women reported feeling depressed or lonely: "I was very depressed. Especially when you have no family near you, no friends, or nobody. It's a very depressing feeling. I was depressed in the first week. I did a lot of crying. I was in my room a lot" (p. 50).

After this initial reaction to the shelter, the women developed new perceptions about their problems (Johnson, 1999). The women reported that they started to see their own lives as being better in comparison with the lives of other women in the shelter. Many reported learning that they had to be strong to take responsibility for providing for their children.

> I'm going to be honest. What helped me was my son. I would look on my son and I'd say, "I have to live for him." That's what picked me up. That's what told me to get going. For him. Find anything—whatever I can get. Go for it because of him. (p. 52)

Other women found that the shelter provided respite from their problems and an opportunity to come to grips with their problems. Finally, the women saw this respite as an opportunity to begin planning for their future.

Johnson found that the women ultimately did not see the shelter as a negative experience; rather, living in a shelter was part of the solution to the crises these women faced in their lives. Living in the shelter provided the women with the time and opportunity to deal with their problems and to restore stability to their family life. The shelter was a place where they received emotional support and tangible help, learned how to navigate social services, and saved money.

Explanatory Research: Why Do People Become Homeless?

Explanatory research seeks to identify causes and effects of social phenomena, and to predict how one phenomenon will change or vary in response to variation in some other phenomenon. In other words, explanatory research is used to understand the causes of a social condition such as homelessness.

Peter Rossi's (1989) work on homelessness was designed to understand why people become homeless. His comparison of homeless people with other extremely poor Chicagoans allowed him to address this explanatory research question. Rossi surveyed a sample of homeless people in shelters and those individuals he and his assistants could find living on the streets. The street sample was something of a challenge. Rossi consulted with local experts to identify which of Chicago's 19,400 blocks were the most likely resting places of homeless people at night. Then he drew samples of blocks from each of the three resulting categories: blocks with a high, medium, and low probability of having homeless people at night. Finally, Rossi's interviewers visited these blocks on several nights between 1 a.m. and 6 a.m. and briefly interviewed people who seemed to be homeless.

After extensive analysis of the data, Rossi (1989) developed a straightforward explanation of homelessness: Homeless people are extremely poor, and all extremely poor people are vulnerable to being displaced because of the high cost of housing in urban areas. Those who are most vulnerable to losing their homes are individuals with problems of substance abuse or mental illness, which leave them unable to contribute to their own support. Extremely poor individuals who have these characteristics and are priced out of cheap lodging by urban renewal and rising housing prices often end up living with relatives or friends. However, the financial and emotional burdens created by this arrangement eventually strain social ties to the breaking point.

Evaluation Research: What Services Help the Homeless?

Evaluation research (program evaluation or practice evaluation) seeks to determine the effects of social policies and the impact of programs. Evaluation research uses the tools of research to do a variety of different tasks, such as describing the clients using a particular program; exploring and assessing the needs of different communities or population groups; evaluating the effectiveness of a particular program or intervention; monitoring the progress of clients; or monitoring the performance of staff. These same tools provide a standard by which we can also evaluate the evaluation.

Because evaluation research or program evaluation uses the same tools as other research, the two often become confused in the minds of readers and even researchers. The distinctions are important, particularly as they relate to the ethical conduct of research, which we discuss in Chapter 2, and specifically to institutional review processes to protect human subjects as required. The intent of research is to develop or contribute to generalizable knowledge, with the beneficiaries of the research usually being society and perhaps the study participants; the intent of evaluation is to assess whether a program is achieving its objectives with a specific group as a means to monitor and improve the program (Snider, 1999). The beneficiaries of the information are the program providers or the clients receiving the services.

The problem of homelessness spawned many programs and, with them, evaluation research to assess the impact of these programs. Should housing or treatment come first for homeless people with serious mental illness and, in particular, for those persons who use or abuse drugs and alcohol? Deborah Padgett, Leyla Gulcur, and Sam Tsemberis (2006) addressed this policy dilemma as part of a 4-year longitudinal study comparing housing-first and treatment-first programs. Participants were randomly assigned to one of the two groups: the *housing-first model*, in which the homeless were given immediate access to housing and were offered an array of services, and in which abstinence was not a prerequisite, or the *treatment-first model*, in which housing was contingent on sobriety. People were randomly assigned to the two types of models so the researchers could be more confident that any differences found between the groups at the study's end had arisen after the subjects were assigned to the housing.

After 4 years, 75% of the housing-first clients were in a stable residence for the preceding 6 months, whereas only 50% of the treatment-first group had a stable residence. In addition, the researchers found that there were no statistically significant differences between the two groups on drug or alcohol use. The researchers concluded that the requirement for abstinence had little impact among mentally ill respondents whose primary concern was for housing.

🔲 QUANTITATIVE AND QUALITATIVE METHODS

In general, research methods can be divided into two different domains called quantitative research methods and qualitative research methods. Did you notice the difference between the types of data the studies used? The primary data collected by Martha Burt et al. (1999) were counts about the homeless population: how many had families, their gender, their race, and other characteristics. Because these data were numerical, we can say this study used **quantitative methods**. Rossi's (1989) survey and Padgett et al.'s (2006) study also used quantitative methods, and they reported their findings as percentages and other statistics that summarized homelessness. In contrast, Johnson (1999) used personal narratives—original text—to understand life in a homeless shelter; because she used actual text, and not counts or other quantities, we say that Johnson used **qualitative methods**.

Quantitative methods Methods such as surveys and experiments that record variation in social life in terms of categories that vary in amount. Data that are treated as quantitative are either numbers or attributes that can be ordered in terms of magnitude.

Qualitative methods Methods such as participant observation, intensive interviewing, and focus groups that are designed to capture social life as participants experience it, rather than in categories predetermined by the researcher. Data that are treated as qualitative are mostly written or spoken words or observations that do not have a direct numerical interpretation.

The distinction between quantitative and qualitative methods involves more than just the type of data collected. Quantitative methods are most often used when the motives for research are explanation, description, or evaluation. Exploration is most often the motive for using qualitative methods, although researchers also use these methods for descriptive and evaluative purposes. The goals of quantitative and qualitative researchers may also differ. Whereas quantitative researchers generally accept the goal of developing an understanding that correctly reflects what is actually happening in the real world, some qualitative researchers instead emphasize the goal of developing an "authentic" understanding of a social process or social setting (Gubrium & Holstein, 1997). An authentic understanding is one that reflects *fairly* the various perspectives of participants in that setting.

As important as it is, we do not want to place too much emphasis on the distinction between quantitative and qualitative orientations or methods. Social work researchers often combine these methods to enhance their research. For example, Hicks-Coolick, Burnside-Eaton, and Peters (2003) used an interview guide with directors of six homeless shelters to understand the kinds of services needed by homeless children and then sent a mail survey to the directors of 600 shelters in order to augment their qualitative data. The use of both methods, called mixed-methods, provided a clearer understanding of the reality of service delivery and needs.

▣ STRENGTHS AND LIMITATIONS OF SOCIAL WORK RESEARCH

These are only four of the dozens of large studies of homelessness done since 1980, but they illustrate some of the questions that social science research can address, several different methods that researchers can use, and ways that research can inform public policy. Notice how each of the four studies was designed to reduce the errors common in everyday reasoning:

- The clear definition of the population of interest in each study and the selection of a broad, representative sample of that population in two studies (Burt's and Rossi's) increased the researchers' ability to draw conclusions without overgeneralizing the findings to groups to which they did not apply.

- The use of surveys in which each respondent was asked the same set of questions reduced the risk of selective or inaccurate observation.

- The risk of illogical reasoning was reduced by carefully describing each stage of the research, clearly presenting the findings, and carefully testing the basis for cause-and-effect conclusions.

- Resistance to change was reduced by utilizing a research design that controls for other explanations.

Nevertheless, we would be less than honest if we implied that we enter the realm of beauty, truth, and light when we engage in social research or when we base our opinions only on the best available social research. Research always has some limitations and some flaws (as does any human endeavor), and our findings are always subject to differing interpretations. Social work research permits us to see more, to observe with fewer distortions, and to describe more clearly to others the basis for our opinions, but it will not settle all arguments. Others will always have differing opinions, and some of those others will be social scientists and social workers who have conducted their own studies and drawn different conclusions. For example, are people encouraged to get off welfare by requirements that they get a job? Some research suggests that they are, other research finds no effect of work incentives, and one major study found positive but short-lived effects. More convincing answers must await better research, more thoughtful analysis, or wider agreement on the value of welfare and work.

But even in areas of research that are fraught with controversy, where social scientists differ in their interpretations of the evidence, the quest for new and more sophisticated research has value. What is most important for improving understanding of the social world is not the result of any particular study but the accumulation of evidence from different studies of related issues. By designing new studies that focus on the weak points or controversial conclusions of prior research, social scientists contribute to a body of findings that gradually expands our knowledge about the social world and resolves some of the disagreements about it.

Whether you plan to conduct your own research projects, read others' research reports, or just think about and act in the social world, knowing about research methods has many benefits. This knowledge will give you greater confidence in your own opinions, improve your ability to evaluate others' opinions, and encourage you to refine your questions, answers, and methods of inquiry about the social world. Also, having the tools of research can guide you to improve the social programs in which you work, to provide better interventions with your clients, and to monitor their progress.

▣ THE VALIDITY OF RESEARCH FINDINGS

A scientist seeks to develop an accurate understanding of empirical reality by conducting research studies that lead to valid knowledge about the world. We have reached the goal of **validity** when our statements or conclusions about empirical reality are correct. The purpose of social work research is not to come up with conclusions that people will like, or to find answers that make our agencies look better or that suit our own personal preferences. Rather, social work research is about (a) conducting research that leads to valid interpretations of the social world; (b) reaching useful conclusions about the impact of social policy; and (c) formulating valid conclusions about the effects of our practice with clients. Therefore, we are concerned with three aspects of validity: measurement validity, generalizability, and causal validity. We learn that invalid measures, invalid generalizations, or invalid causal inferences result in inaccurate conclusions.

Measurement Validity

Measurement validity is our first concern in establishing the validity of research results, because if we have not measured what we think we measured, we really do not know what we are talking about. For example, some researchers have found a high level of serious and persistent mental illness among homeless people based on interviews with samples of homeless people at one point in time. Mental illness has typically been measured by individuals' responses to a series of questions that ask whether they are feeling depressed, anxious, paranoid, and so on. Homeless people more commonly say yes to these questions than do other people, even other extremely poor people who are not homeless.

But for these responses to be considered indicators of mental illness, the responses must indicate relatively enduring states of mind. Critics of these studies note that the living conditions of homeless people are likely to make them feel depressed, anxious, and even paranoid. Feeling depressed may be a normal reaction to homelessness, not an indication of mental illness. Thus, the argument goes, typical survey questions may not provide valid measures of mental illness among the homeless.

Suffice it to say at this point that we must be careful in designing our measures and in evaluating how well they have performed. We must be careful to ensure that the measures are appropriate and comparable for the groups with whom they are used.

Generalizability

The **generalizability** of a study is the extent to which it can be used to inform us about people, places, or events that were not studied. We rarely have the resources to study the entire population that is of interest, so we have to select cases to study. We can never be sure that our propositions will hold under all conditions, so we should be cautious in generalizing to populations that we did not actually sample.

Although most American cities have many shelters for homeless people and some homeless people sleep on the streets to avoid shelters, many studies of "the homeless" are based on surveys of individuals found in just one shelter. When these studies are reported, the authors state that their results are based on homeless people in one shelter, but then they go on to talk about "the homeless this" and "the homeless that," as if their study results represented all homeless people in the city or even in the nation. If every homeless person was like every other one, generalizations based on observations of one homeless person would be valid. But, of course, that is not the case. In fact, homeless people who avoid shelters tend to be different from those who use shelters, and different types of shelters may attract different types of homeless people. We are on solid ground if we question the generalizability of statements about homeless people based on the results of a survey in just one shelter.

Generalizability has two aspects. **Sample generalizability** refers to the ability to take findings obtained from a sample, or subset, of a larger population and apply them to that population. This is the most common meaning of generalizability. A community organizer may study a sample of residents living in a particular neighborhood in order to assess their attitudes toward opening a homeless shelter in their neighborhood and then generalize the findings to all the residents of the neighborhood. The value of the findings is enhanced if what the community organizer learns is representative of all the residents and not just the residents who were surveyed.

Cross-population generalizability refers to the ability to generalize from findings about one group or population or setting to other groups or populations or settings (see Exhibit 1.3).

EXHIBIT 1.3   Sample and Cross-Population Generalizability

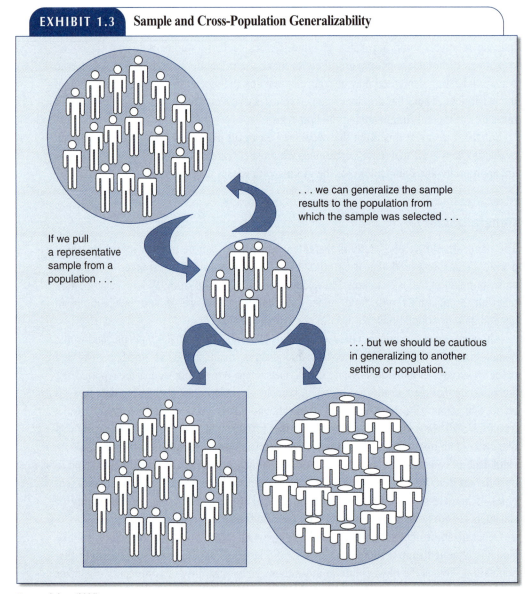

If we pull a representative sample from a population . . .

. . . we can generalize the sample results to the population from which the sample was selected . . .

. . . but we should be cautious in generalizing to another setting or population.

Source: Schutt (2005).

Cross-population generalizability occurs to the extent that the results of a study hold true for multiple populations; these populations may not all have been sampled or they may be represented as subgroups within the sample studied. Consider the debate over whether social support reduces psychological distress among homeless people as it does among housed people (Schutt, Meschede, & Rierdan, 1994). A study based on a sample of only homeless people

> *Sample generalizability* Exists when a conclusion based on a sample, or subset, of a larger population holds true for that population.
>
> *Cross-population generalizability* Exists when findings about one group or population or setting hold true for other groups or populations or settings (see Exhibit 1.3). Also called *external validity.*

could not in itself resolve this debate. But in a heterogeneous sample of both homeless and housed people, the effect of social support on distress among both groups could be tested.

Or consider this when you read about an intervention to help homeless individuals obtain and maintain a permanent residence. It is likely that such a study is done in a particular agency, serving homeless individuals with particular characteristics, living in a particular community. Ideally, you would like to be able to implement that intervention and achieve the same success in your agency, working with your particular clients, in your particular community. You would have greater confidence in implementing the intervention if there is evidence of cross-population generalizability.

Causal Validity

Causal validity refers to the truthfulness of an assertion that A causes B. Most research seeks to determine what causes what, so social scientists frequently must be concerned with causal validity. For example, Gary Cohen and Barbara Kerr (1998) asked whether computer-mediated counseling could be as effective as face-to-face counseling for mental health problems. They could have compared people who had experienced one of these types of treatment, but it is quite likely that individuals who sought out a live person for counseling would differ in important ways from those who were attracted to an opportunity for the less personal computer-mediated counseling. So, instead, they designed an experiment in which individuals seeking counseling were assigned randomly to either computer-mediated or face-to-face counseling. This procedure made it unlikely that people who were less sociable, more educated, and younger were disproportionately in the computer-mediated condition. The differences in counseling outcomes were more likely to be due to the differences in the types of counseling, rather than to differences in the types of people being counseled. Students in both groups benefited to the same degree, so researchers concluded that computer-mediated counseling was as effective in reducing anxiety as face-to-face counseling. (See Exhibit 1.4.)

But causal conclusions can be mistaken because of some factor that was not recognized during planning for the study, even in randomized experiments. If the computer-mediated counseling sessions were conducted in a modern building with all the latest amenities, while face-to-face counseling was delivered in a run-down building, this might have led to different outcomes for reasons quite apart from the type of counseling.

EXHIBIT 1.4   **Partial Evidence of Causality**

Pre-counseling Anxiety Score	Type of Counseling	Post-counseling Anxiety Score
35	Computer-mediated	28
35	Face-to-face	29

| Pre-counseling anxiety score: 35 | Computer-mediated counseling | → | Post-counseling anxiety score: 28 |

| Pre-counseling anxiety score: 35 | Face-to-face counseling | → | Post-counseling anxiety score: 29 |

Source: Engel & Schutt (2005).

   Establishing causal validity can be quite difficult. You will learn in subsequent chapters how experimental designs and statistics can help us evaluate causal propositions, but the solutions are neither easy nor perfect: We always have to consider critically the validity of causal statements that we hear or read.

🖾 SOCIAL WORK RESEARCH IN A DIVERSE SOCIETY

Social work research is being conducted in an increasingly diverse society. In the past, diversity was primarily associated with race and ethnicity (National Association of Social Workers, 2001; Van den Berg & Crisp, 2004) but now includes "people of different genders, social classes, religious and spiritual beliefs, sexual orientation, ages, and physical and mental abilities" (National Association of Social Workers, 2001, p. 8). Although there is much that these groups share, distinct cultural, social, and historical experiences shape and influence group experiences. Just as social work practitioners are expected to engage in culturally competent practice, social work researchers must recognize that cultural norms influence the research process, whether in terms of the willingness to participate in research activities, the meaning ascribed to abstract terms and concepts, the way data are collected, or the interpretation of the findings. The failure by researchers to adequately address the cultural context impacts, in different ways, the research process and, ultimately, the validity and generalizability of research findings.

Historically, women and ethnic minorities have been underrepresented in research studies and, more specifically, in clinical studies testing the impact of health and mental health interventions. The reluctance of different groups to participate in research may be due to different reasons, such as distrust of the motives of the researchers (Beals, Manson, Mitchell, Spicer, & AI-SUPERPFP Team, 2003; Sobeck, Chapleski, & Fisher, 2003), historical experiences, not understanding the research process, not seeing any benefit to participation (Beals et al., 2003), and misuse of findings to the detriment of their communities (Sobeck et al., 2003; Norton & Manson, 1996). Inadequate representation makes it more difficult to conclude, for example, that the results from a primarily White sample can be generalized to other ethnic groups.

Cultural differences given to the meaning of different concepts, particularly psychological concepts, can also impact the validity of the research. Social work researchers use a variety of measurement instruments, but often people of color, women, the poor, and other groups have not been adequately represented in the development or testing of these measurement instruments (Witkin, 2001). It is important to determine whether the concepts being measured have the same meaning and are manifested in the same way across different cultural groups; in other words, is there measurement validity? Measurement bias can result in misidentifying the prevalence of a condition and result in group differences that may not actually exist.

The quality of information obtained from surveys is in part dependent on the questions that are asked; there is an assumption that respondents share a common understanding of the meaning of the question and willingness or unwillingness to answer the question. Yet questions may have different meanings to different groups, may not be culturally appropriate, and even when translated into a different language may lack equivalent connotations (Pasick, Stewart, Bird, & D'Onofrio, 2001). For example, Pasick et al. (2001) found that the concept of routine checkup was unfamiliar to their sample of Chinese Americans, there was no similar concept in the Vietnamese language, and some Latina respondents did not understand the question nor could they offer alternative language.

Data must be analyzed carefully. Often ethnic and racial minorities are compared with the majority population; but in doing so, we may be treating these differences as deficits when in fact they reflect cultural differences. In comparison studies, it is important to control for the impact of socioeconomic status given disparities in economic well-being.

How data are reported must respect confidentiality. Beals et al. (2003) noted that American Indian and Alaska Native communities had experienced research efforts that resulted in negative stereotypes and publicity for their communities; confidentiality, they suggested, needs to extend beyond the individual respondent to the community.

As you can see from this brief introduction, the norms that develop within population subgroups have an impact that cuts across the research process. As you read each chapter, you will learn both the kinds of questions that researchers ask and the strategies they use to ensure that their research is culturally competent.

回 CONCLUSION

We hope this first chapter has given you an idea of what to expect in the rest of the book. Social science provides a variety of methods to reduce the errors common in everyday reasoning. We explore different research methods to understand how they improve our ability to come to valid conclusions which, in turn, can inform social work practice. Whether you plan to conduct your own research projects, read others' research reports, or just think about and act in the social world, knowing about research will give you greater confidence in your own opinions; improve your ability to evaluate others' opinions; and encourage you to refine your questions, answers, and methods of inquiry about the social world. Having the tools of research can guide you to improve the social programs in which you work, to provide better interventions with your clients, and to monitor their progress.

As you read through the studies in this book and as you critically evaluate other research articles, you should continue to ask: How valid are the conclusions? Each research technique must be evaluated in terms of its ability to help us with measurement validity, generalizability, and causal validity. The ensuing chapters are designed to help you learn to assess the validity of research conclusions, whether from your own research or from the research efforts of others.

KEY TERMS

Adherence to authority
Causal validity
Cross-population generalizability
Descriptive research
Evaluation research
Evidence-based practice
Explanatory research
Exploratory research
Generalizability
Illogical reasoning
Inaccurate observation

Measurement validity
Overgeneralization
Qualitative methods
Quantitative methods
Resistance to change
Sample generalizability
Science
Selective observation
Social science
Validity

HIGHLIGHTS

• Five common errors in reasoning are overgeneralization, selective or inaccurate observation, illogical reasoning, resistance to change, and adherence to authority.

• Social science is the use of logical, systematic, documented methods to investigate individuals, societies, and social processes, as well as the knowledge produced by these investigations.

• Social science methods are used by social work researchers and practitioner-researchers to uncover the nature of a social condition, to test the accuracy of assumptions about the causes of the social condition, to identify populations at risk, and to test and evaluate the evidence base of interventions, programs, and policies designed to ameliorate the social condition.

• Evidence-based practice suggests that practice decisions should integrate the best current research evidence, client values, client circumstances, and clinical expertise.

• Social work research can be descriptive, exploratory, explanatory, or evaluative.

• Quantitative methods record variation in social life in terms of categories that vary in amount while qualitative methods are designed to capture social life as participants experience it rather than in predetermined categories.

• The three components of validity are measurement validity, generalizability (both from the sample to the population from which it was selected and from the sample to other populations), and causal validity.

• An important consideration for research practice is social diversity.

DISCUSSION QUESTIONS

1. Select a social issue that is of interest to you. Discuss your beliefs about the causes of the social issue. What is the source of these beliefs? What type of policy, program, and intervention for helping resolve this social issue would be consistent with your beliefs?

2. Develop four research questions related to a topic or issue, one for each of the four types of research—descriptive, exploratory, explanatory, and evaluation.

3. Find a report of social work research in an article in a daily newspaper. What were the major findings? How much evidence is given about the measurement validity, generalizability, and causal validity of the findings? What additional design features might have helped to improve the study's validity?

CRITIQUING RESEARCH

1. Read the abstracts (initial summaries) of each article in a recent issue of a major social work journal. (Ask your instructor for some good journal titles.) On the basis of the abstract only, classify each research project represented in the articles as primarily descriptive, exploratory, explanatory, or evaluative. Note any indications that the research focused on other types of research questions.

MAKING RESEARCH ETHICAL

Throughout the book, we discuss the ethical challenges that arise in social work research. At the end of each chapter, we ask you to consider some questions about ethical issues related to that chapter's focus. We introduce this critical topic formally in Chapter 2, but we begin here with some questions for you to ponder.

1. The chapter began with a brief description from a news article of a homeless person known as "Burt." We think stories like this can provide important information about the social problems that social workers confront. But what would *you* do if you were interviewing homeless persons and one talked of taking his own life out of despair? What if he was only thinking about it? Can you suggest some guidelines for researchers?

2. You read in this chapter that Padgett et al. (2006) found that their housing-first program enabled homeless persons to spend more time housed than those required first to undergo treatment for substance abuse. If you were these researchers, would you announce your findings in a press conference and encourage relevant agencies to eliminate abstinence requirements for homeless persons with substance abuse problems? When would you recommend that social work researchers urge adoption of new policies based on research findings? How strong do you think the evidence should be?

DEVELOPING A RESEARCH PROPOSAL

1. What topic would you focus on if you could design a social work–related research project without any concern for costs or time? What are your reasons for studying this topic?

2. Develop four questions that you might investigate about the topic you just selected. Each question should reflect a different research motive: descriptive, exploratory, explanatory, and evaluation. Be specific.

3. Which question most interests you? Would you prefer to attempt to answer that question with quantitative or qualitative methods? Why?

> To assist you in completing the Web exercises below and to gain a better understanding of the chapter's contents, please access the study site at http://www.sagepub.com/fswrstudy where you will find the Web exercises reproduced with suggested links, along with self-quizzes, e-flash cards, interactive exercises, journal articles, and other valuable resources.

WEB EXERCISES

1. Prepare a 5- to 10-minute class presentation on the U.S. Department of Housing and Urban Development (HUD) report, *Homelessness: Programs and the People They Serve.* Go to the Web site http://www.huduser.org/publications/homeless/homelessness/contents.html and write up a brief outline for your presentation, including information on study design, questions asked, and major findings.

CHAPTER 2

The Process and Problems of Social Work Research

Developing Social Work Research Questions
Examining Research Literature
Finding Literature for Evidence-Based Practice
    Campbell Collaboration
    Government-Supported Resources
Considering Social Diversity

Theory and Social Work Research

Alternative Research Strategies
Deductive Research
Inductive Research
Descriptive Research
Research Paradigms

The Time Element
Cross-Sectional Designs
Longitudinal Designs
    Trend Studies
    Panel Studies
    Cohort Studies

Guidelines for Social Work Research
Scientific Guidelines
Ethical Guidelines
Honesty and Openness
The Uses of Science
Research on People

Conclusion

Key Terms

Highlights

Discussion Questions

Critiquing Research

Making Research Ethical

Developing a Research Proposal

Web Exercises

In this chapter, we introduce how you begin the process of social work research. The first concern in social work research is deciding what to study. A wide variety of theoretical orientations applicable to understanding human behavior at the individual, group, community, and organizational level may help guide us to a research question, elaborate on its implications, and, later, interpret our results. Next, we must decide how to go about answering the research question. Finally, in addition to technical aspects of the research process, we introduce ethical guidelines that should be adhered to no matter what the research strategy. By the chapter's end, you should be ready to formulate a research question and design a general strategy for answering your question.

🔲 DEVELOPING SOCIAL WORK RESEARCH QUESTIONS

A social work research question is a question that you seek to answer through the collection and analysis of firsthand, verifiable, empirical data. There are so many possible research questions that it is more of a challenge to specify what does *not* qualify as a social work research question than to specify what does. That does not mean it is easy to specify a research question. In fact, formulating a good research question can be surprisingly difficult.

Research questions can emanate from a variety of sources. Research questions may emerge from your own experiences, such as volunteering in a women's shelter or the depression of a friend. Other research questions may emerge from your work or field practicum experiences. You might wonder about the effectiveness of the interventions employed at your agency, the causes of some your clients' problems, or how a state policy affects your clients. Other researchers may pose interesting questions for you to study, such as unanswered questions from their research or replicating the research with other samples in other locations. The application of social theory to understanding the causes of a social condition or to designing treatment models may lead to different research questions. Or you may focus on a research question posed by someone else, such as a government agency or a foundation.

The problem is not so much coming up with interesting questions for research as it is focusing on a problem of manageable size. We are often interested in much more than we can reasonably investigate with limited time and resources. A question is unlikely to just spring forth from your pen. You might start by developing a list of possible research questions as you begin to think about conducting a research study. As you read more and think about the possibilities, you can narrow your list to the most interesting and feasible candidates.

Once you have identified one or two questions, you should evaluate the question in terms of three criteria: feasibility, social importance, and scientific relevance (King, Keohane, & Verba, 1994).

- *Feasibility:* Do you have adequate time to complete the study given the resources you have available?

- *Social Importance:* Will an answer to the research question make a difference in improving the well-being of people?

- *Scientific Relevance:* Is the research question grounded in both social work and social science literature? Is the new research question connected to past research?

Here is an example of a research question that met all three criteria. We had a student whose field placement was in a mental health facility. For her research project she asked: Does cognitive-behavioral therapy reduce symptoms of depression among elderly in-patient clients? Given the interest in providing effective interventions, the question was important and there is a body of social work and social science literature to support this research. The challenge for the student was to design the study so that it could be completed in a timely fashion.

Examining Research Literature

As you consider your research question, you should consult the published social work and social science research literature. A review of the literature will connect your work to the efforts of other researchers working in the same area. You may get ideas about your research question, and about how to design your study, select participants, measure concepts, gather information, and analyze results. You will also learn from the researchers' difficulties in carrying out their studies as well as limitations of the studies. Appendix A reviews how to search for information published in peer review journals as well as on the World Wide Web.

Reviewing the literature is really a two-stage process. In the first stage, you must assess each article separately. Keep in mind that you cannot adequately understand a research study if you just treat it as a series of discrete steps involving a marriage of convenience among separate techniques. Any research project is an integrated whole, so you must be concerned with how each component to the research design influenced the others—for example, how the measurement approach might have affected the causal validity of the researcher's conclusions and how the sampling strategy might have altered the quality of measures.

The second stage of the review process is to compare your separate article reviews to assess the implications of the entire set of articles (and other materials) for the relevant aspects of your research question and procedures and then to write an integrated review for your own article or research proposal. Although you can find literature reviews that consist simply of assessments of one published article after another—that never get beyond stage one in the review process—your understanding of the literature and the quality of your own work will be much improved if you make the effort to write an integrated review.

Finding Literature for Evidence-Based Practice

Social work practitioners engaged in evidence-based practice must be able to find research evidence, and they must be able to critically appraise that evidence. In the past, this might have meant doing extensive literature searches or looking for reviews of the literature about the effectiveness of a treatment. Searching for individual articles is time-consuming, and single studies have limited generalizability. Literature reviews of a treatment model generally describe the findings of a variety of studies about an intervention's effectiveness, but these reviews tend to be subjective, and the conclusions tend to be based on the reviewer's opinions about the evidence (Lipp, 2007).

As evidence-based practice has grown, there has been a greater emphasis on **systematic reviews** of research findings. Systematic reviews of an intervention typically set criteria for the kinds of studies to be included based on study design, the population studied, and outcomes (Cook, Sackett, & Spitzer, 1995). For example, the reviewer tries to account for differences in design and participant characteristics, often using statistical techniques such as meta-analysis (which we describe in Chapter 12). These reviews provide better information about the impact of an intervention and how these impacts may vary (Littell, 2005). Although these reviews are believed to be objective, this does not mean that there are not controversies surrounding any particular review, including differences about the inclusion or exclusion of studies and what qualifies as a rigorous study design.

For systematic reviews to be used by social work practitioners, they have to be both easily accessible and understandable. The Internet has eased the access to such studies, and there are now both private and government-supported programs to produce and disseminate systematic reviews.

Campbell Collaboration

In 1999, evaluation researchers founded the **Campbell Collaboration** to publicize and encourage systematic review of evaluation research studies. The Campbell Collaboration encourages systematic reviews of research evidence on interventions and programs in education, criminal justice, social welfare, and research methods. These reviews are accessible to anyone with an Internet connection and can be used to provide evidence about different intervention techniques. For example, reviews conducted about social welfare interventions include *Interventions Intended to Reduce Pregnancy-Related Outcomes Among Teenagers* (Scher, Maynard, & Stagner, 2006); *Multisystemic Therapy for Social, Emotional, and Behavioral Problems in Children and Adolescents Aged 10–17* (Littell, Popa, & Forsythe, 2005); and *Personal Assistance for Older Adults (65+) Without Dementia* (Montgomery, Mayo-Wilson, & Dennis, 2008). The syntheses of intervention effectiveness are available to practitioners and agencies to identify evidence about a particular intervention and are found on the Campbell Collaboration Web site.

Government-Supported Resources

A variety of government agencies have begun to provide registries of effective inter-ventions. For example, the Substance Abuse and Mental Health Services Administration supports the National Registry of Evidence-Based Programs and Practices (NREPP) and can be found at www.nrepp.samhsa.gov. This registry features reviews of different programs including descriptive information about the intervention, ratings of the quality of the research, and ratings about the ease of implementing an intervention in an agency setting. The interventions are rated with respect to individual outcomes so that an intervention may be effective in treating one outcome but less so with another outcome. Search terms in the NREPP database include topics (such as co-occurring disorders), areas of interest (e.g., older adults, homelessness), study design, information about the intervention (e.g., implemented internationally), age, race, gender, settings (e.g., urban, tribal, residential), and availability of materials (e.g., public).

There are other government-supported registries. For example, The Guide to Community Preventive Services (found at www.thecommunityguide.org) is supported by the Centers for Disease Control. The Community Guide provides systematic reviews and interventions to promote community health on a range of topics such as mental health, sexual behavior, and violence. The Office of Juvenile Justice and Delinquency Prevention sponsors a registry of programs (found at www.dsgonline.com/mpg2.5/mpg_index.htm). The Model Program Guide provides ratings on a wide range of topics from prevention programs to reentry programs.

Considering Social Diversity

Finally, as you consider alternative research questions and review the research literature, it is important to remember that we live in a very diverse world. We need to consider whether research questions reflect a social bias or reinforce societal stereotypes. Research questions may reflect a gender, age, ethnic, or heterosexual bias. For example, questions about human aging can reflect negative social stereotypes of the elderly and suggest that aging is a problem (Schaie, 1993). Often questions about aging focus on decline and deficits as opposed to strengths. Behavioral differences or changes are often attributed to age without adequate attention to other factors related to age, such as income or education. Sometimes, questions about ethnic groups are characterized in terms of deficits as opposed to strengths, reinforcing negative stereotypes about those groups. There is a tendency, particularly in comparative research, to phrase questions suggesting a cultural superiority. Differences or gaps may reflect culturally appropriate mechanisms. Questions may reflect a heterosexist bias; conceptualizing a question in strictly heterosexual terms, such as defining a family in terms of parents of the opposite gender, can invalidate lesbian, gay, and bisexual relationships (Herek, Kimmel, Amaro, & Melton, 1991). Language such as comparing lesbians or gay men to the "general population" marginalizes lesbians and gay men.

How we conceptualize our questions and the language we use is therefore critical in the development of a research question. We must be attentive to the choice of language used. Further, it is important to recognize that variables such as age, race, and gender are associated with many other variables such as power, status, or income that may explain group differences.

▣ THEORY AND SOCIAL WORK RESEARCH

As members of an applied profession, social work practitioners and researchers often draw from theories developed in other academic disciplines, such as sociology, psychology, economics, or political science. Theories help us make sense of many interrelated phenomena and predict behavior or attitudes that are likely to occur when certain conditions are met. Theories help us understand how social problems emerge; they guide us in the design of interventions to help individuals, families, groups, or communities; they are used to explain relationships within organizations as well as between organizations; and they are often used to design social policy. Theory helps social work researchers to know what to look for in a study and to specify the implications of their findings for other research.

Theory A logically interrelated set of propositions about empirical reality. Examples of social theories include symbolic interactionism, learning theory, resource dependency, and stress theory.

A **theory** consists of concepts (or constructs) which are mental images that summarize a set of similar observations, feelings, or ideas; concepts have labels designed to describe some phenomena. A theory also includes propositions about the relationships among the concepts. Exhibit 2.1 illustrates a simple model of stress theory. There are two concepts, *stressors* (such as individual, family, or work-related changes) and *stress* (impacts on a person's well-being). The proposition is that the more stressors in a person's life, the more stress, a positive relationship; this is indicated by the "+" in Exhibit 2.1. The theory might be expanded to include a third concept, *resources,* which may alter the relationship between stressors and stress. So, based on this small model of stress theory, the stressors in one's life can lead to poor psychological outcomes, but this depends on how the stressful event is perceived and the coping behaviors available to deal with the stressful event.

Some social work researchers will use theory to examine the relationship between different phenomena. Stress theory led Sands and Goldberg-Glen (2000) to ask whether the availability of social supports (a type of resource) was associated with different levels of anxiety (a type of stress) for older adults who were raising a grandchild (a type of stressor). They thought that people with social supports would experience less distress than people without social supports (see Exhibit 2.1). Support for such a finding would suggest practical applications when working with clients who have experienced a stressful event.

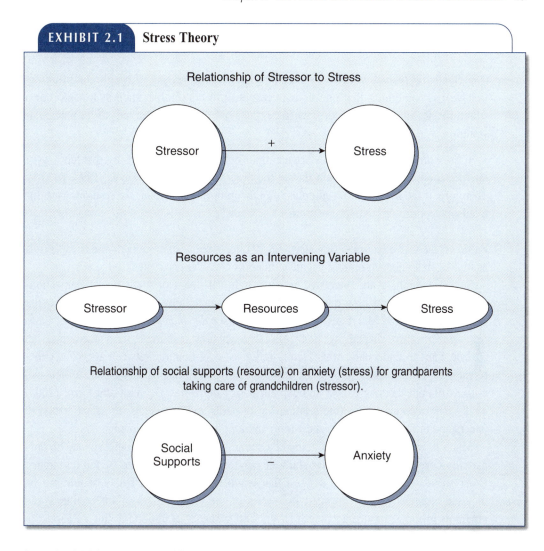

EXHIBIT 2.1   **Stress Theory**

Relationship of Stressor to Stress

Stressor → + → Stress

Resources as an Intervening Variable

Stressor → Resources → Stress

Relationship of social supports (resource) on anxiety (stress) for grandparents taking care of grandchildren (stressor).

Social Supports → − → Anxiety

Source: Engel & Schutt (2005). Adapted from Sands & Goldberg-Glen (2000).

There is no "one theory" of social work practice per se, as different models of social work practice draw from different broader theories often rooted in other disciplines. Therefore, many social work researchers engage in testing and building practice theory. For example, William Bradshaw (1997) evaluated an intervention based on cognitive-behavioral therapy that was designed to improve the psychological functioning of mentally ill individuals while reducing their symptoms and frequency of hospitalization. He noted that "cognitive-behavioral treatments had been applied to a wide range of populations and problems" but not to those suffering with schizophrenia (p. 419). As described by Payne (1997), cognitive-behavioral therapy is based on the following theories:

- *Behavior theory,* which suggests that behavior is learned through conditioning. Behavior is something that one does in response to a stimulus, such as a person or a situation. Conditioning occurs when a behavior becomes linked to a particular stimulus.

- *Cognition theory,* which "argues that behavior is affected by perception or interpretation of the environment during the process of learning" (Payne, 1997, p. 115). Therefore, if the response to a stimulus is an inappropriate behavior, the response was due to misperceptions or misinterpretations.

Based on these two theories, Bradshaw taught clients stress management and social skills, as well as techniques to replace negative thoughts and evaluated client outcomes.

Some researchers are interested in organizational behavior, both how organizations operate internally and how they relate to other organizations in their environment. For example, Rivard and Morrissey (2003) used *resource dependency theory* (which assumes that agencies are shaped by their efforts to obtain resources from their external environment) to understand what factors influence coordination between agencies. Other researchers are interested in both the development and critique of social policies and will utilize different theories to test and explain policy outcomes. Seefeldt and Orzol (2005) used *human capital theory* (the relationship of skills and knowledge to social status) to understand differences between short-term and long-term TANF recipients.

Much social work research is guided by some theory, although the theory may be only partially developed in a particular study or may even be unrecognized by the researcher. Other social work researchers suggest that while theory is important, it should not be imposed, especially when engaged in studies of the effectiveness of interventions and programs in social service agencies (Thyer, 2001). Theory is important, but we can learn from evaluation research studies not driven by a theoretical perspective.

ALTERNATIVE RESEARCH STRATEGIES

When we conduct social work research, we try to connect theory with empirical data—the evidence we obtain from the social world. Researchers use two alternative strategies to make this connection. **Deductive research** starts with a theory and then some of its implications are tested with data. **Inductive research** starts with the researcher first collecting the data and then developing a theory that explains patterns in the data. As Exhibit 2.2 shows, theory and data have a two-way, mutually reinforcing relationship.

Both deductive research and inductive research are essential to social work researchers. We cannot test an idea fairly unless we use deductive research, stating our expectations in

EXHIBIT 2.2	The Links Between Theory and Data

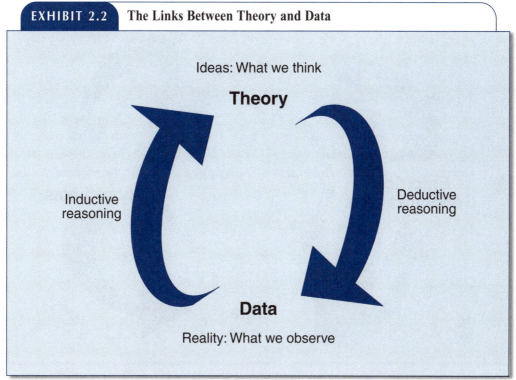

Source: Schutt (2005).

advance and setting up a test in which our idea could be shown to be wrong (falsified). A theory that has not survived these kinds of tests can be regarded only as very tentative. Yet theories cannot make useful predictions for every social situation or research problem. Moreover, we may find unexpected patterns in the data we collect, called **serendipitous findings** or **anomalous findings**. In either situation, we should reason inductively, making whatever theoretical sense we can of our unanticipated findings. Then, if the new findings seem sufficiently important, we can return to deductive reasoning and plan a new study to formally test our new ideas.

The process of conducting research, moving from theory to data and back again, or from data to theory and back again, is commonly called the **research circle** (see Exhibit 2.3). It mirrors the relationship between theory and data shown in Exhibit 2.2 and it comprises three main research strategies: deductive research, inductive research, and descriptive research.

Deductive Research

In deductive research we start with a theory and from the theory derive a specific expectation; data are then collected to test the specific expectation (see Exhibit 2.3). For

EXHIBIT 2.3   **The Research Circle**

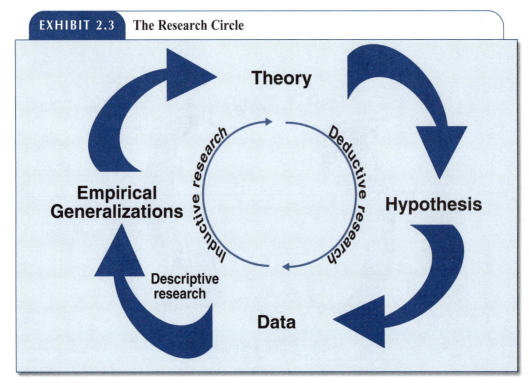

Source: Schutt (2005).

Hypothesis A tentative statement about empirical reality involving a relationship between two or more variables.

Example of a hypothesis: The higher the poverty rate in a community, the higher the percentage of community residents who are homeless.

Variables Characteristics or properties that can take on different values or attributes.

Examples of a variable: Poverty rate, percentage of homeless community residents.

Independent variable A variable that is hypothesized to cause, or lead to, variation in another variable.

Example of an independent variable: Poverty rate.

Dependent variable A variable that is hypothesized to vary depending on or under the influence of another variable.

Example of a dependent variable: Percentage of community residents who are homeless.

example, when people have more human capital, that is, work-related skills and education, they are likely to have higher incomes. We can deduce from this relationship a **hypothesis**, that is, a specific expectation; for example, using human capital theory, we might deduce that persons who graduate from college should have a higher income than persons who do not graduate from college. We then collect data about level of education and income to test the hypothesis.

A hypothesis proposes a relationship between two or more concepts or **variables.** A variable is a characteristic or property that can vary. Variation in one variable is proposed to predict or cause variation in the other variable. In the above example, we are proposing that having a college degree will predict income level. "College graduate" as the proposed influence is called the **independent variable;** its effect or consequence, in this case income level, is the **dependent variable.** After the researchers formulate one or more hypotheses and develop research procedures, they collect data with which to test the hypothesis.

Hypotheses can be worded in several different ways, and identifying the independent and dependent variables is sometimes difficult. When in doubt, try to rephrase the hypothesis as an "if-then" statement: "*If* the independent variable increases (or decreases), *then* the dependent variable increases (or decreases)." Exhibit 2.4 presents several hypotheses with their independent and dependent variables and their "if-then" equivalents.

Exhibit 2.4 demonstrates another feature of hypotheses: **direction of association**. When researchers hypothesize that one variable increases as the other variable increases, the direction of association is positive (Hypothesis 1); when one variable decreases as the other variable decreases, the direction of association is also positive (Hypothesis 3). But when one variable increases as the other decreases, or vice versa, the direction of association is negative, or inverse (Hypothesis 2). Hypothesis 4 is a special case in which the independent variable is categorical: It cannot be said to increase or decrease. In this case, the concept of direction of

EXHIBIT 2.4	**Examples of Hypotheses**			
Original Hypothesis	*Independent Variable*	*Dependent Variable*	*IF-THEN Hypothesis*	*Direction of Association*
1. As the number of stressors increases, the number of depressive symptoms increases.	Number of stressors	Depressive symptoms	IF the number of stressors is higher, THEN the number of depressive symptoms is higher.	Positive
2. As social support increases, caregiver stress decreases.	Social support level	Caregiver stress	IF social support is higher, THEN caregiver stress is less.	Negative
3. As years of education decrease, income decreases.	Years of education	Income	If years of education decrease, THEN income decreases.	Positive
4. Property crime is higher in urban areas than in suburban or rural areas.	Urbanization	Rate of property crimes	IF areas are urban, THEN property crime is higher compared with crime in suburban or rural areas.	NA
5. Depressive symptoms are higher for adolescents and older adults than for persons age 20 to 65.	Age of person	Depressive symptoms	IF people are age 13 to 19 or 65 or older, THEN their number of depressive symptoms is higher compared with people age 20 to 65.	Curvilinear

Source: Schutt (2005).

association does not apply, and the hypothesis simply states that one category of the independent variable is associated with higher values on the dependent variable. Some hypotheses, such as Hypothesis 5, are not linear but rather curvilinear, meaning that the relationship does not reflect a straight line but a curve of some sort. Hypothesis 5 suggests that the percentage of people who are depressed is highest among teenagers and older adults, whereas it is lower for people between the ages of 20 and 65.

Explanatory and evaluative research studies are types of deductive research. In both types of research, researchers explicitly state their hypotheses or their statements of expectations. The research is designed to test these expectations. Deductive researchers show their hand by stating their expectations in advance and then by letting "the chips fall where they may;" the researcher accepts the resulting data as a fairly objective picture of reality.

Inductive Research

In contrast to deductive research, inductive research begins with specific data, which are then used to develop (induce) a general explanation (a theory) to account for the data. One way to think of this process is in terms of the research circle (Exhibit 2.3): Rather than starting at the top of the circle with a theory, the researcher starts at the bottom of the circle with data and then develops the theory. Researchers most committed to an inductive approach even put off formulating a research question before they begin to collect data—the idea is to let the question emerge from the situation itself (Brewer & Hunter, 1989).

A motivation for inductive research is exploration. In Chapter 1, you read about Johnson's (1999) exploratory study describing what it was like to live in a homeless shelter. Johnson did not develop a theory from her work but did identify themes to understand life in a homeless shelter.

In strictly inductive research, researchers know what they have found when they start theorizing or attempting to explain what accounts for their findings. The result can be new insights and provocative questions. But the adequacy of an explanation formulated after the fact is necessarily less certain than an explanation presented prior to the collection of data. Every phenomenon can always be explained in some way. Inductive explanations are thus more trustworthy if they are tested subsequently with deductive research.

The very nature of the research circle suggests that some research studies will include strategies to do both inductive and deductive research. For example, a study by Garland, Rogers, and Yancey (2001) of collaboration between faith-based organizations and secular organizations included two phases: An inductive research phase followed by a deductive research phase. For the inductive research, the research team conducted in-depth interviews with different stakeholders at 16 organizations to learn about the meaning and nature of the collaborative process and to identify potential relationships between and among ideas and concepts. In the second phase, the researchers developed a closed-ended survey based on the concepts developed in the first phase that was sent to a national sample of faith-based organizations. Using this instrument, they tested the relationships that were identified in the inductive phase of the research.

Descriptive Research

You have learned in Chapter 1 that some social work research is purely descriptive. Such research does not involve connecting theory and data, but it is still part of the research circle; it begins with data and proceeds only to the stage of making empirical generalizations based on those data (refer to Exhibit 2.3).

Valid description is important in its own right and is a necessary component of all investigations. Much important research for the government and public and private organizations is primarily descriptive: How many poor people live in this community? Is the health of the elderly improving? Where do the uninsured go to obtain medical treatment? Simply put, good description of data is the cornerstone of the scientific research process. Good descriptive research can also stimulate more ambitious deductive and inductive research. For example, knowing the prevalence of homelessness has motivated many researchers to examine the causes of homelessness and to test interventions and to test interventions and programs to serve the homeless.

Research Paradigms

Deductive research is often associated with a positivist or postpositivist perspective. Researchers with a **positivist** philosophy believe that there is an objective reality that exists apart from the perceptions of those who observe it; the goal of science is to better understand this reality. Positivists believe that a well-designed test of a theoretically based prediction—the test of the prediction that young adults with more education will be tolerant of other ethnic groups, for example—can move us closer to understanding actual social processes.

Postpositivists believe that there is an external, objective reality, but they are sensitive to the complexity of this reality and to the limitations of the researchers who study it and, in particular, for social workers, the biases they bring to the study of social beings like themselves (Guba & Lincoln, 1994). The goal of science is to achieve intersubjective agreement, that is, an agreement by different observers on what is happening in the natural or social world about the nature of reality (Wallace, 1983).

Inductive research is often guided by a very different philosophy: **interpretivism.** Interpretive social scientists believe that social reality is socially constructed and that the goal of social scientists is to understand the meanings people give to reality, not to determine how reality works apart from these interpretations. This philosophy rejects the positivist belief that there is a concrete, objective reality that scientific methods help us to understand (Lynch & Bogen, 1997); instead, interpretivists believe that scientists construct an image of reality based on their own preferences and prejudices and their interactions with others. The empirical data we collect comes to us through our own senses and must be interpreted with our own minds. This suggests that we can never be sure that we have understood reality properly.

The **constructivist paradigm** extends interpretivist methodology by emphasizing the importance of exploring how different stakeholders in a social setting construct their beliefs (Guba & Lincoln, 1989). It gives particular attention to the different goals of researchers and other participants in a research setting and seeks to develop a consensus among participants about how to understand the focus of inquiry. The constructivist research report will highlight different views of the social program or other issue and explain how a consensus can be reached among participants.

▣ THE TIME ELEMENT

You have reached the point of thinking about the design of the study. This means that you have settled upon a research question that you think sufficiently important and doable. You may or may not have linked your research question to a particular theory. And you have decided on the approach you wish to use to answer your question. You are now at the stage of considering an overall strategy to design the research. You will need to consider whether data will be collected at one point in time—a **cross-sectional research design**—or whether data are to be collected at two or more time points—a **longitudinal research design**.

Cross-Sectional Designs

In a cross-sectional research design, data are collected at one point in time. It is like taking a still photo snapshot as you see a picture of what exists at that point in time but not what came before or after. Cross-sectional designs do not allow you to examine the impact of time on a variable. For example, you might find that in a sample of adolescent girls those who had given birth had also dropped out of school. What you do not know is which event came first: Did these girls drop out and then become pregnant? (or) Did these girls become pregnant and then drop out of school? You cannot determine the time order of events, so you do not know what causes what. You might think the time order is not important, but if you were designing programs, it would become important. Do you provide outreach to those who have dropped out and offer programs to prevent pregnancy? Do you provide school-based child care to enable girls to continue in school? As a result, cross-sectional designs do not let you determine the impact of one variable on another variable.

Longitudinal Designs

In longitudinal research, data are collected over time. By measuring the value of cases on an independent variable and a dependent variable at each of these different times, the researcher can determine whether changes in the independent variable precede changes in the dependent variable. This design strategy enables researchers to test hypotheses that the independent variable does in fact come before changes in the dependent variable. Using a cross-sectional design, you cannot be sure which came first, but in a longitudinal design you can measure the independent variable and then see at a later time the effect on the dependent variable. Following the same group of high school girls over several years would clarify whether dropping out precedes or follows becoming an adolescent mother.

It is more difficult to collect data at two or more points in time than at one time, and often researchers simply cannot, or are unwilling to, delay completion of a study in order to collect follow-up data. Yet, as you can imagine, there are many research questions that really should involve a much longer follow-up period. The value of longitudinal data is so great that every effort should be made to develop longitudinal research designs when they are appropriate for the research question asked.

In some longitudinal designs, the same sample (or panel) is followed over time; in other designs, sample members are rotated or completely replaced. The three major types of longitudinal designs are trend studies, panel designs, and cohort designs (see Exhibit 2.5).

Trend Studies

Trend studies, also known as repeated cross-sectional studies, involve gathering data at two or more points in time from different samples (or groups of respondents) of the same population. Trend studies are appropriate when the goal is to determine whether a population has changed over time. For example, every month the government reports the unemployment rate and labor force participation as well as annual poverty rates. One source of these reports is the Current Population Survey (CPS), which is a monthly survey jointly

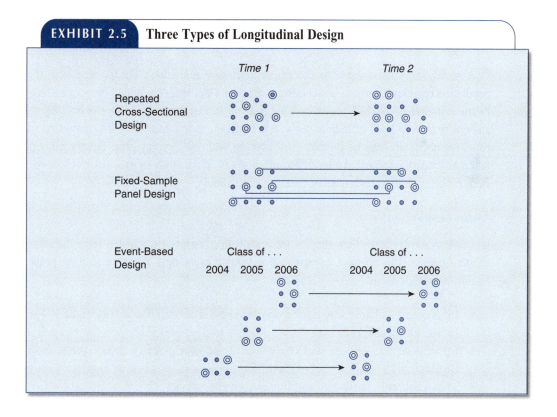

EXHIBIT 2.5 **Three Types of Longitudinal Design**

conducted by the U.S. Census Bureau and the U.S. Bureau of Labor Statistics of 50,000 households designed to represent the civilian, noninstitutional population. Each survey represents a different sample of households. In general, trend studies involve the following:

1. Drawing a sample from a population at Time 1, and collecting data from the sample.

2. As time passes, some people leaving the population and others entering it.

3. At Time 2, drawing a different sample from this population.

Panel Studies

When we want to know whether individuals within the population have changed, we use a **panel study**. Another U.S. Census Bureau–sponsored survey, called the Survey of Income and Program Participation, is a survey of 14,000 to 36,700 households, depending on the panel, in which the same individuals are interviewed every 4 months for 30 consecutive months about labor force participation, sources of income, and social program participation. A panel study involves the following:

1. A sample is drawn from a population at Time 1, and data are collected from the sample.

2. At Time 2, data are collected from the same people as at Time 1—except for those people who cannot be located.

A panel study allows you to determine both how individuals change and how the population changes. However, panel designs are also a challenge to implement successfully because of three major difficulties: expense, subject fatigue, and attrition. It can be difficult and costly to keep track of individuals over a long period, and inevitably the proportion of panel members who can be located for follow-up will decline over time. Panel members may grow weary of repeated interviews and drop out of the study or give stock responses. Both problems lead to high rates of participant attrition.

Cohort Studies

In a **cohort study,** follow-up samples (at one or more times) are selected from the same cohort—people who all have experienced a similar event or a common starting point. Examples include these:

- Birth cohorts—Those who share a common period of birth (those born in the 1940s, 1950s, 1960s, and so on)
- Seniority cohorts—Those who have worked at the same place for about 5 years, about 10 years, and so on
- School cohorts—Freshmen, sophomores, juniors, seniors

A cohort study can be either a type of trend study or a type of panel study. In a trend study, separate samples are drawn from the same cohort at two or more different times. In a cohort panel study, the same individuals from the same cohort are studied at two or more different times.

GUIDELINES FOR SOCIAL WORK RESEARCH

The guidelines followed by researchers fall into two categories: Those that help keep research scientific and those that keep research ethical. Both sets of guidelines are essential.

Scientific Guidelines

The following guidelines are applicable to all forms of scientific inquiry. Adhering to these guidelines will enable you to avoid mistakes about understanding the social world and prevent your investigations from being nothing more than a reflection of your own beliefs.

1. *Test ideas against empirical reality without becoming too personally invested in a particular outcome.* This guideline requires a commitment to testing, as opposed to reacting to events as they happen, being swayed by the popularity or status of others, or looking for what we want to see (Kincaid, 1996). When testing ideas, researchers have to recognize that what they find from their studies may not confirm what they had predicted the studies would find. Empirical testing requires a neutral and open mind.

2. *Plan and carry out investigations systematically.* Social work researchers have little hope of conducting a careful test of their ideas if they do not think through in advance how they should go about the test and then proceed accordingly. But a systematic approach is not always easy and the best plans can go awry. Kathryn Edin developed a structured interview to learn about how low-income families financially made ends meet, but most respondents refused to offer information. To get accurate responses, Edin had to switch approaches and arranged a series of informal semi-structured interviews (Edin & Lein, 1997).

3. *Document all procedures and disclose them publicly.* Social work researchers should disclose the methods on which their conclusions are based so that others can evaluate for themselves the likely soundness of these conclusions. Such disclosure is a key feature of science. It enables researchers to react to each other's work and provides the best guarantee against purely self-interested conclusions (Kincaid, 1996). Furthermore, by documenting procedures, other researchers will know how the study was completed and can replicate the study.

4. *Clarify assumptions.* No investigation is complete unto itself; whatever the researcher's method, the research rests on some background assumptions. By definition, research assumptions are not tested, so we do not know for sure whether they are correct.

By taking the time to think about and disclose their assumptions, researchers provide important information for those who seek to evaluate the validity of research conclusions.

5. *Specify the meaning of all terms.* Words often have multiple or unclear meanings. *Alienation, depression, strengths, information and referral, welfare,* and so on can mean different things to different people. Thus the terms used in scientific research must be defined explicitly and used consistently.

6. *Maintain a skeptical stance toward current knowledge.* The results of any particular investigation must be examined critically. A general skepticism about current knowledge stimulates researchers to improve the validity of research results and expand the frontier of knowledge. Often even in their own studies, researchers will conclude with a discussion of the limitations of their study designs.

7. *Replicate research and build social theory.* No one study is definitive by itself. We cannot fully understand it apart from the larger body of knowledge to which it is related, and we cannot place much confidence in it until it has been replicated. Theories organize the knowledge accumulated by numerous investigations into a coherent whole and serve as a guide to future inquiries. Different models of social work practice must be tested by repeated applications of a treatment modality with different participants, in different settings, and with different types of concerns.

8. *Search for regularities or patterns.* Positivist and postpositivist scientists assume that the natural world has some underlying order of relationships, so that unique events and individuals can be understood, at least in part, in terms of general principles (Grinnell, 1992). The goal of elaborating individual cases is to understand the social patterns that may characterize many individuals.

These general guidelines are ideals for much social work research, but no particular investigation is going to follow every guideline exactly. Real investigations by social work researchers do not always include much attention to theory, specific definitions of all terms, and so forth.

Ethical Guidelines

The previous section dealt with technical considerations; now we consider the ethics of conducting the study. Every scientific investigation has an ethical dimension to it. The scientific concern with validity requires that scientists be honest and reveal their methods. Researchers also have to consider the uses to which their findings will be put. Often social work research deals with topics that challenge social conditions or social policy, which places an added burden on ensuring the research is done well. In addition, protecting respondents is paramount as social work research is often conducted with vulnerable populations, such as the elderly, children, or people with a mental illness, who may or may not be able to consent to research. Other research includes historically oppressed populations such as people of color, women, or sexual minorities, who have reasons to distrust research efforts despite the assurances of researchers. As you can see, social work researchers often confront unique ethical challenges.

Honesty and Openness

Research distorted by political or personal pressures to find particular outcomes or to achieve the most marketable results is unlikely to be carried out in an honest and open fashion, but distinguishing between unintentional error and deliberate fraud can be very difficult. For example, a 1963 report of the U.S. Senate's Subcommittee on Problems of the Aged and Aging concluded that a study of elderly persons' health needs, publicized by the American Medical Association, was a "supposedly objective, scientific, academic study" but really a "pseudo-scientific half-effort" (Cain, 1967, pp. 78–79). The researchers were accused of having an upper-class bias in the design of their sample and of using some questions that underestimated elders' health needs. Yet the researchers were convinced they had adhered to scientific guidelines.

Openness about research procedures and results goes hand-in-hand with honesty in research design. Openness is also essential if researchers are to learn from the work of others. Despite the need for openness, some researchers may hesitate to disclose their procedures or results to prevent others from building on their ideas and taking some of the credit. You may have heard of the long legal battle between a U.S. researcher and a French researcher about how credit for discovering the AIDS virus should be allocated. Although such public disputes are unusual, concerns with priority of discovery are common. Scientists are like other people in their desire to be first. Enforcing standards of honesty and encouraging openness about research is the best solution for these problems.

The Uses of Science

Scientists must also consider the uses to which their research is put. Although many scientists believe that personal values should be left outside the laboratory, some feel that it is proper for scientists in their role as citizens to attempt to influence the way their research is used. Social scientists who identify with a more critical tradition question the possibility of setting our values aside and instead urge researchers to use research to achieve goals that they believe are worthy.

Sometimes it is difficult to separate research and advocacy given the nature of many of the kinds of questions social work researchers pursue. Some social work research is conducted to monitor the impacts of social legislation: for example, research to monitor changes in health care policy or the effects of welfare reform. The findings from such studies are likely to be used to help shape changes in policy or to reinforce current policy. Regardless of whether the researchers enter into the research with an opinion, the methods they use should be objective, and their reporting of the data should be accurate and honest. This will lend credibility to the conclusions reported by the researcher.

Social work researchers who conduct research on behalf of organizations and agencies may face additional difficulties when the organization, not the researcher, controls the final report and the publicity it receives. If organizational leaders decide that particular research results are unwelcome, the researcher's desire to have findings used appropriately and reported fully can conflict with contractual obligations. Researchers can often anticipate such dilemmas in advance and resolve them when the contract for research is negotiated—or simply decline a particular research opportunity altogether. But often such problems come up only after a report has been drafted, or they are ignored by a researcher who needs to have a job or to maintain particular personal relationships. These possibilities cannot be avoided entirely, but because of them, it is always important to acknowledge the source of research funding in reports.

Research on People

Social work researchers must concern themselves with the way their human subjects are treated in the course of research. This treatment may involve comparisons of different interventions in social service agencies, different tests to determine effective social policy, sensitive questions in survey research, observations in field studies, or analyses of personal data. Here we will review briefly current ethical standards for the treatment of human subjects and identify some of the issues in their application. As you read subsequent chapters, you will learn about specific ethical issues as they arise.

The federal government, professional associations, special university review boards, and ethics committees in other organizations all set standards for the treatment of human subjects. Federal regulations require that every institution seeking federal funding for biomedical or behavioral research on human subjects have an **institutional review board (IRB)** that reviews research proposals. IRBs at universities and other agencies apply ethics standards that are set by federal regulations but can be expanded or specified by the IRB (Sieber, 1992). To promote adequate review of ethical issues, the regulations require that IRBs include members with diverse backgrounds. The Office for Protection From Research Risks in the National Institutes of Health (NIH) monitors IRBs, with the exception of research involving drugs (the responsibility of the Federal Drug Administration). In addition, in October 2000, the NIH began to require that all researchers (and key study investigators) who seek funding complete an educational program on the protection of human research participants.

The National Association of Social Workers has incorporated these standards into its ethical code. The National Association of Social Workers (1999) *Code of Ethics* evaluation and research standards include the following:

- Social workers engaged in evaluation and research should follow guidelines developed for the protection of evaluation and research participants. They should consult with appropriate Institutional Review Boards.

- Research should cause no harm to participants.

- Participants must give their informed consent to participate in the research, if capable. If not, then assent must be obtained from an appropriate proxy.

- Participation in research should be voluntary and participants should be informed of their right to withdraw at any time without penalty.

- Researchers should fully disclose their identity. Social workers doing research should avoid conflicts of interest and reveal possible conflicts with potential participants.

- Anonymity or confidentiality must be maintained for individual research participants. Participants should be told about any limits of confidentiality and the methods to ensure confidentiality.

- Findings should be reported accurately; errors later found should be corrected.

- The benefits of a research project should outweigh any foreseeable risks.

- Social workers should take steps to ensure that participants have access to appropriate supportive services. (National Association of Social Workers, 1999)

As simple as these guidelines may seem, they are difficult to interpret in specific cases and harder yet to define in a way agreeable to all social work researchers. For example, how should "no harm to subjects" be interpreted? Does it mean that participants should not be harmed at all, psychologically as well as physically? That they should feel no anxiety or distress whatsoever during the study or only after their involvement ends? Should the possibility of any harm, no matter how remote, deter research?

Consider the question of possible harm to the participants of a well-known prison simulation study (Haney, Banks, & Zimbardo, 1973). The study was designed to investigate the impact of social position on behavior—specifically, the impact of being either a guard or a prisoner in a prison, a "total institution." The researchers selected apparently stable and mature young male volunteers and asked them to sign a contract to work for 2 weeks as a guard or a prisoner in a simulated prison. Within the first 2 days after the prisoners were incarcerated by the "guards" in a makeshift basement prison, the prisoners began to be passive and disorganized, whereas the guards became verbally and physically aggressive. Five "prisoners" were soon released for depression, uncontrollable crying, fits of rage, and in one case a psychosomatic rash; on the 6th day, the researchers terminated the experiment. Through discussions in special post-experiment encounter sessions, feelings of stress among the participants who played the role of prisoner seemed to be relieved; follow-up during the next year indicated no lasting negative effects on the participants and some benefits in the form of greater insight.

Would you ban such experiments because of the potential for harm to participants? Does the fact that the experiment yielded significant insights into the effect of a situation on human behavior—insights that could be used to improve prisons—make any difference (Reynolds, 1979)? Do you believe that this benefit outweighed the foreseeable risks?

The requirement of **informed consent** means that potential participants receive all the information they need to decide whether to participate in a research study. Potential participants should learn the purpose of the study, the length of the study, the procedures used in the study, a description of the possible risks or discomforts that might be encountered in the study, the benefits for the participant and others, how confidentiality will be protected, and the voluntary nature of participation. But to be informed is more difficult to define than it first appears.

To be informed, consent must be given by persons who are competent in that they understand what they have been told, recognize the significance of the information, can adequately weigh the benefits and costs, and voluntarily consent to participate or not (Grisso & Appelbaum, 1995; Zayas, Cabassa, & Perez, 2005). Who is competent to give consent? What does "competent" mean? Children cannot legally give consent to participate in research, but they must have the opportunity to give or withhold their *assent* to participate in research to which their legal guardians have consented (Sieber, 1992). Are persons with a mental illness competent to give consent or does the nature of their specific illness preclude their ability to comprehend the nature of the research, their rights as research participants, and the benefits and costs of participating in the research?

Consent must be given voluntarily without coercion, that is, without forcing persons to participate. Coercion need not be explicit; rather, coercion may be subtle and implicit. Where there are differences in power between the researchers and the participants, implicit coercion may be a problem. Clients in human service agencies may feel that they are better served by the agency if they agree to participate, or they may worry that by refusing to participate in the research, their services will be altered. To the extent possible, clients must be reassured that there is no penalty or other consequence for refusing to participate in the research. The researcher's actions and body language must help to convey his verbal assurance that consent is voluntary. This also means that participants can withdraw at any time during the study without penalty.

Inducements such as money may also affect the voluntary nature of participation. Even small amounts of money may be sufficient to induce persons with low incomes to participate in research activities that they might otherwise have refused. Inducements should be kept to a level that acknowledges the subject's participation and inconvenience but is not so large as to entice people to participate. Payments, if offered, should be given even if the subject terminates participation without fully completing the research.

Fully informed consent may also reduce participation in research and, because signing consent forms prior to participation may change participants' responses, produce biased results (Larson, 1993). Experimental researchers whose research design requires some type of subject deception try to get around this problem by withholding some information before the experiment begins but then debriefing participants at the end. To conduct the study, the researcher must convince an institutional review board that the risks are minimal and the benefits of carrying out the study are substantial. In the **debriefing,** the researcher explains to the participant what happened in the experiment and why and responds to questions (Sieber, 1992).

Maintaining **confidentiality** is another key ethical obligation; a statement should be included in the informed consent agreement about how each participant's privacy will be protected (Sieber, 1992). Confidentiality means that someone, usually the researcher, can link particular responses to an individual. This contrasts with a promise of **anonymity,** in which there is no way to link an individual with his or her responses. To ensure confidentiality, procedures such as locking records and creating special identifying codes must be created to minimize the risk of access by unauthorized persons. The researcher must also be careful when reporting results to ensure that persons cannot be identified from the findings. However, statements about confidentiality should be realistic: Laws allow research records to be subpoenaed and may require reporting child abuse; a researcher may feel compelled to release information if a health- or life-threatening situation arises and participants need to be alerted. The need to report such information should be included in the informed consent process. Also, the standard of confidentiality does not apply to observation in public places and information available in public records.

The potential of withholding a beneficial treatment from some participants is also cause for ethical concern. Differential outcomes in welfare-to-work experiments mean that some individuals might well have higher earnings in both the short and long run. Experiments comparing treatment methods, such as intensive case management with traditional case management, might mean that some children have less chance of being reunified with their parents. These are not trivial consequences for the participants. The justification for such study designs, however, is quite persuasive: The researchers do not know prior to the experiment which method will be better.

However, just because a treatment approach is new does not make it automatically a better approach. That is why it is being tested to begin with—to determine whether it is beneficial. The researchers are not withholding a known, successful treatment from some participants. You will read in many social work intervention studies that rather than withhold a treatment, one set of participants will likely get the regular intervention rather than no intervention.

The evaluation of ethical issues in a research project should be based on a realistic assessment of the overall potential for harm and benefit to research participants rather than an apparent inconsistency between any particular aspect of a research plan and a specific ethical guideline. For example, full disclosure of "what is really going on" in an experimental study is unnecessary if participants are unlikely to be harmed. Nevertheless, researchers should make every effort to foresee all possible risks and to weigh the possible benefits of the research against these risks.

CONCLUSION

Selecting a worthy research question does not guarantee a worthwhile research project. The simplicity of the research circle presented in this chapter belies the complexity of the social research process. In the following chapters, we focus on particular aspects of that process. As you encounter these specifics, do not lose sight of the basic guidelines that researchers need to follow to overcome the most common impediments to social work research.

Owning a large social science toolkit is no guarantee of making the right decisions about which tools to use and how to use them in the investigation of particular research problems.

Ethical issues must be considered when evaluating research proposals and conducting research studies. As the preceding examples show, ethical issues in social work research are no less complex than the other issues that researchers confront. It is inexcusable to jump into research on people without any attention to ethical considerations.

You are now forewarned about, and thus hopefully forearmed against, the difficulties that social scientists face in their work. We hope that you will return often to this chapter as you read the subsequent chapters, when you critique the research literature, and when you design your own research projects.

KEY TERMS

Anomalous findings
Anonymity
Campbell Collaboration
Cohort study
Confidentiality
Constructivist paradigm
Cross-sectional research design
Debriefing
Deductive research
Dependent variable
Direction of association
Hypothesis
Independent variable
Inductive research

Informed consent
Institutional review board
Interpretivism
Longitudinal research design
Panel study
Positivist
Postpositivism
Research circle
Serendipitous findings
Systematic reviews
Theory
Trend studies
Variables

HIGHLIGHTS

• Research questions should be feasible (given the time and resources available), socially important, and scientifically relevant.

• Research questions should avoid reflecting a social bias or reinforcing societal stereotypes.

• Social work researchers often engage in testing and building practice theory. Often practice theory is derived from broader social theory developed by other disciplines.

• The type of reasoning in most research can be described as primarily deductive or inductive. Research based on deductive reasoning proceeds from general ideas, deduces specific expectations from these ideas, and then tests the ideas with empirical data. Research based on inductive reasoning begins with specific data and then develops general ideas or theories to explain patterns in the data.

• It may be possible to explain unanticipated research findings after the fact, but such explanations have less credibility than those that have been tested with data collected for the purpose of the study.

• The scientific process can be represented as circular, with a path from theory to hypotheses, to data, and then to empirical generalizations. Research investigations may begin at different points along the research circle and traverse different portions of it. Deductive research begins at the point of theory; inductive research begins with data, but ends with theory. Descriptive research begins with data and ends with empirical generalizations.

• Research designs may involve gathering data at one time point or at two or more time points.

• Social work researchers should structure their research so that their own ideas can be proved wrong, should disclose their methods for others to critique, and should recognize the possibility of error.

• Scientific research should be conducted and reported in an honest and open fashion. Contemporary ethical standards also require that social work research cause no harm to participants, that participation be voluntary as expressed in informed consent, that researchers fully disclose their identity, that benefits to participants outweigh any foreseeable risks, and that anonymity or confidentiality be maintained for participants unless it is voluntarily and explicitly waived. These standards are incorporated into the NASW *Code of Ethics*.

DISCUSSION QUESTIONS

1. What are the steps involved in a comprehensive literature review? What should you look for in journal articles? What cautions should you bear in mind when conducting searches on the Web?

2. Discuss the relationship of social theory to practice theory.

3. Describe the relationship between inductive and deductive research.

4. Describe the debate between positivism and interpretivism. What are the guidelines for these research philosophies and their associated goals? What do you think about each of these philosophies?

5. Discuss the relationship of social work research ethics to the NASW *Code of Ethics* statements on research. How are they similar? How are they different?

CRITIQUING RESEARCH

Locate a research article on a particular social issue such as homelessness, poverty, domestic violence, or child welfare. Consider the following questions:

1. What is the social condition under study? What is the basic research question or problem? Try to state it in just one sentence.

2. How did the author(s) explain the importance of the research question? Is the research question relevant to social work practice and/or social welfare policy?

3. What prior literature was reviewed? Was it relevant to the research problem? To the theoretical framework? Does the literature review appear to be adequate? Are you aware of (or can you locate) any important omitted studies? Is the literature review up-to-date?

4. Was a theoretical framework presented? What was it? Did it seem appropriate for the research question addressed? Can you think of a different theoretical perspective that might have been used?

5. Were any hypotheses stated? Were these hypotheses justified adequately in terms of the theoretical framework? In terms of prior research?

6. What were the independent and dependent variables in the hypothesis or hypotheses? What direction of association was hypothesized? Were any other variables identified as potentially important?

MAKING RESEARCH ETHICAL

1. Evaluate the study you found in Critiquing Research for its adherence to each of the ethical guidelines for research on people. How would you weigh the study's contribution to practice and social policy against its potential risks to human subjects?

DEVELOPING A RESEARCH PROPOSAL

Now it is time to start writing the proposal. These next exercises are very critical steps.

1. What is the problem for research? Why is this important for social workers to address? If you have not identified a problem for study, or if you need to evaluate whether your research problem is doable, a few suggestions should help to get the ball rolling and keep it on course:
    a. Jot down questions that have puzzled you in some area having to do with social issues or social work practice. These may be questions that have come to mind while reading textbooks or research articles or things you might have heard about in the news. Try to identify questions that really interest you.
    b. Now take stock of your interests, your opportunities, and the work of others. Which of your research questions no longer seem feasible or interesting? What additional research questions come to mind? Pick out a question that is of interest and seems doable.

2. What is known about the problem? Search the literature (and the Web) on the research question you identified. Try to identify recent citations to articles (with abstracts from *Social Work Abstracts* or other indexes). Get the articles and remember to inspect the article bibliographies for additional sources. Write a brief description of each article and Web site you consulted. As you read the literature, try to identify the theories used to explain the problem, the methodological approaches used to study the problem, and the results of the studies. What additions or changes to your thoughts about the research question are suggested by the various articles?

3. How does your proposed study build on the current literature? What will be the specific objective of your study?

4. Write out your research question in one sentence and elaborate on it in one paragraph. Identify the specific aims or hypotheses that will be addressed by your study. List at least three reasons that it is a good research question for you to investigate.

5. Which standards for the protection of human subjects might pose the most difficulty for researchers on your proposed topic? Explain your answers and suggest appropriate protection procedures for human subjects.

To assist you in completing the Web exercises below and to gain a better understanding of the chapter's contents, please access the study site at http://www.sagepub.com/fswrstudy where you will find the Web exercises reproduced with suggested links, along with self-quizzes, e-flash cards, interactive exercises, journal articles, and other valuable resources.

WEB EXERCISES

1. Try your hand at developing a hypothesis of your own. Pick a theorist from the wide range of personality theorists at http://webspace.ship.edu/cgboer/perscontents.html. Read some of what you find and think about the behavioral phenomena on which this theorist focuses. What hypotheses seem consistent with his or her theorizing? Describe a hypothetical research project to test one of these hypotheses.

2. You have been assigned to write a paper on domestic violence and the law. To start, you would like to find out what the American Bar Association's stance is on the issue. Go to the American Bar Association Commission on Domestic Violence's Web site (http://www.abanet.org/domviol/screening toolcdv.pdf). What is the American Bar Association's definition of domestic violence? How do they suggest one can identify a person as a victim of domestic violence? What do they identify as "basic warning signs"? Write your answers in a one- or two-page report.

3. Go to the National Registry of Evidence-Based Programs and Practices Web site (http://nrepp .samhsa.gov) and find a review of a mental health intervention for older African American adults that used an experimental design and had a quality of research rating of at least 3.0.

CHAPTER 3

Conceptualization and Measurement

Defining Concepts
Concepts and Variables
Operationalization
Scales
Treatment as a Variable
Combining Measurement
Operations

Characteristics of Variables
Nominal Level of Measurement
Ordinal Level of Measurement
Interval Level of Measurement
Ratio Level of Measurement
The Case of Dichotomies
Mathematical Comparisons

Measurement Error

Assessing Measurement Accuracy
Measurement Reliability
Test-Retest Reliability
Internal Consistency
Alternate-Forms Reliability
Interrater Reliability
Intrarater Reliability

Measurement Validity
Face Validity
Content Validity
Criterion Validity
Construct Validity
*Reliability and Validity of Existing
Measures*

Using Scales to Describe a Clinical Status

Measurement in a Diverse Society

**Measurement Implications for Evidence-
Based Practice**

Conclusion

Key Terms

Highlights

Discussion Questions

Critiquing Research

Making Research Ethical

Developing a Research Proposal

Web Exercises

Measurement is crucial to establishing the evidence base of social work practice. When you think of measurement in social work practice, you typically think of "assessment," whereby you are collecting information about a client system; the assessment often includes key concepts and measures of these concepts. When evaluating a program's outcomes, broadly stated goals and objectives are translated into something that can be measured. In each situation, you are making decisions that have consequences for clients and agency programs. Therefore, it is important to use accurate methods to assess clients or measure program outcomes.

In reviewing or designing a research study, how key concepts are defined and measured is critically important in order to evaluate the validity of the research. Judgments about the evidence to support a particular intervention are not just about the demonstration of successful outcomes but also entail considerations about the quality of the measures of these outcomes.

Therefore, you will have to answer three questions: (1) What do the main concepts mean? (2) How are the main concepts measured? (3) Is the measurement method accurate and valid?

In this chapter, we first address the issue of conceptualization, or how you define key terms. The next section focuses on the characteristics, or levels of measurement, reflected in different measures. This section is followed by a discussion of measurement error. Subsequently, we discuss different methods to assess the quality of measures, specifically the techniques used to assess reliability and validity. We then consider the implications of measurement for diverse population groups as well as evidence-based practice. By the chapter's end, you should have a good understanding of measurement and the crucial role it plays for social work research.

▣ DEFINING CONCEPTS

In 2007, the nation's official poverty rate was 12.5%, a percentage not very different from 2004; the percentage translated into 37.3 million people living in poverty (DeNavas-Walt, Proctor, & Smith, 2008). What does "poverty" mean? The Official Poverty Line definition used in this report is conceptualized as an absolute standard, based on the amount of money required to purchase an emergency diet adequate for about 2 months. But other social scientists reject the notion that a poverty measure should be based on an emergency diet and suggest that poverty means having sufficient income to purchase adequate amounts of goods such as housing, food, shelter, transportation, and the like in a particular geographical region (Bangs, Kerchis, & Weldon, 1997). Still other researchers disagree with absolute standards and have urged adoption of a relative poverty standard, defining those persons who live in poverty based on their incomes relative to the general population. In fact, the **concept** of poverty means different things to different people, and its measurement has always been somewhat

Concept A mental image that summarizes a set of similar observations, feelings, or ideas.

controversial. These discussions are important, because different notions about poverty shape estimates of how prevalent it is and what can be done about it.

Many of the topics social work researchers study involve abstract concepts or ideas, not just simple objects. Some concepts, such as age or gender, are straightforward, and there is little confusion about their meaning. When we refer to concepts like homelessness, mental health, poverty, or community empowerment, we cannot count on others knowing exactly what we mean. Even the experts may disagree about the meaning of frequently used concepts, just as we saw with the different definitions of poverty. That is okay. The point is not that there can be only one definition of a concept, but that we have to specify clearly what we mean when we use a concept. This is what is meant by **conceptualization**.

> *Conceptualization* The process of specifying what we mean by a term. In deductive research, **conceptualization** helps to translate portions of an abstract theory into testable hypotheses involving specific variables. In inductive research, conceptualization is an important part of the process used to make sense of related observations.

Since many concepts of interest are abstract, a beginning step in measurement is to define the concept. We have to turn to social theory and prior research to review appropriate definitions. We may need to identify the different dimensions or aspects of the concept. We should understand how the definition we choose fits within the theoretical framework guiding the research and what assumptions underlie this framework.

Researchers start with a **nominal definition** by which the concept is defined in terms of other concepts. Nominal definitions are like those definitions found in dictionaries: You get an understanding of the word and its dimensions, but you still do not have a set of rules to use to measure the concept. For example, child abuse might be defined as evident when either severe physical or emotional harm is inflicted on a child or there is contact of a sexual nature. The nominal definition of child abuse includes concepts such as severe harm, physical abuse, and emotional abuse, but the definition does not provide the set of rules to identify the forms of abuse or distinguish between severe and not severe harm. The actual measures of child abuse should be consistent with the nominal definition.

Concepts and Variables

After we define the concepts in a study, we can identify corresponding variables and develop procedures to measure them. Consider the concept of substance abuse, which is defined in the *DSM-IV-TR (Diagnostic and Statistical Manual of Mental Disorders,* 4th ed., text revision) as the "repeated use of a substance to the extent that it interferes with adequate social, vocational, or self-care functioning" (American Psychiatric Association [APA], 2004). This concept can be converted to a variable in different ways. One variable might be the count of alcoholic drinks; an alternative variable might involve asking about the presence of blackouts; a third variable may ask about binge drinking; and a fourth variable might reflect a score on a rating scale of 10 questions. Each of these variables is a plausible measure of substance abuse. If we are to study variation in substance abuse, we must identify the variables to measure that are most pertinent to the research question.

Where do variables fit in the continuum from concepts to operational indicators? Think of it this way: Usually, the term *variable* is used to refer to some specific aspect of a concept that varies and for which we then have to select even more concrete indicators. For example, research on the concept of social support might focus on the variable *level of perceived support*. We might then select as our indicator the responses to a series of statements about social support, such as the following statement from Zimet, Dahlem, Zimet, and Farley's (1988) Multidimensional Scale of Perceived Social Support: "There is a special person around when I am in need" (p. 35). Identifying the variables that we will measure is a necessary step on the road to developing our specific measurement procedures.

Concepts vary in their level of abstraction, and this in turn affects how readily we can specify the variables pertaining to the concept. We may not think twice before we move from a conceptual definition of age as time elapsed since birth to the variable, *years since birth*. Binge drinking is also a relatively concrete concept, but it requires a bit more thought. We may define binge drinking conceptually as episodic drinking and select for our research on binge drinking the variable, *frequency of five or more drinks in a row*. That is pretty straightforward.

A very abstract concept like social status may have a clear role in social theory but a variety of meanings in different social settings. Variables that pertain to social status may include level of esteem in a group, extent of influence over others, level of income and education, or number of friends. It is very important to specify what we mean by an abstract concept like social status in a particular study and to choose appropriate variables to represent this meaning.

Not every concept in a particular study is represented by a variable. If we were to study clients' alcohol abuse at an in-patient treatment unit, there is no variation; rather, all the clients are clients. In this case, *client* is called a constant; it is always the same and therefore is not a variable. Of course, this does not mean we cannot study differences, such as gender, among the clients. In this case, gender is the variable and client is still a constant.

It is very tempting to try to "measure everything" by including in a study every variable we can think of that might have something to do with our research question. This haphazard approach will inevitably result in the collection of data that are useless and the failure to collect some data that are important. In choosing variables for a study, examine relevant theories to identify key concepts, review prior research to learn how useful different indicators have been, and assess the resources available for adequately measuring variables in the specific setting to be studied.

Operationalization

Once we have defined our concepts in the abstract—that is, once we have provided a nominal definition—and we have identified the specific variables we want to measure, we must develop measurement procedures. The goal is to devise operations that actually measure the concepts we intend to measure, that is, to achieve measurement validity. **Operationalization** is the process of connecting concepts to observations. Researchers provide an **operational**

definition, which includes what is measured, how the indicators are measured, and the rules used to assign a value to what is observed and to interpret the value.

Previously we provided a nominal definition of alcoholism. An operational definition for alcoholism might include the following content:

> The Michigan Alcoholism Screening Test (MAST) is a 24-item instrument that includes a variety of indicators of symptoms such as seeing drinking as a problem, seeking treatment for problem drinking, delirium tremens, severe shaking, hearing voices, complaints from others about drinking, memory loss from drinking, job loss due to drinking, social problems from drinking, arrests for drunk driving or for drunken behavior, guilt feelings about drinking, and ability to stop drinking. The scale may be administered orally or may be self-administered. Respondents respond yes or no to each item and each item is given a weighted score ranging from 0 to 5. There are four items for which the alcoholic response is "no." The weighted item responses are summed, with a score of 0 to 3 indicating no problem with alcoholism, 4 considered to be suggestive of a problem and 5 or above an indication of alcoholism. (Adapted from Selzer, 1997)

As you can see from this definition, we are provided with the specific indicators included in the measure, the method(s) for data collection, specific scoring of the responses, and the interpretation of scale scores.

Exhibit 3.1 represents one part of the operationalization process in three studies. The first researcher defines the concept *income* and chooses one variable, annual earnings, to represent it. This variable is then measured with responses to a single question or item: What was your total income from all sources in 1998? The second researcher defines the concept *poverty* as having two aspects or dimensions, subjective poverty and absolute poverty. Subjective poverty is measured with responses to a survey question: Do you consider yourself poor? Absolute poverty is measured by comparing family income to the poverty threshold. The third researcher decides that the concept *social class* is defined by a position on three measured variables: income, education, and occupational prestige.

One consideration is the precision of the information that is necessary. The first researcher in Exhibit 3.1 is seeking information that is quite precise. She assumes that respondents will be able to accurately report the information. As an alternative, she might have asked respondents: "Please identify the income category that includes your total income from all sources in 1998." For this question, she will get less exact information. Generally, the decision about precision is based on the information that is needed for the research. It may also be based on what the researcher believes people can recall and the content people may be willing to report.

The variables and particular measurement operations chosen for a study should be consistent with the research question. Take this research question: Are self-help groups more effective in increasing the likelihood of abstinence among substance abusers than hospital-based treatments? We may operationalize the variable, *form of treatment,* in terms of participation in these two types of treatment, self-help or hospital-based. However, if we

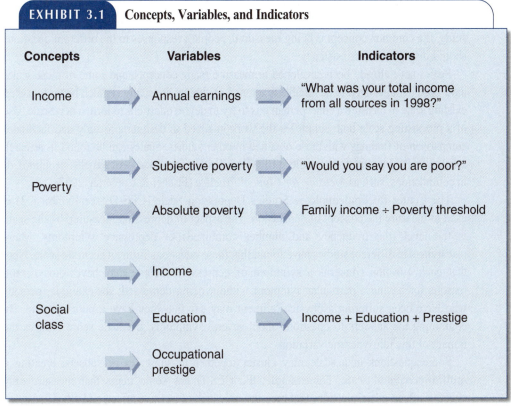

EXHIBIT 3.1   **Concepts, Variables, and Indicators**

Concepts	Variables	Indicators
Income	Annual earnings	"What was your total income from all sources in 1998?"
Poverty	Subjective poverty	"Would you say you are poor?"
	Absolute poverty	Family income ÷ Poverty threshold
Social class	Income	
	Education	Income + Education + Prestige
	Occupational prestige	

Source: Schutt (2008).

are answering the question, "What influences the success of substance abuse treatment?" we should probably consider what it is about these treatment alternatives that is associated with successful abstinence. Prior theory and research suggest that some of the important variables that differ between these treatment approaches are level of peer support, beliefs about the causes of alcoholism, and financial investment in the treatment.

Scales

When several questions are used to measure one concept, the responses may be combined by taking the sum or average of responses. A composite measure based on this type of sum or average is termed a **scale** (or index). The idea is that idiosyncratic variation in response to particular questions will average out so that the main influence on the combined measure will be the concept on which all the questions focus. Each item is an indicator of the concept, but the item alone is often not a sufficient measure of the concept. Therefore, the scale is a more complete measure of the concept than any single component question.

Creating a scale is not just a matter of writing a few questions that seem to focus on a concept. Questions that seem to you to measure a common concept might seem to respondents to concern several different issues. The only way to know that a given set of questions does form a scale is to administer the questions to people like those you plan to study. If a common concept is being measured, people's responses to the different questions should display some consistency.

Scales have already been developed to measure many concepts, and some of these scales have been demonstrated to be reliable in a range of studies. It usually is much better to use an existing scale to measure a concept than it is to try to devise questions to form a new scale. Use of a preexisting scale both simplifies the work involved in designing a study and facilitates comparison of findings with those obtained in other studies. Scales can be found in research articles, on the Internet, for example at ERIC/AE Test Locator (www.ericae.net/testcol.htm), or in compilations, such as *Measure for Clinical Practice* (Fischer & Corcoran, 2007).

The Center for Epidemiologic Studies Depression Scale (CES-D; see Exhibit 3.2) is used to measure the concept of depression. The aspect of depression measured by the scale is the level (the frequency and number combined) of depressive symptoms. Many researchers in different studies have found that these questions form an accurate scale. Note that each question concerns a symptom of depression. People may have idiosyncratic reasons for having a particular symptom without being depressed; for example, persons who have been suffering a physical ailment may say that they have a poor appetite. By combining the answers to questions about several symptoms, the scale score reduces the impact of this idiosyncratic variation.

Some questions in a scale may cluster together in subscales or subsets, creating a **multidimensional scale**. For example, the CES-D has some items that measure only negative affect, other questions that measure only lack of positive affect, and other questions measuring somatic symptoms. Each of these concepts is an indicator of depression. Researchers may choose to use a variable that summarizes the total scale score, or they may chose to use variables that summarize the subscale scores.

Some scales have questions that are more central to the concept being measured than other questions and so may be given greater weight when computing the scale score. For example, the MAST asks questions that are assigned different weights. The question "Have you ever been in a hospital because of your drinking?" is given more points (weighted higher) than the question "Do you feel you are a normal drinker?"

Treatment as a Variable

Frequently, social work researchers will examine the effectiveness of an intervention or compare two different intervention approaches. When an intervention is compared with no intervention or when two or more interventions are compared, the intervention is a variable. The intervention becomes the independent variable that you assume will cause a change in a status or condition. It is important that a researcher provide a very clear nominal definition of the intervention. For example, it is not enough for the researcher to say that the study is comparing one method to another, such as "traditional" case management to "intensive" case management. Although the general meaning of such an approach may be

| EXHIBIT 3.2 | Example of a Scale: The Center for Epidemiologic Studies Depression Scale (CES-D) |

Below is a list of the ways you might have felt or behaved. Please indicate how often you have felt this way during the past week (*circle one number on each line*).

During the past week . . .	*Rarely or none of the time (less than 1 day)*	*Some or a little of the time (1–2 days)*	*Occasionally or a moderate amount of time (3–4 days)*	*All of the time (5–7 days)*
1. I was bothered by things that usually don't bother me.	0	1	2	3
2. I did not feel like eating; my appetite was poor.	0	1	2	3
3. I could not shake off the blues even with help from my family or friends.	0	1	2	3
4. I felt I was just as good as other people.	0	1	2	3
5. I had trouble keeping my mind on what I was doing.	0	1	2	3
6. I felt depressed.	0	1	2	3
7. I felt everything I did was an effort.	0	1	2	3
8. I felt hopeful about the future.	0	1	2	3
9. I thought my life had been a failure.	0	1	2	3
10. I felt fearful.	0	1	2	3
11. My sleep was restless.	0	1	2	3
12. I was happy.	0	1	2	3
13. I talked less than usual.	0	1	2	3
14. I felt lonely.	0	1	2	3
15. People were unfriendly.	0	1	2	3
16. I enjoyed life.	0	1	2	3
17. I had crying spells	0	1	2	3
18. I felt sad.	0	1	2	3
19. I felt people disliked me.	0	1	2	3
20. I could not "get going."	0	1	2	3

Source: Radloff (1977).

familiar to you, the researcher must define what each approach involves. For example, case management may include full support, so that the social worker provides a variety of services and supports including rehabilitation, social skill building, counseling, linking to resources, identifying work and social opportunities, and money management, whereas another social worker providing case management may only assess the client, link the client to other services, and periodically reassess the client.

Nominal definitions of an intervention only provide the characteristics or components of the intervention but fail to fully describe how the intervention was implemented. Researchers provide varying amounts of specificity regarding the actual operationalization of the intervention. For example, Mitchell (1999) operationalized his cognitive-behavioral group therapy approach by designating the length of the groups (8-week program) and the content covered in each of the weekly sessions. This amount of detail provides a much clearer sense of the nature of the intervention, but it would still not be possible to repeat the research or to implement the intervention in your agency without additional information.

Combining Measurement Operations

The choice of a particular measurement method is often determined by available resources and opportunities, but measurement is improved if this choice also takes into account the particular concept or concepts to be measured. Responses to such questions as "How socially engaged were you at the party?" or "How many days did you use sick leave last year?" are unlikely to provide information as valid, respectively, as direct observation or agency records. However, observations at social gatherings may not answer questions about why some people do not participate; we may just have to ask them.

Triangulation—the use of two or more different measures of the same variable—can strengthen measurement considerably (Brewer & Hunter, 1989). When we achieve similar results with different measures of the same variable, particularly when the measures are based on such different methods as survey questions and field-based observations, we can be more confident in the validity of each measure. If results diverge with different measures, it may indicate that one or more of these measures are influenced by more measurement error than we can tolerate. Divergence between measures could also indicate that they actually operationalize different concepts.

▣ CHARACTERISTICS OF VARIABLES

The final part of operationalization is to assign a value or symbol to represent the observation. Each variable has categories of some sort, and we need to know how to assign a value—typically a number—to represent what has been observed or learned. A variable's categories impart different types of information. We may have a **discrete variable**, whereby the symbol represents a separate category or a different status. The variable may be a **continuous variable**, for which the symbol represents a quantity that can be described in terms of order, spread between the numbers, and/or relative amounts.

Part of operationalization is to decide the variable's **level of measurement** that will be used in the research. When we know a variable's level of measurement, we can better understand how cases vary on that variable and so understand more fully what we have measured. Level of measurement also has important implications for the type of mathematical operations and statistics that can be used with the variable. There are four levels of measurement: nominal, ordinal, interval, and ratio. Exhibit 3.3 depicts the differences among these four levels.

> *Level of measurement* The mathematical precision with which the values of a variable can be expressed. The nominal level of measurement, which is qualitative, has no mathematical interpretation; the quantitative levels of measurement—ordinal, interval, and ratio—are progressively more precise mathematically.

Nominal Level of Measurement

The **nominal level of measurement** identifies variables whose values have no mathematical interpretation; they vary in kind or quality but not in amount. The variable *gender* has two categories or attributes: male and female. We might represent male with the value 1 and female with the value 2, but these numbers do not tell us anything about the difference between male and female except that they are different. Female is not one unit more of "gender" than male, nor is it twice as much "gender."

Nominal-level variables are commonplace in social work research. Client characteristics such as ethnicity (e.g., African American, Hispanic, Asian American, White, Native American), marital status (e.g., Married Spouse Present, Married Spouse Absent, Widowed, Divorced, Separated, Never Married), or mental health diagnosis (e.g., Mood Disorder, Personality Disorder) are nominal-level variables. Service-related variables such as referral source, types of service used, or type of abuse are nominal variables. In each case, the variable has a set of categories whose order has no meaning.

Although the attributes of nominal variables do not have a mathematical meaning, they must be assigned to cases with great care. The attributes we use to categorize cases must be mutually exclusive and exhaustive:

- A variable's attributes or values are **mutually exclusive** if every case can have only one attribute.

- A variable's attributes or values are **exhaustive** when every case can be classified into one of the categories.

When a variable's attributes are mutually exclusive and exhaustive, every case corresponds to one and only one attribute.

The only mathematical operation we can perform with nominal-level variables is a count. We can count how many current clients are females and how many are males. From this count, we can calculate the percentage or proportion of females to males among our clients. If the agency serves 150 women and 100 men, then we can say that 60% of the

EXHIBIT 3.3 **Levels of Measurement**

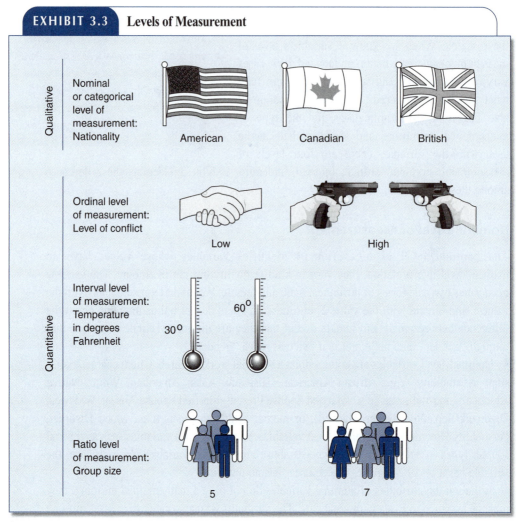

Source: Schutt (2008).

clients are female. But we cannot identify an average gender nor can we add or subtract or compute any other kind of number.

Ordinal Level of Measurement

The first of the three quantitative levels is the **ordinal level of measurement**. At this level, the numbers assigned to cases specify only the order of the cases, permitting greater-than and less-than distinctions. The gaps between the various responses do not have any particular meaning. As with nominal variables, the different values of a variable measured at the ordinal level must be mutually exclusive and exhaustive.

The properties of variables measured at the ordinal level are illustrated in Exhibit 3.3 by the contrast between the levels of conflict in two groups. The first group, symbolized by two people shaking hands, has a low level of conflict. The second group, symbolized by two persons pointing guns at each other, has a high level of conflict. To measure conflict, we would put the groups "in order" by assigning the number 1 to the low-conflict group and the number 2 to the high-conflict group. The numbers thus indicate only the relative position or order of the cases. Although low level of conflict is represented by the number 1, it is not one less unit of conflict than high level of conflict, which is represented by the number 2.

A common ordinal measure used in social service agencies is client satisfaction. Often, agencies will ask a client a global question about satisfaction with the services provided by the agency using a rating system such as 4 = *very satisfied,* 3 = *satisfied,* 2 = *dissatisfied,* and 1 = *very dissatisfied.* Someone who responds very satisfied, coded as 4, is clearly more satisfied than someone who responds dissatisfied, coded as 2, but the respondent with a 4 is not twice as satisfied as the respondent with a 2. Nor is the respondent with a 4 two units more satisfied than the respondent with a 2. We do know that the first person is more satisfied than the second person, and therefore, the order has meaning. We can count the number of clients who fall into each category. We can also compute an average satisfaction, but the average is not a quantity of satisfaction; rather, the number summarizes the relative position of the group on the scale.

Agencies sometimes use goal attainment scales to evaluate client outcomes. These scales are usually developed by describing the worst indicators, the best indicators, and several steps in between. The gap between the steps has no meaning, but the scoring represents the progress of the client. Exhibit 3.4 provides an example of a goal attainment scale to measure self-esteem and mother's attitude toward children. The social worker evaluates the extent to which there is improvement in self-esteem based on the nature of the verbal and nonverbal responses of the client. There is an order to the levels of achievement, and we can describe how many clients fall into each category, but we cannot calculate the average level of achievement using this scale.

Interval Level of Measurement

The values of a variable measured at the **interval level of measurement** represent fixed measurement units, but have no absolute or fixed zero point. An interval level of measurement also has mutually exclusive categories, the categories are exhaustive, and there is an order to the responses. This level of measurement is represented in Exhibit 3.3 by the difference between two Fahrenheit temperatures. Although 60 degrees is 30 degrees hotter than 30 degrees, 60 in this case is not twice as hot as 30. Why not? Because "heat" does not begin at 0 degrees on the Fahrenheit scale. Therefore, the numbers can be added and subtracted, but ratios between them (2 to 1 or "twice as much") are not meaningful.

There are few true interval-level measures in social work, but many social work researchers treat scales created by combining responses to a series of ordinal-level variables

EXHIBIT 3.4	Example of a Goal Attainment Scale			
Problem Area	Client Outcome Goal	No Achievement (Score = 0)	Some Achievement (Score = 1)	Major Achievement (Score = 2)
Self-esteem	To develop increased feeling of self-esteem	• Makes only negative statements • Does not identify strengths • No verbal expression of confidence • No sense of self-worth	• Some positive statements • Some negative statements • Can identify some strengths but overly critical about self • Emerging confidence • Emerging self-worth	• Makes many positive statements • Few to no negative statements • Can identify strengths without qualifying statements • Is confident • Has self-worth
Mother's attitude toward child	Less of a negative attitude toward child	• Resists child's affection constantly • Shows anger verbally and nonverbally constantly • Shows frustration constantly • Shows hostility constantly • Impatient constantly	• Occasional affection • Occasional anger • Occasional frustration • Occasional hostility • Occasional impatience	• Accepts child's affection • No verbal or nonverbal signs of anger, hostility, frustration • Patient

Source: Engel & Schutt (2005).

as interval-level measures. This is frequently done because there are more mathematical operations associated with interval-level variables. For example, a scale of this sort could be created with responses to Attkisson's (Larsen, Attkisson, Hargreaves, & Nguyen, 1979) Client Satisfaction Questionnaire (see Exhibit 3.5 for the CSQ-8). The questions in this scale have different response categories, but the same response numbers. Each question can be used independently of the other questions to provide useful information: an ordinal level of measurement. The responses to the eight questions can be summed to reflect overall satisfaction. The scale would then range from 8 to 32, with higher scores representing greater satisfaction. A score of 24 could be treated as if it were 12 more units than a score of 12, but that does not mean that one respondent is twice as satisfied as the other respondent.

EXHIBIT 3.5	**Example of an Interval-Level Measure: Client Satisfaction Questionnaire (CSQ-8)**

Circle your answer:

1. How would you rate the quality of service you have received?

4	3	2	1
Excellent	Good	Fair	Poor

2. Did you get the kind of service you wanted?

1	2	3	4
No, definitely not	No, not really	Yes, generally	Yes, definitely

3. To what extent has our program met your needs?

4	3	2	1
Almost all of my needs have been met	Most of my needs have been met	Only a few of my needs have been met	None of my needs have been met

4. If a friend were in need of similar help, would you recommend our program to him or her?

1	2	3	4
No, definitely not	No, I don't think so	Yes, I think so	Yes, definitely

5. How satisfied are you with the amount of help you have received?

1	2	3	4
Quite dissatisfied	Indifferent or mildly dissatisfied	Mostly satisfied	Very satisfied

6. Have the services you received helped you to deal more effectively with your problems?

4	3	2	1
Yes, they helped a great deal	Yes, they helped	No, they really didn't help	No, they seemed to make things worse

7. In an overall, general sense, how satisfied are you with the service you received?

4	3	2	1
Very satisfied	Mostly satisfied	Indifferent or mildly dissatisfied	Quite dissatisfied

8. If you were to seek help again, would you come back to our program?

1	2	3	4
No, definitely not	No, I don't think so	Yes, I think so	Yes, definitely

Ratio Level of Measurement

The **ratio level of measurement** represents fixed measuring units and an absolute zero point (zero means absolutely no amount of whatever the variable indicates). On a ratio scale, 10 is 2 points higher than 8 and is also 2 times greater than 5. Ratio numbers can be added and subtracted; because the numbers begin at an absolute zero point, they can be multiplied and divided (so ratios can be formed between the numbers). For example, people's ages can be represented by values ranging from 0 years (or some fraction of a year) to 120 or more. A person who is 30 years old is 15 years older than someone who is 15 years old ($30 - 15 = 15$) and is twice as old as that person ($30/15 = 2$). Of course, the numbers also are mutually exclusive, are exhaustive, have an order, and there are equal gaps.

Exhibit 3.3 displays an example of a variable measured at the ratio level. The number of people in the first group is 5, and the number in the second group is 7. The ratio of the two groups' sizes is then 1.4, a number that mirrors the relationship between the sizes of the groups. Note that there does not actually have to be any group with a size of 0; what is important is that the numbering scheme begins at an absolute zero—in this case, the absence of any people.

Ratio-level variables are common in social work research. We can count the number of clients in a program, the time spent in a particular activity, or the number of hot meals delivered to homebound elderly. We can describe a community by the number of community development organizations, the number of after-school programs, or the number of low-income households. In each case, the answer *zero* is meaningful, representing the complete absence of the variable.

The Case of Dichotomies

Dichotomies, variables having only two values, are a special case from the standpoint of levels of measurement. The values or attributes of a variable, such as depression, clearly vary in kind or quality, not in amount. Thus, the variable *depression* is categorical— measured at the nominal level. Yet in practical terms, we can think of the variable in a slightly different way, as indicating the presence of the attribute *depressed* or *not depressed.* Viewed in this way, there is an inherent order; a depressed person has more of the attribute (it is present) than a person who is not depressed (the attribute is not present). Nonetheless, although in practical terms there is an order, we treat dichotomous variables as nominal variables.

Mathematical Comparisons

Exhibit 3.6 summarizes the types of comparisons that can be made with different levels of measurement, as well as the mathematical operations that are legitimate. All four levels of measurement allow researchers to assign different values to different cases. All three quantitative measures allow researchers to rank cases in order.

EXHIBIT 3.6 **Properties of Measurement Levels**

Examples of Comparison Statements	Appropriate Math Operations	Relevant Level of Measurement			
		Nominal	Ordinal	Interval	Ratio
A is equal to (not equal to) *B*	= (≠)	✓	✓	✓	✓
A is greater than (less than) *B*	> (<)		✓	✓	✓
A is three more than (less than) *B*	+ (−)			✓	✓
A is twice (half) as large as *B*	× (÷)				✓

Source: Schutt (2005).

Researchers choose levels of measurement in the process of operationalizing the variables; the level of measurement is not inherent in the variable. Many variables can be measured at different levels, with different procedures. For example, a variable to describe alcoholic drinking can be measured by asking respondents to identify how many alcoholic drinks they had in the last week (a ratio variable) or answer the same question by checking *none, 1 to 4, 5 to 9,* or *10 or more* (an ordinal variable). A nominal variable about drinking could be created by asking, "Did you consume any alcoholic drink in the last week," with response categories *yes* or *no.*

It is a good idea to try to measure variables at the highest level of measurement possible. The more information available, the more ways we have to compare cases. There are more possibilities for statistical analysis with quantitative than with qualitative variables. You can create ordinal or nominal variables from ratio-level variables, but you cannot go in the reverse direction. If you know the actual age, you can combine the ages into categories at a later time, but if you ask respondents to check the category, you cannot later modify that variable to reflect their actual age.

Be aware, however, that other considerations may preclude measurement at a high level. For example, many people are reluctant to report their exact incomes even in anonymous questionnaires. So asking respondents to report their income in categories (such as less than $10,000, $10,000–19,999, $20,000–29,999, or $30,000 and higher) will result in more responses, and thus more valid data, than asking respondents for their income in dollars.

MEASUREMENT ERROR

No matter how carefully we operationalize and design our measures, no measure is perfect, and there will be some error. It might be that the measurement instrument needs to be corrected or reevaluated. Sometimes people are simply inconsistent in the way they respond to questions. What respondents report (the reported score) is not necessarily the true response (the true score) because of the imperfections of measurement. The true response differs from the reported response because of measurement error, of which there are two types: systematic error and random error.

Systematic error is generally considered to be a predictable error in that we can predict the direction of the error. Think about weighing yourself on a scale each day. If you put a scale on a particular part of the floor in your house, it may always show that you weigh less (reported score) than you actually do (true score). The direction of the error is predictable: In this case, your scale will always underreport your true weight.

There are different forms of systematic error, and each of these forms of systematic error reflects some bias. The various forms include the following:

• *Social desirability.* Social desirability bias occurs when respondents wish to appear most favorable in the eyes of the interviewer or researcher.

• *Acquiescence bias.* There is a tendency for some respondents to agree or disagree with every statement, regardless of whether they actually agree.

• *Leading questions.* Leading questions have language that is designed to influence the direction of a respondent's answer. There are many different ways in which this might be done, such as using words that have a negative connotation in society (e.g., government regulation or liberal), using the names of controversial people, or including some but not all responses to a question in the actual question.

• *Differences in subgroup responses according to gender, ethnicity, or age.* Differences in cultural beliefs or patterns, socialization processes, or cohort effects may bias findings from what otherwise might be a set of neutral questions.

To avoid systematic error requires careful construction of scales and questions and the testing of these questions with different population groups. We explore these methods in depth in Chapter 7.

Unlike systematic error, **random error** is unpredictable in terms of its effects. Random error may be due to the way respondents are feeling that particular day. Respondents may be having a great day or they may be fatigued, bored, or not in a cooperative mood. Perhaps the weather is making them less willing to cooperate. Respondents may also be affected by the conditions of the testing. The lighting may be bad, the room may be noisy, the seating may be cramped, the lack of walls in the cubicle may mean other people can hear, there may be other people in the room, or the respondent may not like the looks of the person gathering the information.

Another form of random error is *regression to the mean.* This is the tendency of persons who score very high on some measure to score lower the next time, or the reverse, for persons who score very low to score higher. What might have influenced the high or low score on the first test may not operate in the second test.

Random error might occur when researchers rating behavior are not adequately trained to do the rating. For example, two people grading an essay test might come up with different grades if they have not discussed the grading criteria beforehand. A field supervisor and a beginning student might assess a client differently given the variation in their years of experience.

As we have already said, the effects of random error cannot be predicted: Some responses overestimate the true score, whereas other responses underestimate the true score. Many researchers believe that if the sample size is sufficiently large, the effects of random error cancel each other out. Nonetheless, we want to use measurement scales and questions that are stable to minimize the effects of random error as much as possible.

▣ ASSESSING MEASUREMENT ACCURACY

Do the operations to measure our concepts provide stable or consistent responses—are they reliable? Do the operations developed to measure our concepts actually do so—are they valid? Why are these questions important? When we test the effectiveness of two different interventions or when we monitor a client's progress, we want the changes we observe to be due to the intervention and not the measurement instrument. We also want to know that the measure we use is really a measure of the outcome and not a measure of some other outcome. If we have weighed our measurement options, carefully constructed our questions and observational procedures, and carefully selected from the available data indicators, we should be on the right track. But we cannot have much confidence in a measure until we have evaluated with data its reliability and validity.

Measurement Reliability

Reliability means that a measurement procedure yields consistent or equivalent scores when the phenomenon being measured is not changing. If a measure is reliable, it is affected less by random error or chance variation than if it is unreliable. Reliability is a prerequisite for measurement validity: We cannot really measure a phenomenon if the measure we are using gives inconsistent results. The methods to evaluate measurement reliability include test-retest reliability, internal consistency, alternate forms, and interrater and intrarater reliability.

Test-Retest Reliability

When researchers measure a phenomenon that does not change between two points in time, the degree to which the two measurements are related is the **test-retest reliability** of the measure. If you take a test of your research knowledge and retake the test 2 months later, the test is performing reliably if you receive a similar score both times, presuming that nothing happened during the 2 months to change your knowledge of research. We hope to find a correlation between the two tests of about .7 and prefer even a higher correlation, such as .8.

Of course, if events between the test and the retest have changed the variable being measured, then the difference between the test and retest scores should reflect that change. As the gap in time between the two tests increases, there is a greater likelihood that real change did occur. This also presumes that you were not affected by the conditions of the testing (a **testing effect**). The circumstances of the testing, such as how you were given the test, or environmental conditions, such as lighting or room temperature, may impact test scores. The testing effect may extend to how you felt the first time you took the test; because you did not know what to expect the first time, you may have been very nervous, as opposed to the second time, when you knew what to expect.

Internal Consistency

When researchers use multiple items to measure a single concept, they are concerned with **internal consistency**. For example, if the items comprising the CES-D reliably measure depression, the answers to the items should be highly associated with one another. The stronger the association among the individual items and the more items that are included, the higher the reliability of the scale.

One method to assess internal consistency is to divide the scale into two parts, to determine its **split-half reliability**. We might take a 20-item scale, such as the CES-D, sum the scores of the first 10 items, sum the scores of the second 10 items (items 11 through 20), and then find the correlation between the summed scores of the first 10 items and the summed scores of the second 10 items. If there is internal consistency, the correlation should be fairly high, such as .8 or .9. The correlation typically gets higher the more items there are in the scale.

There are countless ways in which you might split the scale, and in practical terms, it is nearly impossible to split the scale by hand into every possible combination. Statistical software can be used to calculate a score that splits the scale in every combination. A summary score, such as **Cronbach's alpha coefficient**, is the average score of all the possible split-half combinations.

Alternate-Forms Reliability

Researchers are testing **alternate-forms reliability** (or parallel-forms reliability) when they compare subjects' answers to slightly different versions of survey questions (Litwin, 1995). A researcher may reverse the order of the response choices in a scale, modify the question wording in minor ways, or create a set of different questions. The two forms are then administered to the subjects. If the two sets of responses are not too different, alternate-forms reliability is established. For example, you might remember taking the SATs or ACTs when you were in high school. When you compared notes with your friends, you found that each of you had taken a different test. The developers had evaluated these tests to ensure that they were equivalent and comparable.

Interrater Reliability

When researchers use more than one observer to rate the same people, events, or places, **interrater reliability** is their goal. If observers are using the same instrument to rate the same thing, their ratings should be similar. If they are similar, we can have much more confidence that the ratings reflect the phenomenon being assessed rather than the orientations of the raters.

Intrarater Reliability

Intrarater reliability occurs when a single observer is assessing an individual at two or more points in time. It differs from test-retest reliability in that the ratings are done by the observer as opposed to the subjects. Intrarater reliability is particularly important when you are evaluating a client's behavior or making judgments about the client's progress.

Measurement Validity

Measurement validity refers to the extent to which measures indicate what they are intended to measure. More technically, a valid measure of a concept is one that is (1) closely related to other apparently valid measures; (2) closely related to the known or supposed correlates of that concept; and (3) not related to measures of unrelated concepts (Brewer & Hunter, 1989). A good measure of your current age should correspond to your age calculated from your birth certificate. Measurement validity is assessed with four different approaches: face, content, criterion, and construct validation.

Face Validity

Researchers apply the term **face validity** to the confidence gained from careful inspection of a concept to see whether it is appropriate "on its face." A measure has face validity if it obviously pertains to the meaning of the concept being measured more than to other concepts (Brewer & Hunter, 1989). For example, a count of how many drinks people consumed in the past week would be a face-valid measure of their alcohol consumption.

Although every measure should be inspected in this way, face validation in itself does not provide very convincing evidence of measurement validity. The question "How much beer or wine did you have to drink last week?" looks valid on its face as a measure of frequency of drinking, but people who drink heavily tend to underreport the amount they drink. So the question would be an invalid measure in a study that includes heavy drinkers.

Content Validity

Content validity establishes that the measure covers the full range of the concept's meaning. To determine that range of meaning, the researcher may solicit the opinions of experts and review literature that identifies the different aspects or dimensions of the concept. Like face validity, content validity lacks empirical support, and experts may disagree with the range of content provided in a scale.

Criterion Validity

Criterion validity is established when the scores obtained on one measure are similar to the scores obtained with a more direct or already validated measure of the same phenomenon (the criterion). The criterion that researchers select can itself be measured either at the same time as the variable to be validated or after that time. **Concurrent validity** exists when a measure yields scores that are closely related to scores on a criterion measured at the same time. A measure of blood-alcohol concentration or a urine test could serve as the criterion for validating a self-report measure of drinking as long as the questions we ask about drinking refer to the same period. **Predictive validity** is the ability of a measure to predict scores on a criterion measured in the future. SAT or ACT scores as a measure of academic success can be validated when compared with college grades.

Criterion validation greatly increases confidence that the measure is measuring what was intended. It is a stronger form of validity than face or content validity as it is based on research evidence rather than subjective assessment.

Construct Validity

Measurement validity can be established by showing that a measure is related to a variety of other measures as specified in a theory. This validation approach, known as **construct validity,** is commonly used in social work research when no clear criterion exists for validation purposes. The construct validation process relies on using a deductive theory with hypothesized relationships among the constructs (Koeske, 1994). The measure has construct validity (or theoretical construct validity) if it "behaves" as it should relative to the other constructs in the theory. For example, Hann, Winter, and Jacobsen (1999) compared subject scores on the CES-D to a number of indicators that they felt from previous research and theory should be related to depression: fatigue, anxiety, and global mental health. They found that individuals with higher CES-D scores tended to have more problems in each of these areas, giving us more confidence in the CES-D's validity as a measure.

There are other approaches to establish construct validity that you are likely to encounter when reading research literature. With **discriminant validity**, scores on the measure to be validated are compared with scores on another measure of the same variable and with scores on variables that measure different but related concepts. Discriminant validity is achieved if the measure to be validated is related strongly to its comparison measure and less so to the measures of other concepts. The CES-D would demonstrate discriminant validity if the scale scores correlated strongest with the Beck Depression Inventory (a validated scale to measure depression) and correlated less strongly with the Beck Anxiety Inventory (a validated scale to measure anxiety).

Convergent validity is when you can show a relationship between two measures of the same construct that are assessed using different methods (Koeske, 1994). For example, the CES-D scale scores should correlate with the scores obtained from a clinical protocol used by social work practitioners. **Known-groups validity** is demonstrated by comparing the scale scores to groups with and without the characteristic measured by the scale. We would expect the CES-D scores to be higher among people who are clinically depressed than among those who have a clinical diagnosis of anxiety.

The distinction between criterion and construct validation is not always clear. Opinions can differ about whether a particular indicator is indeed a criterion for the concept that is to be measured. A key difference is simply that with criterion validity, "the researcher's primary concern is with the criterion in a practical context, rather than with the theoretical properties of the construct measure" (Koeske, 1994, p. 50). What if you need to validate a question-based measure of social support that people receive? Even if you could observe people in the act of counseling or otherwise supporting their friends, can an observer be sure that the interaction is indeed supportive? There is not really a criterion here, just related concepts that could be used in a construct validation strategy.

What construct and criterion validation have in common is the comparison of scores on one measure with scores on other measures that are predicted to be related. It is not so important that researchers agree that a particular comparison measure is a criterion rather than a related construct. But it is very important to think critically about the quality of the comparison measure and whether it actually represents a different view of the same phenomenon.

Reliability and Validity of Existing Measures

A reliable measure is not necessarily a valid measure, as Exhibit 3.7 illustrates. This discrepancy is a common flaw of self-report measures of substance abuse. Most respondents answer questions in a consistent manner, so the scales are reliable. However, a number of respondents will not admit that they drink even though they drink a lot. Their answers to the questions are consistent, but they are consistently misleading. So the scales based on self-report are reliable but invalid. Unfortunately, many measures are judged to be worthwhile on the basis only of a reliability test.

The reliability and validity of measures in any study must be tested after the fact to assess the quality of the information obtained. If it turns out that a measure cannot be considered reliable and valid, little can be done to save the study. Hence, it is important to select in the first place measures that are likely to be reliable and valid. Consider the different strengths of different measures and their appropriateness to your study. Conduct a pretest in which you use the measure with a small sample and check its reliability. Provide careful training to ensure a consistent approach if interviewers or observers will administer the measure. In most cases, however, the best strategy is to use measures that have been used before and whose reliability and validity have been established in other contexts. But

| EXHIBIT 3.7 | The Difference Between Reliability and Validity: Drinking Behavior |

Measure: "How much do you drink?"

Subject 1

Not at all.

Not at all.

Measure is reliable and valid.

Time 1

Time 2

Subject 2

Not at all.

Not at all.

Measure is reliable but invalid.

Time 1

Time 2

Source: Schutt (2005).

the selection of "tried and true" measures still does not absolve researchers of the responsibility of testing the reliability and validity of the measure in their own studies.

USING SCALES TO DESCRIBE A CLINICAL STATUS

Many scales do not just measure the range or intensity of some phenomenon but are also used by researchers and practitioners as screening tools to make educated guesses about the presence or absence of clinical conditions. For example, the CES-D has been used to determine the extent of depression in the community. CES-D scale scores may range from 0 to 60; people with scores 16 or higher may be classified as depressed whereas people scoring below 16 may be classified as not depressed. This score is called a **cut-off score**.

Cut-off score A scale score used to define the presence or absence of a particular condition.

Cut-off scores should be as accurate as possible. If not, we risk expending limited resources on what may turn out to be an inaccurate assessment, we risk missing individuals with the condition, and we risk labeling clients with a condition they might not actually have. Typically, the validity of a cut-off score is assessed by comparing the scale's classifications to an established clinical evaluation method. The CES-D cut-off score might be compared with a clinical diagnosis using the DSM-IV-TR.

A summary of the analysis of the validity of a cut-off is presented in Exhibit 3.8. If the cut-off scale provides an accurate assessment, there should be a high proportion of cases classified as either a **true negative** (Cell a) or a **true positive** (Cell d). A true negative occurs when based on the scale the client is assessed as not having a problem and really does not have the problem. A true positive occurs when it is determined from the obtained scale score that the client has a problem, and the client really does have the problem based on the clinical evaluation. There should be few **false negative** (Cell b) cases, when based on the scale score you conclude that the client does not have the problem, but the client really does have the problem, and few **false positive** (Cell c) cases, when you conclude from the scale score that the client does have a significant problem, but in reality the client does not have the problem.

Researchers use different measures to establish the validity of the cut-off scores. **Sensitivity** describes the true positive cell; it reflects a proportion based on the number of people who are assessed as having the condition (d) relative to the number of people who actually have the condition (b + d), or d/b + d. **Specificity** describes the true negative cell. It is a proportion based on the number of people assessed as not having a condition (Cell a) relative to the number who really do not have the condition (a + c); its mathematical formula is a/(a + c). False negative rates and false positive rates are similarly calculated.

EXHIBIT 3.8   **Outcomes of Screening Scale Versus Clinical Assessment**

Screening Scale Result	**Actual Diagnosis for the Clinical Condition**		
	Client does not have clinical condition	Client has clinical condition	Total
Assessed as not having condition	True negative (a)	False negative (b)	a + b
Assessed as having the condition	False positive (c)	True positive (d)	c + d
Total	a + c	b + d	

Source: Engel & Schutt (2005).

Ideally, we would like the sensitivity and specificity of the scale's cut-off scores to be very high so that we make few mistakes. Yet there are trade-offs. To identify all the true positives, the cut-off score would need to be eased; in the case of the CES-D, it would need to be lowered. This will increase sensitivity but will also likely result in more false positives, which means a lower specificity. Making it more difficult to test positive requires setting a higher score; this will increase the specificity but will also produce more false negatives, and the sensitivity score will decline.

▣ MEASUREMENT IN A DIVERSE SOCIETY

Although it is crucial to have evidence of reliability and validity, it is also important that such evidence generalize to the different populations social workers serve. Often people of color, women, the poor, and other groups have not been adequately represented in the development or testing of various measurement instruments (Witkin, 2001). Just because a measure appears valid does not mean that you can assume cross-population generalizability.

It is reasonable to consider whether the concepts we use have universal meaning or differ across cultures or other groups. Hui and Triandis (1985) suggest that there are four components that must be evaluated to determine whether a concept differs across cultures:

1. *Conceptual equivalence.* The concept must have the same meaning, have similar precursors and consequences, and relate to other concepts in the same way.

2. *Operational equivalence.* The concept must be evident in the same way so that the operationalization is equivalent.

3. *Item equivalence.* Items used must have the same meaning to each culture.

4. *Scaler equivalence.* The values used on a scale mean the same in intensity or magnitude.

Take for example the concept of self-esteem. Bae and Brekke (2003) note that cross-cultural research has found that Asian Americans typically have lower self-esteem scores than other ethnic groups. They hypothesized that Korean Americans would have lower scores on positively worded items than other ethnic groups but would have similar scores on negatively worded items. They suggested that this response pattern was due to culture: "Giving high scores on the positive items is intrinsically against their collective culture in which presenting the self in a self-effacing and modest manner is regarded as socially desirable behavior to maintain social harmony" (p. 28). Bae and Brekke found that overall self-esteem scores were lower among Korean Americans and that it was due to Korean Americans scoring lower on the positively worded items while scoring the same or higher than other ethnic groups on the negatively worded items.

Similar concerns have been noted for scales measuring depression. For example, Newmann (1987) has argued that gender differences in levels of depressive symptoms may reflect differences in the socialization process of males and females. Newmann suggests that some scales ask questions about behaviors and feelings, such as crying, being lonely, and feeling sad, that are more likely to be answered in the affirmative by women than by men because men are socialized to not express such feelings. Similarly, Ortega and Richey (1998) note that people of color may respond differently to questions used in depression scales. Some ethnic groups report feelings of sadness or hopelessness as physical complaints, and therefore have high scores on these questions but low scores on emotion-related items. Ortega and Richey also note that some items in depression scales, such as suicidal ideation, are not meaningful to some ethnic groups. The elderly are more likely to endorse some items that also measure physical changes as opposed to changes brought about by depression (Schein & Koenig, 1997; Schulberg et al., 1985).

Biased scores can result in practical problems. For example, many scales include cut-off scores to demonstrate the presence or absence of a condition. If there is a response bias, the result could be the treatment of a condition that does not exist or not identifying a condition that does exist (Bae & Brekke, 2003; Ortega & Richey, 1998). The failure to measure correctly may affect the ability to identify effective interventions. Further, the relationship of different phenomena may be distorted because of measurement bias. Therefore, it is important to assess the samples used for validation and to use measures that have been validated with the population group to whom they will be administered.

▣ MEASUREMENT IMPLICATIONS FOR EVIDENCE-BASED PRACTICE

Measurement is an essential ingredient in social work practice whether it be your assessment of a client or your monitoring and evaluation of your practice. Further, the studies you review depend, in part, on the quality of the measurement; systematic errors can negate the validity of a particular study (Johnston, Sherer, & Whyte, 2006). You need to be confident that the evidence presented is due to the intervention and not the instability of the measurement instrument.

What should you consider when you examine the efficacy of a measure for your agency? In the previous sections, we have stressed the importance of measurement reliability and validity. That alone is insufficient because there should be evidence of the appropriateness of the measure for the population with whom it will be used. Therefore, when you review research about the reliability and validity of a measure, you need to look at the samples that were used in the studies. Too often these studies are done without consideration of gender, race, ethnicity, or age. It may be that the samples used in the studies look nothing like the population you are serving. If that is the case, the instrument may not be appropriate for your agency or setting.

The same holds true for scales that can also be used for cut-off scores. Earlier, we described the CES-D as a commonly used scale with a more or less acceptable cut-off score of 16. On further inspection, researchers found that this score was too low to be useful with the elderly. Some item reports in the CES-D can be due to physical conditions that are common among the elderly. As a result, an appropriate cut-off score for elderly people with physical ailments has been determined to be at least 20 (Schein & Koenig, 1997). The bottom line is to take nothing for granted about cut-off scores described in the literature.

Of course, there are other practical considerations including ease of administration, cost, sensitivity, reactivity, and acceptability to staff. Different methods of administration require different amounts of time to complete, as well as skill to gather the data. The measure should be affordable. Many useful measures and scales can be found in the public domain, but many other scales have to be purchased, and sometimes you must also pay for their scoring. The measure you use should be sufficiently sensitive to pick up changes in the outcome and should have a sufficient number of items that you are able to identify changes. To the extent possible, you want nonreactive measures that do not influence the responses that people provide. Finally, the measures have to be accepted by staff as measures that will provide valid information.

All of these were considerations we had to take into account when we were asked by a family service agency's senior adult unit to recommend a short and simple screen for pathological gambling. The agency uses a 25- to 30-minute psychosocial assessment at intake, screening for a variety of social, economic, health, and mental health concerns, so the staff did not want something that would add terribly to the length of the assessment. At the same time, they wanted something that would be accurate and easy to use, and that would not offend their older clients. Ultimately, we found a reliable and valid two-item screen that could be added to the intake assessment.

As you read intervention research or other types of research studies or you develop a research proposal, there are important questions for you to consider. You should identify the major concepts in the study and assess whether the measure is clearly defined. Next, you should examine how the concepts are operationalized. Is the operational definition sufficient to capture the various dimensions of the concept? When scales are used, is there evidence of reliability and validity as well as the scale's appropriateness for the specific study population? Our confidence in the measure is enhanced when the author reports methods used to enhance the reliability of the measure, such as the specific training in collecting the information or using multiple measures.

CONCLUSION

Remember always that measurement validity is a necessary foundation for social work research and professional practice. Gathering data without careful conceptualization or conscientious efforts to operationalize key concepts often is a wasted effort. The difficulties of achieving valid measurement vary with the concept being operationalized and the circumstances of the particular study.

Planning ahead is the key to achieving valid measurement in your own research; careful evaluation is the key to sound decisions about the validity of measures in others' research. Statistical tests can help to determine whether a given measure is valid after data have been collected, but if it appears after the fact that a measure is invalid, little can be done to correct the situation. If you cannot tell how key concepts were operationalized when you read a research report, do not trust the findings. If a researcher does not indicate the results of tests used to establish the reliability and validity of key measures, remain skeptical.

KEY TERMS

Alternate-forms reliability	Level of measurement
Concept	Multidimensional scale
Conceptualization	Mutually exclusive
Concurrent validity	Nominal definition
Construct validity	Nominal level of measurement
Content validity	Operational definition
Continuous variable	Operationalization
Convergent validity	Ordinal level of measurement
Criterion validity	Predictive validity
Cronbach's alpha coefficient	Random error
Cut-off score	Ratio level of measurement
Discrete variable	Reliability
Discriminant validity	Scale
Exhaustive	Sensitivity
Face validity	Specificity
False negative	Split-half reliability
False positive	Systematic error
Internal consistency	Test-retest reliability
Interrater reliability	Testing effect
Interval level of measurement	Triangulation
Intrarater reliability	True negative
Known groups validity	True positive

HIGHLIGHTS

• Conceptualization plays a critical role in research. In deductive research, conceptualization guides the operationalization of specific variables.

• Concepts may refer to either constant or variable phenomena. Concepts that refer to variable phenomena may be very similar to the actual variables used in a study, or they may be much more abstract.

- Concepts should have a nominal definition and an operational definition. A nominal definition defines the concept in terms of other concepts, while the operational definition provides the specific rules by which you measure the concept.

- In social work research, a treatment or intervention is often a variable. The intervention should have an operational definition, that is, a description of the intervention process.

- Scales measure a concept by combining answers to several questions and so reducing idiosyncratic variation. Several issues should be explored with every scale: Does each question actually measure the same concept? Does combining items in a scale obscure important relationships between individual questions and other variables? Is the scale multidimensional?

- Measures are not perfect, and there may be two types of measurement error. Systematic error refers to predictable error and should be minimized. Random error is unpredictable in terms of effect on measurement.

- Level of measurement indicates the type of information obtained about a variable and the type of statistics that can be used to describe its variation. The four levels of measurement can be ordered by complexity of the mathematical operations they permit: nominal (least complex), ordinal, interval, and ratio (most complex). The measurement level of a variable is determined by how the variable is operationalized.

- The validity of measures should always be tested. There are four basic approaches: face validation, content validation, criterion validation, and construct validation.

- Measurement reliability is a prerequisite for measurement validity, although reliable measures are not necessarily valid. The forms of reliability include test-retest, internal consistency, parallel forms, interrater, and intrarater.

- Some scales are used to screen for the presence or absence of a clinical condition and, therefore, use cut-off scores. The accuracy of cut-off scores is assessed using measures of sensitivity and specificity.

- In examining studies of measurement reliability and validity, it is important to look at the samples to ensure that there is evidence of reliability and validity for different population subgroups.

DISCUSSION QUESTIONS

1. Describe the relationship between a nominal definition and an operational definition of a concept. How are these two types of definitions related?

2. Describe the elements of an operational definition. What information about the measurement process is provided in an operational definition?

3. What are the relative merits of the different forms of measurement reliability and validity?

CRITIQUING RESEARCH

Using one of the articles provided on the Web site *Learning From Journal Articles* (http://www.sagepub.com/fswrstudy), answer the following questions:

1. What are the major concepts used in the study? What are the nominal definitions? Does the author provide clear and complete nominal definitions for each concept? Are some concepts treated as unidimensional that you think might best be thought of as multidimensional?

2. What are the variable operational definitions? Are the operational definitions adequate? Do the measures of the variables seem valid and reliable? How does the author establish measurement reliability and measurement validity? Is there evidence that the reliability and validity of the measurements have been assessed with populations or samples similar to the study sample?

MAKING RESEARCH ETHICAL

1. Why is it important that the reliability and validity of any scale be evaluated with different populations?

DEVELOPING A RESEARCH PROPOSAL

At this point you can begin the process of conceptualization and operationalization.

1. Identify the concepts you will use in the study. Provide a nominal definition for each concept. When possible, this definition should come from the existing literature—either a book you have read for a course or a research article.

2. How will the concepts be operationalized? Identify the variables you will use to study the research question. Which of these variables are independent or dependent variables? What is the level of measurement for each variable? How will these variables be coded?

3. Develop measurement procedures or identify existing instruments that might be used. If you are using a new measure, what procedures will you use to determine the reliability and validity of the measure? If you are using an existing instrument, report the evidence for the instrument's reliability and validity.

> To assist you in completing the Web exercises below and to gain a better understanding of the chapter's contents, please access the study site at http://www.sagepub.com/fswrstudy where you will find the Web exercises reproduced with suggested links, along with self-quizzes, e-flash cards, interactive exercises, journal articles, and other valuable resources.

WEB EXERCISES

1. How would you define alcoholism? Write a brief definition. Based on this conceptualization, describe a method of measurement that would be valid for a study of alcoholism (as you define it). Now go to the Center of Alcohol Studies (CAS) home page (http://alcoholstudies.rutgers.edu). Choose "Library," then scroll down and choose "Library Resources (more . . .)." Then, scroll and click on the heading, "Miscellaneous Internet Resources." Then, choose "National Council on Alcohol and Drug Dependence"; choose "Facts"; choose "Medical/Scientific Information"; and finally click on "Definition of Alcoholism."

What is the definition of alcoholism used by the National Council on Alcohol and Drug Dependence (NCADD)? How is alcoholism conceptualized? Based on this conceptualization, give an example of one method that would be a valid measurement in a study of alcoholism.

Now look at some of the other related links accessible from the CAS and NCADD Web sites. What are some of the different conceptualizations of alcoholism that you find? How does the chosen conceptualization affect one's choice of methods of measurement?

2. Compare two different measures of substance abuse. A site maintained by the University of New Mexico's Center on Alcoholism, Substance Abuse, and Addictions (http://casaa.unm.edu/inst.html) provides a number of measures. Pick two of them. What concept of substance abuse is reflected in each measure? Is either measure multidimensional? What do you think the relative advantages of each measure might be? What evidence is provided about their reliability and validity, or if none is available, how might you go about testing these?

CHAPTER 4

Sampling

Why Sample?
Preparing to Sample
  Evaluate Generalizability
  Assess the Homogeneity of the Population
Sampling Methods
  Probability Sampling Methods
    Simple Random Sampling
    Systematic Random Sampling
    Stratified Random Sampling
    Cluster Sampling
  Nonprobability Sampling Methods
    Availability Sampling
    Quota Sampling
    Purposive Sampling
    Snowball Sampling

The Sampling Distribution
Unit of Analysis
Enhancing Participation of Diverse Populations
Implications for Evidence-Based Practice
Conclusion
Key Terms
Highlights
Discussion Questions
Critiquing Research
Making Research Ethical
Developing a Research Proposal
Web Exercises

In this chapter, you will learn about the rationale for sampling methods in social work research and evaluation of practice. We start by defining different terms and discuss concepts important to understanding two alternatives to sampling. We then turn to specific sampling methods and when they are most appropriate.

WHY SAMPLE?

It is a common technique in journalism to put a "human face" on a story. For instance, a reporter for *The New York Times* went to an emergency assistance unit near Yankee Stadium to ask homeless mothers about new welfare policies that require recipients to work. One woman with three children suggested, "If you work a minimum wage job, that's nothing. . . . Think about paying rent, with a family." In contrast, another mother with three children remarked, "It's important to do it for my kids, to set an example."

These are interesting comments, but we do not know whether they represent the opinions of most homeless people in the United States, in New York City, or even in the emergency assistance unit near Yankee Stadium. Even if the reporter had interviewed 10 homeless single mothers with children, we would not know how representative their opinions were. Because we have no idea whether these opinions are widely shared or quite unique, we cannot really judge what they tell us about the impact of welfare reform on single mothers. We would not want to develop programs to help single mothers based on these two comments alone. In other words, we do not know whether these comments are generalizable.

The same concerns apply to social work research. Perhaps you read a research study about the effectiveness of a particular cognitive-behavioral treatment conducted with depressed teenagers and you wonder whether the treatment might work with the teens in your unit. Perhaps your agency collects information from key community stakeholders about the most prevalent community needs, and you think that residents might have a different perspective. These are issues of generalizability. How we choose people from whom to gather information (or households, organizations, or even something as mundane as client records) has ramifications for the conclusions that can be made. Are the findings true for only those who provided the information, or can the findings from some sample be generalized to the population from which the sample was drawn? This is really the most basic question to ask about a sample.

▣ PREPARING TO SAMPLE

Let's say we are designing a study of a topic that involves a lot of people (or other entities such as households, agencies, or communities), which are the **elements** in your study. We do not have the time or the resources to study the entire **population** or the set of individuals (or other entities) in which you are interested. Therefore we decide to study a **sample**, a subset of the population in which we are interested.

In many instances we collect our data directly from the elements in our sample. For example, we may be interested in our clients' satisfaction with agency procedures, so we collect the information directly from the clients. Some studies are not so simple. The entities that we can easily reach are not the same as the elements from whom we want information. For example, we may have a list of households in a neighborhood but not a list of the entire adult population of that neighborhood, although the adults are the elements that we actually want to sample. We could draw a sample of households so that we could then identify

Population The entire set of individuals or other entities (elements) in which you are interested.

Elements The individual members of the population whose characteristics are to be measured.

Sample A subset of elements from the larger population.

the adult individuals in these households. The households are termed **enumeration units**, and the adults in the households are the elements (Levy & Lemeshow, 1999).

In other studies, the individuals or other entities from which we collect information are not actually the elements in our study. A researcher who wants to obtain information about child welfare services might sample child welfare agencies for a survey and then interview a sample of staff within each sampled organization. The child welfare agencies and the staff are both termed **sampling units**, because we sample from both (Levy & Lemeshow, 1999). The child welfare agencies are selected in the first stage, so they are the *primary sampling units* and in this case they are also the elements in the study. The staff members are *secondary sampling units* but they are not elements, although they do provide information about the entire organization (see Exhibit 4.1).

EXHIBIT 4.1   Sample Components in a Two-Stage Study

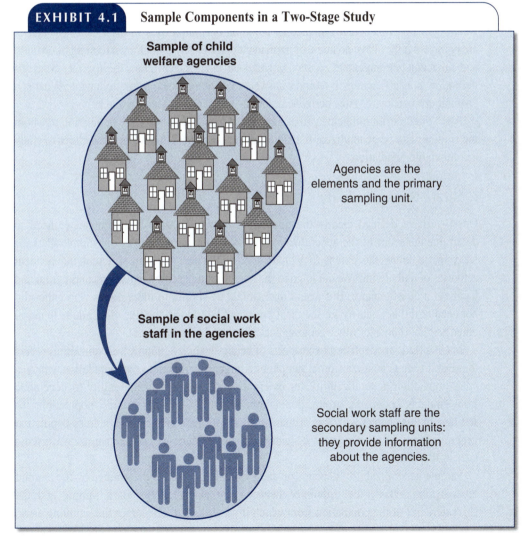

Source: Schutt (2005).

It is important to know exactly how the population is defined. Surveys of older adults may reasonably be construed as including individuals over the age of 65, but always be alert to ways in which the population may have been narrowed or expanded by the sample selection procedures. If we use a list provided by the American Association for Retired Persons, *older* would be defined as 50 and above. In some surveys, older adults living in skilled nursing homes or personal-care homes are excluded. Sometimes age is capped so that only people ages 65 to 84 are surveyed. In each survey, the sample is based on a somewhat different population. The population for a study is the aggregation of elements that we actually sample from, not some larger aggregation that we really wish we could have studied.

Some populations, such as the homeless, are not identified by a simple criterion such as age, a geographic boundary, or an organizational membership. If we were interested in the needs of homeless people, we would require a clear definition of "homeless." Such a definition is difficult but quite necessary, since in any research anyone should be able to determine just what population was actually studied. A common definition used in the 1980s was: People are homeless if they have no home or permanent place to stay of their own (renting or owning) and no regular arrangement to stay at someone else's place (Burt, 1996). Yet, even this definition is insufficient as it requires answers to questions such as the following: What is a "regular arrangement"? How permanent does a "permanent place" have to be?

An explicit definition helps you as a reader of research to know the population to whom the findings can be generalized. It enables other researchers to develop procedures to study a comparable population.

Evaluate Generalizability

Once we have defined clearly the population from which we will sample, we need to determine the scope of the generalizations we will seek to make from our sample. Perhaps we want to know the extent to which older adults can perform different independent activities of daily living. We could go to the neighborhood senior center's meal program and hand out a questionnaire. But would that sample be similar to older adults who either did not need or did not qualify for the meal program? Would they be like older adults living in other neighborhoods or other geographical locations? Obviously not.

In Chapter 1 we identified two aspects of generalizability. Sample generalizability refers to the ability to generalize from a sample of a larger population to that population, whereas cross-population generalizability (or external validity) refers to the ability to generalize from findings about one group, population, or setting to other groups, populations, or settings. In this chapter we focus primarily on sample generalizability, but cross-population generalizability is an important consideration in evidence-based practice, as we discuss later in this chapter.

Sample generalizability depends on sample quality, which is determined by the amount of **sampling error**—the difference between the characteristics of a sample and the characteristics of the population from which it was selected. The larger the sampling error, the less representative the sample, and therefore, the less generalizable the findings. To assess sample quality when you are planning or evaluating a study, ask yourself these questions:

Sampling error Any difference between the characteristics of a sample and the characteristics of the population from which it was drawn. The greater the sampling error, the less representative the sample.

- From what population were the cases selected?

- What method was used to select cases from this population?

- Do the cases that were studied represent, in the aggregate, the population from which they were selected?

Sometimes researchers project their theories onto groups or populations much larger than, or simply different from, those they have actually studied. The **target population** is a set of elements larger than or different from the population that was sampled and to which the researcher would like to generalize any study findings. The validity of cross-population generalizations cannot be tested empirically, except by conducting more research in other settings and with other populations. When we generalize findings to target populations, we must be somewhat speculative. We must carefully consider the validity of claims that the findings can be applied to other subgroups of the population, geographic areas, cultures, or times.

Assess the Homogeneity of the Population

Sampling is unnecessary if all the units in the population are identical. Physicists do not need to select a representative sample of atomic particles to learn about basic physical processes. They can study a single atomic particle because it is identical to every other particle of its type. Similarly, biologists do not need to sample a particular type of plant to determine whether a given chemical has toxic effects on that particular type.

What about people? The social world and the people in it are too diverse to be considered identical units. In the past, researchers assumed that psychological and social processes were similar and generalizations could be made. The problem with this assumption is that there is no way to know for sure whether the processes being studied are identical across all people. Generalizing the results of single experiments and intervention studies is risky because such research often studies a small number of people who do not represent any particular populations.

The larger point is that social work researchers as well as other social scientists rarely can skirt the problem of demonstrating the generalizability of their findings. If a small sample has been studied in a particular agency, in an experiment, or in a field research project, the study should be replicated in different settings or, preferably, with a **representative sample** of the population to which generalizations are sought (see Exhibit 4.2).

EXHIBIT 4.2 | Representative and Unrepresentative Samples

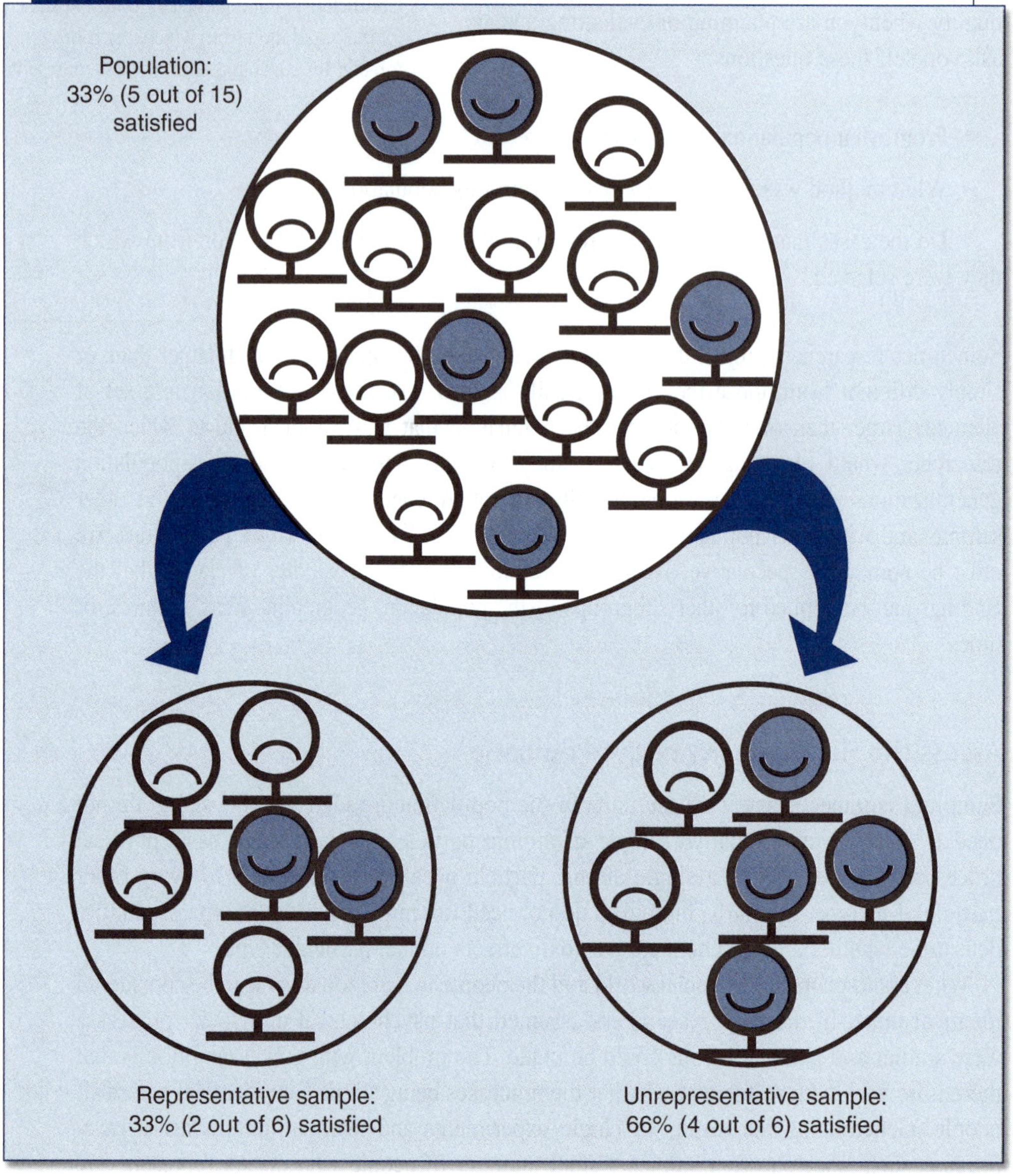

Population:
33% (5 out of 15)
satisfied

Representative sample:
33% (2 out of 6) satisfied

Unrepresentative sample:
66% (4 out of 6) satisfied

Source: Schutt (2005).

▣ SAMPLING METHODS

Certain features of samples make them more or less likely to represent the population from which they are selected. The most important distinction made about sampling methods is whether they are based on a probability or a nonprobability sampling method. Sampling methods that allow us to know in advance how likely it is that any element of a population will be selected for the sample are termed **probability sampling methods**. Sampling methods that do not let us know the likelihood in advance are termed **nonprobability sampling methods**.

Probability Sampling Methods

Probability sampling methods are used when we want to be able to generalize the results from a sample to the broader population. Because they are based on probability theory, we can estimate the extent to which the sample is actually representative of the broader population.

Probability sampling methods rely on a random selection procedure (or **random sampling**), which is in principle the same as flipping a coin to decide which of two people "wins" and which one "loses." Heads and tails are equally likely to turn up in a coin toss, so both people have an equal chance to win. That chance, their **probability of selection**, is 1 out of 2, or .5. Flipping a coin is a fair way to select one of two people, because the selection harbors no systematic bias; that is, nothing but chance determines which person is included in the sample.

There is a tendency to confuse the concept of random selection, in which cases are selected only on the basis of chance, with a haphazard method of sampling. "Leaving things up to chance" seems to imply not exerting any control over the sampling method. But to ensure that nothing but chance influences the selection of cases, the researcher must proceed methodically. The researcher must follow carefully controlled procedures if a purely random process is to occur. When reading about a sampling method in a study, do not assume that a random sample was obtained just because the researcher used a probability sampling method. Two particular problems are issues of concern: selecting elements from an incomplete list of the total population and failing to obtain an adequate response rate.

> *Probability of selection* The likelihood that an element will be selected from the population for inclusion in the sample. In a census of all the elements of a population, the probability that any particular element will be selected is 1.0. If half the elements in the population are sampled on the basis of chance (say, by tossing a coin), the probability of selection for each element is one-half, or .5. As the size of the sample as a proportion of the population decreases, so does the probability of selection.
>
> *Systematic bias* Nothing but chance determines which elements are included in the sample.

The list from which the elements of the population are selected is the **sampling frame**. Sampling frames or lists come from a variety of sources, such as state maltreatment report registries (Leiter, 2007), Temporary Assistance for Needy Families (TANF) recipients registered by the state (Sullivan, Larrison, Nackerud, Risler, & Bodenschatz, 2004), social workers licensed by a state department (Cole, Panchanadeswaran, & Daining, 2004), or social service agencies compiled by a human service consortium (Engel, Rosen, & Soska, 2008). If the sampling frame is incomplete, a sample selected randomly from that list will not really be a random sample of the population. You should always consider the adequacy of the sampling frame. Each of the above lists likely did not include the entire population. Even for a simple population like a university's student body, the registrar's list is likely to be at least a bit out-of-date at any given time. The sampling frame for a city, state, or nation is always likely to be incomplete because of constant migration into and out of the area. Omissions from the sampling frame can bias a sample against particular groups within the population.

Even a study using an inclusive sampling frame may still yield a biased sample if many sampled elements cannot be located or refuse to participate. Nonresponse is a major hazard in survey research because nonrespondents are likely to differ systematically from those who take the time to participate. You should not assume that findings from a randomly selected sample will be generalizable to the population from which the sample was selected if the nonresponse rate is considerable (certainly not if it is much above 30%).

Although a random sample has no systematic bias, it will certainly have some sampling error due to chance. Imagine selecting randomly a sample of 10 clients from an agency program comprising 50 men and 50 women. Just by chance, you find that your sample of 10 clients includes 8 women and only 2 men. The sample was selected in an unbiased fashion, but it is still unrepresentative. Fortunately, we can determine mathematically the likely degree of sampling error in an estimate based on a random sample (as we discuss later in this chapter)—assuming that the sample's randomness has not been destroyed by a high rate of nonresponse or by poor control over the selection process.

In general, both the size (number of cases) of the sample and the homogeneity (sameness) of the population affect the degree of error due to chance. Specifically,

- *The larger the sample, the more confidence we can have in the sample's representativeness.* If we randomly pick five people to represent the entire population of our city, our sample is unlikely to be very representative of the entire population in terms of age, gender, race, attitudes, and so on. But if we randomly pick 100 people, the odds of having a representative sample are much better; with a random sample of 1,000, the odds become very good indeed.

- *The more homogeneous the population, the more confidence we can have in the representativeness of a sample of any particular size.* Let's say we plan to draw samples of 50 from each of two communities to estimate mean family income. One community is diverse, with family incomes varying from $12,000 to $85,000. In the other, more homogeneous community, family incomes are concentrated in a narrow range, from $41,000 to $64,000. The estimated mean family income based on the sample from the homogeneous community is more likely to be representative than is the estimate based on the sample from the more heterogeneous community. With less variation to represent, fewer cases are needed to represent the homogeneous community.

The fraction of the total population that a sample contains does not affect the sample's representativeness unless that fraction is large. The number of cases is more important than the proportion of the population represented by the sample. We can regard any sampling fraction less than 2% with about the same degree of confidence (Sudman, 1976). In fact, sample representativeness is not likely to increase much until the sampling fraction is quite a bit higher. Other things being equal, a sample of 1,000 from a population of 1 million (with a sampling fraction of 0.001, or 0.1%) is much better than a sample of 100 from a population of 10,000 (although the sampling fraction is 0.01, or 1%, which is 10 times higher). The size of the sample is what makes representativeness more likely, not the proportion of the whole that the sample represents.

Because they do not disproportionately exclude or include particular groups within the population, random samples that are successfully implemented avoid systematic bias. Random sampling error can still be considerable, however, and different types of random samples vary in their ability to minimize it. The four most common methods for drawing random samples are simple random sampling, systematic random sampling, stratified random sampling, and cluster sampling.

Simple Random Sampling

Simple random sampling requires a procedure that identifies cases strictly on the basis of chance. Flipping a coin and rolling a die can be used to identify cases strictly on the basis of chance, but these procedures are not efficient tools for drawing a sample. A **random numbers table,** like the one reproduced in Exhibit 4.3, simplifies the process considerably. The researcher numbers all the elements in the sampling frame and then uses a systematic procedure for picking corresponding numbers from the random numbers table. (Exercise 2 at the end of this chapter explains the process step by step.) For a large sample, a computer program can easily produce a random sample of any size by generating a random selection of numbers within the desired range.

Organizations that conduct phone surveys often draw random samples with another automated procedure, called **random digit dialing**. A machine dials random numbers within the phone prefixes corresponding to the area in which the survey is to be conducted. Random digit dialing is particularly useful when a sampling frame is not available. The researcher simply replaces any inappropriate numbers, such as those that are no longer in service, with the next randomly generated phone number.

The key characteristic of a true simple random sample is that the probability of selection is equal for each element. If a sample of 40 agency case files is selected from a population of 600 (that is, a sampling frame of 600), then the probability of selection for each element is 40/600, or .0667. Every element has an equal chance of being selected, just like the odds in a toss of a coin (1/2) or a roll of a die (1/6). Thus, simple random sampling is an equal probability of selection method (EPSEM).

Systematic Random Sampling

Systematic random sampling is a variant of simple random sampling. The first element is selected randomly from a list or from sequential files and then every *n*th element is selected. This is a convenient method for drawing a random sample when the population elements are

	EXHIBIT 4.3		**Random Numbers Table**										

(1)	(2)	(3)	(4)	(5)	(6)	(7)	(8)	(9)	(10)	(11)	(12)	(13)	(14)
10480	15011	01536	02011	81647	91646	69179	14194	62590	36207	20969	99570	91291	90700
22368	46573	25595	85393	30995	89198	27982	53402	93965	34095	52666	19174	39615	99505
24130	48360	22527	97265	76393	64809	15179	24830	49340	32081	30680	19655	63348	58629
42167	93093	06243	61680	07856	16376	39440	53537	71341	57004	00849	74917	97758	16379
37570	39975	81837	16656	06121	91782	60468	81305	49684	60672	14110	06927	01263	54613
77921	06907	11008	42751	27756	53498	18602	70659	90655	15053	21916	81825	44394	42880
99562	72905	56420	69994	98872	31016	71194	18738	44013	48840	63213	21069	10634	12952
96301	91977	05463	07972	18876	20922	94595	56869	69014	60045	18425	84903	42508	32307
89579	14342	63661	10281	17453	18103	57740	84378	25331	12566	58678	44947	05585	56941
85475	36857	43342	53988	53060	59533	38867	62300	08158	17983	16439	11458	18593	64952
28918	69578	88231	33276	70997	79936	56865	05859	90106	31595	01547	85590	91610	78188
63553	40961	48235	03427	49626	69445	18663	72695	52180	20847	12234	90511	33703	90322
09429	93969	52636	92737	88974	33488	36320	17617	30015	08272	84115	27156	30613	74952
10365	61129	87529	85689	48237	52267	67689	93394	01511	26358	85104	20285	29975	89868
07119	97336	71048	08178	77233	13916	47564	81056	97735	85977	29372	74461	28551	90707
51085	12765	51821	51259	77452	16308	60756	92144	49442	53900	70960	63990	75601	40719
02368	21382	52404	60268	89368	19885	55322	44819	01188	65255	64835	44919	05944	55157
01011	54092	33362	94904	31273	04146	18594	29852	71585	85030	51132	01915	92747	64951
52162	53916	46369	58586	23216	14513	83149	98736	23495	64350	94738	17752	35156	35749
07056	97628	33787	09998	42698	06691	76988	13602	51851	46104	88916	19509	25625	58104

Source: Beyer (1979, pp. 480-481).

arranged sequentially. It is particularly efficient when the elements are not actually printed (i.e., there is no sampling frame) but instead are represented by folders in filing cabinets.

Systematic random sampling requires three steps:

- The total number of cases in the population is divided by the number of cases required for the sample. This division yields the **sampling interval**, the number of cases between one sampled case and the next sampled case. If 50 cases are to be selected out of 1,000, the sampling interval is 20; that is, every 20th case is selected.

- A number is selected randomly using the entire range; in this case from 1 to 1,000. This number identifies the first case to be sampled. A random numbers table or a computer can be used to decide upon a starting number.

- After the first case is selected, every *n*th case is selected for the sample, where *n* is the sampling interval. If the sampling interval is not a whole number, you may round to define the sampling interval. But no matter the decimal, you must round up even if the interval is 30.1; rounding down precludes some elements from having any chance of being selected.

In almost all sampling situations, systematic random sampling yields what is essentially a simple random sample. The exception is a situation in which the sequence of elements is affected by *periodicity*—that is, the sequence varies in some regular, periodic pattern. Some couples' research suffered from this problem when the couples were listed systematically by gender and an even number was used for the sampling interval. But in reality, periodicity and the sampling interval are rarely the same.

Stratified Random Sampling

Stratified random sampling uses information known about the total population prior to sampling to make the sampling process more efficient. First, all elements in the population (i.e., in the sampling frame) are distinguished according to their value on some relevant characteristic. That characteristic forms the sampling strata. Next, elements are sampled randomly from within these strata. For example, race may be the basis for distinguishing individuals in some population of interest. Within each racial category, individuals are then sampled randomly. Of course, to use this method, more information is required prior to sampling than is the case with simple random sampling. It must be possible to categorize each element in one and only one stratum, and the size of each stratum in the population must be known. To compare the effectiveness of social work trained and non–social work trained child welfare workers, Perry (2006) stratified the population of child protective service workers by position (child protective investigator and child protective service worker) and college major.

This method is more efficient than drawing a simple random sample because it ensures appropriate representation of elements across strata. Imagine that you plan to draw a sample of 500 from an ethnically diverse neighborhood. The neighborhood population is 15% Black, 10% Hispanic, 5% Asian, and 70% White. If you drew a simple random sample, you might end up with disproportionate numbers of each group. But if you created sampling strata based on race and ethnicity, you could randomly select cases from each stratum: 75 Blacks (15% of the sample), 50 Hispanics (10%), 25 Asians (5%), and 350 Whites (70%). Using **proportionate stratified sampling** eliminates any possibility of error in the sample's distribution of ethnicity. Each stratum would be represented exactly in proportion to its size in the population from which the sample was drawn (see Exhibit 4.4).

In **disproportionate stratified sampling**, the proportion of each stratum that is included in the sample is intentionally varied from what it is in the population. In the case of the sample stratified by ethnicity, you might select equal numbers of cases from each racial or ethnic group: 125 Blacks (25% of the sample), 125 Hispanics (25%), 125 Asians (25%), and 125 Whites (25%). In this type of sample, the probability of selection of every case is known but unequal between strata. You know what the proportions are in the population, and so you can easily adjust your combined sample statistics to reflect these true proportions. For instance, if you want to combine the ethnic groups and estimate the average income of the total population, you would have to weight each case in the sample. The weight is a number you multiply by the value of each case based on the stratum it is in. For example, you would multiply the incomes of all Blacks in the sample by 0.6 (75/125), the incomes of all Hispanics by 0.4 (50/125), and so on.

EXHIBIT 4.4   **Stratified Random Sampling**

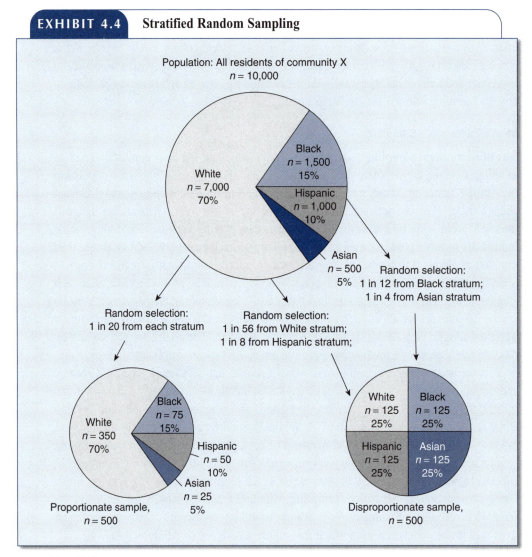

Source: Schutt (2005).

Why would anyone select a sample that is so unrepresentative in the first place? The most common reason is to ensure that cases from smaller strata are included in the sample in sufficient numbers. Only then can separate statistical estimates and comparisons be made between groups (strata). And remember that one of the determinants of sample quality is sample size. If the number of elements in a subgroup is too small, the sample may not accurately reflect the subgroup. Therefore, if few members of a particular minority group are in the population, they need to be oversampled.

Cluster Sampling

Cluster sampling is useful when a sampling frame (list of elements) is not available, as often is the case for large populations spread out across a wide geographic area or among many different organizations. A **cluster** is a naturally occurring, mixed aggregate of elements of the population, with each element appearing in one and only one cluster. Schools could serve as clusters for sampling students; blocks could serve as clusters for sampling city residents; counties could serve as clusters for sampling the general population; and agencies could serve as clusters for sampling social work staff.

Cluster sampling is at least a two-stage procedure and may involve multiple stages. First, the researcher draws a random sample of clusters. A list of clusters should be much easier to obtain than a list of all the individuals in each cluster in the population. Next, the researcher draws a random sample of elements within each selected cluster. Because only a fraction of the total clusters is involved, obtaining the sampling frame at this stage should be much easier. For example, in a needs assessment of residents of a particular neighborhood, blocks could be the first-stage clusters. Next, someone could walk around each selected block and record the addresses of all occupied dwelling units. The sample would be drawn from the occupied dwellings.

How many clusters and how many individuals within clusters should be selected? As a general rule, cases in the sample will be closer to the true population value if the researcher maximizes the number of clusters selected and minimizes the number of individuals within each cluster. Unfortunately, this strategy also maximizes the cost of the sample. The more clusters selected, the higher the travel costs. It also is important to take into account the homogeneity of the individuals within clusters—the more homogeneous the clusters, the fewer cases needed per cluster.

Cluster sampling is a popular method among survey researchers, but it has one drawback: Sampling error is greater in a cluster sample than in a simple random sample. This error increases as the number of clusters decreases, and it decreases as the homogeneity of cases per cluster increases.

Nonprobability Sampling Methods

Unlike probability sampling, nonprobability sampling techniques do not use a random selection procedure, and therefore elements within the population do not have a known probability of being selected. We cannot expect a sample selected using a nonprobability sampling method to yield a representative sample. Nonetheless, these methods are useful when random sampling is not possible, with a research question that does not concern a large population or require a random sample, or for a preliminary, exploratory study. These methods are often applied to experimental studies testing the effectiveness of different treatment or intervention methods. The four nonprobability sampling methods commonly used are availability sampling, quota sampling, purposive sampling, and snowball sampling.

Availability Sampling

Elements are selected for **availability sampling** (or convenience sampling) because they are available or easy to find. Newspaper reporters, like the *New York Times* reporter whose story introduced the chapter, often talk to one or two people to provide a personal perspective to a story. But their responses are not generalizable to other people or the broader community.

Availability sampling is appropriate when a researcher is exploring a new setting and trying to get some sense of prevailing attitudes or when a survey researcher conducts a preliminary test of a new set of questions. Availability samples are common techniques used when observing behavior in a social setting. There are many ways to select elements for an availability sample, such as sitting in the waiting room as clients come to the agency or asking passersby to answer a few questions. You may have been part of an availability sample when a professor asked you to complete a survey.

Availability sampling often masquerades as a more rigorous form of research. Popular magazines periodically survey their readers by printing a questionnaire for readers to fill out and mail in. A follow-up article then appears in the magazine under a title such as "What You Think About Intimacy in Marriage." If the magazine's circulation is large, a large sample can be attained in this way. The problem is that usually only a tiny fraction of readers return the questionnaire, and these respondents are probably unlike other readers who did not have the interest or time to participate. Although the follow-up article may be interesting, we have no basis for thinking that the results describe the readership as a whole—much less the population at large.

Quota Sampling

Quota sampling is intended to overcome the most obvious flaw of availability sampling—that the sample will consist of only whoever or whatever is available, without any concern for its similarity to the population of interest. The distinguishing feature of a quota sample is that quotas are set to ensure that the sample represents certain characteristics in proportion to their prevalence in the population. Similar to stratified sampling, **quota sampling** involves dividing the population into groups and deciding what proportion of the population with a particular characteristic is desired for the sample. Unlike in stratified sampling, respondents are not randomly selected; rather, they are selected by their availability.

Suppose that you wish to sample adult residents of a city in a study of support for building a casino. You know from the city's annual report what the proportions of the residents are in terms of gender, employment status, age, and race. You think that each of these characteristics might influence support for building a casino, so you want to be sure that the sample includes men, women, people who work, people not in the labor force, older people, younger people, and various ethnic groups in proportion to their numbers in the town population.

This is where quotas come in. Let's say that 48% of the city's adult residents are men and 52% are women and that 60% are employed, 5% are unemployed, and 35% are out of the labor force. These percentages and the percentages corresponding to the other characteristics become the quotas for the sample. If you plan to include a total of 500 residents in your sample, 240 must be men (48% of 500), 260 must be women, 300 must be employed, and so on. You may even set more refined quotas, such as certain numbers of employed women, employed men, unemployed women, and so on. With the quota list in hand, you (or your research staff) can now go out into the community looking for the right number of people in each quota category. You may go door to door or go bar to bar, or you can just stand on a street corner until you have surveyed 240 men, 260 women, and so on.

One problem is that even when we know that a quota sample is representative of the particular characteristics for which quotas have been set, we have no way of knowing whether the sample is representative of any other characteristics. In Exhibit 4.5, for example, quotas have been set for gender only. Under the circumstances, it is no surprise that the sample is representative of the population only in terms of gender, not in terms of race.

Another limitation of quota sampling is that you must know the characteristics of the entire population to set the right quotas. In most cases, researchers know what the population looks like in terms of no more than a few of the characteristics relevant to their concerns. In some cases, they have no such information on the entire population. So researchers can set quotas for a small fraction of characteristics relevant to the study.

EXHIBIT 4.5   Quota Sampling

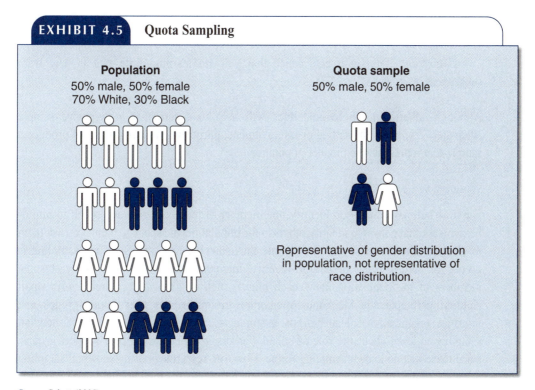

Population
50% male, 50% female
70% White, 30% Black

Quota sample
50% male, 50% female

Representative of gender distribution in population, not representative of race distribution.

Source: Schutt (2005).

Purposive Sampling

In **purposive sampling,** each sample element is selected for a purpose, usually because of the unique position of the sample elements. Purposive sampling may involve studying the entire population of some limited group (directors of shelters for homeless adults) or a subset of a population (caseworkers with a reputation for effectiveness). Purposive sampling may be used to examine the effectiveness of some intervention with clients who have particular characteristics, such as a specific diagnosis. A purposive sample may be used in a key informant survey, targeting individuals who are particularly knowledgeable about the issues under investigation.

Rubin and Rubin (1995) suggest three guidelines for selecting informants when designing any purposive sampling strategy. Informants should be

- Knowledgeable about the cultural arena or situation or experience being studied
- Willing to talk
- Represent[ative of] the range of points of view. (p. 66)

In addition, Rubin and Rubin (1995) suggest continuing to select interviewees until you can pass two tests:

- *Completeness.* "What you hear provides an overall sense of the meaning of a concept, theme, or process." (p. 72)

- *Saturation.* "You gain confidence that you are learning little that is new from subsequent interview[s]." (p. 73)

Although adhering to these guidelines will help to ensure that a purposive sample adequately represents the setting or issues studied, purposive sampling does not produce a sample that represents the broader population.

Snowball Sampling

For **snowball sampling**, you identify one member of the population and speak to him or her; you ask that person to identify others in the population and speak to them; you ask them to identify others, and so on. The sample thus snowballs in size. Snowball sampling is useful for hard-to-reach or hard-to-identify, interconnected populations (at least some members of the population know each other), such as drug users, parents with small children, participants in Alcoholics Anonymous groups or other peer support groups, and informal organizational leaders. For example, Carolyn Pryor (1992) used snowball sampling to learn about the role of social workers in school-based peer support groups, since there was no known sampling frame. However, researchers using snowball sampling normally cannot be confident that their sample represents the total population of interest.

One caveat to using a snowball sampling technique is that you are asking people to identify other people with a similar status without the knowledge or consent of the people being identified. The people who are identified may not want others to know that they have a particular status. This is particularly a concern when snowball sampling is used to identify subgroups of the population who may experience oppression or discrimination because they hold a particular status. In class, we often use a sampling exercise that requires students to identify a nonprobability sample technique to gather information from gay and lesbian members of the community with the purpose of identifying their social service needs. Often students will suggest a snowball sampling without realizing that what they are doing is asking people to "out" their acquaintances without permission of those being identified.

▣   THE SAMPLING DISTRIBUTION

The use of a probability sampling method does not guarantee that a sample is representative of the population from which it was selected even when we have avoided the problems of nonresponse. Random sampling (probability-based selection techniques) is an unbiased method of sample selection and so minimizes the odds that a sample is unrepresentative, but there is always some chance that the sample differs substantially from the population. Random samples are subject to sampling error due just to chance. To deal with that problem, social researchers take into account the properties of a **sampling distribution,** a hypothetical distribution of a statistic across all the random samples that could be drawn from a population. Any single random sample can be thought of as just one of an infinite number of random samples that, in theory, could have been selected from the population.

What does a sampling distribution look like? Because a sampling distribution is based on some statistic calculated for different samples, we need to choose a statistic. Let's focus on the arithmetic average or mean. To calculate a mean, you add up the values of all the cases and divide by the total number of cases. Let's say you draw a random sample of 500 families and find that their average (mean) family income is $36,239. Imagine that you then draw another random sample. That sample's mean family income might be $31,302. Imagine marking these two means on graph paper and drawing more random samples and marking their means on the graph. The resulting graph would be a sampling distribution of the mean.

We do not actually observe sampling distributions; instead, researchers just draw the best sample they can—one sample, not a distribution of samples. A sampling distribution is a theoretical distribution. However, we can use the properties of sampling distributions to calculate the amount of sampling error that was likely with the random sample used in a study. **Inferential statistics** is a mathematical tool for estimating how likely it is that a statistical result based on data from a random sample is representative of the population from which the sample is assumed to have been selected.

Sampling distributions for many statistics, including the mean, have a normal shape. A graph of a **normal distribution** looks like a bell, with one hump in the middle, centered around the population mean, and the number of cases tapering off on both sides of the mean. Note that a normal distribution is symmetric: If you folded it in half at its center (at the population mean), the two halves would match perfectly. This shape is produced by random sampling error. The value of the statistic varies from sample to sample because of chance, so higher and lower values are equally likely. Exhibit 4.6 shows what the sampling distribution of family incomes would look like if it formed a perfectly normal distribution.

Systematic sampling error Overrepresentation or underrepresentation of some population characteristics in a sample due to the method used to select the sample. A sample shaped by **systematic sampling error** is a biased sample.

Random sampling error (chance sampling error) Differences between the population and the sample that are due only to chance factors (random error), not to systematic sampling error. Random sampling error may or may not result in an unrepresentative sample. The magnitude of sampling error due to chance factors can be estimated statistically.

The properties of a sampling distribution facilitate the process of statistical inference, that is, of generalizing what we observe in our sample to the population of interest. In the sampling distribution, the most frequent value of the **sample statistic,** or the statistic (such as the mean) computed from sample data, is identical to the **population parameter**—the statistic computed for the entire population. We can have a lot of confidence that the value at the peak of the bell curve represents the norm for the entire population.

In a normal distribution, a predictable proportion of cases also fall within certain ranges under the curve. Inferential statistics takes advantage of this feature and allow researchers to estimate how likely it is that, given a particular sample, the true population value will be within some range of the statistic. For example, a statistician might conclude from a sample of 30 families that we can be 95% confident that the true mean

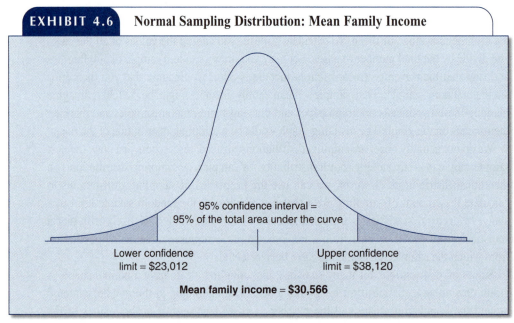

| EXHIBIT 4.6 | Normal Sampling Distribution: Mean Family Income |

95% confidence interval =
95% of the total area under the curve

Lower confidence
limit = $23,012

Upper confidence
limit = $38,120

Mean family income = $30,566

Source: Schutt (2005).

family income in the total population is between $23,012 and $38,120. The interval from $23,012 to $38,120 would then be called the 95% **confidence interval** for the mean. The upper ($38,120) and lower ($23,012) bounds of this interval are the *confidence limits*. Exhibit 4.6 marks such confidence limits, indicating the range that encompasses 95% of the area under the normal curve; 95% of all samples would fall within this range.

Although all normal distributions have the same basic features, they differ in the extent to which they cluster around the mean. If the sample size had been greater than 30 families, the sampling distribution would have been more compact. Stated another way, we can be more confident in estimates based on larger random samples because we know that a larger sample creates a more compact sampling distribution. The confidence interval for a sample of 100 families was $25,733 and $35,399, which is narrower than the confidence level for the 30 families.

▣ UNIT OF ANALYSIS

In social work research, we obtain samples from many different units including individuals, families, households, organizations, neighborhoods, and towns. When we make generalizations to the population, it is important to keep in mind the units under study and about whom we want to make conclusions. This is referred to as the **units of analysis**.

You may collect survey data from individuals, analyze the data, and then report on, say, how many individuals felt socially isolated and whether substance abuse by individuals was related to their feelings of social isolation. The unit of analysis is the individual. Or you may collect income data about a family from an individual family member and then compare family incomes. Your unit of analysis is the family, as this is the unit about which you are making conclusions.

It is important to distinguish the concept of units of analysis from the *units of observation*. In many studies, the units of observation and the units of analysis are the same, but this is not always the case. In a study comparing family income, data are typically collected from one member of the family—this is the unit of observation. The collected data are used to describe the family—the unit of analysis. Whether we are drawing conclusions from data or interpreting others' conclusions, it is important to be clear about which relationship is being referred to.

A researcher who draws conclusions about individual-level processes from group-level data is making what is termed an **ecological fallacy** (see Exhibit 4.7). The conclusions may or may not be correct, but we must recognize that group-level data do not describe individual-level processes. For example, a researcher may compare communities across different characteristics and find that a community has high rates of poverty. Researchers would commit an ecological fallacy if they concluded that an individual resident of that community is likely to be poor.

EXHIBIT 4.7   **Errors in Causal Conclusions**

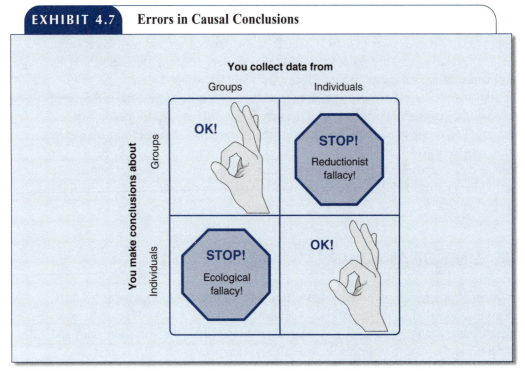

Source: Schutt (2005).

Readers of research must also beware not to confuse the unit of analysis, even when the researcher has presented it correctly. The term *underclass* first referred to neighborhoods or communities with certain characteristics, such as high rates of unemployment, poverty, out-of-wedlock births, welfare recipiency, and lower educational attainment. The term began to be misused when the people living in such communities were described as members of the underclass.

Bear in mind that conclusions about individual processes based on group-level data are not necessarily wrong. We just do not know for sure. Say we find that communities with higher average incomes have lower crime rates. The only thing special about these communities may be that they have more individuals with higher incomes, who tend to commit fewer crimes. Even though we collected data at the group level and analyzed them at the group level, they reflect a causal process at the individual level (Sampson & Lauritsen, 1994).

When data about individuals are used to make inferences about group-level processes, a problem occurs that can be thought of as the mirror image of the ecological fallacy: the *reductionist fallacy* (see Exhibit 4.7). You may have been on a team with really skilled individual players and so you thought that the team (group-level unit) would also do very well; but you might have been wrong. Such predictions are often wrong, as we know that groups do not work like individuals.

▣ ENHANCING PARTICIPATION OF DIVERSE POPULATIONS

One of the challenges for researchers is to ensure the representation of diverse populations in research studies. Different subgroups of the population, whether distinguished by gender, ethnicity, age, class, or sexual orientation, have been underrepresented in research efforts. Studies of published research in journals have found disproportionately few studies having an explicit focus on people of color or a separate analysis by race (Cauce, Ryan, & Grove, 1998; Graham, 1992). Sampling bias and gender have been discussed in critiques of studies about the diagnostic categories of the *Diagnostic and Statistical Manual of Mental Disorders* (Hartung & Widiger, 1998) and addictions research (Brett, Graham, & Smythe, 1995). Given that social work research can inform treatment effectiveness, intervention methods, and policy directions, it is important that what is learned pertains to and is useful to all segments of society (Miranda, Azocar, Organista, Munoz, & Lieberman, 1996).

A common response is that it is hard to recruit minorities to participate in research. There have been legitimate reasons for minority communities to distrust research efforts, whether it is the exploitation of African American participants in the Tuskegee experiments on syphilis or the misuse of findings to the detriment of minority communities (Norton & Manson, 1996). Too often research studies have not benefited the participating communities, and by couching comparative studies as evidence of "deficits," researchers have sometimes stigmatized ethnic communities.

When appropriate efforts are made, people of color do participate at high rates in research activities (Milburn, Gary, Booth, & Brown, 1992; Thompson, Neighbors, Munday, & Jackson, 1996; Yamatani, Mann, & Wright, 2000).The following are common themes to recruit and retain participants.

- *Involve key community members, organizations, and institutions to obtain credibility and gain acceptance.* Norton and Manson (1996) describe the importance of first gaining the approval of the tribe before seeking individual permission of American Indians to participate in research. To recruit elderly African American and Hispanic participants, Arean and Gallagher-Thompson (1996) solicited the support of the directors of community centers and ministers of neighborhood churches. After gaining their approval, they met with potential participants with the leaders present. Milburn et al. (1992) in a study of Black households contacted key individuals from the Urban League, pastors of Black churches, and directors of local health and community centers.

- *Demonstrate that there is a benefit to the community.* Many ethnic communities have seen research efforts that have had adverse impacts on the community. Norton and Manson (1996) suggest that two benefits to Native American tribes include employing local community members to help with the research and working with local service providers to translate the findings into action.

- *Understand cultural barriers.* Miranda et al. (1996) identify several different cultural norms among Latinos that may preclude or facilitate participation in treatment research, including importance of family, respect toward older adults, respect toward professionals, and warmth in interactions between professionals/researchers and clients/participants. They suggest that recruitment procedures that are too informal or cold will fail as opposed to "treating older Latinos with respect using formal titles, while being warm and personable" (p. 870).

- *Training of interviewers.* Thompson et al. (1996) suggest that the interviewers practice "how to approach [participants], how to provide a general overview of the study, and the best method of presenting topics such as confidentiality and voluntary participation" (p. 863). The training should not be a one-way street; rather, input from those trained can also enhance the overall study.

- *Go to where the potential participants are.* Often recruitment seems to be centered in the wrong locations. For example, African Americans and Latinos have lower rates of usage of mental health provider services and therefore recruitment should be at settings that they frequent such as community hospitals or primary care providers.

- *Understanding cultural differences is important in decisions about the choice of interviewers.* In a multistage cluster study of an African American neighborhood, Yamatani et al. (2000) achieved a high response rate in part by using local members of the community to conduct the interviews. Do this judiciously since using interviewers from the same tribe may impose on some Native American tribes' sense of privacy and confidentiality (Norton & Manson, 1996).

Difficulties of recruitment are not limited to people of color. Other subgroups of the population have legitimate fears of being stigmatized and facing discrimination if they are identified. For example, there has been recent discussion of how to recruit gay males and lesbians to research studies. Silvestre (1994) describes a brokering technique that was used to recruit nearly 3,000 gay and bisexual men to an ongoing longitudinal epidemiological study of HIV among gay and bisexual men. The process included the following steps:

- Hiring a community organizer and having publicly known leaders in the gay community participate in the search.

- Establishing a community advisory board reflecting the diversity of interests in the community.

- Engaging in the exchange of goods and services between the researchers and the formal and informal gay leadership.

Roger Roffman et al. (1997) describe a different method to recruit gay and bisexual males to an intervention and research project. Potential participants were given the choice of enrolling by a confidential option or anonymously. Those enrolling through the confidential option were asked for a phone number and instructions about the type of message that could be left; then, they were interviewed over the phone. To enroll anonymously, participants were asked to rent a postal box using either a real name or a pseudonym, and they were sent a money order to pay for the postal box with no name written on the payee line. All subsequent communications about treatment, data collection, and incentive payments were conducted through the postal box.

IMPLICATIONS FOR EVIDENCED-BASED PRACTICE

There are several lessons for evidenced-based practice implicit in the evaluations of the sampling methods. Remember, our goal is to make conclusions about a measure, a treatment, or a policy finding and to determine its appropriateness for practice. Therefore, it is important that what is learned pertains to and is useful to all segments of society (Miranda et al., 1996). Because issues of sampling cut across various research topics, we summarize these lessons in this chapter, but we return to these lessons in other chapters.

We cannot evaluate the quality of a sample if we do not know what population it is supposed to represent. If the population is unspecified because the researchers were never clear about just what population they were trying to sample, then we can safely conclude that the sample is no good. We cannot evaluate the generalizability of a sample if we do not know how cases in the sample were selected from the population. If the method was specified, we then need to know whether cases were selected in a systematic fashion and on the basis of chance.

Sample quality is determined by the sample actually obtained, not just by the sampling method. Even if we have chosen to sample in the best possible way, if many of the people selected for our sample are nonrespondents or people (or other entities) who do not participate in the study, although they have been selected for the sample, the quality of our sample is undermined. Those who chose to participate may be unlike those who chose not to participate in ways that limit the generalizability of the findings. Therefore, the response rate, the percentage of the sample that actually responds, is critically important; we return to this issue in Chapter 7.

We need to be aware that even researchers who obtain good samples may talk about the implications of their findings for some group that is larger than or just different from the population they actually sampled—what we have described as cross-population generalizability. As you evaluate their claims, you must consider the relevance of the population sampled to your own practice context—the particular setting, the location, or the type of clients. For example, findings from a representative sample of students in one university often are discussed as if they tell us about university students in general. Maybe they do; we just do not know.

The sample size may influence statistical conclusions about the findings. The sample size may lack statistical power—that is, it may be too small to find a statistically significant relationship even when there appears to be a relationship. However, as we discuss in Chapter 11, many statistical tests are influenced by sample size. A large sample may produce a statistically significant relationship even if the relationship is trivial or not clinically significant.

◲ CONCLUSION

Sampling is a powerful tool for social work research. Probability sampling methods allow researchers to use the laws of chance or probability to draw samples from which population parameters can be estimated with a high degree of confidence. When probability sampling methods are used, findings from a small number of cases can be generalized to a much larger population. Many researchers rely on these techniques when they are interested in describing population groups, understanding the impacts of different social welfare policies, or learning about community needs or attitudes.

There are many different research questions that are not easily answered by a probability sampling technique, particularly as we seek answers about questions from vulnerable populations. Most studies designed to provide evidence for a practice intervention rely on nonprobability sampling techniques. As a result, replication studies at both the same and different agencies are required for social workers to be confident that they have the best evidence.

Social work researchers and other social scientists often seek to generalize their conclusions from the population that they studied to some larger target population. The validity of generalizations of this type is necessarily uncertain because having a representative sample of a particular population does not at all ensure that what we find will hold true in other populations. Nonetheless, the accumulation of findings from studies based on local or otherwise unrepresentative populations can provide important information about broader populations.

KEY TERMS

Availability sampling	Probability sampling methods
Cluster	Proportionate stratified sampling
Cluster sampling	Purposive sampling
Confidence interval	Quota sampling
Disproportionate stratified sampling	Random digit dialing
Elements	Random numbers table
Enumeration units	Random sampling
Inferential statistics	Random sampling error
Nonprobability sampling methods	Representative sample
Normal distribution	Sample
Population	Sample statistic
Population parameter	Sampling distribution
Probability of selection	Sampling error

Sampling frame
Sampling interval
Sampling units
Simple random sampling
Snowball sampling

Systematic bias
Systematic random sampling
Systematic sampling error
Target population
Units of analysis

HIGHLIGHTS

- Sampling theory focuses on the generalizability of descriptive findings to the population from which the sample was drawn. It also considers whether statements can be generalized from one population to another.

- Sampling is unnecessary when the elements that would be sampled are identical, but the complexity of the social world makes it difficult to argue very often that different elements are identical. Conducting a complete census of a population also eliminates the need for sampling, but the resources required for a complete census of a large population are usually prohibitive.

- To ensure the representation of diverse populations in research studies, a variety of different methods can and should be used to encourage participation of people of color, women, the elderly, and sexual minorities.

- Nonresponse undermines sample quality: It is the obtained sample, not the desired sample, that determines sample quality.

- Probability sampling methods rely on a random selection procedure to ensure that there is no systematic bias in the selection of elements. In a probability sample, the odds of selecting elements are known, and the method of selection is carefully controlled.

- A sampling frame (a list of elements in the population) is required in most probability sampling methods. The adequacy of the sampling frame is an important determinant of sample quality.

- Simple random sampling and systematic random sampling are equivalent probability sampling methods in most situations. However, systematic random sampling is inappropriate for sampling from lists of elements that have a regular, periodic structure.

- Stratified random sampling uses prior information about a population to make sampling more efficient. Stratified sampling may be either proportionate or disproportionate. Disproportionate stratified sampling is useful when a research question focuses on a stratum or on strata that make up a small proportion of the population.

- Cluster sampling is less efficient than simple random sampling but is useful when a sampling frame is unavailable. It is also useful for large populations spread out across a wide area or among many organizations.

- Nonprobability sampling methods can be useful when random sampling is not possible, when a research question does not concern a larger population, and when a preliminary exploratory study is appropriate. However, the representativeness of nonprobability samples cannot be determined.

• The likely degree of error in an estimate of a population characteristic based on a probability sample decreases when the size of the sample and the homogeneity of the population from which the sample was selected increases. Sampling error is not affected by the proportion of the population that is sampled, except when that proportion is large. The degree of sampling error affecting a sample statistic can be estimated from the characteristics of the sample and knowledge of the properties of sampling distributions.

DISCUSSION QUESTIONS

1. Underrepresentation of different subgroups can significantly limit the generalizability of social work research findings and their subsequent applications. Suppose you were conducting a study of barriers to health care access in urban areas. What are some of the strategies you might employ to encourage minority participation in your research project?

2. The State Department of Aging representative involved in a service audit of a Seniors Unit at a local community agency used a nonprobability sampling method. Discuss the potential weaknesses of this approach in reaching a conclusion about the entire agency's filing compliance. Identify instances in which the use of an availability sample might be more appropriate or required.

3. Although probability-based selection techniques minimize the odds of sample unrepresentativeness, there remains a chance that the sample does differ substantially from the population. What do confidence limits tell us about the statistic we have derived from our sample and the likelihood of it being true for the population? How is the confidence interval impacted by sample size?

4. What ethical issues might you confront when using snowball sampling?

5. Select a random sample using the table of random numbers in Exhibit 4.3. Compute a statistic based on your sample, and compare it with the corresponding figure for the entire population. Here's how to proceed:

   a. First, go to http://www.census.gov/hhes/www/hlthins/liuc07.html to find rates of low-income uninsured children by state.
   b. The next step is to create your sampling frame, a numbered list of all the elements in the population. When using a complete listing of all elements, as from a U.S. Census Bureau publication, the sampling frame is the same as the list. Just number the elements by writing a number next to the name of each state.
   c. Now calculate the average value of the percentage of children at or below 200% of the poverty level for the total population of states. You do this by adding up the values for each state in that column and dividing by the number of states.
   d. Decide on a method of picking numbers out of the random numbers table in Exhibit 4.3, such as taking every number in each row, row by row (or you may move down or diagonally across the columns). Use only the first (or last) digit in each number if you need to select no more than 9 cases, or use only the first (or last) two digits if you want 10 to 99 cases.

e. Pick a starting location in the random numbers table. It is important to pick a starting point in an unbiased way, perhaps by closing your eyes and then pointing to some part of the page.

f. Record the numbers you encounter as you move from the starting location in the direction you decided on in advance, until you have recorded as many random numbers as the number of cases you need in the sample. If you are selecting states, 10 might be a good number. Ignore numbers that are too large (or small) for the range of numbers used to identify the elements in the population. Discard duplicate numbers.

g. Calculate the average value in your sample by adding up the values of the percentage of children at or below 200% of the poverty level for each of the states (elements) in the sample you have just selected and dividing by the number of elements in the sample.

h. How close is the sample average to the population average you calculated in Step c?

i. Guesstimate the range of sample averages that would be likely to include 90% of the possible samples of the same size.

6. Locate one or more newspaper articles reporting the results of an opinion poll. What information does the article provide on the sample that was selected? What additional information do you need to determine whether the sample was a representative one?

CRITIQUING RESEARCH

1. Select five scholarly journal articles that describe social work research using a sample of respondents. Identify the type of sample used in each study, and note any strong and weak points in how the sample was actually drawn. Did the researchers have a problem due to nonresponse? How confident are you in the validity of generalizations about the population based on the sample? Do you need additional information to evaluate the sample? Do you think a different sampling strategy would have been preferable? What larger population were the findings generalized to? Are these generalizations warranted? Why or why not?

MAKING RESEARCH ETHICAL

1. Silvestre (1994) recruited nearly 3,000 gay and bisexual men to an ongoing longitudinal epidemiological study of HIV among gay and bisexual men. Do you believe that the researchers had any ethical obligation to take any action whatsoever when they learned that a respondent was currently engaging in risky sexual practices? Are any of the ethical guidelines presented in Chapter 2 relevant to this situation? How would a decision to take action to reduce the risk of harm to others affect the promise to preserve the anonymity of respondents?

DEVELOPING A RESEARCH PROPOSAL

1. Propose a sampling design that would be appropriate for your research study. Define the population, identify the sampling frame (if any), and specify the elements. Indicate the exact

procedure for selecting people to be included in the sample. Specify any specific selection criteria. How many subjects will you need?

2. Develop appropriate procedures for the recruitment of human subjects in your study. Include a recruitment form with these procedures.

To assist you in completing the Web exercises below and to gain a better understanding of the chapter's contents, please access the study site at http://www .sagepub.com/fswrstudy where you will find the Web exercises reproduced with suggested links, along with self-quizzes, e-flash cards, interactive exercises, journal articles, and other valuable resources.

WEB EXERCISES

1. Research on health care concerns has increased in recent years as health care costs have risen. Search the Web for sites that include the words *medically uninsured* and see what you find. You might try limiting your search to those that also contain the word *census*. Pick a site and write a paragraph about what you learned from it.

2. Check out the people section of the U.S. Bureau of the Census Web site: www.census.gov. Based on some of the data you find there, write a brief summary of some aspect of the current characteristics of the American population.

CHAPTER 5

Group Experimental Designs

Causal Explanation
Association
Time Order
Nonspuriousness
Mechanism
Context
True Experimental Designs
Types of True Experimental Designs
"Difficulties" in True Experiments in Agency-Based Research
Quasi-experimental Designs
Nonequivalent Control Group Designs
Time Series Designs
Designs to Monitor Programs
Types of Nonexperimental Designs
Threats to the Validity of Group Designs
Threats to Internal Validity
Noncomparable Groups
Endogenous Change
External Events
Contamination
Treatment Misidentification

Generalizability
Sample Generalizability
External Validity
Reactivity
Implications for Evidence-Based Practice
Diversity, Group Design, and Evidence-Based Practice
Ethical Issues Unique to Experimental Research
Deception
Selective Distribution of Benefits
Conclusion
Key Terms
Highlights
Discussion Questions
Critiquing Research
Making Research Ethical
Developing a Research Proposal
Web Exercises

Do intensive, in-home, family-based interventions result in higher rates of family reunification than traditional services? Or are any observed differences due to some other factor unrelated to the interventions? Can we conclude that the intervention *caused* improved family reunification rates or are the differences due to something else? These were questions Walton and colleagues (Walton, Fraser, Lewis, Pecora, & Walton, 1993; Lewis, Walton, & Fraser, 1995; Walton, 2001) asked in a series of studies of children in substitute care. The answers to such questions are crucial for agencies looking to implement effective services. Similarly, understanding causality is essential for understanding the roots of a social condition or examining the implications of social policy.

This chapter considers the meaning of causality, the criteria for achieving causally valid explanations, and the ways in which researchers seek to meet these criteria using group research designs. By the end of this chapter, you should be able to weigh the evidence from experimental group research studies about the effectiveness of social work interventions and begin to design experimental group research projects. In subsequent chapters, we will show how causal criteria are established in other research designs.

回 CAUSAL EXPLANATION

A cause is an explanation for some characteristic, attitude, or behavior of groups, individuals, or other entities (such as families, organizations, or communities). A **causal effect** means that the variation in an independent variable will be followed by variation in the dependent variable, when all other things are equal. We recognize that you can legitimately argue that "all" other things cannot literally be equal. We will not be able to compare the same people at the same time in exactly the same circumstances except for the variation in the independent variable (King, Keohane, & Verba, 1994). However, we can design research to create conditions that are very comparable so that we can isolate the impact of the independent variable on the dependent variable. For example, Walton et al. (1993) tested whether the type of intervention (independent variable) impacts the rate of family reunification (dependent variable) and tried to create comparable conditions so that the only difference was the type of intervention received by participants.

Causal effect The finding that change in one variable leads to change in another variable, *ceteris paribus* (other things being equal).

Example: Families receiving intensive, in-home, family-based services have higher rates of reunification with their children than families receiving traditional casework services.

Five criteria must be considered when deciding whether a causal connection exists. The first three of the criteria must be established to identify a causal effect: empirical association, time order, and nonspuriousness. Evidence that meets the other two criteria—identifying a causal mechanism and specifying the context in which the effect occurs—can considerably strengthen causal explanations.

Research designs to establish these criteria require careful planning, implementation, and analysis. Many times researchers have to leave one or more of the criteria unmet and are left with some important doubts about the validity of their causal conclusions, or they may avoid even making any causal assertions.

Association

The first criterion for identifying a causal effect is an observed (empirical) **association** (or correlation) between the independent and dependent variables. This means that when the independent variable changes, the dependent variable also changes; if there is no association between two variables, there cannot be a causal relationship. Exhibit 5.1 displays the association that Walton et al. (1993) found between the type of intervention and the rate of family reunification. Family reunification after 90 days was much more common among families receiving intensive, in-home, family-based services than among families receiving traditional casework services. Therefore, variation in treatment (the independent variable) is associated with family reunification (the dependent variable). An empirical association is typically demonstrated by using statistical techniques to show that the relationship between an independent and a dependent variable is not due to chance.

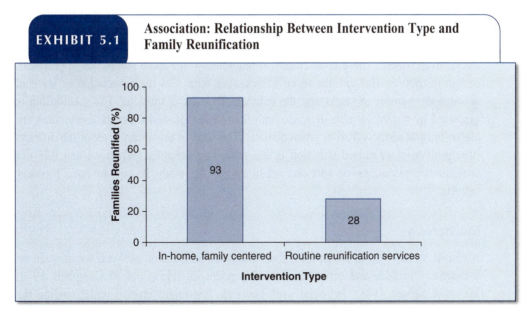

EXHIBIT 5.1 | **Association: Relationship Between Intervention Type and Family Reunification**

Source: Adapted from Walton et al. (1993).

Time Order

Association is a necessary criterion for establishing a causal effect, but it is not sufficient. We must also ensure that the variation in the dependent variable occurred after the variation in the independent variable. This is the criterion of **time order**. Walton's study satisfied this criterion because all participants started with the same status—families with children out of the home. Walton et al. (1993) measured changes in that status, both during the 90 days of the study period and after the 90 days were finished. It was only during and after the interventions that children could return home.

As you can imagine, we cannot be so sure about time order when we use a cross-sectional research design (see Chapter 2) to test a causal hypothesis. For example, there was evidence from cross-sectional studies that women who had given birth as teenagers had fewer years of schooling than women who first gave birth after they were in their 20s (or older). What the research could not answer was whether teenage moms had fewer years of education because they dropped out of school when they had a child, or whether teenage girls who dropped out of school were more likely to become pregnant than those who stayed in school. You cannot establish a causal relationship until you establish which comes first.

Nonspuriousness

Even when research establishes that two variables are associated and that variation in the independent variable precedes variation in the dependent variable, we cannot be sure that we have identified a causal relationship between the two variables. Before we can conclude that a causal relationship exists, we must have reason to believe that the relationship is **nonspurious**, that is, that the relationship is not due to any other variable. For example, do storks bring babies? There is an empirical relationship; the more storks that appeared in certain districts in Holland, the more babies were born. But the association in Holland between the number of storks and the number of babies is spurious. The relationship is explained by a third variable, because both the number of storks and the birth rate were higher in rural districts than in urban districts. The rural or urban character of the districts (the third variable) caused variation in the other two variables. When we can rule out alternative explanations or spurious relationships, the study is said to have **internal validity**.

Mechanism

A **causal mechanism** is the process that creates the connection between variation in an independent variable and variation in the dependent variable (Cook & Campbell, 1979; Marini & Singer, 1988). In social work research, this might involve understanding the theoretical components of the intervention model, or it might be to understand the underlying process, the essential actions, that will lead to the desired changes. For example, Lewis et al. (1995) found that family reunification using in-home, family-based services is more effective when caseworkers have the time to focus on communication skills, parenting skills, and anger management, while less effective when caseworkers devote their time to providing transportation, defusing crises, and managing conflicts.

Figuring out some aspects of the process by which the independent variable influenced the variation in the dependent variable can increase confidence in our conclusion that there was a causal effect (Costner, 1989). However, there may be many components to the causal mechanism and we cannot hope to identify them all in one study.

Context

No cause has its effect apart from some larger **context** involving other variables. For whom, when, and in what conditions does this effect occur? A cause is really one among a set of interrelated factors required for the effect (Hage & Meeker, 1988; Papineau, 1978). Identification of the context in which a causal effect occurs is not a criterion for a valid causal conclusion and it is not always attempted, but it does help us to understand the causal relationship. It is important to consider when assessing the applicability of an intervention to different settings.

Walton et al. (1993) noted the possibility that contextual factors influenced their findings. The study was done in Utah and the authors suggested that Utah's unique religious and social characteristics might have influenced the findings (and limited the generalizability of the findings). Furthermore, they suggested that the decision to place a child is not just the result of the family situation but of many system-level factors that could play a role in placement decisions.

▣ TRUE EXPERIMENTAL DESIGNS

Experimental research provides the most powerful design for testing causal hypotheses, because it allows us to confidently establish the first three criteria for causality: association, time order, and nonspuriousness. **True experimental research designs** (or randomized clinical trials) are used when a social work researcher wants to show that an intervention (independent variable) caused a change in an outcome (the dependent variable). True experiments have at least three features that help provide the strongest evidence about an intervention's effectiveness:

1. Two comparison groups (in the simplest case, an experimental and a control group) to establish association.

2. Random assignment to the two (or more) comparison groups to control for alternative explanations.

3. Variation in the independent variable before assessment of change in the dependent variable to establish time order.

The combination of these features enables researchers and consumers of research to have much greater confidence in the validity of causal conclusions than is possible in other research designs.

To establish an association between an independent variable and a dependent variable, true experimental designs have at least two groups. One group, called the **experimental group**, receives some treatment or manipulation of the independent variable. The second group, the **control group**, does not receive the treatment, or as is often the case in social work research, the second group is a **comparison group,** which typically receives the traditional intervention (or treatment as usual). The experimental group and the control group (or comparison group) scores on the outcome or dependent variable are compared in order to establish an association.

A study can have more than one experimental group if the goal is to test several versions of the treatment (the independent variable) or several combinations of different treatments. For example, a researcher testing different interventions for depression might include a control group, a group receiving medication, a group receiving counseling, and a group receiving both medication and counseling. But there is still a comparison group either not receiving any treatment or receiving treatment as usual.

It is crucial that the two groups be more or less equal at the beginning of the study. **Randomization**, or **random assignment**, is used to make the experimental group and the control group similar at the beginning of the experiment (see Exhibit 5.2). You randomly sort the participants into the two groups. You can do this by flipping a coin for each participant, pulling names out of a hat, or using a random number table. In any case, the subjects should not be free to choose the group nor should you (the researcher) be free to put subjects into whatever group you want.

| EXHIBIT 5.2 | Random Assignment to One of Two Groups |

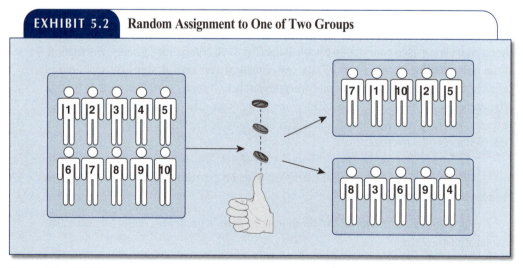

Source: Schutt (2005).

Note that the random assignment of subjects to experimental and comparison groups is not the same as random sampling of individuals from some larger population (see Exhibit 5.3). In fact, random assignment does not help at all to ensure that the research subjects are representative of some larger population; instead, representativeness is the goal of random sampling. What random assignment does is to ensure internal validity, not generalizability.

EXHIBIT 5.3   **Random Sampling Versus Random Assignment**

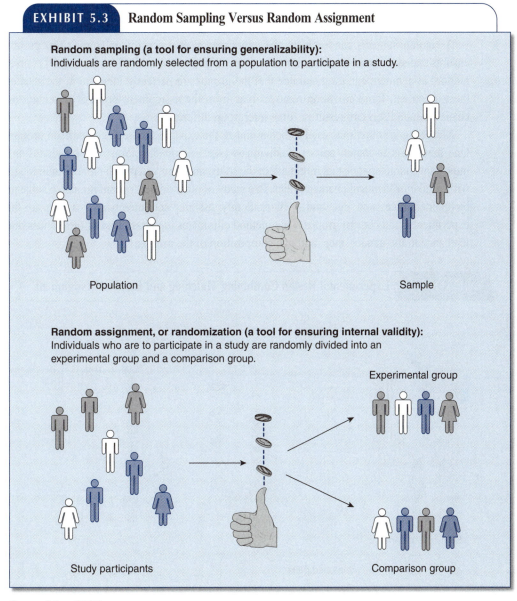

Random sampling (a tool for ensuring generalizability):
Individuals are randomly selected from a population to participate in a study.

Population

Sample

Random assignment, or randomization (a tool for ensuring internal validity):
Individuals who are to participate in a study are randomly divided into an experimental group and a comparison group.

Experimental group

Study participants

Comparison group

Source: Schutt (2005).

Why is random assignment useful for ensuring internal validity? The underlying assumption of random assignment is that if chance is used to determine who goes into a particular group, equivalent groups are created. The groups are believed not only to be more or less equal in demographic makeup and to have similar scores on the dependent variable (something we can check), but also to be more or less equal with regard to the impact of different threats to internal validity. For example, some people are highly motivated, whereas others are less motivated. Using random assignment improves the probability that highly motivated participants are more or less equally distributed into the two groups and therefore, motivation for change does not explain the treatment's effects.

Assigning subjects randomly to the experimental and control or comparison groups ensures that systematic bias does not affect the assignment of subjects to groups. Of course, random assignment cannot guarantee that the groups are perfectly identical at the start of the experiment. Randomization removes bias from the assignment process by relying on chance, which itself can result in some intergroup differences.

Matching is sometimes used to better equate the experimental and comparison groups. One method is to match pairs of individuals (see Exhibit 5.4). You start by identifying important characteristics that might affect the study, and then you match pairs of individuals with similar or identical characteristics. In a study of older adults, you might match subjects by gender, race, and age and then randomly assign each member of a pair to the experimental and control groups. This method eliminates the possibility of differences due to chance in the gender, race, and age composition of the groups.

EXHIBIT 5.4	Experimental Design Combining Matching and Random Assignment

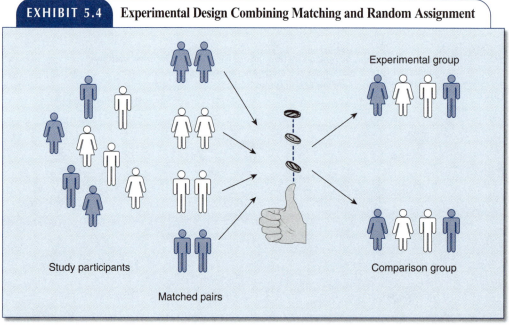

Source: Schutt (2005).

The basic problem is that, as a practical matter, individuals can be matched on only a few characteristics; unmatched differences between the experimental and comparison groups may still influence outcomes. However, matching combined with randomization can reduce the possibility of differences due to chance. A second problem occurs when one of the matched pair drops out of the study, unbalancing the groups. In this case, researchers will often exclude the findings of the individual who remained in the study.

Block matching is used when participants are grouped by their characteristics. Rather than creating pairs of older adults, the researcher might group by age and gender, so that there is a group of men between the ages of 65 and 74, a second group between the ages of 75 and 84, and a third group ages 85 and older. The same grouping by age would be done with female participants. Within each group, the members are randomly assigned into the experimental and treatment group.

Aggregate matching is matching by group. Older residents living in a high-rise might be grouped by floor. Random assignment into each group would be done by floor. Of course, this assumes that there are no systematic differences among the floors, such as apartment types.

Finally, to establish that the change in the dependent variable occurred after the intervention (in other words, time order), all true experiments have a **posttest**, that is, a measurement of the outcome in both groups after the experimental group has received the treatment. Many true experiments also have **pretests** that measure the dependent variable prior to the experimental intervention. Generally, the pretest measurement of the dependent variable is exactly the same as the posttest measurement of the dependent variable. We say *generally* because sometimes the measurement methods used for the pretest and posttest differ, although both methods must be equivalent measures of the same construct.

Strictly speaking, a true experiment does not require a pretest. When researchers use random assignment, the groups' initial scores on the dependent variable and all other variables are likely to be similar. Any difference in outcome between the experimental and comparison groups should be due to the intervention (or to other processes occurring during the experiment), and the likelihood of a difference just on the basis of chance can be calculated. The advantage of having a pretest score is that the researcher can verify that randomization did produce similar groups.

Types of True Experimental Designs

A common true experimental design is the *Pretest–Posttest Control Group Design* (sometimes referred to as the Classical Experimental Design or Randomized Before/After Control Group Design). Harris and Franklin (2003) used this design (see Exhibit 5.5a) to test whether a cognitive-behavioral group for Mexican American pregnant and parent adolescents would improve problem solving and coping skills and academic achievement. The experimental group participated in an 8-session task-centered, cognitive-behavioral group and received case management, while the comparison group received only case management services.

EXHIBIT 5.5a	Examples of True Experimental Designs

a. Pretest-Posttest Control Group Design:
Effects of a cognitive-behavioral, school-based, group intervention with Mexican American pregnant and parenting adolescents

Subjects:	Random Assignment (R)	Pretest Measures (O_1)	Intervention (X)	Posttest Measures (O_2)
Pregnant or parenting adolescents	Group A	Social problem-solving skills Problem-focused coping School attendance Grade average	Cognitive-behavior group and case management	Social problem-solving skills Problem-focused coping School attendance Grade average
	Group B	Social problem-solving skills Problem-focused coping School attendance Grade average	Case management	Social problem-solving skills Problem-focused coping School attendance Grade average

Source: Harris & Franklin (2003).

To establish an *association,* there are two groups, one receiving the intervention and the other group receiving services as normal. You can make two different types of comparisons to demonstrate the association. If you want to assume that the Time 1 observations are more or less equal, you only need to compare O_{2a} with O_{2b}. But in this case, you are making an assumption that is not necessary; instead, it is common to compare the change between observations in Group A (ΔO_A) with the change in Group B (ΔO_B). *Time order* is demonstrated by measuring outcomes at the point of initial assignment into one of the two groups and after the intervention is provided.

To establish *internal validity* (or nonspuriousness), Harris and Franklin (2003; see Exhibit 5.5a) randomly assigned participants into the cognitive-behavioral group or the comparison group. Since participants were randomly assigned to the groups, any group differences should be due to chance, and there should be little to no likelihood that a third variable impacts the findings. They did test the comparability of the two groups on a variety of demographic variables and found no differences.

The weakness of the Pretest-Posttest Control Group Design is that a pretest measurement might affect the posttest scores. It is possible that the test can sensitize respondents to the treatment and therefore make the treatment effective or more effective than it would have been without the test. The *Posttest-Only Control Group Design* (Randomized Control Group After-Only Design) safeguards against the reactive effects of testing and treatment. There is no pretest; rather, the researcher assumes that the pretest measures are more or less equal because random assignment is used. But because random assignment is based on probability, there is the possibility that unequal groups were formed; the lack of a pretest makes it impossible to check whether the groups are comparable initially. Walton (2001) used this design (see Exhibit 5.5b) to evaluate the effectiveness of two different methods to investigate allegations of child abuse and to develop service places. In particular, the design safeguarded against the outcomes of the assessment of parenting attitudes being influenced by a pretest measurement.

The *Solomon Four Group Design* enables researchers to determine whether there is a testing effect or a test-treatment interaction by combining the features of the preceding designs. There are four groups, two with a pretest and posttest and two with a posttest only. If a testing or a test-treatment interaction exists, there should be a difference in outcome scores for the two experimental groups and the two comparison groups.

EXHIBIT 5.5b   **Examples of True Experimental Designs**

b. Posttest Control Group Design:
Combining abuse and neglect interventions with intensive family preservation services: An innovative approach to protecting children

Subjects:	Random Assignment (R)	Pretest Measures (O_1)	Intervention (X)	Posttest Measures (O_2)
Families with alleged child abuse or neglect	Group A	None	Investigative and family preservation services	Parenting attitudes Satisfaction with services In-home status of children Number of days in-home Investigation findings Crises
	Group B	None	Routine services	Parenting attitudes Satisfaction with services In-home status of children Number of days in-home Investigation findings Crises

Source: Walton (2001).

Generally, this kind of interaction is problematic. When social workers apply research findings to practice, they do not want to have to recreate the research conditions. The interaction of testing and treatment might be an exception to this concern. It is common for clients to receive an initial test that we typically might refer to as an initial assessment or even a follow-up assessment. The testing effect may be beneficial if it adds to the effectiveness of the intervention.

"Difficulties" in True Experiments in Agency-Based Research

If true experimental designs are powerful tools to demonstrate causality, why are they typically the province of social work researchers and used less often by agencies to evaluate their programs? Implementing true experimental designs requires expertise, sufficient numbers of clients, and plenty of time. In addition, there are real and imagined criticisms, such as these:

- The program cannot change during the course of the experiment or evaluation (Weiss, 1998). This poses a problem because administrators want continual improvement. Weiss recommends that if a program does change, it is important to note the timing of the changes and to keep accurate records of outcomes at different points in time as the program changes.

- Even if the program or treatment does not change, implementation depends on staff with different skill levels, such as their ability to engage clients or provide services.

- The more controlled the conditions under which the treatment or program is provided, the less generalizable it will be to other times or locations. This is certainly a concern and points to the importance of being able to describe the context and conditions under which the research is undertaken. One solution is to replicate the intervention in different sites and with different samples.

- Staff may complain about threats to professional judgment. Posavac and Carey (1997) refer to these problems as, "I know what is best for my client" (p. 184). This concern manifests itself in two ways. One concern is about random assignment. Typically, social workers choose clients for treatment based on need or when someone comes to seek help. Many social workers (including our students) object to letting chance (randomization) dictate who gets help and who has to wait; rather, they want to base their decisions on their professional judgment. The second concern is that an experiment defines the intervention that is provided to clients and how the intervention is provided. Some social workers believe this threatens their ability to make decisions about how to best meet their clients' needs.

- Staff may say, "If the experimental approach is believed to be so good, I want all my clients to get it." The reason for trying a new method is based on some belief—whether anecdotal or theoretical—that suggests that the model is indeed better. Staff want their clients to receive the best service, so they argue, "Why delay implementing what we know should work?" Yet social workers have an ethical responsibility to have evidence that the new intervention is better before it is widely implemented.

- Clients may say, "Don't experiment on me" (Posavac & Carey, 1997, p. 183). People are suspicious of experimentation, and clients, who are particularly vulnerable, may be even more suspicious of experimentation. This makes recruitment and retention more difficult. With proper human subject protections, such as the use of informed consent, these fears can be mitigated.

回 QUASI-EXPERIMENTAL DESIGNS

Sometimes, using an experimental design to test hypotheses about the impact of service delivery, the effectiveness of a treatment modality, or the manner in which services are provided is not feasible with the desired subjects and in the desired setting. A true experiment may be too costly or take too long to carry out, it may not be ethical to randomly assign subjects to different conditions, or it may presume ability to manipulate an intervention that already has occurred. Researchers use quasi-experimental designs to overcome these problems.

A **quasi-experimental design** is one in which we may be able to rule out at least some threats to internal validity. In a quasi-experimental design, there is no random assignment when a comparison group is used. Instead, the comparison group is predetermined to be comparable to the treatment group in critical ways, like being eligible for the same services or being in the same school cohort (Rossi & Freeman, 1989). As a result, we cannot be as confident in the comparability of the groups as in true experimental designs.

Nonequivalent Control Group Designs

The *Nonequivalent Control Group Design* (see Exhibit 5.6) is exactly like the Pretest-Posttest Control Group Design except that there is no random assignment into the groups. There are two groups: One is exposed to the independent variable, whereas the other is not exposed to the independent variable. Researchers also may use this design to compare two (or more) interventions.

In this type of quasi-experimental design, researchers select a comparison group as similar as possible to the experimental treatment group. This technique may employ individual matching and aggregate matching used in true experimental designs; however, the key difference is that once the matches have been made, there is no attempt to utilize chance to randomly assign participants into the groups. The individuals or groups serving as the matched group become part of the comparison group.

Where are "matches" to be found? One potential source for finding matches is an agency waiting list. Persons on the waiting list are as yet not receiving services from the agency and, therefore, are a comparison group that is likely to be similar to the treatment group. Another alternative is to locate similar individuals in the community who are willing to serve as a control group. A third option is to compare client outcomes in one agency with client outcomes in another agency, assuming of course that the second agency is serving a similar population group.

EXHIBIT 5.6	Nonequivalent Group Designs

Nonequivalent Control Group Design:
Treatment of anxiety in a managed care setting

Subjects	Pretest Measures (O_1)	Intervention (X)	Posttest Measures (O_2)
Group A: Willing to be treated	Anxiety measures	Medication Eight weeks cognitive behavioral therapy	Anxiety measures
Group B: Unwilling to be treated	Anxiety measures	Medication only	Anxiety measures

Source: Mitchell (1999).

Mitchell's (1999) study of the impact of an 8-week cognitive-behavioral group treatment on treating panic disorders illustrates the use of a waiting list to create a matched group (see Exhibit 5.6). Mitchell wanted to examine whether medication and the cognitive-behavioral therapy group would reduce anxiety to a lower level than medication only. The sample included 56 people seeking treatment at an HMO (health maintenance organization). Comparisons were made between the 30 participants who received medications and participated in therapy groups and the 26 people who were on the waiting list for the group therapy or who had declined therapy but were receiving medication.

Nonequivalent control or comparison group designs are particularly useful for researchers (and evaluators). Because of the pretest and posttest, both *time-order* and a *statistical association* can be demonstrated, suggesting that if not causal, there is a correlation between the treatment and outcome. Further, if the selection process appears sound, you might rule out other explanations. The key is whether you are convinced that the matched comparison group has been chosen and evaluated in such a way that you are willing to accept the comparability between the two groups despite the lack of random assignment.

Time Series Designs

A *Time Series Design* is unlike the other research designs we have described up until now in that no control or comparison group is needed. A time series design typically involves only one group for which multiple observations of data have been gathered both prior to and after the intervention. Although many methodologists distinguish between Repeated Measures Panel Designs, which include several pretest and posttest observations, and time series designs, which include many (preferably 30 or more) such observations in both pretest and posttest periods, we do not make this distinction here.

A common design is the *Interrupted Time-Series Design,* in which three or more observations are taken before and after the intervention. It looks like this:

Experimental Group	O_1	O_2	O_3	X	O_4	O_5	O_6

As with other designs, there are variations on this basic design, including time series designs with comparison or control groups and time series designs in which observations are also gathered during the course of the intervention.

One advantage of a time series design is that there is only one group, so a second group need not be created. A second advantage is that, depending on the question, both the pretest and posttest observations need not occur prospectively; rather, the impacts of programmatic or policy changes can be based on data already collected.

A time series design is based on the idea that, by taking repeated measures prior to an intervention or programmatic change, you have the opportunity to identify a pattern. A pattern may show a trend reflecting an ongoing increase or decline or it may simply stay flat. The pattern may be seasonal, with differences based on time of year, such as the use of a homeless shelter, which declines in the summer and peaks in the winter and slowly declines again. Having identified the pre-intervention pattern, the question is whether an intervention or program altered the nature of the pattern to what is considered to be a more favorable state.

What can you say about causality when using a time series design? The before-after comparison enables you to determine whether an *association* exists between the intervention and the dependent variable. You can determine whether the change in the dependent variable occurred after the intervention, so *time* order is not a problem. However, there is no control group, so spuriousness may be a problem; some other event may have occurred during the intervention that resulted in a change in posttest scores. But the multiple pretest scores do enable you to discount other explanations, as they are likely to be observed in the pretest scores.

🔲 DESIGNS TO MONITOR PROGRAMS

Nonexperimental designs (or pre-experimental research designs) are classified as such because they provide less evidence for causality. To the extent that social work researchers are trying to demonstrate that different treatment modalities cause a change, the lack of control over internal threats to validity is a glaring weakness. This weakness often leads researchers and consumers of research to discount the utility of these designs and the findings from studies using these designs. Yet the simplicity of these designs makes them extraordinarily useful for the evaluation of programs within agencies.

Types of Nonexperimental Designs

The *One Group Pretest-Posttest Design* (Before-After One Group Design) (see Exhibit 5.7) is characterized by the absence of a comparison group; unlike the time series design, it lacks repeated pretest measures. All cases are exposed to the experimental treatment. The basis for comparison is provided by the pretest.

EXHIBIT 5.7	Pretest–Posttest Design

Pretest-Posttest Group Design:
Evaluating the outcomes of family-based intervention for troubled children: A
pretest-posttest study

Subjects	Pretest Measures (O_1)	Intervention (X)	Posttest Measures (O_2)
Treatment group	Measures of family cohesion, family conflict, time spent together and in community, parenting styles, parent mental health, parent-child agreement	12-week intervention for parents and children and three weekend activities	Measures of family cohesion, family conflict, time spent together and in community, parenting styles, parent mental health, parent-child agreement

Source: Harrison, Boyle, & Farley (1999).

It is possible to demonstrate a time order because there is a pretest and a posttest. Having pre- and posttest scores means statistical analyses can be used to determine whether there is an association between the independent and dependent variables. The weakness of this design is that spuriousness is a problem; there are many different threats to the internal validity of the design.

This is a popular form of design for program evaluation both for its ease of use and for the types of questions that you might answer. It is far simpler to implement than group designs because no comparison group is needed. The design flows from a typical practice model of assessment, intervention, and evaluation of the impact of the intervention (follow-up assessment). The conformity to a practice model is more easily understood by and more comfortable for agency directors and practitioners.

The One Group Pretest-Posttest Design is used to answer a variety of questions that interest social service agency staff and the funders of social services. For example, this design demonstrates whether improvement occurred, how much change occurred, and how many individuals improved. It can be used to determine how well clients are functioning and the number of clients who have achieved some minimum standard of functioning at the end of the program.

Harrison, Boyle, and Farley (1999) used a pretest-posttest design to study the effectiveness of a 12-week, family-based intervention for children (see Exhibit 5.7). The intervention was a course for parents and children that emphasized learning and practicing new skills, such as parenting behaviors, communication skills, and anger and stress management. In addition, there were three weekend outdoor recreational activities to practice the skills. Harrison and colleagues selected one particular agency because it had a comprehensive program and available subjects. Several positive changes were identified between pre- and posttest scores.

A less rigorous one group design is the *After-Only Design* (Posttest-Only; Cross-sectional group; One-Shot Only). This design is characterized by only one group without a control or comparison group, and it includes no pretest observations so that there are no benchmarks with which the posttest scores can be compared. The After-Only Design has little utility for researchers trying to illustrate causation. Because there is no pretest, both time order and association cannot be determined. The researcher does not know if the final outcomes are higher, lower, or equal to the pre-intervention level. Further, it is impossible to rule out other explanations.

The After-Only Design may be used to provide factual information for agency-based program evaluation. It is the typical design used for client satisfaction. It is also used to describe participant functioning at the end of the program, such as how many clients are no longer depressed or how many are employed after a job training program. Nonetheless, changes in depression or employment cannot be attributed solely to the program. This design is also useful for researchers piloting and developing measures, or developing hypotheses about relationships that then require more rigorous designs, and may provide some sense of attrition related to the treatment.

A third nonexperimental design is the *Static-Group Design.* It includes two groups without random assignment: One group gets the treatment and the other group does not receive the treatment, and there is no pretest or baseline. This design is frequently used when a program has already begun and baseline information cannot be obtained.

The central issue of this design is finding a comparable group. If an agency waiting list is used, perhaps an argument might be made about the comparability of Group B. Or one might find nonparticipants who are eligible for the program to use as a comparison group. The problem persists that without a pretest, the comparability of the groups cannot be evaluated. Without such a test, it is a leap of faith to be able to say that comparing posttest scores provides evidence of a time order and an association, let alone controls for internal threats to validity.

THREATS TO THE VALIDITY OF GROUP DESIGNS

Research experiments must be evaluated for their ability to yield valid conclusions. True experiments are particularly well-suited to producing valid conclusions about causality (internal validity), but they are less likely to achieve generalizability. Quasi-experiments may provide more generalizable results than true experiments, but they are more prone to problems of internal validity. Nonexperimental designs permit even less certainty about internal validity.

Threats to Internal Validity

An experiment's ability to yield valid conclusions about causal effects is determined by the comparability of its experimental and comparison groups. First, of course, a comparison group must be created. Second, this comparison group must be so similar to the experimental group that it will show what the experimental group would be like if it did not receive the experimental treatment.

There are five basic threats to the internal validity of a research design:

1. *Noncomparable groups.* When characteristics of the experimental and comparison group differ.

2. *Endogenous change.* When the subjects develop or change during the experiment as part of an ongoing process independent of the experimental treatment.

3. *External events.* When something occurs during the experiment, other than the treatment, that influences outcome scores.

4. *Contamination.* When either the experimental group or the comparison group is aware of the other group and is influenced in the posttest as a result (Mohr, 1992).

5. *Treatment misidentification.* When variation in the independent variable is associated with variation in the observed outcome, but the change occurs through a process that the researcher has not identified.

Noncomparable Groups

You may already realize that the lack of similarity between groups may offer an alternative explanation for an experiment's findings as opposed to the effect of the independent variable on the dependent variable. **Selection bias** occurs when a comparison group and an experimental group are initially different and is related to the methods used to assign subjects to the groups. When subjects are assigned randomly (by chance) to treatment and comparison groups, the threat of selection bias is reduced; whereas, when subjects are assigned using other methods besides random assignment, the threat of selection bias is great. Imagine assigning highly motivated subjects to one group and less motivated subjects to a second group. The highly motivated subjects are apt to perform better than the less motivated subjects. Even if the researcher selects a comparison group that matches the treatment group on important variables (e.g., demographic characteristics), there is no guarantee that the groups are similar initially in terms of the dependent variable or some other characteristic that influences scores taken after the treatment.

Even when random assignment works as planned, the groups can become different over time because of *mortality* or differential attrition. The groups become different when subjects are more likely to drop out of one of the groups. There are different reasons why participants drop out: (a) the study may be too lengthy; (b) participants in the experimental group may become more motivated than comparison subjects to continue in the experiment; or (c) participants receiving some advantageous program benefit may be more likely to stay in the experiment than participants who are not receiving program benefits.

Endogenous Change

Endogenous change occurs when natural developments in the subjects, independent of the experimental treatment, account for some or all of the observed change between a pretest and posttest. Endogenous change includes three specific threats to internal validity:

- *Testing.* Taking a pretest can influence posttest scores. Subjects may learn something or may be sensitized to an issue by the pretest and, as a result, respond differently the next time they are asked the same questions on the posttest. Just taking a test the first time often reduces anxiety provoked by the "unknown" and subjects will be more comfortable with subsequent testing.

- *Maturation.* Changes in outcome scores during experiments that involve a lengthy treatment period may be due to *maturation*. Subjects may age, gain experience, or grow in knowledge, all as part of a natural maturational experience, and therefore respond differently on the posttest than on the pretest. For example, after the death of a cherished family pet, feelings of depression and sadness become less intense with the passing of time.

- *Statistical Regression.* People experience cyclical or episodic changes that result in different posttest scores, a phenomenon known as a *statistical regression*. Subjects who are chosen for a study because they received low scores on a test may show improvement in the posttest simply because some of the low scorers were having a bad day when they were assessed.

External Events

External events during the experiment (things that happen outside the experiment) could change subjects' outcome scores. One type of problem is **history**, or an event that subjects are exposed to during the course of the experiment or evaluation. For example, a new cook is hired at a nursing home and the food improves at the same time a researcher is testing a group intervention to improve the morale of residents.

Broader social or economic trends may also impact the findings of a study, creating a problem called **secular drift.** For example, trends in the economy may have impacted the outcomes of welfare reform in 1996. The decline in the number of people receiving cash assistance from Aid to Families with Dependent Children began prior to 1996. It is reasonable to wonder if the Temporary Assistance for Needy Families (TANF) program produced the subsequent decline or if the reduction reflected a trend that had already begun as the economy improved.

Another possibility is **instrumentation**. When the same method of measurement is used for the pretest and posttest, the measures must be stable (demonstrate measurement reliability), otherwise the findings may reflect the instability of the measurement and not the effect of the treatment. When different methods of measurement are used, such as a paper measure for the pretest and behavioral observations for the posttest, the two methods must be equivalent (again measurement reliability); otherwise any changes might be due to the lack of equivalency.

Contamination

Contamination occurs in an experiment when the comparison group is in some way affected by, or affects, the treatment group. When comparison group members are aware that they are being denied some advantage, they may increase their efforts to compensate, creating a problem termed **compensatory rivalry** (Cook & Campbell, 1979). Comparison group members may become demoralized (called **resentful demoralization**) if they feel that they have been left out of some valuable treatment and perform worse than they would have outside the experiment. The treatment may seem, in comparison, to have had a more beneficial effect than it actually did. Both compensatory rivalry and resentful demoralization may distort the impact of the experimental treatment. Another form of contamination occurs when treatment and control (comparison) groups interact and the nature of the treatment becomes known to the control group. This problem, called **diffusion of treatment**, may result in the control group sharing in the benefits of the treatment.

Treatment Misidentification

Treatment misidentification occurs when some process that the researcher is not aware of is responsible for the apparent effect of treatment. Treatment misidentification has at least two sources:

- *Expectancies of experimental staff.* Change among experimental subjects may be due to the positive expectancies of the experimental staff who are delivering the treatment rather than the treatment itself. Even well-trained staff may convey their enthusiasm for an experimental program to the subjects in subtle ways. Such positive staff expectations create a self-fulfilling prophecy. Staff providing services to the comparison group may feel that it is unfair and, therefore, work harder or do more than they might have if there had been no experiment. This effect is called **compensatory equalization of treatment.** To counter these effects, some researchers use **double-blind procedures**, in which neither staff nor participants know whether they are in the group getting the treatment or the comparison group.

- *Placebo effect.* A **placebo effect** may occur when subjects receive a treatment that they consider likely to be beneficial and improve because of that expectation rather than because of the treatment. Medical research indicates that the placebo effect produces positive health effects in two-thirds of patients suffering from relatively mild medical problems (Goleman, 1993).

Process analysis is a technique researchers use to avoid treatment misidentification. A researcher might review audio- or videotapes of the intervention to determine whether the intervention was delivered as planned.

Generalizability

The need for generalizable findings can be thought of as the Achilles' heel of group experimental design. The design components that are essential to minimize the threats to internal validity make it more difficult to achieve sample generalizability (being able to apply the findings to some clearly defined larger population) and cross-population generalizability (generalizability across subgroups and to other populations and settings).

Sample Generalizability

Participants who can be recruited for a laboratory experiment, randomly assigned to a group, and kept under carefully controlled conditions for the study's duration are unlikely to be a representative sample of any large population of interest to social work researchers. Can they be expected to react to the experimental treatment in the same way as members of the larger population?

Researchers can take steps both before and after an experiment to increase a study's generalizability. Participants can be selected randomly from the population of interest, and thus, the researchers can achieve results generalizable to that population. Some studies of the effects of income supports on the work behavior of poor people have randomly sampled people within particular states before randomly assigning participants to experimental and comparison groups. But in most experiments, neither random selection from the population nor selection of the entire population is possible. Potential subjects must make a conscious decision to participate—probably resulting in an unrepresentative pool of volunteers.

External Validity

Researchers are often interested in determining whether treatment effects identified in an experiment hold true for subgroups of subjects and across different populations, times, or settings. Of course, determining that a relationship between the treatment and the outcome variable holds true for certain

> *External validity* The applicability of a treatment effect (or noneffect) across subgroups within an experiment and/or across different populations or settings.

subgroups does not establish that the relationship also holds true for these subgroups in the larger population, but it suggests that the relationship might be **externally valid**.

Evidence of an overall sample effect does not mean that the effect holds true for subgroups within the study. For example, Roger Roffman et al. (1997) examined the effectiveness of a 17-session HIV prevention group with gay and bisexual males. The researchers found that subjects in the treatment group had better outcomes than subjects in the control group. But within the treatment group, outcomes were better for exclusively gay males than for bisexual males. This study shows that an interaction effect can limit the generalizability of the findings.

Reactivity

A variant on the problem of external validity, called **reactivity**, occurs when the experimental treatment has an effect only when the particular conditions created by the experiment occur. Without the experimental conditions, there would be no effect. This is a problem as social work providers try to translate research findings into practice. The agency does not want to have to re-create the experimental conditions in order to provide an effective treatment. Reactivity takes several different forms:

- *Interaction of testing and treatment.* One such problem occurs when the treatment has an effect only if subjects have had the pretest. The pretest sensitizes the subjects to some issue, so that when they are exposed to the treatment, they react in a way they would not have reacted if they had not taken the pretest. In other words, testing and treatment interact to produce the outcome.

- *Reactive effects of experimental arrangement.* Members of the treatment group change in terms of the dependent variable because their participation in the study makes them feel special. Experimental group members could feel special simply because they are in the experiment. This is called a *Hawthorne effect*, named after a famous productivity experiment at the Hawthorne electric plant outside Chicago. No matter what conditions researchers changed in order to improve or diminish productivity, the workers seemed to work harder simply because they were part of a special experiment.

- *Interaction of selection and treatment.* This effect occurs when the results are related to selection biases in who receives the treatment and who serves in the comparison group. For example, voluntary clients often do better than involuntary clients. If the treatment group consists of voluntary clients and the comparison group consists of involuntary clients, the findings of the study are likely to be influenced by the biased assignment.

- *Multiple treatment interference.* This refers to clients or subjects who have been exposed to other interventions prior to the experiment. The question of multiple treatment interference is this: Was the intervention successful on its own or was it successful because of the subject's cumulative experience with other treatments or interventions? For example, chronically mentally ill individuals are likely to have had past treatment experiences, both in the community and in an institutional setting. If multiple treatment interference is a problem, the generalizability of the findings may be limited to a population having experienced a similar treatment pattern.

▣ IMPLICATIONS FOR EVIDENCE-BASED PRACTICE

The types of designs described throughout this chapter provide varying degrees of evidence to support the notion that a particular intervention resulted in the desired change in some outcome. There is a hierarchy among these group designs based on the three criteria for causality. True experimental designs (or randomized clinical trials) are commonly accepted as the gold standard in offering evidence about the efficacy of an intervention because they are organized to meet the criteria of association, time order, and internal validity (American Psychological Association, 2006; Gambrill, 2006; Johnston et al., 2006). Ideally, there are a number of randomized experimental trials of the intervention's effectiveness relative to a particular outcome. Quasi-experimental and nonexperimental designs provide less conclusive evidence about the effectiveness of the intervention.

But we do not mean to suggest that you need not look critically at the evidence learned from a true experiment, let alone quasi-experimental and nonexperimental designs. Throughout this chapter, we have suggested that there are specific issues you should consider as you read the results of research studies, including the following:

- *Randomization process.* Many authors report using random assignment of participants to the experimental and comparison groups without clarifying how the actual assignment was made. This is important information as you assess the findings' internal validity.

- *Sample size.* In Chapter 4, we briefly mentioned the concept of statistical power; the study needs to have a sample size that is sufficient to detect a statistically significant difference. With small samples, the chances of finding no treatment effect are greater than with a larger sample size; in other words, there may indeed be a treatment effect but the sample size may be too small to detect the impact of the treatment.

- *Attrition.* It is likely that some participants will drop out of the study, and there may be differential rates of attrition for the experimental and comparison groups. You should consider how attrition is handled in the analysis.

Even after you are convinced that the results are meaningful and not the outcome of a poor process of random assignment, small sample size, or attrition, you will have to address the external validity of the findings. Remember, you are taking research-derived knowledge and applying that knowledge to your individual clients. McNeil (2006) notes that "clinical expertise is indispensable for deciding whether external evidence applies to an individual client and, if so, how it should be integrated into treatment" (p. 151). Will the treatment's effects hold true for your clients who, for example, may differ by race, gender, social class, or sexual orientation from the people in the intervention studies? Does the study's setting and location impact the findings? These are all considerations in determining an appropriate intervention.

▣ DIVERSITY, GROUP DESIGN, AND EVIDENCE-BASED PRACTICE

In Chapter 4, we described how historically racial minorities and women had not been adequately represented in research studies. Under the provisions of the *NIH Revitalization Act of 1993* (Pub. L. No. 103-43), women and minorities must be included in clinical research supported by the National Institute of Health. We described recruitment strategies in Chapter 4. In this section, we highlight the link between adequate representation in research and evidence-based practice.

The most important consideration is the external validity of the findings from group research designs. For what population groups has the intervention been determined to be effective? Although social work research extends to many different areas, the evidence about the inclusion of people of color and women is probably best developed in the evaluations of mental health studies. Miranda, Nakamura, and Bernal (2003) found that between 1986 and 1997 there were few minority participants in studies using true experimental designs to test the effectiveness of treatment for depression, bipolar disorder, schizophrenia, and ADHD; of nearly 10,000 participants, they could only identify 561 African Americans, 99 Latinos, 11 Asian Americans and Pacific Islanders, and no American Indians or Alaska Natives (U.S. Department of Health and Human Services, 2001; Miranda et al., 2003). A more recent analysis of 379 National Institute of Mental Health–funded studies reported that women were adequately included whereas only Whites and African Americans were adequately represented (Mak, Law, Alvidrez, & Perez-Stable, 2007).

Therefore, as you review the available research and try to answer the "for whom" question, it is necessary to identify the characteristics of those who participated in the research. This is likely to be challenging because many of the studies described by Miranda and Mak included no information about ethnicity or lumped all those who were not White into a single category.

Representation alone is insufficient, because there needs to be a sufficient number of participants so that subgroups can be analyzed. Researchers often fail to do an analysis just for women in their sample or just for African Americans. Rather, the results are often only analyzed for the entire sample; different treatment effects for women or people of color may not be reported or observed.

Finally, the broad categories we use to depict racial or ethnic groups tend to imply that all African Americans, all Latinos, or all Asian Americans share the same cultural, social, and historical legacies. Yet, within these groups, there are differences in cultural definitions, language, history, and immigration experience. For example, Vega et al. (1998) found that Mexican immigrants have lower rates of depression than do Mexican Americans born in the United States. You can see that even within what seems like a narrowly defined ethnic group—Mexican Americans—there can be significant differences, in this case based on birthplace. Given that there can be so many variations, evaluating the evidence becomes even more difficult. Therefore, any intervention should at least have a theoretical base, and there is some evidence to link that theoretical base to culture (Miranda et al., 2003).

ETHICAL ISSUES UNIQUE TO EXPERIMENTAL RESEARCH

Social science experiments often involve subject deception. Primarily because of this feature, some experiments have prompted contentious debates about research ethics.

Experimental evaluations of social programs also pose ethical dilemmas because they require researchers to withhold possibly beneficial treatment from some of the subjects just on the basis of chance. In this section, we give special attention to the problems of deception and the distribution of benefits in experimental research.

Deception

Deception occurs when subjects are misled about research procedures to determine how they would react to the treatment if they were not research subjects. Deception is a critical component of many social experiments, though it occurs less frequently in social work research. One reason deception is used is because of the difficulty of simulating real-world stresses and dilemmas in a laboratory setting. Aronson and Mills (1959), for example, wanted to learn how severity of initiation to real social groups influences liking for those groups. But they could not practically design a field experiment on initiation. Their alternative, which relied on a tape-recorded discussion staged by the researcher, was of course deceptive. In many experiments, if subjects understood what was really happening to them, the results would be worthless.

The ethical dilemma posed by deceptive research is whether it precludes potential subjects from offering informed consent, given that they will not have full information about the experiment. In other words, if subjects do not have full information about the experiment, it limits their ability to weigh the risks of participation.

Aronson and Mills's (1959) study of severity of initiation (at an all-women's college in the 1950s) is a good example of experimental research that does not pose greater-than-everyday risks to subjects. The students who were randomly assigned to the *severe initiation* experimental condition had to read a list of embarrassing words. We think it is fair to say that, even in the 1950s, reading a list of potentially embarrassing words in a laboratory setting and listening to a taped discussion are unlikely to increase the risks to which students are exposed in their everyday lives. Moreover, the researchers informed subjects that they would be expected to talk about sex and could decline to participate in the experiment if this requirement would bother them. None dropped out.

To further ensure that no psychological harm was caused, Aronson and Mills (1959) explained the true nature of the experiment to subjects after the experiment. This procedure is called **debriefing,** and it is usually a good idea. Except for those who are opposed to any degree of deception whatsoever in research (and there are some), the minimal deception in the Aronson and Mills experiment, coupled with the lack of any ascertainable risk to subjects and a debriefing, would meet most standards of ethical research.

Selective Distribution of Benefits

Experiments conducted to evaluate social programs also can involve issues of informed consent (Hunt, 1985). One ethical issue that is somewhat unique to these experiments is the *distribution of benefits*: How much are subjects harmed by the way treatments are distributed in the experiment? For example, participation in a study of different models of case management for TANF recipients could have serious implications. The requirements of TANF impose a lifetime limit on participation so persons receiving a potentially less adequate method of case management could lose valuable time if one method helped people find work faster than the other method.

Is it ethical to give some potentially advantageous or disadvantageous treatment to people on a random basis? Random distribution of benefits is justified when the researchers do not know whether some treatment actually is beneficial—and, of course, it is the goal of the experiment to find out. Chance is as reasonable a basis for distributing the treatment as any other. Also, if insufficient resources are available to fully fund a benefit for every eligible person, distribution of the benefit on the basis of chance to equally needy persons is ethically defensible (Boruch, 1997).

🔲 CONCLUSION

True experiments play a critical role in social work research. They are the best research designs to provide evidence that an intervention is effective. Such studies are imperative for building the evidence base of social work practice. Even when conditions preclude use of a true experimental design, many research designs can be improved by adding some experimental components. Nevertheless, the lack of random sampling limits the generalizability of the results.

Just because it is possible to test a hypothesis with an experiment does not mean it will be desirable to do so. When a social program is first being developed and its elements are in flux, it is not a good idea to begin a large research study that cannot possibly succeed unless the program design remains constant. Researchers should wait until the program design stabilizes somewhat. It also does not make sense for researchers engaged in program evaluation to test the impact of programs that cannot actually be implemented or to test programs that are unlikely to be implemented in the real world because of financial or political problems (Rossi & Freeman, 1989).

Many forms of social work research, particularly research and evaluation done in agencies, will require design decisions about what is feasible. As you can see from the contents of this chapter, there are many components and factors to consider in choosing a group design. Regardless of the design used, it is important to understand the limits of the conclusions that can be made, in terms of both the internal validity of the design and the generalizability of the findings.

KEY TERMS

After-only design	Nonequivalent control group design
Aggregate matching	Nonexperimental designs
Association	Nonspuriousness
Block matching	One group pretest-posttest design
Causal effect	Placebo effect
Causal mechanism	Posttest
Comparison group	Posttest-only control group design
Compensatory equalization of treatment	Pretest
Compensatory rivalry	Pretest-posttest control group design
Context	Process analysis
Control group	Quasi-experimental design
Debriefing	Random assignment
Diffusion of treatment	Randomization
Distribution of benefits	Reactivity
Double-blind procedures	Repeated measures panel designs
Endogenous change	Resentful demoralization
Experimental group	Secular drift
External validity	Selection bias
Hawthorne effect	Solomon four group design
History	Spuriousness
Instrumentation	Static group design
Internal validity	Statistical regression
Interrupted time series design	Time order
Matching	Time series design
Maturation	True experimental research designs
Mortality	

HIGHLIGHTS

• Causal explanation relies on a comparison. The value of cases on the dependent variable is measured after they have been exposed to variation in an independent variable. This measurement is compared with what the value of cases on the dependent variable would have been if they had not been exposed to the variation in the independent variable.

• Three criteria are necessary to identify a causal relationship: association between the variables, proper time order, and nonspuriousness of the association. In addition, the basis for concluding that a causal relationship exists is strengthened by identification of a causal mechanism and the context.

• Association between two variables is in itself insufficient evidence of a causal relationship.

- True experimental research designs have three essential components: use of at least two groups of subjects for comparison, measurement of the change that occurs as a result of the experimental treatment, and use of random assignment.

- Random assignment of subjects to experimental and comparison groups eliminates systematic bias in group assignment. The odds of a difference between the experimental and comparison groups on the basis of chance can be calculated.

- Random assignment involves placing predesignated subjects into two or more groups on the basis of chance. Matching can improve the comparability of groups when it is used to supplement randomization.

- The independent variable in an experiment is represented by a treatment or other intervention. Some subjects receive one type of treatment; others may receive a different treatment or no treatment.

- Causal conclusions derived from experiments can be invalid because of selection bias, endogenous change, external events, cross-group contamination, or treatment misidentification. In true experiments, randomization should eliminate selection bias and bias due to endogenous change. External events, cross-group contamination, and treatment misidentification can threaten the validity of causal conclusions in both true experiments and quasi-experiments.

- The external validity of causal conclusions is determined by the extent to which they apply to different types of individuals and settings. When causal conclusions do not apply to all the subgroups in a study, they are not generalizable to corresponding subgroups in the population—and so they are not externally valid with respect to those subgroups. Causal conclusions can also be considered externally invalid when they occur only under the experimental conditions.

- Quasi-experimental group designs control for some threats to internal validity while nonexperimental group designs tend to control for few or no threats to internal validity. It is common to find both types of designs in agency settings.

- Subject deception is common in laboratory experiments and poses unique ethical issues. Researchers must weigh the potential harm to subjects and debrief subjects who have been deceived. Another common ethical problem is selective distribution of benefits. Random assignment may be the fairest way of allocating treatment when treatment openings are insufficient for all eligible individuals and when the efficacy of the treatment is unknown.

DISCUSSION QUESTIONS

1. A program has recently been funded to provide casework intensive services to the homeless. The mission of the program is to provide skills that will lead to self-sufficiency and employment. Develop a research study using

    Experimental design

    Quasi-experimental design

    Nonexperimental design

Be specific in describing the procedures you would have to do to implement your design. This may mean specifying how you will assign clients to groups (if you have more than one group) or where you would find clients for your control/comparison groups (if you have such groups).

2. Identify the benefits and weaknesses of each of the specific designs you chose for Exercise 1.

3. Search for a research study using a true experimental design to examine the effects of hospice care. Diagram the experiment using the exhibits in this chapter as a model. How generalizable do you think the study's results are to the population from which cases were selected? To other populations? To specific subgroups in the study? To other settings? How thoroughly do the researchers discuss these issues?

CRITIQUING RESEARCH

1. Go to the book's study site (http://www.sagepub.com/fswrstudy) and choose two research articles that include some attention to causality (as indicated by a check in that column of the article matrix). For each article describe the following:

   a. What type of design was used? How does the author describe the design? Was it suited to the research question posed and the specific hypotheses tested, if any? Why do you suppose the author chose the particular design?

   b. Did the design eliminate threats to internal validity? How did the design do this? Are you satisfied with the internal validity conclusions stated by the author? Why or why not?

   c. What is the setting for the study? Does the setting limit the generalizability of the results to other similar settings or to the broader population? Is reactivity a problem? Are there other threats to external validity?

MAKING RESEARCH ETHICAL

1. Randomization and double-blind procedures are key features of experimental design that are often used by studies to investigate the efficacy of new treatments for serious and often incurable, terminal diseases. What ethical issues do these techniques raise in studies of experimental treatments for incurable, terminal diseases?

2. Under what conditions do you think that randomized assignment of subjects to a specific treatment is ethical in social work research? Was it ethical for Walton et al. (1993) to randomly assign families into two different treatment groups? What about randomly assigning some welfare recipients to receive higher payments than others?

3. Critique the ethics of one of the experiments presented in this chapter. What specific rules do you think should guide researchers' decisions about subject deception and the selective distribution of benefits?

DEVELOPING A RESEARCH PROPOSAL

If you are planning to use a group design,

1. What specific design will you use? How long will the study last? At what time points will data be collected? How will the data be collected?

2. If you are using a design with more than one group, describe how participants are assigned to each group.

3. Discuss the extent to which each source of internal validity is a problem in the study.

4. How generalizable would you expect the study's findings to be? What can be done to improve generalizability?

5. Develop appropriate procedures for the protection of human subjects in your study. Include in these procedures a consent form.

> To assist you in completing the Web exercises below and to gain a better understanding of the chapter's contents, please access the study site at http://www.sagepub.com/fswrstudy where you will find the Web exercises reproduced with suggested links, along with self-quizzes, e-flash cards, interactive exercises, journal articles, and other valuable resources.

WEB EXERCISES

1. Try out the process of randomization. Go to the Web site http://www.randomizer.org. Type numbers into the randomizer for an experiment with 2 groups and 20 individuals per group. Repeat the process for an experiment with 4 groups and 10 individuals per group. Plot the numbers corresponding to each individual in each group. Does the distribution of numbers within each group truly seem to be random?

2. Participate in a social psychology experiment on the Web (go to http://www.socialpsychology.org/expts.htm). Pick an experiment in which to participate and follow the instructions. After you finish, write up a description of the experiment and evaluate it using the criteria discussed in the chapter.

CHAPTER 6

Single-Subject Design

Features of Single-Subject Design
Repeated Measurement
Baseline Phase
Internal Validity
Treatment Phase
Graphing
Measuring the Targets of Intervention
Analyzing and Interpreting Results
Interpreting Visual Patterns
Types of Single-Subject Designs
Basic Design (A-B)
Withdrawal Designs
A-B-A Design
A-B-A-B Design
Multiple Baseline Designs
Multiple Treatment Designs
Monitoring Designs

Implications for Evidence-Based Practice

Single-Subject Design in a Diverse Society

Ethical Issues in Single-Subject Design

Conclusion

Key Terms

Highlights

Discussion Questions

Critiquing Research

Making Research Ethical

Developing a Research Proposal

Web Exercises

Jody was a 40-year-old married White female who had been ill since 22 years of age. She had multiple hospitalizations, including 1 year in the state hospital. In the past year, she had six hospitalizations. She suffered from hallucinations, delusions, psychomotor retardation, apathy, flat affect, and avoidance of people and social situations. She was suicidal, inactive, and unable to do minimal self-care. She lived with her husband, who took care of her. She was a high school graduate and had attended 1 year of training as a dental assistant before her illness forced her to drop out of school. She took neuroleptic medications interspersed with brief periods of noncompliance due to paranoid ideas about the medicine (Bradshaw, 1997, p. 438).

It is not unusual for social work practitioners to have clients such as Jody who have a mental health condition such as schizophrenia. As practitioners, we often think we "know" when a client is improving. Yet when we use our own subjective conclusions, we are prone to human error. In this chapter, you learn how single-subject designs can be used to systematically test the effectiveness of a particular intervention as Bradshaw (1997, 2003; Bradshaw & Roseborough, 2004) did with Jody and subsequently with other participants, as well as how it can be used to monitor client progress.

Single-subject research designs (sometimes referred to as single-case or single-system designs) offer an alternative to experimental group designs. The focus is on a single participant as opposed to a group of participants. The structure of these designs, which are easily adapted to social work practice, makes them useful for research on interventions in direct and community practice. The process of assessment, establishing intervention goals and specific outcomes, providing the intervention, and evaluating progress prior to termination parallels the process of using single-subject designs, which depend on identifying the focus of the intervention, taking preintervention measures, providing the intervention, taking additional measures, and making decisions about the efficacy of the intervention. Because of these similarities, single-subject designs are easily adapted to evaluating practice and monitoring a client's progress.

In this chapter, we first take you through the components of single-subject designs, including their basic features, measurement of the target of the intervention, and interpretation of the findings. We then describe different designs and connect them to their different roles for social work research, practice evaluation, and client monitoring. Finally, we end the chapter with a discussion about the implications of single-subject designs for evidence-based practice and the ethical issues associated with single-subject designs.

FEATURES OF SINGLE-SUBJECT DESIGN

The underlying principle of single-subject design as a social work research method is that if an intervention with a client, agency, or community is effective, it should be possible to see a change in status from the period prior to the start of the intervention to the period during and after it. At a minimum, single-subject research designs include

- repeated measurements to identify a client's status;
- the baseline phase or the time period prior to the start of the intervention; and
- the treatment phase or the time period during the intervention.

Furthermore, the baseline and treatment phase measurements are typically displayed using graphs.

Repeated Measurement

Single-subject designs require the repeated measurement of a dependent variable, or in other words, the **target** or the focus of the intervention such as a status, condition, or problem. The target is measured at regular time intervals such as hours, days, weeks, or months, prior to the intervention and during the intervention. The preferred method is to take measures of the target with the client prior to implementing the intervention, for example during the assessment process, and then continue during the course of the intervention. Gathering information may mean withholding the intervention until the repeated measures can be taken. Alternatively, repeated measures of the dependent variable can begin when the client is receiving an intervention for other concerns. For example, a child may be seen for behavioral problems but eventually communication issues will be a concern. The repeated measurement of the communication issues could begin prior to that specific intervention focus.

There are times when it is not possible to delay the intervention either because there is a crisis or because to delay intervention would not be ethically appropriate. Yet you may still be able to construct a set of preintervention measures using data already collected or by asking about past experiences. Client records may have information from which a baseline can be produced, although you are limited to the information that is available in the record. Another option is to ask the client or, if permission is granted, significant members of the client's network about past behaviors, such as how many alcoholic drinks were consumed by the client in the last several weeks. Trying to construct measures by asking clients or family members assumes that the information is both remembered and reported accurately. Generally, behaviors and events are easier to recall than moods or feelings, yet the recall of even behaviors or events becomes more difficult with the passage of time and probably should be limited to the previous month.

There are other times when using retrospective data is feasible. Agencies often collect data about their operations, and these data can be used to obtain repeated measurements. For example, if an agency director was trying to find an outreach method that would increase the number of referrals, previous monthly referral information could be used and the intervention begun immediately. Or if an organizer was interested in the impact of an empowerment zone on levels of employment in a community, the preintervention employment data are likely to exist.

Baseline Phase

The **baseline phase** (abbreviated by the letter A), represents the period in which the intervention to be evaluated is not offered to the subject. During the baseline phase, repeated measurements of the dependent variable are taken or reconstructed. These measures reflect the status of the client (or agency or community) on the dependent variable prior to the intervention. The baseline phase measurements provide two aspects of control analogous to a control group in a group design. First, in a group design we expect the treatment group to have different scores than the control group after the intervention. In a single-subject design, the subject serves as the control, as the repeated baseline measurements establish the pattern of scores that we expect the intervention to change. Without the intervention, researchers assume that the baseline pattern of scores would continue its course. Second, in a control group design, random assignment controls for threats to internal validity. In a single-subject design, the repeated baseline measurements allow the researcher to discount some of the threats to the internal validity of the design.

In the baseline phase, measurements are taken until a *pattern* emerges. You have found a pattern when you can predict with some certainty what might be the next score. Predicting the next score requires a minimum of three observations in the baseline stage. When there are only two measures, the next data point could be higher or lower, or it could stay the same as the previous data points (see Exhibit 6.1a). With three measures, your certainty increases about the nature of the pattern. But even three measures might not be enough, depending on the pattern that is emerging. Is the pattern in Exhibit 6.1b predictable? You probably should take at least two more baseline measures, but three or four additional measures may be necessary to see a pattern emerge. As a general rule, the more data points, the more certain you will be about the pattern; it takes at least three consecutive measures that fall in some pattern for you to have confidence in the shape of the baseline pattern.

The three common types of patterns are a stable line, a trend line, and a cycle. A **stable line** (see Exhibit 6.2a) is a relatively flat line, with little variability in the scores so that the scores fall in a narrow band. This kind of line is desirable because changes can easily be detected, and it is likely that there are few problems of testing, instrumentation, statistical regression, and maturation in the data. A wider band or range of scores (see Exhibit 6.2b) is more difficult to interpret than a stable line with little variation.

A **trend** occurs when the scores are either increasing or decreasing during the baseline phase. When there is a linear trend (see Exhibit 6.2c), the scores tend to increase (or decrease) at more or less a constant rate over time. A trend may also be curvilinear (see Exhibit 6.2d) so that the rate of change is accelerating over time, rather than scores increasing or decreasing at a constant rate.

A **cycle** (see Exhibit 6.2e) is a pattern in which there are increases and decreases in scores depending on the time of year (month or week) when the measures are taken. For example, homeless shelter occupancy varies by the time of the year, with increased use in winter months and lower use in summer months.

There are situations in which no pattern is evident (see Exhibit 6.2f). With such baseline patterns, it is important to consider the reasons for the variability in scores. Is it due to the lack of reliability of the measurement process? If so, then an alternative measure might be sought. The participant may be using a good measure but not reporting information consistently, such as completing a depression scale at different times of day. Or the variability in scores may be due to some changing circumstance in the life of the participant.

Stable line A stable line is a line that is relatively flat with little variability in the scores so that the scores fall in a narrow band.

Trend An ascending or descending line.

Cycle A pattern reflecting ups and downs depending upon time of measurement.

EXHIBIT 6.1   **Predicting a Pattern**

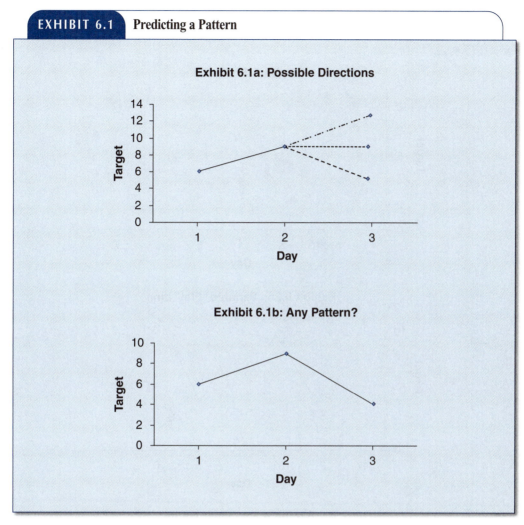

Exhibit 6.1a: Possible Directions

Exhibit 6.1b: Any Pattern?

Source: Engel & Schutt (2005).

Internal Validity

Findings of causality depend on the internal validity of the research design. Identifying a pattern by taking repeated baseline measures can control for several threats to the internal validity of single-subject designs. The alternative explanations posed by maturation, instrumentation, statistical regression, and testing may be evaluated because patterns illustrative of these threats to internal validity should appear in the baseline.

When baseline measures are stable lines, these threats may be ruled out, but it is more difficult to rule out some threats if the pattern is a trend, particularly if the trend is in the desired direction. For example, if maturation is a problem, you would expect to find a trend line and not a horizontal line. Perhaps you have a client who has experienced a loss and you

EXHIBIT 6.2 Different Baseline Patterns

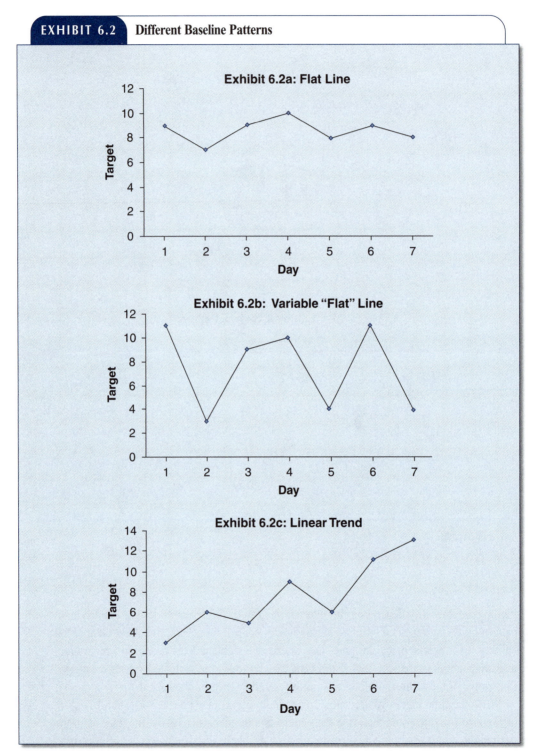

Source: Engel & Schutt (2005).

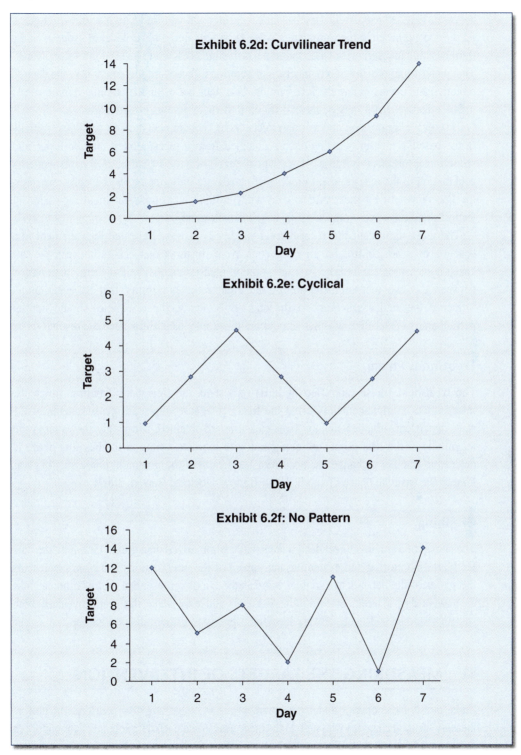

Source: Engel & Schutt (2005).

are measuring sadness. At the first baseline measurement you find a high degree of sadness. At the second baseline measurement a week later, you find a lower level of sadness, and a third baseline measurement finds sadness has declined below the level of the second week. This pattern suggests that there may be a maturation effect as improvement is in the desired direction and occurs before the intervention. This does not mean that an intervention would not be effective, but it may be more difficult to demonstrate its effectiveness.

If statistical regression and testing effects occur, their impact is likely to appear initially in the baseline measures. A high score obtained from a measurement may be lower in a second measurement because of statistical regression or because of the respondent's acclimation to the measurement process. If there were only one or two baseline measures, the line might reflect these effects. But with multiple measures, statistical regression or testing should disappear once a stable baseline pattern appears.

The most significant threat to internal validity is history. Repeated measurement in a baseline does not control for an extraneous event (history) that occurs between the last baseline measurement and the first intervention measurement. The longer the time period between the two measurement points, the greater the possibility that an event might influence the subject's scores. At the end of the study, the researcher should debrief participants to determine whether some other event may have influenced the results.

Treatment Phase

The **treatment phase** (signified by a B) represents the time period during which the intervention is implemented. During the treatment phase, repeated measurements of the same dependent variable using the same measures are obtained. Ultimately, the patterns and magnitude of the data points are compared with the data points in the baseline phase to determine whether a change has occurred. The length of the treatment phase should be as long as the baseline phase (Tripodi, 1994; Barlow, Nock, & Hersen, 2009).

Graphing

The phases of a single-subject design are usually summarized on a graph. Graphing the data facilitates monitoring and evaluating the impact of the intervention. The y-axis represents the scores of the dependent variable, whereas the x-axis represents a unit of time, such as an hour, a day, a week, or a month. Although you may make the graph by hand, both statistical and spreadsheet software have the capacity to present data on graphs.

▣   MEASURING THE TARGETS OF INTERVENTION

Three questions to answer about measurement are (a) what target to measure, (b) how to measure the target, and (c) who will do the measuring. With each decision, there are important issues to consider. For social work research as well as for other uses of single-subject design, there should be some certainty based on theoretical literature, empirical support, or practice experience to suggest that the chosen intervention is an appropriate method to address the target.

The dependent variable in a single-subject design is the target or concern that is the focus of the intervention. The target and intervention are usually established as part of the research project. In contrast, social work practitioners using single-subject design methods to evaluate practice or monitor their work typically arrive at the target through their interaction with clients or client systems.

The target may focus on one specific concern or several. For example, with an adolescent who is having behavioral problems in school, you may decide to measure the frequency of the behavioral problems. Or you may hypothesize that the adolescent's behavioral problems are caused by poor family communication and low self-esteem, so you may choose to measure all three problems. The targets can be measured simultaneously or sequentially.

Once the target or outcome of the intervention has been identified, you must determine how you will operationalize the outcome. Generally, in a research study, operationalization occurs prior to the beginning of the study; when evaluating practice or monitoring clients, operationalization occurs through client-practitioner interactions. For example, if you are evaluating the impact of positive parenting techniques on altering a child's behavior, you would identify jointly with the parents a behavior such as tantrums. You would then guide the parents to distinguish a tantrum from other behaviors or verbal expressions. This engagement is particularly important because there may be gender and ethnic differences in how a general problem may manifest itself (Nelson, 1994).

Measures of behaviors, status, or functioning are often characterized in four ways: frequency, duration, interval, and magnitude.

1. **Frequency** refers to counting the number of times a behavior occurs or the number of times people experience different feelings within a particular time period. Frequency counts are useful for measuring targets that happen regularly but can be burdensome if the behavior occurs too often. However, if the behavior happens only periodically, the counts will not be meaningful.

2. **Duration** refers to the length of time an event or some symptom lasts and usually is measured for each occurrence of the event or symptom. A measure of duration requires fewer episodes than do frequency counts of the target. It also requires a clear definition as to what constitutes the start and finish of the event.

3. The **interval**, or the length of time between events, may be measured. This kind of measure may not be appropriate for events or symptoms that happen frequently unless the intent of the intervention is to delay their onset.

4. The **magnitude** or intensity of a behavior or psychological state can be measured. Often magnitude or intensity measures are applied to psychological symptoms or attitudes, such as measures of depressive symptoms, quality of peer interactions, or self-esteem.

Social work researchers and practitioners have a variety of alternative methods available to measure the target. Standardized instruments and rapid assessment tools cover a wide range of psychological dimensions, family functioning, individual functioning, and the like. Another option is to collect data based on clinical observations. Observations are particularly useful when the target involves a behavior. A third option is to develop measures within the agency, such as a goal attainment scale. Regardless of how the data are collected, the measures should be reliable and valid.

Who will gather the data? You might ask participants to keep logs and to record information in the logs or to complete instruments at specified time points, either through self-administration or by an interview. You may choose to observe the participant's behavior. Regardless of which method you choose, reactivity may be a concern since the measurement process may influence a participant's responses or behaviors. If you ask a subject to keep a log and to record each time a behavior occurs, the act of keeping the log may reduce the behavior. Observing a father interacting with his children might change the way the father behaves with the children. Staff, knowing that supervisors are looking for certain activities, may increase the number of those activities.

Yet reactivity is not always an issue either for research or practice, as it may have clinical implications for practice interventions. If keeping a log enhances the impact of the intervention, then this finding could be integrated into the actual intervention. But we would still have to test whether different methods of gathering data produce different outcomes.

There are other considerations about the choice of measurement. Repeatedly taking measures can be cumbersome, inconvenient, and difficult. Repeated measurement may be too time-consuming for the subject or the researcher, and continuous measurements may reduce the incentive of the subject to participate in the research or treatment.

The choice of measurement must be sensitive enough to detect changes. If the measurement scale is too global, it may be impossible to detect incremental or small changes, particularly in targets such as psychological status, feelings, emotions, and attitudes. In addition, whatever is measured must occur frequently enough or on a regular basis so that repeated measurements can be taken. Unless the research is designed to last a long time, it will be impractical to take repeated measures of an infrequent event or behavior.

Bradshaw (1997) chose to measure three outcomes simultaneously: symptomatology, psychosocial functioning, and hospitalizations. The symptoms measure was based on the severity of the symptoms (magnitude); the psychosocial functioning measure had behavioral anchors and was characterized by magnitude; and hospitalizations were the actual number that occurred in each month (frequency). The ratings were done by a psychotherapist and two case managers trained to use the measures.

ANALYZING AND INTERPRETING RESULTS

How might we analyze data from a single-subject design? One option is to use a statistical technique, such as the two-standard-deviation band, chi-square analysis, or time-series to analyze the data (see Barlow et al., 2009; Bloom, Fischer, & Orme, 2009; Borckardt et al., 2008; Franklin, Allison, & Gorman, 1997). The most common method is to visually examine the graphed data. Visual analysis is the process of looking at a graph of the data points to determine whether the intervention has altered the subject's preintervention pattern of scores. Three concepts that guide visual analysis are level, trend, and variability.

Level refers to the amount or magnitude of the target variable. Has the amount of the target variable changed from the baseline to the intervention phase? Changes in level are typically used when the observed scores fall along relatively stable lines. A simple method to describe changes in level is to inspect the actual data points (see Exhibit 6.3a). It appears that the actual amount of the target variable—anxiety—has decreased.

Alternatively, the level of the phase scores may be summarized by drawing a line at the typical score for each phase separately. For example, the level may be summarized into a single observation using the mean (the average of the observations in the phase), or the median (the value at which 50% of the scores in the phase are higher and 50% are lower). The mean of the baseline scores is calculated, and a horizontal line is drawn across the baseline phase at the mean. Then the mean of the intervention scores is calculated, and a horizontal line is drawn at the mean score across the intervention phase. The summary line for the baseline phase is compared with the summary line for the intervention phase (see Exhibit 6.3b).

When the data points reflect trend lines instead of stable lines, there are two different questions depending on the nature of the lines. The first question is this: Has the intervention altered the direction of the trend? If the baseline trend line is ascending, is the trend line descending in the treatment phase? When the direction does not change, you may be interested in whether the rate of increase or decrease in the trend has changed. You might ask, Does the intervention alter the slope of the line?

Visually inspecting the lines might provide an answer, but trends can also be represented by summary lines. One approach is to use Ordinary Least Squares (OLS) regression (see Exhibit 6.4a) to calculate a regression line that summarizes the scores in the baseline and another regression line to summarize the scores in the intervention phase. The baseline OLS regression line is extended into the intervention phase, and the two lines are visually examined to determine whether the trend has changed. In Exhibit 6.4a, the increasing level of anxiety reflected in the baseline has stopped and the level of anxiety has dropped. Since the actual computation is quite complicated, statistical software can be used to produce OLS regression lines.

Nugent (2000) has suggested a simpler approach to represent the trend in a phase (see Exhibit 6.4b). When the trend is linear, draw a straight line connecting the first and last data points in the baseline phase with an arrow at the end to summarize the direction. A similar line would then be drawn for the points in the intervention phase. These two lines could then be compared. In the case of an outlier, Nugent recommends that the line be drawn from either the second point to the last point, if the first point is an outlier, or from the first point to the second to last point, if the last point is an outlier. The same methods can be used to summarize nonlinear trends, except that two lines are drawn in the baseline phase, one representing the segment of the first point to the lowest (or highest) point and the second line from the lowest (or highest) point to the last data point.

EXHIBIT 6.3   Level

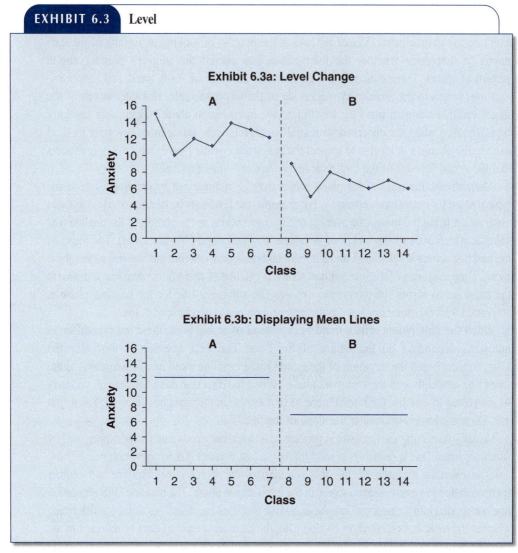

Source: Engel & Schutt (2005).

Finally, the **variability** of scores, or how different the scores are in the baseline and intervention phases, may be evaluated. Widely divergent scores in the baseline make the assessment of the intervention more difficult, as do widely different scores in the intervention phase. There are some conditions and concerns for which the lack of stability is the problem and so creating stability may represent a positive change. One way to summarize variability with a visual analysis is to draw range lines, as was done in Exhibit 6.5. As you can see, the only change has been a reduction in the spread of the points. But this does not mean that the intervention has not been effective, because it depends on the goal of the intervention.

EXHIBIT 6.4 **Displaying Trend Lines**

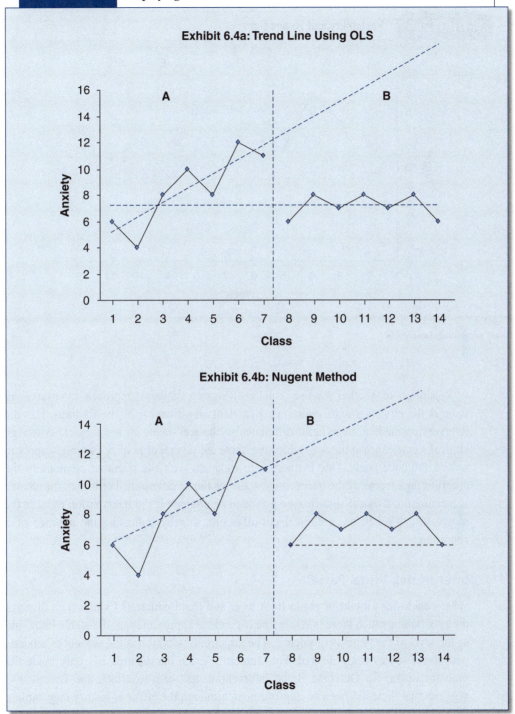

Exhibit 6.4a: Trend Line Using OLS

Exhibit 6.4b: Nugent Method

Source: Engel & Schutt (2005).

EXHIBIT 6.5	Variability and Range Bars

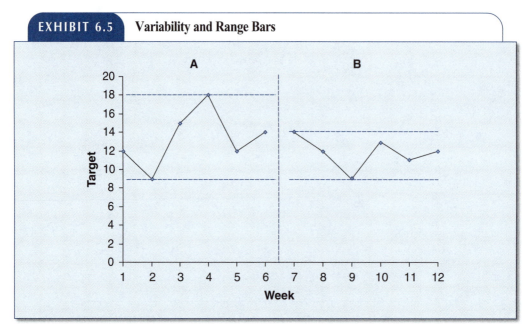

Source: Engel & Schutt (2005).

Regardless of whether you use visual analysis or a statistical approach, the overriding issue is the *clinical significance* (i.e., **practical significance**) of the findings. Has the intervention made a meaningful difference in the well-being of the subject? Although clinical significance at times is subjective, there are several principles you might apply to reduce the uncertainty. One method is to establish with the client or community the criterion for success. If the intervention achieves the predetermined criterion, the change is meaningful. Clinical significance may also be attained if the intervention reduces the scores to a level below a clinical cut-off score, thereby indicating the absence of a condition.

Interpreting Visual Patterns

What conclusions might be made from level and trend patterns? Exhibit 6.6a displays the situation in which there is stable line (or a close approximation of a stable line), and so the level of the target is of interest. The target in this exhibit is the amount of anxiety, with lower scores being desired. For Outcome A, the intervention has only made the problem worse, for Outcome B the intervention has had no effect, and Outcome C suggests that there has been an improvement, although the effect of history may explain the change. Exhibit 6.6b illustrates outcomes of a stable baseline and a trend line in the

EXHIBIT 6.6   Typical Baseline-Intervention Patterns

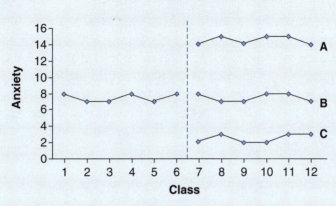

Exhibit 6.6a: Stable Line Display

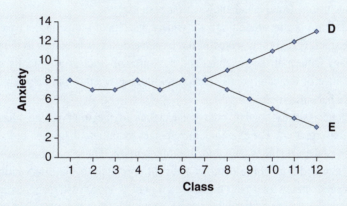

Exhibit 6.6b: Stable Baseline and Trends

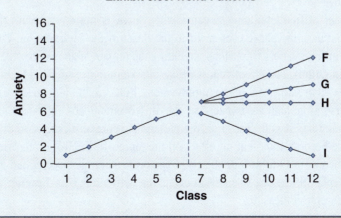

Exhibit 6.6c: Trend Patterns

Source: Engel & Schutt (2005).

treatment phase; Outcome D represents a deteriorating trend, while Outcome E reflects an improving trend.

Exhibit 6.6c displays common patterns when there is a trend in the baseline; the baseline phase is marked by an increase in anxiety from week to week. In the case of Outcome F, the intervention had no effect on the level of anxiety. For Outcome G, there was no change in the direction of the trend, but the rate of increase of anxiety has slowed, suggesting that the intervention has been effective at least in slowing the increase of the problem but has not alleviated it. Outcome H represents the situation in which the intervention has improved the situation only to the extent that it is not getting worse. Finally, for Outcome I, the intervention has resulted in an improvement in the subject's status.

In real practice research or evaluation, you are less likely to obtain such clear patterns. Because you are relying on visual judgment, there is the real possibility of coming to the wrong conclusion even if you are using systematic approaches like those suggested by Nugent (Borckardt, Murphy, Nash, & Shaw, 2004). There are several possible concerns that make conclusions from visual analysis less certain.

One concern occurs when there are widely discrepant scores in the baseline as was the case in Exhibit 6.2f. When scores in the baseline differ, it is harder to determine whether there is any pattern at the baseline, and measures of level or a typical score may not be representative of the data points. Therefore, judging whether the intervention has made a difference becomes more difficult.

A second issue is how to interpret changes in the intervention phase that are not immediately apparent. For example, the changes in anxiety displayed in Exhibits 6.7a and 6.7b took place several weeks into the intervention. These changes may be due to the intervention or due to some extraneous event unrelated to the intervention. There is no easy answer as many treatment modalities do not produce instantaneous improvement. It depends on the nature of the intervention and when it is hypothesized that change will occur. The alternative interpretation that something happened (i.e., history) is equally plausible.

Another difficult judgment occurs when there is improvement in the target scores during the baseline phase even prior to the onset of the intervention. This improvement may occur for a variety of reasons, including the impact of an event or the passage of time (i.e., maturation). The effectiveness of the intervention may depend on whether there is a shift in level or in the rate of the improvement. In Exhibit 6.8a, you see a pattern in which the intervention had no impact, as the improvement continues unchanged after the intervention has begun. Based on the pattern of scores in Exhibits 6.8b and 6.8c, there may have been an intervention effect on the target. In Exhibit 6.8b, there was a shift in level, whereas in Exhibit 6.8c the rate of improvement has accelerated. Of course, these changes may still be due to an event occurring between the last baseline measure and the first intervention measure.

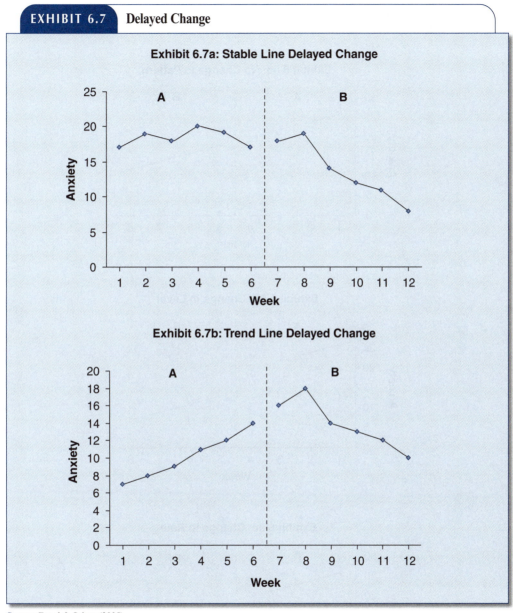

EXHIBIT 6.7   **Delayed Change**

Exhibit 6.7a: Stable Line Delayed Change

Exhibit 6.7b: Trend Line Delayed Change

Source: Engel & Schutt (2005).

The act of graphing can create visual distortions that can lead to different conclusions. In Exhibit 6.9, three different pictures of the baseline data appear, with the lines becoming increasingly flat. Furthermore, the nature of the graph may prevent small but meaningful changes from being visually evident. Therefore, when constructing a graph, it is important to make the axes as proportionate as possible to minimize distortions.

EXHIBIT 6.8 Improvement in the Baseline

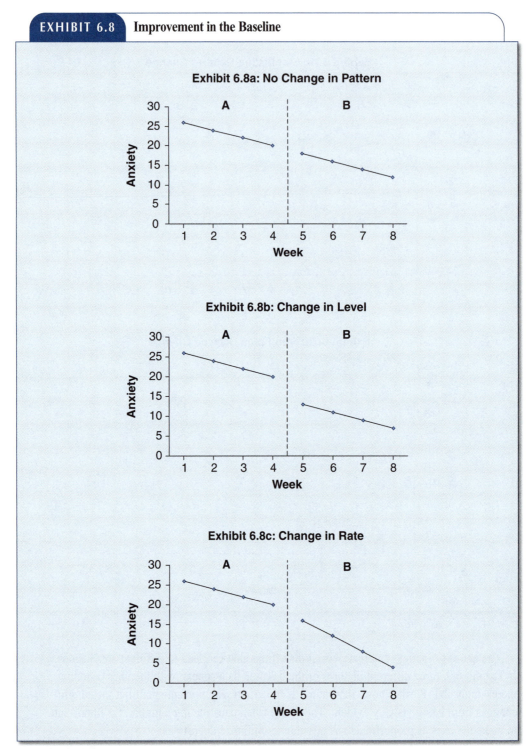

Source: Engel & Schutt (2005).

EXHIBIT 6.9 | **Distorted Pictures**

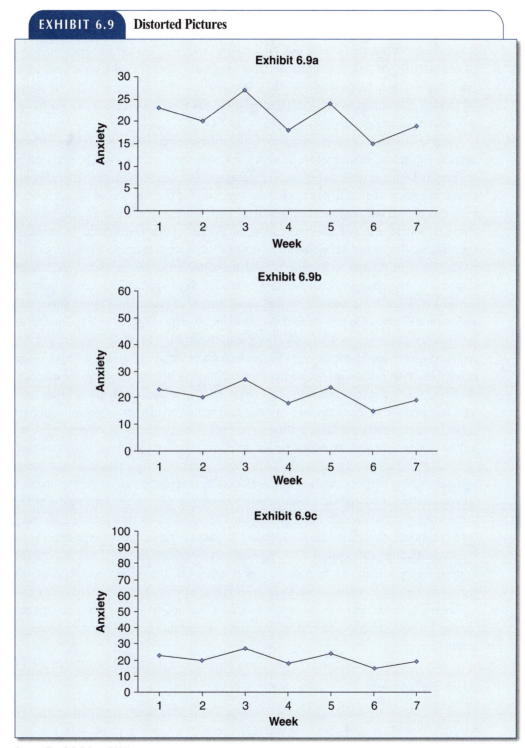

Source: Engel & Schutt (2005).

▣ TYPES OF SINGLE-SUBJECT DESIGNS

Single-subject designs are used to test interventions (research), evaluate program outcomes (assess practice outcomes), and monitor client progress. There are more constraints when using single-subject design when the goal is research than when using single-subject design for practice evaluation; monitoring client progress has even fewer constraints than those imposed on practice evaluation.

The goal of a research experiment is to test the efficacy of an intervention on a particular target and, therefore, to enhance social work knowledge about what works. The intervention has already been specified, as has (have) the target(s) that will be evaluated. The measures should be reliable and valid indicators of the target(s). The baseline should include at least three data points, and measurement should continue until there is a pattern. The baseline measures should also be collected during the course of the experiment. To establish causality, the design should control for all internal validity threats, including history.

The focus of practice evaluation is to describe the effectiveness of the program or particular intervention approach. Increasing knowledge about a particular treatment approach may be a goal, but that is secondary to the overall purpose of evaluation. Practice or program evaluation is conducted to provide feedback about the program to agency staff and funders so that demonstrating a causal relationship is less important. The specific target and the appropriate intervention emerge from the interactions of the social worker with the client, rather than being established before the interaction. As in a research study, the measures should be reliable and valid indicators of the target. Ideally, the baseline should include at least three measures and be characterized by a stable pattern, but this may not be possible; only one or two measures may be available. Unlike the case in a research design, the baseline measures may be produced through the recollection of the client, significant others, or client records.

The purpose of monitoring is to systematically track a client's progress. Monitoring provides ongoing feedback that may be more objective than just relying on the practitioner's impressions. Monitoring provides information about whether the intervention should continue without change or whether the intervention should be modified. As with practice evaluation, the target(s) and intervention are not specified in advance; rather, they emerge through the client-social worker interaction. Ideally, the measures are reliable and valid indicators. There may not be any baseline, or the baseline may be limited to a single assessment. When the techniques are used to monitor a client's progress, threats to internal validity are not a concern.

Keep these distinctions in mind as you read about the various designs. Some designs can be used for both research and practice evaluation while other designs are more suited to monitoring.

Basic Design (A-B)

The *A-B design* is the basic single-subject design and is often used for all three purposes: research, evaluation, and client monitoring. There is a baseline phase with repeated measurements and an intervention phase continuing the same measures. Bradshaw (1997) used an A-B design to test the effectiveness of Cognitive-Behavioral Treatment (CBT) with four participants with schizophrenia. Bradshaw collected 3 months of baseline data on symptomatology and psychosocial functioning using standardized instruments. This was followed by 18 months of intervention, with data collected monthly. He used visual analysis to assess the effectiveness of CBT on these two outcomes. As a research study, Bradshaw (a) set the length of the study and the particular outcomes prior to contact with the participants, (b) used standardized measures for which there was evidence of reliability and validity, and (c) had a minimum of three baseline measures.

The A-B design can also be used to monitor a client's progress. Consider a case in which a social worker wants to test the benefits of negative rewards in changing adolescent behavior. The subject is a 17-year-old daughter who has been squabbling with her brother and being rude and sarcastic with her parents. Points will be accrued for poor behavior, and after a certain number of points are attained, the child will begin to lose certain privileges. The parents are instructed to count and record the total number of rude and sarcastic comments, as well as sibling arguments begun by the child, every 3 days over a 15-day period. The intervention begins on the 16th day with the parents explaining how the child might get negative points and face the consequences of accumulating points.

The results of the intervention are displayed in Exhibit 6.10. There is a significant improvement. The question is whether the improvement is due to the intervention alone. The parents thought so, but in a debriefing with the social worker it appears that other factors might have been involved. For example, each day during the first week, the child asked her parents whether they were proud of her behavior. The parents lavished praise on the child. The threat associated with the negative consequences may have been confounded by the positive reinforcement provided by the parents. It also turned out that, at about the time the intervention began, the child stopped hanging out with two peers who had begun to tease her. So the changes could be attributable to the child's removing herself from a negative peer group.

These two examples point to the limits of the A-B design as a tool for research. The design cannot rule out other extraneous events, so it is impossible to conclude that the treatment *caused* the change. The A-B design does provide evidence of an association between the intervention and the change, and given that some threats to internal validity are controlled, it is analogous to a quasi-experimental design. The researcher may have more confidence that history did not impact the findings if after debriefing the subjects, there appear to be no influential external events.

Withdrawal Designs

There are two withdrawal designs: the *A-B-A design* and the *A-B-A-B design*. By withdrawal, we mean that the intervention is concluded and there is a planned, systematic follow-up (A-B-A design) or the intervention is stopped for some period of time before it

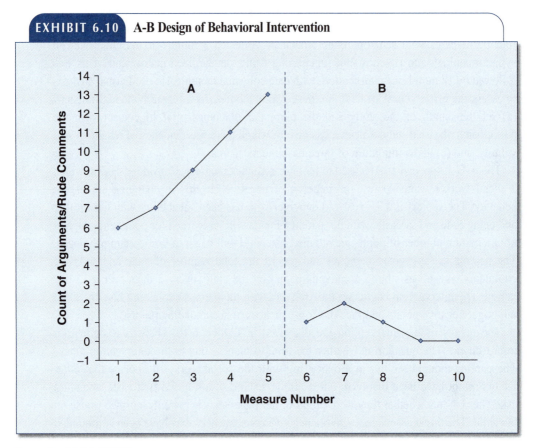

EXHIBIT 6.10   **A-B Design of Behavioral Intervention**

Source: Engel & Schutt (2005).

is begun again (A-B-A-B design). The premise is that if the intervention is effective, the target should only be improved during the course of intervention and the target scores should worsen when the intervention is removed. If this assumption is correct, then the impact of an extraneous event (history) between the baseline and intervention phase would not explain the change.

This premise, however, is problematic for social work research. Ideally, the goal of the intervention is to reduce or eliminate the target without the need for ongoing intervention. We would like the impact of the intervention to be felt long after the client has stopped the intervention. Practice theories, such as behavioral or cognitive-behavioral treatment, are based on the idea that the therapeutic effects will persist. This concern, referred to as the **carryover effect**, may inhibit the use of these designs for research. To be used for research, the implementation of each of the withdrawal designs may necessitate limiting the length of the intervention and ending it prematurely. Or this design can be used to test the assumption that the impact of the treatment continues after treatment is discontinued. If the designs are being used for evaluation, it is unnecessary to prematurely withdraw the intervention; rather, the second baseline provides important follow-up information.

A-B-A Design

The A-B-A design builds on the A-B design by integrating a post-treatment follow-up that would typically include repeated measures. This design answers the question left unanswered by the A-B design: Does the effect of the intervention persist beyond the period in which treatment is provided? Depending on the length of the follow-up period, it may also be possible to learn how long the effect of the intervention persists.

The follow-up period should include sufficient multiple measures until a follow-up pattern emerges. This arrangement is built into the research study. For practice evaluation, the practicality of this depends upon whether the relationship with the client extends beyond the period of the actual intervention and the ease of collecting information.

A-B-A-B Design

The A-B-A-B design builds in a second intervention phase. The intervention in this phase is identical to the intervention used in the first B phase. The replication of the intervention in the second intervention phase makes this design useful for social work practice research. For example, if, during the follow-up phase, the effects of the intervention began to reverse (see Exhibit 6.11a), then the effects of the intervention can be established by doing it again. If there is a second improvement, the replication reduces the possibility that an event or history explains the change.

Just as with the A-B-A design, there is no guarantee that the effects will be reversed by withdrawing the intervention. If the practice theory holds, then it is unlikely that the effects will actually be reversed. So it may be that this first intervention period has to be short and ended just as evidence of improvement appears. Even if the effect is not reversed, reintroducing the intervention may demonstrate a second period of additional improvement (see Exhibit 6.11b). This pattern suggests that the changes between the no-treatment and treatment phases are due to the intervention and not the result of history.

Multiple Baseline Designs

In the three previous designs, the individual baseline scores serve as the control for the impact of the intervention. An alternative is to add additional subjects, targets, or settings, to the study. This method provides social work researchers with a feasible method of controlling for the effects of history.

The basic format of a *concurrent multiple baseline design* is to implement a series of A-B designs (though A-B-A or A-B-A-B designs could also be used) at the same time for at least three cases (clients, targets, or settings). The unique feature of this design is that the length of the baseline phase is staggered (see Exhibit 6.12) to control for external events across the three cases. The baseline phase for the second case extends until the intervention

EXHIBIT 6.11 A-B-A-B Designs

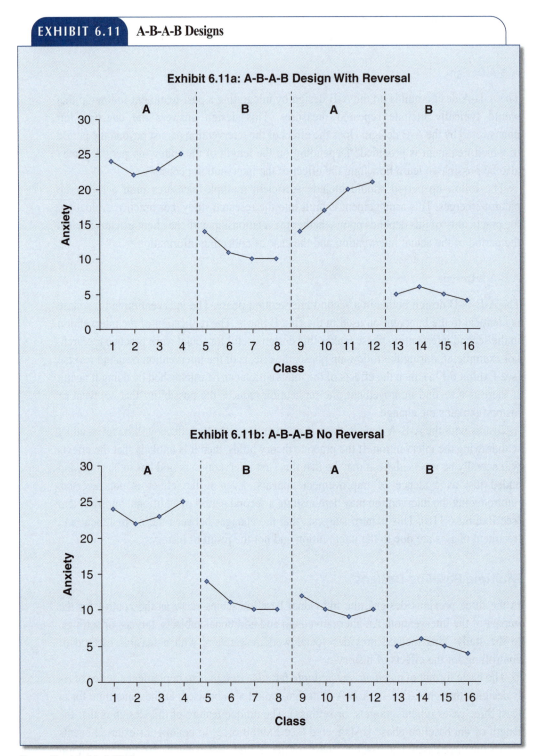

Exhibit 6.11a: A-B-A-B Design With Reversal

Exhibit 6.11b: A-B-A-B No Reversal

Source: Engel & Schutt (2005).

EXHIBIT 6.12   **Multiple Baseline Design**

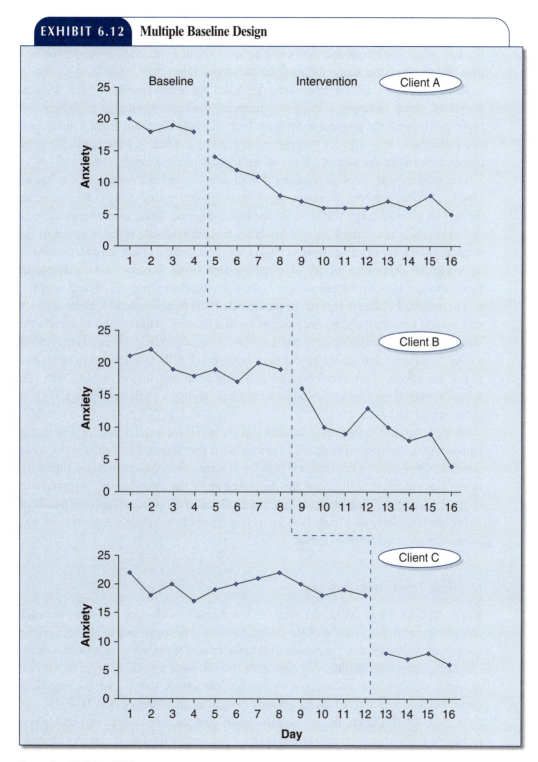

Source: Engel & Schutt (2005).

data points for the first case become more or less stable. Similarly, the intervention for the third case does not begin until the second case's data points in the intervention phase become stable. The second and third cases act as a control for external events for the first case, and the third case acts as a control for the second case.

After Bradshaw's (2003) first study, he tested the effectiveness of CBT with an additional seven participants using a concurrent multiple baseline A-B design. All participants started the program at the same time. The baseline phase lasted 6 months for two participants, 9 months for two participants, and 12 months for the remaining three participants. During the baseline phase, all participants received treatment as usual.

One problem with a design requiring that all subjects start at the same time is having enough available subjects. In a *nonconcurrent multiple baseline design*, the researcher decides on different lengths of time for the baseline period. Then, as clients or subjects meeting the selection criteria become available, they are randomly assigned to one of the baseline phases. For example, Jensen (1994) used this approach to test the effectiveness of an integrated short-term model of Cognitive-Behavioral Therapy and Interpersonal Psychotherapy. Jensen randomly assigned clients to a baseline phase of 3, 4, or 5 weeks.

The multiple baseline design can be implemented with three (or more) subjects in which each subject receives the same intervention but at a different starting point to address the same target. Or the design can be implemented with one subject, with the same intervention applied to different, but related, problems or behaviors. Finally, this design can be applied to test the effects of an intervention as it is applied to one subject, dealing with one behavior, such as arriving on time, but sequentially applied to different settings, such as home, school, and work.

Multiple baseline designs have features that are useful for research studies. The design introduces two replications so that if consistent results are found, the likelihood that some external event is causing the change is reduced. If some extraneous event might impact all three cases, the effect of the event may be picked up by the control cases. The pattern of change in Exhibit 6.13 suggests that some event influenced the outcomes not only for Client A, but simultaneously for Clients B and C as they reported changes and improvement even before they received the intervention.

Multiple Treatment Designs

In a multiple treatment design, the nature of the intervention changes over time, and each change represents a new phase of the design. One type of change that might occur is the *intensity* of the intervention. For example, the actual amount of contact you have with a family may change over time, starting with counseling sessions twice a week, followed by a period of weekly sessions, and concluding with monthly interactions. In this case, the amount of contact declines over time. Changing intensity designs are characterized by $A\text{-}B_1\text{-}B_2\text{-}B_3$.

In an A-B-C-D design, the actual intervention changes over time so that each phase represents a different intervention. For example, an agency director designed a study to

EXHIBIT 6.13 **Multiple Baseline Design With History**

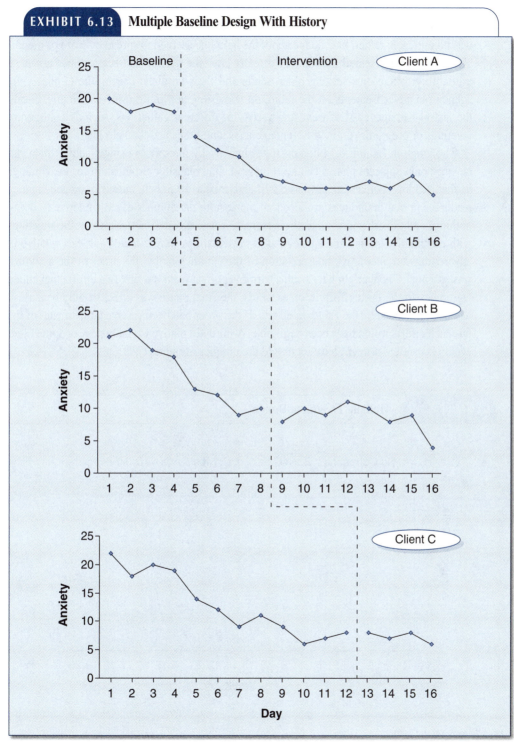

Source: Engel & Schutt (2005).

determine the effectiveness of outreach efforts on the number of phone calls received by a help line (information and referral). The baseline period represented a time in which there was no outreach; rather, knowledge about the help line seemed to spread by word of mouth. The B phase represented the number of calls after the agency had sent notices about its availability to agencies serving older adults and their families. During the C phase, the agency ran advertisements on the radio, on television, and in print media. Finally, during the last phase, agency staff went to a variety of different gatherings, such as community meetings or programs run by different agencies, and described the help line.

The graph in Exhibit 6.14 demonstrates how tricky interpreting single-subject data can be since only adjacent phases can be compared. One plausible explanation for the findings is that sending notices to professionals and media efforts at outreach wasted agency resources in that the notices produced no increase in the number of calls relative to doing nothing, and advertising produced no increase relative to the notices. Only the meetings with community groups and agency-based presentations were effective, at least relative to advertising. An alternative interpretation of the findings is that the order of the activities was essential. There might have been a carryover effect from the first two efforts that added legitimacy to the third effort. In other words, the final phase was effective only because it had been preceded by the first two efforts. If the order had been reversed, the impact of the outreach efforts would have been negligible. A third alternative is that history or some other event occurred that might have increased the number of phone calls.

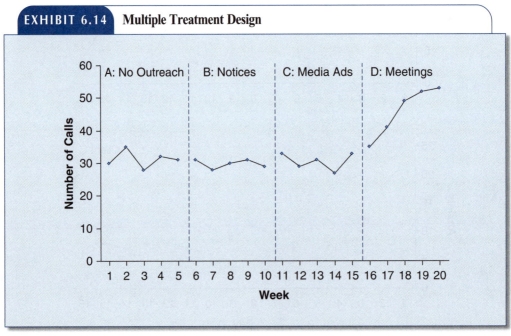

EXHIBIT 6.14 **Multiple Treatment Design**

Source: Engel & Schutt (2005).

Multiple treatment designs might also include interactions where two treatments are combined. An interaction design often parallels experiences with clients or agency activities, in which interventions are combined or done simultaneously. In the previous example, the agency outreach effort might have included its baseline (A), notices to agencies (B), media efforts (C), and then a combination of the two (B-C).

Monitoring Designs

When monitoring a client's progress, the A-B design is recommended for the baseline information it provides. But there are times when establishing a baseline is not possible, other than to have a single point based on an initial assessment. Nonetheless, to ascertain whether a client is making progress, a form of monitoring should be done. Therefore, a social worker might use the B or the B-A design.

The *B design* (see Exhibit 6.15a) only has an intervention phase; during the course of intervention, you take repeated measurements. This design can be used to determine whether the client is making progress in the desired direction. If the client is not making progress, you may decide to change the type of intervention or the intensity of the intervention. With a B design, the actual improvement cannot be attributed to the intervention. There is no baseline, and therefore changes might be due to different threats to internal validity, reactivity to the measurement process, or reactivity to the clinical setting.

If a period of follow-up measurements can be introduced, then a *B-A design* is a better alternative (see Exhibit 6.15b). The intervention period is followed by a period of no intervention for the specific problem. Although it is harder to get repeated measurements of a client after the intervention has concluded, if treatment about other concerns continues, then follow-up measures are possible. This design enables the social worker to see whether the impact of the intervention continues after ceasing treatment.

▣ IMPLICATIONS FOR EVIDENCE-BASED PRACTICE

Single-subject designs offer a range of evidence to assess the impact of different interventions. The most rigorous designs control for threats to internal validity, while monitoring designs demonstrate client outcomes but without the ability to suggest it was the intervention that mattered. Therefore, understanding the differences in these designs is crucial to weighing the evidence derived from such studies.

One benefit of single-subject design is the focus on the individual as opposed to a group. The evidence derived from single-subject designs differs from that of group designs in that the question of interest is different (Johnston et al., 2006). In a single-subject design the question is whether an intervention works for an individual. In contrast, the questions in a group design include the following: Does the group average change? Does the treatment group average differ in comparison with a second group? In a group design, the impact on any one individual is obscured by the impact on the group.

EXHIBIT 6.15 **Two B Designs**

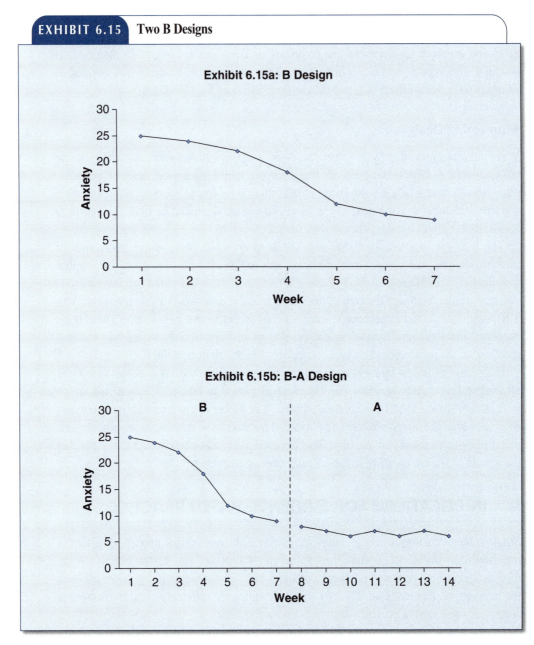

Source: Engel & Schutt (2005).

This different focus is particularly important for social workers because much of their practice involves interventions with individuals. Given the focus on the individual, cultural and other contextual variables are considered in evaluating outcomes (Arbin & Cormier, 2005). Single-subject designs are likely to pay greater consideration to client characteristics, such as gender, age, ethnicity, sexual orientation, or class. Therefore, the evidence may be quite compelling because it reflects more accurately findings from actual practice.

However, the strength of single-subject design with its focus on an individual is also its weakness. How are we to judge findings about a single individual? How is evidence about that single individual relevant to other clients? We can think about this criticism as a statistical problem or as a problem about building the generalizability of the findings. The statistical problem is being addressed by statisticians who are developing meta-analytic methods to assess single-subject design research; these methods are designed to take the findings of many single-subject design studies and aggregate them (Jenson, Clark, Kircher, & Kristjansson, 2007).

The problem of generalizability of single-subject design research is not unlike that of group design research—it is an issue of external validity. Ideally, we want to take what has been tested in one research context and apply the findings to different settings, clients, or communities; to other providers; and to other problems related to the target concern of the research. To do so when the sample consists of a single subject engaged in a particular intervention provided by a particular individual is challenging. To demonstrate the external validity of single-subject design requires replication of both the same research conditions and then other research conditions.

Barlow et al. (2009) suggest that three sequential replication strategies be used to enhance the external validity of single-subject design. These are direct replication, systematic replication, and clinical replication.

- *Direct replication.* **Direct replication** involves repeating the same procedures, by the same researchers, including the same providers of the treatment, in the same setting, and in the same situation, with different clients who have similar characteristics (Barlow et al., 2009). The strength of the findings is enhanced by having successful outcomes with these other clients. When the results are inconsistent, differences in the clients can be examined to identify characteristics that may be related to success or failure.

- *Systematic replication.* The next step is **systematic replication,** which involves repeating the experiment in different settings, using different providers, and other related behaviors (Barlow et al., 2009). Systematic replication also increases the number and type of clients exposed to the intervention. Through systematic replication, the applicability of the intervention to different conditions is evaluated. Like direct replication, systematic replication helps to clarify conditions in which the intervention may be successful and conditions in which the intervention may not be successful.

- *Clinical replication.* The last stage is **clinical replication,** which Barlow et al. (2009) define as combining different interventions into a clinical package to treat multiple problems. The actual replication takes place in the same setting and with clients who have the same types of problems. In many ways, findings from practice evaluation can enhance clinical replications.

For any replication effort to be successful, the treatment procedures must be clearly articulated, identified, and followed. Failing to adhere to the treatment procedures changes the intervention, and therefore there is not a true replication of the experiment.

Bradshaw's efforts at demonstrating the effectiveness of CBT to treat schizophrenia represent the contribution such systematic research makes to advancing practice-related knowledge. His initial study (1997) was completed with 4 participants who had been referred for outpatient therapy after being discharged from psychiatric hospitalizations. His next study (2003) included 10 participants (3 did not complete the study) randomly selected from a county mental health system. In this study, the intervention period was twice as long as in the first study, but followed the same model of CBT. Finally, in collaboration with David Roseborough, Bradshaw reported findings from a third study of 30 clients (8 left the study) who received CBT for 18 months (2004). The ongoing replication and findings of positive results has provided support for this intervention with clients with schizophrenia.

▣   SINGLE-SUBJECT DESIGN IN A DIVERSE SOCIETY

Special attention must be paid to issues of diversity. Researchers and practitioners must understand that how problems are identified and defined may depend on client characteristics, such as gender, ethnicity, sexual orientation, and class. Measures must be acceptable and applicable (reliable and valid) to different population subgroups. Similarly, issues regarding informed consent are relevant for all population subgroups (Martin & Knox, 2000; Nelson, 1994).

Single-subject design may be a useful method for engaging diverse groups who have been underrepresented in research and in particular experimental group designs or clinical research trials. Because it is often practice-based, it may be easier to mitigate distrust of the researcher. Because it focuses on the individual, as opposed to the group, single-subject designs can more easily incorporate cultural factors and test for cultural variation (Arbin & Cormier, 2005).

▣   ETHICAL ISSUES IN SINGLE-SUBJECT DESIGN

Like any form of research, single-subject designs require the informed consent of the participant. The structure of single-subject designs for research involves particularly unique conditions that must be discussed with potential participants. As we discussed in Chapter 2, all aspects of the research, such as the purpose, measurement, confidentiality, and data collection, are a part of the information needed for informed consent. In particular, the need for repeated baseline measurements and the possibility of premature withdrawal of treatment are particularly unique to single-subject design research.

Participants must understand that the onset of the intervention is likely to be delayed until either a baseline pattern emerges or some assigned time period elapses. Until this condition is met, a needed intervention may be withheld. Furthermore, the length of the baseline also depends on the type of design. In a multiple baseline design, the delay in the intervention may be substantial. The implications of this delay must be discussed as part of obtaining informed consent.

When a withdrawal or reversal design is used, there are additional considerations. The structure of such designs means that the intervention may be withdrawn just as the research subject is beginning to improve. The risks associated with prematurely ending treatment may be hard to predict. If there is a carryover effect, the subject's condition may not worsen, but it is possible that the subject's condition or status may indeed worsen. Given this possibility, the use of an A-B-A-B design as opposed to the A-B-A design is preferable for the purpose of research.

Obtaining informed consent may not be limited to the use of single-subject design for research purposes. As we noted in Chapter 2, the NASW Code of Ethics (1999) does not distinguish between the need for informed consent in research and the need for informed consent for practice evaluation. Specifically,

> Social workers engaged in evaluation or research should obtain voluntary and written informed consent from participants, when appropriate, without any implied or actual deprivation or penalty for refusal to participate; without undue inducement to participate; and with due regard for participants' well-being, privacy, and dignity. Informed consent should include information about the nature, extent, and duration of the participation requested and disclosure of the risks and benefits of participation in research. (5.02[e])

Others suggest that informed consent may not be necessary. For example, Royse, Thyer, Padgett, and Logan (2006) suggest that written informed consent is not necessarily required for practice evaluation because the intent is not to provide generalized knowledge or to publish the results.

Even if written informed consent is not required when using these tools for practice evaluation and monitoring, social workers using these tools should be guided by practice ethics. According to the NASW Code of Ethics (1999), social work practitioners should, as a part of their everyday practice with clients,

> Provide services to clients only in the context of a professional relationship that is based on valid informed consent. Social workers should use clear and understandable language to inform clients of the purpose of the services, risks related to the services, limits to services because of the requirements of a third-party payer, relevant costs, reasonable alternatives, clients' right to refuse or withdraw consent, and the time frame covered by the consent. (1.03[a])

Therefore, if such techniques are going to be used as part of the overall intervention, clients should be aware of the procedures.

回 CONCLUSION

Single-subject designs are useful for research, evaluating practice, and monitoring client progress, though the characteristics of these designs suggest that you as a researcher or a consumer of research must reflect on the factors that might influence the association between the intervention and the outcome. Done systematically, the success or failure of different interventions can be evaluated with distinct clients and under differing conditions. Furthermore, single-subject designs may be useful for understanding the process of change and how change occurs with particular clients. Applying these techniques to your own practice can be beneficial to your clients. As Rosen (2003) warns, "Uncertainty regarding the effectiveness of any intervention for attaining any outcome pervades all practice situations, regardless of the extent and quality of empirical support" (p. 203). Therefore, if you monitor what you do, you will add to your own practice experience, which enhances your work with future clients.

KEY TERMS

Baseline phase (A)	Level
Carryover effect	Magnitude
Clinical replication	Nonconcurrent multiple baseline design
Clinical significance	Practical significance
Concurrent multiple baseline design	Stable line
Cycle	Systematic replication
Direct replication	Target
Duration	Treatment phase (B)
Frequency	Trend
Interval	Variability

HIGHLIGHTS

• Single-subject designs are tools for researchers and practitioners to evaluate the impact of an intervention on a single system such as an individual, community, or organization.

• Single-subject designs have three essential components: the taking of repeated measurements, a baseline phase (A), and a treatment phase (B).

• Repeated measurement controls for many of the potential threats to internal validity. The period between the last baseline measure and the first treatment measure is susceptible to the effect of history.

• The baseline phase typically continues, if practical, until there is a predictable pattern. To establish a pattern requires at least three measurements. The pattern may include a stable line, an increasing or decreasing trend line, or a cycle of ups and downs dependent on time of measurement.

- Researchers often measure behaviors, status, or level of functioning. These measures are typically characterized by frequency (counts), duration (length of time), interval (time between events), or magnitude (intensity).

- Reactivity to the process of measurement may impact the outcomes, and efforts to limit reactivity are important.

- Data analysis typically involves visually inspecting graphs of the measurements. A researcher may look for changes in level (magnitude), rate or directional changes in the trend line, or reductions in variability. The most important criterion is whether the treatment has made a practical (or clinical) difference in the subject's well-being.

- Generalizability from single-subject designs requires direct replication, systematic replication, and clinical replication.

DISCUSSION QUESTIONS

1. Visual analysis is used to communicate the impact of an intervention in visual form. What are the three primary ways that the pattern of scores established during a baseline or intervention stage may be viewed? When is each of them best used? What information is conveyed and what information may be omitted by choosing each one of them over the others?

2. Single-subject designs lack the inclusion of additional subjects serving as controls to demonstrate internal validity. How do the measurements during the baseline phase provide another form of control?

3. Social work research seeks to confirm an intervention's effectiveness by observing scores when clients no longer receive the intervention. Yet the carryover effect may necessitate using a withdrawal design—ending a treatment prematurely—to do this successfully. Debate the merits of the withdrawal design in social work research. What are the advantages and disadvantages? Do the benefits outweigh the risks or vice versa?

4. How can a researcher enhance the external validity of a single-subject design?

5. Stress is a common occurrence in many students' lives. Measure the frequency, duration, interval, and magnitude of school-related stress in your life in a 1-week period of time. Take care to provide a clear operational definition of stress and construct a meaningful scale to rate magnitude. Did you notice any issues of reactivity? Which of the measurement processes did you find most feasible? Finally, do you believe that your operational definition was sufficient to capture your target and detect changes?

6. Patterns detected in the baseline phase of single-subject designs also emerge in the larger population. Obtain a copy of a national newspaper and locate stories describing contemporary issues that can be described as having the pattern of a stable line, a trend, and a cycle. Is information provided about the number of observations made? If so, does this number seem sufficient to warrant the conclusion about what type of pattern it is?

CRITIQUING RESEARCH

1. Go to the book's study site (http://www.sagepub.com/fswrstudy) and choose two research articles that include some attention to causality (as indicated by a check in that column of the article matrix). For each article describe the following:

    a. What type of design was used? How does the author describe the design? Was it suited to the research question posed and the specific hypotheses tested, if any? Why do you suppose the author chose the particular design?

    b. Did the design eliminate threats to internal validity? How did the design do this? Are you satisfied with the internal validity conclusions stated by the author? Why or why not?

    c. What is the setting for the study? Does the setting limit the generalizability of the results to other similar settings or to the broader population? Is reactivity a problem? Are there other threats to external validity?

2. Search *Social Work Abstracts* for articles describing single-subject designs. Try to identify the type of design used. Read over the article. How well did this design satisfy the need for internal validity?

MAKING RESEARCH ETHICAL

1. Use of single-subject methodology requires frequent measurement of symptoms or other outcomes. Practitioners should discuss with clients before treatment begins the plan to use de-identified data in reports to the research community. Clients who do not consent still receive treatment—and data may still be recorded on their symptoms in order to evaluate treatment effects. Should the prospect of recording and publishing de-identified data on single subjects become a routine part of clinical practice? What would be the advantages and disadvantages of such a routine?

2. The A-B-A design is a much more powerful single-subject design than the A-B design because it reduces the likelihood that the researcher will conclude that an improvement is due to the treatment when it was simply due to a gradual endogenous recovery process. Yet the A-B-A design requires stopping the very treatment that may be having a beneficial effect. Under what conditions do you think it is safe to use an A-B-A design? Why do some clinicians argue that an A-B-A-B design lessens the potential for ethical problems? Are there circumstances when you would feel it is unethical to use an A-B-A-B design?

DEVELOPING A RESEARCH PROPOSAL

If you are planning to use a single-subject design,

1. What specific design will you use? How long will the study last? How will the data be collected? How often?

2. Discuss the extent to which each source of internal validity is a problem in the study. Will you debrief with participants to assess history?

3. Discuss the extent to which reactivity is a problem. How will you minimize the effects of reactivity?

4. How generalizable would you expect the study's findings to be? What can be done to improve generalizability?

5. Develop appropriate procedures for the protection of human subjects in your study. Include a consent form.

To assist you in completing the Web exercises below and to gain a better understanding of the chapter's contents, please access the study site at http://www.sagepub .com/fswrstudy where you will find the Web exercises reproduced with suggested links, along with self-quizzes, e-flash cards, interactive exercises, journal articles, and other valuable resources.

WEB EXERCISES

1. Visit the Northwest Regional Education Laboratory's archives and read Close Up #9, Schoolwide and Classroom Discipline (http://www.nwrel.org/archive/sirs/5/cu9.html). Select three of the techniques that educators use to minimize disruption in educational settings and then suggest a single-subject design that could be used to evaluate the effectiveness of each technique. Bear in mind the nature of the misbehavior and the treatment. Which of the designs seems most appropriate? How would you go about conducting your research? Think about things such as operationalizing the target behavior, determining how it will be measured (frequency, duration, magnitude, etc.), deciding on the length of the baseline and treatment periods, and accounting for threats to internal validity.

2. Access the PsycINFO database through your university library's Web site. Perform a search using the words *comparative single-subject research*. Click on the link to the full text version of the article by Holcombe, Wolery, and Gast (1994). Review the description of the designs used and then the discussion of the problems faced in each of these. Can you think of any other issues the authors may have neglected? Which of these methods would you employ? Why?

CHAPTER 7

Survey Research

Why Is Survey Research So Popular?

Errors in Survey Research

Questionnaire Design
Maintain Consistent Focus
Build on Existing Instruments
Order the Questions

Writing Questions
Write Clear Questions
Avoid Confusing
Phrasing
Avoid Vagueness
Provide a Frame of
Reference
Avoid Vague Words
Avoid Negative Words and
Double Negatives
Avoid Double-Barreled
Questions
Avoid Jargon
Reduce the Risk of Bias
Memory Questions
Closed-Ended and Open-Ended
Questions
Closed-Ended Questions and
Response Categories
Avoid Making Agreement
Agreeable
Social Desirability

Minimize Fence-
Sitting and Floating
Filter Questions
Utilize Likert-Type
Response Categories
Matrix Questions
Scales
Sensitive Questions

Pretest!

Survey Design Alternatives
Mail Surveys
Group-Administered Surveys
Telephone Surveys
Maximizing Response to
Phone Surveys
In-Person Interviews
Maximizing Response to
Interviews
Web Surveys
Mixed-Mode Surveys
A Comparison of Survey Designs

Secondary Data

Survey Research Design in a
Diverse Society
Translating Instruments
Interviewer-Respondent
Characteristics

**Implications for Evidence-Based
    Practice**
Ethical Issues in Survey Research
Conclusion
Key Terms
Highlights

Discussion Questions
Critiquing Research
Making Research Ethical
Developing a Research Proposal
Web Exercises

In this chapter, we will introduce you to survey research. Survey research is one of the most popular designs used in social work research. You will learn about the challenges of designing a survey, some basic rules of question construction, and the ways in which surveys can be administered. This is followed by issues of survey design related to our diverse society and the utility of survey methods for evidence-based practice. We conclude with a discussion about specific ethical issues surrounding surveys. By the chapter's end, you should be well on your way to becoming an informed consumer of survey reports and a knowledgeable developer of survey designs.

We hope that you will have an increased appreciation for the fact that designing a survey involves a great deal of thought and planning and is much more difficult than putting a few questions together. This holds true whether the survey is part of a research project or the information an agency collects from clients such as a biopsychosocial assessment or phone interviews as part of a community needs assessment.

WHY IS SURVEY RESEARCH SO POPULAR?

Survey research involves the collection of information from a sample of individuals through their responses to questions. As you probably have observed, a great many researchers choose this method of data collection. In fact, surveys have become such a vital part of our social fabric that we cannot assess much of what we read in the newspaper or see on TV without having some understanding of survey research (Converse, 1984).

Regardless of its scope, survey research owes its continuing popularity to its versatility, efficiency, and generalizability. First and foremost is the *versatility* of survey methods. Social work researchers have used survey methods to investigate every field of social work practice, including (but not limited to) child welfare, gerontology, health, mental health, income maintenance, community building, and community development. Surveys are used in agencies to assess the impact of policy changes, assess community needs, track changes in community characteristics, monitor and evaluate program effectiveness, and assess client satisfaction with programs.

Surveys are *efficient* in that many variables can be measured without substantially increasing the time or cost. Survey data can be collected from many people at relatively low cost and, depending on the survey design, relatively quickly.

Survey methods lend themselves to probability sampling from large populations. Thus, survey research is appealing when *sample generalizability* is a central research goal. In fact, survey research is often the only means available for developing a representative picture of the attitudes and characteristics of a large population. Surveys are also the method of choice when cross-population generalizability is a key concern because they allow a range of social contexts and subgroups to be sampled. The consistency of findings can be examined across various sampled subgroups.

▣ ERRORS IN SURVEY RESEARCH

It might be said that surveys are too easy to conduct. Organizations and individuals often decide that a survey would help to solve some important problem because it seems so easy to prepare a form with some questions and send it out. But without careful attention to sampling, measurement, and overall survey design, the effort is likely to be a flop. Such flops are too common for comfort, and the responsible survey researcher must take the time to design surveys properly and convince sponsoring organizations that this time is worth the effort (Turner & Martin, 1984).

For a survey to succeed, it must minimize the risk of two types of error: poor measurement of cases that are surveyed (*errors of observation*) and omission of cases that should be surveyed (*errors of nonobservation*) (Groves, 1989). Measurement error was a key concern in Chapter 3, but there is much more to be learned about how to minimize these errors of observation in the survey process. Potential problems that can lead to errors of observation stem from the way questions are written, the characteristics of the respondents who answer the questions, the way questions are presented in questionnaires, and the interviewers used to ask the questions. The potential measurement errors that survey researchers confront in designing questions and questionnaires are summarized in Exhibit 7.1; we discuss each of these sources of error throughout this chapter.

There are three sources of errors of nonobservation:

• Coverage of the population can be inadequate due to a poor sampling frame.

• The process of random sampling can result in sampling error—differences between the characteristics of the sample members and the population that arise due to chance.

• Nonresponse can distort the sample when individuals refuse to respond or cannot be contacted. Nonresponse to specific questions can distort the generalizability of the responses to those questions.

We considered the importance of a good sampling frame and the procedures for estimating and reducing sampling error in Chapter 4; we only add a few more points here. We focus more attention in this chapter on procedures for reducing nonresponse in surveys.

EXHIBIT 7.1   **Measurement Errors Associated With Surveys**

Question Wording: Does the question have a consistent meaning to respondents? Problems can occur with

- *Lengthy wording* Words are unnecessarily long and complicated.
- *Length of question* Question is unnecessarily long.
- *Lack of specificity* Question does not specify the desired information.
- *Lack of frame of reference* Question does not specify what reference comparisons should be made to.
- *Vague language* Words and phrases can have different meanings to respondents.
- *Double negatives* Question uses two or more negative phrases.
- *Double barreled* Question actually asks two or more questions.
- *Using jargon and initials* Phrasing uses professional or academic discipline-specific terms.
- *Leading questions* Question uses phrasing meant to bias the response.
- *Cultural differences in meaning* Phrases or words have different meanings to different population subgroups.

Respondent Characteristics: Characteristics of respondents may produce inaccurate answers. These include

- *Memory recall* Problems remembering events or details about events.
- *Telescoping* Remembering events as happening more recently than when they really occurred.
- *Agreement of acquiescence bias* Tendency for respondents to "agree."
- *Social desirability* Tendency to want to appear in a positive light and therefore providing the desirable response.
- *Floaters* Respondents who choose a substantive answer when they really do not know.
- *Fence-sitters* People who see themselves as being neutral so as not to give the wrong answer.
- *Sensitive questions* Questions deemed too personal.

Presentation of Questions: The structure of questions and the survey instrument may produce errors including

- *Open-ended questions* Response categories are not provided, left to respondent to provide.
- *Closed-ended questions* Possible response categories are provided.
- *Agree-disagree* Tendency to agree when only two choices are offered.
- *Question order* The context or order of questions can affect subsequent responses as respondents try to remain consistent.
- *Response set* Giving the same response to a series of questions.
- *Filter questions* Questions used to determine if other questions are relevant.

Interviewer: The use of an interviewer may produce error.

- Mismatch of interviewer-interviewee demographic characteristics.
- Unconscious judgmental actions to responses.

Source: Engel & Schutt (2008).

Unfortunately, nonresponse is an increasing concern for survey researchers. For reasons that are not entirely understood, but may include growing popular cynicism and distrust of government, nonresponse rates have been growing in the United States and Western Europe since the early 1950s (Groves, 1989; Groves & Couper, 1998).

We can anticipate problems that lead to survey errors and identify possible solutions if we take enough time to think about the issue theoretically. A well-designed survey will maximize the social rewards, minimize the costs for participating in the survey, and establish trust that the rewards will outweigh the costs. The next two sections focus on principles to develop a well-designed survey.

▣ QUESTIONNAIRE DESIGN

Survey questions are answered as part of a **questionnaire** (or **interview schedule,** as it is sometimes called in interview-based studies). The context created by the questionnaire has a major impact on how individual questions are interpreted and answered. As a result, survey researchers must carefully design the questionnaire, as well as individual questions. There is no precise formula for a well-designed questionnaire. Nonetheless, some key principles should guide the design of any questionnaire, and some systematic procedures should be considered for refining it.

> *Questionnaire* The survey instrument containing the questions in a self-administered survey.
>
> *Interview schedule* The survey instrument containing the questions asked by the interviewer in an in-person or phone survey.

Maintain Consistent Focus

The contents of a survey should be guided by a clear conception of the research problem under investigation and the population to be sampled. Throughout the process of questionnaire design, the research objective should be the primary basis for making decisions about what to include and exclude and what to emphasize or treat in a cursory fashion. The questionnaire should be viewed as an integrated whole in which each section and every question serves a clear purpose related to the study's objective and each section complements other sections.

Build on Existing Instruments

If another researcher already has designed a set of questions to measure a key concept and evidence from previous surveys indicates that this measure is reliable and valid, then use that instrument. Your review of the literature can provide useful information about existing instruments. Resources like *Measures for Clinical Practice and Research: A Sourcebook* (Fischer & Corcoran, 2007) can give you many ideas about existing instruments.

There is a trade-off. Questions used previously may not concern quite the right concept or may not be appropriate in some ways to your population. Scales developed much earlier may no longer be appropriate for your population as times change. A good rule of thumb is to use a previously designed instrument if it measures the concept of concern to you and if you have no clear reason for thinking it is inappropriate with your survey population.

Order the Questions

The order in which questions are presented will influence how respondents react to the questionnaire as a whole and how they may answer some questions. As a first step, the individual questions should be sorted into broad thematic categories, which then become separate sections in the questionnaire. Both the sections and the questions within the sections must then be organized in a logical order that would make sense in a conversation.

The first question deserves special attention, particularly if the questionnaire is to be self-administered. This question signals to the respondent what the survey is about, whether it will be interesting, and how easy it will be to complete. It is not the time to ask a sensitive question as this might turn off a potential respondent. Finally, the first question should apply to everyone in the sample (Dillman, 2000).

Question order can lead to **context effects** when one or more questions influence how subsequent questions are interpreted (Schober, 1999). The potential for context effects is greatest when two or more questions concern the same issue or closely related issues. Often, respondents will try to be consistent with their responses, even if they really do not mean the response.

▣ WRITING QUESTIONS

The centerpiece of survey research is asking people questions. In principle, survey questions can be a straightforward and efficient means to measure demographic characteristics, levels of knowledge, opinions and attitudes, feelings and symptoms, and behaviors, but in practice, survey questions can result in misleading or inappropriate answers. All questions proposed for a survey must be screened carefully for their adherence to basic guidelines and then tested and revised until the researcher feels some confidence that they will be clear to the intended respondents (Fowler, 1995).

Write Clear Questions

All hope for achieving measurement validity is lost unless the questions in a survey are clear and convey the intended meaning to respondents. You may be thinking that you ask people questions all the time and have no trouble understanding the answers you receive, but you may also remember misunderstanding or being confused by some questions. Consider just a few of the differences between everyday conversations and standardized surveys:

- Survey questions must be asked of many people, not just one person.

- The same survey question must be used with each person, not tailored to the specifics of a given conversation.

- Survey questions must be understood in the same way by people who differ in many ways.

- You will not be able to rephrase a survey question if someone does not understand it, because that would result in a different question for that person.

- Survey respondents do not know you and so cannot be expected to share the nuances of expression that help you and your friends and family to communicate.

Every question considered for inclusion in a survey must be reviewed carefully for its clarity and ability to convey the intended meaning. Questions that were clear and meaningful to one population may not be so to another. Nor can you simply assume that a question used in a previously published study was carefully evaluated. Several basic principles will go a long way toward developing clear and meaningful questions.

Avoid Confusing Phrasing

In most cases, a simple direct approach to asking a question minimizes confusion. Use shorter rather than longer words: *brave* rather than *courageous; job concerns* rather than *work-related employment issues* (Dillman, 2000). Use shorter sentences when you can. A lengthy question often forces the respondent to have to "work hard," that is, to have to read and reread the entire question. Lengthy questions can go unanswered or can be given only a cursory reading without much thought.

Avoid Vagueness

Questions should not be abbreviated in a way that results in confusion. The simple statement

    Residential location: _____

does not provide sufficient focus; rather, it is a general question when a specific kind of answer is desired. There are many reasonable answers to this question, such as Squirrel Hill (a neighborhood), Pittsburgh (a city), or Forbes Avenue (a street). Asking, "In what neighborhood of Pittsburgh do you live?" provides specificity so that respondents understand that the intent of the question is about their neighborhood.

Provide a Frame of Reference

Questions often require a frame of reference that provides specificity about how respondents should answer the question. The question

    Overall, the performance of this caseworker is
      _____   Excellent
      _____   Good
      _____   Average
      _____   Poor

lacks a frame of reference. In this case, the researcher does not know the basis of comparison the respondent is using. In formulating an answer, some respondents may compare the caseworker with other caseworkers, whereas some respondents may use a personal "absolute scale" about a caseworker's performance. To avoid this kind of confusion, the basis of comparison should be specifically stated: "Compared with other caseworkers you have had, the performance of this caseworker is . . ."

Avoid Vague Words

It is important to avoid vague language; there are words whose meaning may differ from respondent to respondent. The question

Do you usually or occasionally attend programs at the community center?

will not provide useful information, for the meaning of usually or occasionally can differ for each respondent. A better alternative is to define the two terms such as *usually (2 or 3 times a week)* and *occasionally (2 or 3 times a month)*. A second option is to ask respondents how many times they attended programs at the community center in the last month; the researcher can then classify the responses into categories.

Avoid Negative Words and Double Negatives

Try answering, "Do you disagree that juveniles should not be tried as adults if they commit murder?" Respondents have a hard time figuring out which response matches their sentiments because the statement is written as a double negative. Such errors can easily be avoided with minor wording changes.

Avoid Double-Barreled Questions

Double-barreled questions produce uninterpretable results because they actually ask two questions but allow only one answer. For example, the question "Do you support increased spending on schools and social services?" is really asking two questions—about support for schools and about support for social services. It is perfectly reasonable for someone to support increased spending on schools but not on social services. A similar problem can also show up in response categories.

Avoid Jargon

Avoid using jargon or technical language related to a profession or academic discipline. Words like *social justice, empowering,* and *strengths* may appear in social work literature, but they do not necessarily have a shared meaning in the profession, let alone the broader community. Using initials to abbreviate phrases is also a form of professional jargon. For example, to some social work students (particularly those students specializing in gerontology) AAA refers to the Area Agency on Aging, but to other social work students and the general population, the initials are as likely to refer to the American Automobile Association.

Reduce the Risk of Bias

Specific words in survey questions should not trigger biases unless that is the researcher's conscious intent. Such questions are referred to as *leading questions* because they lead the respondent to a particular answer. Biased or loaded words and phrases tend to produce misleading answers as certain responses become less attractive. There are words such as *welfare* or *liberal* that have taken on meanings that stir reactions in at least some people. Surveys have found that support for "programs to assist the poor" is 39% higher than when the word "welfare" is used (Smith, 1984).

Responses can also be biased when response categories do not reflect the full range of possible alternatives. For example, the Detroit Area Study (Turner & Martin, 1984) asked the following question: "People feel differently about making changes in the way our country is run. In order to keep America great, which of these statements do you think is best?" When the only response choices were "We should be very cautious of making changes" and "We should be free to make changes," only 37% said that we should be free to make changes. However, when a response choice was added that suggested we should "constantly" make changes, 24% picked that response and another 32% chose the "free to make changes" response, for a total of 56% who seemed open to making changes in the way our country is run. Including the more extreme positive alternative ("constantly" make changes) made the less extreme positive alternative more attractive (p. 252).

A similar bias occurs when some but not all possible responses are included in the question. "What do you like about your community, such as the parks and schools?" focuses respondents on those categories, and other answers may be ignored. It is best left to the respondent to answer the question without such response cues.

Memory Questions

Some questions require respondents to try to remember an event. Remembering an event is affected by the length of time since the event occurred and how important the event was to the respondent. **Recall loss** occurs when a respondent does not remember an event or behavior or can remember only some aspects of the event. This problem is not unusual. Events important to the respondent are likely to be remembered, even if they happened long ago, whereas events unimportant to the respondent, even if they happened recently, are likely to be forgotten. For example, one survey asked, "During the past 12 months, about how many times did you see or talk to a medical doctor?" When official records were checked, respondents forgot about 60% of their doctor visits (Goleman, 1993). In general, when information about mundane or day-to-day activities is solicited, reference periods should be no longer than in the past month.

Researchers face a second issue called a **telescoping effect**, in which an event is thought to have happened during a particular time period, although it actually happened before that time period. Sometimes, we remember an event "just like it happened yesterday" because it was so meaningful or important. Unfortunately, the event can be reported that way too. Researchers may choose to use a life history calendar with which respondents sequence the timing of personal events by using standardized visual cues including years (or months) and other events like births, job changes, or moves (Axinn, Pearce, & Ghimire, 1999).

Closed-Ended and Open-Ended Questions

Questions can be designed with or without explicit response choices. When explicit response categories are offered, the type of question is a **closed-ended question**. For example, the following question asked in a survey of agencies providing mental health and/or substance abuse treatment is closed-ended because the desired response categories are provided. Mental health providers were asked,

What type of mental health care does your organization provide?
_____ In-patient care only
_____ Out-patient care only
_____ Both

Most surveys of a large number of people contain primarily closed-ended questions, which are easy to process with computers and analyze with statistics. Including the response choices reduces ambiguity, and respondents are more likely to answer the question that the researcher really wants them to answer. However, closed-ended questions can obscure what people really think unless the choices are designed carefully to match the range of possible responses to the question.

Most important, closed-ended response choices should be mutually exclusive and exhaustive so that every respondent can find one and only one choice that applies to him or her (unless the question is of the "Check all that apply" format). To make response choices exhaustive, researchers may need to offer at least one option with room for ambiguity. For example, mental health providers were asked about why they did not treat problem gambling. The list included six different reasons but concluded with a category "Other (please specify _____)" because the researchers were not sure they had all the possible reasons on their list. If respondents do not find a response option that corresponds to their answer to the question, they may skip the question entirely or choose a response option that does not indicate what they are really thinking.

Open-ended questions are questions without explicit response choices so that the respondents provide their own answers in their own words. This type of question is usually used when there is little knowledge about a particular topic, and you want to learn as much as possible without limiting the responses. For example, if you are interested in learning the perceptions of agency directors about potential problems brought out by the opening of a casino, you might ask,

> What difference will the opening of the new casino make on the services provided by your agency?

The information obtained from a question such as this could be used as response categories for closed-ended questions in future surveys.

Open-ended questions may also be used to explain what a particular concept means to a respondent. For example, in a questionnaire dealing with psychiatric conditions, respondents were asked a "Yes-No" question: "In the last 2 weeks, have you had thoughts that you would be better off dead or of hurting yourself in some way?" They were then asked: "Can you tell me about it?" The purpose of the second question was to expand on the first question and help the analyst to determine whether there was a threat of suicide.

Although open-ended questions provide a wealth of information, they also require careful consideration. Administering, analyzing, and summarizing open-ended questions can be time-consuming and difficult. Some respondents do not like to write a lot and may find open-ended questions taxing. Interviewing is not necessarily the solution: The amount of information provided by a respondent may depend on the respondent's personality—some respondents may provide short or cursory answers, whereas other respondents may provide extensive answers with a great deal of relevant (and irrelevant) information.

Closed-Ended Questions and Response Categories

When writing response categories for closed-ended questions, there are several guidelines that might help improve the questions. We have already mentioned that it is important to ensure that the responses are mutually exclusive and that the list is exhaustive. We offer these additional guidelines to consider when designing questions.

Avoid Making Agreement Agreeable

The tendency for some respondents to agree with a statement just to avoid seeming disagreeable is referred to as **acquiescence** (or agreement) **bias**. You can see the impact of this human tendency in a 1974 Michigan Survey Research Center survey that asked who was to blame for crime and lawlessness in the United States. When one question stated that individuals were more to blame than social conditions, 60% of the respondents agreed. But when the question was rephrased so respondents were asked, in a balanced fashion, whether individuals or social conditions were more to blame, only 46% chose individuals (Schuman & Presser, 1981).

To reduce the likelihood of agreement bias, you should present both sides of attitude scales in the question (Dillman, 2000). The response choices to the question "In general, do you believe that *individuals* or *social conditions* are more to blame for poverty in the United

States?" should be phrased to make each one seem socially acceptable. You should also consider replacing a range of response alternatives with other alternatives that focus on the word *agree*. For example, the question "To what extent do you support or oppose the new health care plan?" (response choices range from *strongly support* to *strongly oppose*) is probably a better approach than the question "To what extent do you agree or disagree with the statement: The new health care plan is worthy of support?" (response choices range from *strongly agree* to *strongly disagree*).

Social Desirability

Social desirability is the tendency for individuals to respond in ways that make them appear in the best light to the interviewer. The error, in this case, is that respondents are not providing their true opinions or answers. Social desirability effects are likely to occur when people are discussing issues that are controversial or expressing views that are not popular.

Minimize Fence-Sitting and Floating

Two related problems in question writing stem from people's desire to choose an acceptable answer, even if they do not know or have no opinion. There are **fence-sitters** who see themselves as being neutral and whose responses may skew the results if you force them to choose between opposites. Adding an explicit neutral response option is appropriate when you want to find out who is a fence-sitter. But adding a neutral response may provide an easy escape for respondents who do not want to reveal their true feelings.

Floaters are respondents who choose a substantive answer when they really do not know. Because there are so many floaters in the typical survey sample, the decision to include an explicit *"Don't know"* option for a question is important. *"Don't know"* responses are offered more often by those with less education—except for questions that are really impossible to decipher, to which more educated persons are likely to say they do not know (Schuman & Presser, 1981). Unfortunately, the inclusion of the *"Don't know"* response choice leads some people who do have a preference to take the easy way out and choose *"Don't know."*

Filter Questions

The use of **filter questions** is important to ensure that questions are asked only of relevant respondents. If you ask questions about work, you first need to determine who is working and who is not working. These filter questions create **skip patterns.** Based on the response to a filter question, respondents will be asked to either skip one or more questions or to answer those questions. The questions asked of the more limited group of people are referred to as **contingency questions.** Skip patterns should be indicated clearly with arrows or other direction in the questionnaire as demonstrated in Exhibit 7.2.

EXHIBIT 7.2   **Filter Questions and Skip Patterns**

3. Are you currently employed in a social work position?

   1 _____ Yes

   2 _____ No –> GO TO QUESTION 10

4. What type of agency is your current employer?

   1 _____ Public Service

   2 _____ Private, Nonprofit

   3 _____ Private for Profit

   4 _____ Other (specify)

Utilize Likert-Type Response Categories

Likert-type responses generally ask respondents to indicate the extent to which they agree or disagree with statements. The response categories list choices for respondents to select their level of agreement with a statement from *strongly agree* to *strongly disagree*. The questions in Exhibit 7.3 have Likert-type response categories.

Matrix Questions

Some question formats lend themselves to be presented in a matrix format. **Matrix questions** are actually a series of questions that concern a common theme and that have the same response choices. The questions are written so that a common initial phrase applies to

---

EXHIBIT 7.3   **Matrix Questions Using Likert-Type Responses**

15. In general, how well did: (Please circle one response for each question)

	Strongly agree				Strongly disagree
a. MSW classes prepared me for my social work position.	1	2	3	4	5
b. Field education experiences prepared me for my social work position.	1	2	3	4	5
c. MSW classes prepared me for attaining a social work license.	1	2	3	4	5

each one (see Exhibit 7.3). This format shortens the questionnaire by reducing the number of words that must be used for each question. It also emphasizes the common theme among the questions and so invites answering each question in relation to other questions in the matrix. It is important to provide an explicit instruction to "Circle one response on each line" in a matrix question, since some respondents will think that they have completed the entire matrix after they have responded to just a few of the specific questions.

Matrix questions are susceptible to another form of error called a **response set**. When scales are used (or a set of single questions for that matter) with the same set of response categories, there is the possibility that, rather than reading and answering each question, the respondent simply circles the same response down the entire set of questions. To avoid this problem, researchers often phrase some questions in the opposite direction; if the questions are worded using positive language, they will ask some questions using negative language. The assumption is that if the respondent then answers all the questions with the same response, it is clear he or she was just circling them without thinking.

Scales

Writing single questions that yield usable answers is always a challenge, whether the response format is closed- or open-ended. Simple though they may seem, single questions are prone to problems due to idiosyncratic variation, which occurs when individuals' responses vary because of their reactions to particular words or ideas in the question. Differences in respondents' backgrounds, knowledge, and beliefs almost guarantee that they will understand the same question differently. If some respondents do not know some of the words in a question, we will not know what their answers mean—if they answer at all. If a question is too complex, respondents may focus on different parts of the question. If prior experiences or culturally based orientations lead different groups to interpret questions differently, answers will not have a consistent meaning.

If just one question is used to measure a variable, the researcher may not realize that respondents had trouble with a particular word or phrase in the question. One solution is to phrase questions more carefully; the guidelines for writing clear questions should help to reduce idiosyncratic variation due to different interpretations of questions. But the best option is to devise multiple rather than single questions to measure concepts, as we discussed in Chapter 3. Therefore, you might choose to use a scale that includes multiple questions to measure the concept.

Because of the popularity of survey research, scales already have been developed to measure many concepts, and some of these scales have been demonstrated to be reliable in a range of studies. Use of a preexisting scale both simplifies the work involved in designing a survey and facilitates comparison of findings to those obtained in other studies.

Sensitive Questions

Respondents may consider some topics, such as drug use, sexual activity, or the use of mental health services, to be too sensitive or embarrassing to discuss. Some respondents will be reluctant to agree that they have ever engaged in such activities. In this situation, the goal is to write a question and response choices that will reduce the anxiety or threat of providing an answer. To do so may violate some of the guidelines we have mentioned.

One way is to make agreement seem more acceptable. For example, Dillman (2000) suggests that we ask, "Have you ever taken anything from a store without paying for it?" rather than "Have you ever shoplifted something from a store?" (p. 75). Asking about a range of behaviors or attitudes that run the gamut from socially acceptable to socially unacceptable will also soften the impact of agreeing with those that are socially unacceptable. The behavior will also be softened by asking, "How often have you. . . ?" rather than using a filter question "Have you ever. . . ?"

回 PRETEST!

Adhering to the preceding guidelines will go a long way toward producing a useful questionnaire. However, simply asking what appear to you to be clear questions does not ensure that people have a consistent understanding of what you are asking. You need some external feedback.

No questionnaire should be considered ready for use until there has been a **pretest**. Try answering the questionnaire yourself, and then revise it. Try it out on some colleagues or other friends, and then revise it. Then select a small sample of individuals from the population you are studying or one very similar to it, and try out the questionnaire with them.

Researchers are increasingly getting feedback from guided discussions among potential respondents, called *focus groups,* to check for consistent understanding of terms and to identify the range of events or experiences about which people will be asked to report. By listening to and observing the focus group discussions, researchers can test their assumptions about what level of vocabulary is appropriate and what people are going to be reporting (Fowler, 1995). Focus group techniques are particularly useful for developing questionnaires with different economic and ethnic groups because participants will answer in their own terms and language (to learn more about focus groups, see Chapter 8).

Professional survey researchers have also developed a technique for evaluating questions called the **cognitive interview** (Dillman, 2000; Fowler, 1995). Although the specifics vary, the basic approach is to ask people to "think aloud" as they answer questions. The researcher asks a test question and then probes with follow-up questions to learn how the question was understood and whether its meaning varied for different respondents. Another technique is **behavior coding**: A researcher observes several interviews or listens to taped interviews and codes according to strict rules the number of times that difficulties occur with questions. Such difficulties include respondents asking for clarification and interviewers rephrasing questions rather than reading them verbatim (Presser & Blair, 1994).

Conducting a pilot study is the final stage of questionnaire preparation. In a **pilot study**, you draw a small sample of individuals from the population you are studying or one similar to it and carry out the survey procedures with them. You may include in the pretest version of a written questionnaire some space for individuals to add comments on each key question or, with in-person interviews, audiotape the test interviews for later review.

Review the distribution of responses to each question, listen to the audiotapes, or read all the comments, and then code what you heard or read to identify problems in question wording or delivery. Revise any questions that respondents do not seem to interpret as you had intended or that are not working well for other reasons. If the response rate is relatively low, consider whether it can be improved by some modifications in procedures.

▣ SURVEY DESIGN ALTERNATIVES

The five basic social science survey designs are mail surveys, group administered surveys, telephone surveys, in-person surveys, and electronic surveys. Exhibit 7.4 summarizes the typical features of the five different survey designs. Each design differs from the others in one or more important features.

- *Manner of administration.* Mail, group, and electronic surveys are completed by the respondents. During phone and in-person interviews, the researcher or a staff person asks the questions and records the respondent's answers.

- *Setting.* Most mail and electronic questionnaires and phone interviews are intended for completion by only one respondent. The same is usually true of in-person interviews, although sometimes researchers interview several respondents at once. However, a variant of the standard survey is a questionnaire distributed simultaneously to a group of respondents, who complete the survey while the researcher waits.

- *Questionnaire structure.* Most mail, group, phone, and electronic surveys are highly structured, fixing in advance the content and order of questions and response choices. Some

EXHIBIT 7.4	Typical Features of the Five Survey Designs			
Design	Manner of Administration	Setting	Questionnaire Structure	Cost
Mail survey	Self	Individual	Mostly structured	Low
Group survey	Self	Group	Mostly structured	Very low
Phone survey	Professional	Individual	Structured	Moderate
In-person interview	Professional	Individual	Structured or unstructured	High
Web survey	Self	Individual	Mostly structured	Very low

Source: Engel & Schutt (2008).

of these types of surveys, particularly mail surveys, may include some open-ended questions. In-person interviews range from the highly structured, including both closed-ended and open-ended questions, to the relatively unstructured in which the interviewer covers the same topics but varies questions according to the respondent's answers to previous questions.

• *Cost.* In-person interviews are the most expensive type of survey. Phone interviews are much less expensive, but surveying by mail is even cheaper. Electronic surveys are now the least expensive method because there are no interviewer costs, no mailing costs, and, for many designs, almost no costs for data entry. Of course, extra staff time and expertise are required to prepare an electronic questionnaire.

Because of their different features, the five designs vary in the types of errors to which they are most prone and the situations in which they are most appropriate. The rest of this section focuses on their unique advantages and disadvantages.

Mail Surveys

A **mail survey** is conducted by mailing a questionnaire to respondents, who then administer the survey. The central concern in a mail survey is maximizing the response rate. Even an attractive questionnaire full of clear questions requires additional efforts to maximize the response rate. A response rate of 70% or higher is desirable; lower response rates call into question the representativeness of the sample.

Sending follow-up mailings to nonrespondents is the single most important requirement for obtaining an adequate response rate to a mail survey. Follow-up mailings explicitly encourage initial nonrespondents to return a completed questionnaire; implicitly, they convey the importance of the effort. Dillman (2000) has demonstrated the effectiveness of a mailing process that includes the following:

1. A few days before mailing the questionnaire, send a brief letter that notifies sample members of the importance of the survey.

2. Include a personalized cover letter (see the next section) and a self-addressed stamped return envelope with the questionnaire.

3. Send a friendly reminder postcard to all sample members 2 weeks after the initial mailing. The postcard is written to thank respondents and remind nonrespondents. Include a phone number for those people who may not have received the questionnaire or may have lost it.

4. Send a replacement questionnaire with a new cover letter only to nonrespondents 2 to 4 weeks after the initial questionnaire mailing and again after 6 to 8 weeks.

The **cover letter** is critical to the success of a mail survey since it sets the tone for the entire questionnaire. A carefully prepared cover letter (see Exhibit 7.5) should increase the response rate and result in more honest and complete answers to the survey questions. The cover letter should be personalized to the respondent and signed by the researcher. The contents of the letter should establish the credibility of the research, catch the interest of the respondent, and note ethical obligations, such as confidentiality and voluntary participation. The letter should also include a phone number to call if the respondent has any questions.

EXHIBIT 7.5   **Sample Questionnaire Cover Letter**

University of Massachusetts at Boston
May 24, 2003

Jane Doe
AIDS Coordinator
Shattuck Shelter

Dear Jane:

AIDS is an increasing concern for homeless people and for homeless shelters. The enclosed survey is about the AIDS problem and related issues confronting shelters. It is sponsored by the Life Lines AIDS Prevention Project for the Homeless—a program of the Massachusetts Department of Public Health.

As an AIDS coordinator/shelter director, you have learned about homeless persons' problems and about implementing programs in response to these problems. The Life Lines Project needs to learn from your experience. Your answers to the questions in the enclosed survey will improve substantially the base of information for improving AIDS prevention programs.

Questions in the survey focus on AIDS prevention activities and on related aspects of shelter operations. It should take about 30 minutes to answer all the questions.

Every shelter AIDS coordinator (or shelter director) in Massachusetts is being asked to complete the survey. And every response is vital to the success of the survey. The survey report must represent the full range of experiences.

You may be assured of complete confidentiality. No one outside of the university will have access to the questionnaire you return. (The ID number on the survey will permit us to check with nonrespondents to see if they need a replacement survey or other information.) All information presented in the report to Life Lines will be in aggregate form, with the exception of a list of the number, gender, and family status of each shelter's guests.

Please mail the survey back to us by Monday, June 4, and feel free to call if you have any questions.

Thank you for your assistance.

Yours sincerely,

Project Director   Project Assistant

Source: Schutt (2009).

There are other strategies to increase the response rate (Fowler, 1988; Mangione, 1995; Miller & Salkind, 2002). The individual questions should be clear and understandable to all the respondents. There should only be a few open-ended questions because respondents are likely to be put off by the idea of having to write out answers. Having a sponsor known to respondents may increase the response rate. Enclosing a token incentive such as a coupon or ticket worth $1 or $2 may help. Finally, include a stamped, self-addressed return envelope with the questionnaire.

Another concern for mail surveys is the hazard of incomplete response. Some respondents may skip some questions or just stop answering questions at some point in the questionnaire. Fortunately, this problem does not occur often with well-designed questionnaires. Potential respondents who have decided to participate in the survey usually complete it.

Finally, there is no control over the manner in which the respondent answers the questions. Despite efforts to create a meaningful order to the questions, the respondent chooses the order in which the questions are answered. The respondent can choose to answer all the questions at once or answer them over several days. The respondent may even discuss the questions with significant others, family, friends, and coworkers.

Group-Administered Surveys

A **group-administered survey** is completed by individual respondents assembled together. The response rate is not usually a major concern in surveys that are distributed and collected in a group setting because most group members will participate. The real difficulty with this method is that it is seldom feasible because it requires what might be called a captive audience. With the exception of students, employees, members of the armed forces, and some institutionalized populations, most populations cannot be sampled in such a setting.

A special concern with group-administered surveys is the possibility that respondents will feel coerced to participate and as a result will be less likely to answer questions honestly. Also, because administering a survey in this way requires approval of the setting's administrators, respondents may infer that the researcher is not at all independent of the sponsor. No complete solution to this problem exists, but it helps to make an introductory statement emphasizing the researcher's independence and giving participants a chance to ask questions about the survey.

The person administering the survey to the group must be careful to minimize comments that might bias answers or that could vary between different groups in the same survey (Dillman, 2000). A standard introductory statement should be read to the group that expresses appreciation for their participation, describes the steps of the survey, and emphasizes (in classroom surveys) that the survey is not the same as a test. A cover letter like the one used in mailed surveys also should be distributed with the questionnaires. To emphasize confidentiality, respondents should be given an envelope in which to seal their questionnaire after it is completed.

Telephone Surveys

In a **phone survey**, interviewers question respondents over the phone and then record their answers. Phone interviewing is a popular method of conducting surveys in the United States because almost all families have phones. But two matters may undermine the validity of a phone survey: not reaching the proper sampling units and not getting enough complete responses to make the results generalizable.

Most telephone surveys use **random digit dialing** to contact respondents. A machine calls random phone numbers within the designated exchanges regardless of whether the numbers are published. When the machine reaches an inappropriate household (such as a business in a survey that is directed to the general population), the phone number is simply replaced with another. When the households are contacted, the interviewers must ask a series of questions at the start of the survey to ensure that they are speaking to the appropriate member of the household.

Maximizing Response to Phone Surveys

Three issues require special attention in phone surveys to maximize participant response. First, because people often are not home, multiple callbacks are needed for many sample members. If you are doing the calling yourself, you will find that you need to make multiple callbacks during the day and evening. Survey research organizations may call back households as many as 20 times. Second, interviewers must be prepared to deal with distractions as the respondent is interrupted by other household members. Finally, sprinkling interesting questions throughout the questionnaire may help to maintain respondent interest. In general, rapport between the interviewer and the respondent is likely to be lower with phone surveys than with in-person interviews, and so respondents may tire and refuse to answer all the questions (Miller & Salkind, 2002).

Researchers using phone surveys also must cope with difficulties due to the impersonal nature of phone contact. Careful interviewer training is essential. Visual aids cannot be used, so the interviewer must be able to convey verbally all information about response choices and skip patterns. Interviewers must know how to ask each question, how to answer questions posed by the respondent, and how to code responses. Exhibit 7.6 illustrates an example of interviewer instructions for a survey to measure symptoms of stress.

Procedures can be standardized more effectively, quality control maintained, and processing speed maximized when phone interviewers are assisted by computers using a computer-assisted telephone interview (CATI). In using CATI, the survey is programmed into the computer, including all relevant skip patterns, and the interviewer reads the questions and enters the responses directly into the computer.

Computerized interactive voice response (IVR) technology allows even greater control over interviewer-respondent interaction. In a survey, respondents receive automated calls and answer questions by pressing numbers on their touch-tone phones or speaking numbers that are interpreted by computerized voice recognition software. These surveys can also record verbal responses to open-ended questions for later transcription. Although they present some

---

EXHIBIT 7.6   **Sample Interviewer Instructions**

Question:

41. On how many of the past 7 days have you . . .

                                                                          Number of days

    a. Worried a lot about little things?   _____

    b. Felt tense or anxious?   _____

Instructions for interviewers:

Q41 For the series of "On how many of the past 7 days," make sure the respondent gives the numerical answer. If he/she responds with a vague answer like "not too often" or "just a few times," ask *again,* "On how many of the past 7 days would you say?" Do *not* lead the respondent with a number (e.g., "would that be 2 or 3?"). If R says, "all of them," verify that the answer is "7."

Question:

45. In the past 12 months about how many times have you gone on a diet to lose weight?

Never	0
Once	1
Twice	2
Three times or more	3
Always on a diet	4

Instructions for interviewers:

Q45 Notice that this question ends with a question mark. That means that you are *not* to read the answer categories. Rather, wait for R to respond and circle the appropriate number.

---

difficulties when many answer choices must be used or skip patterns must be followed, IVR surveys have been used successfully with short questionnaires and when respondents are highly motivated to participate (Dillman, 2000). When these conditions are not met, potential respondents may be put off by the impersonal nature of this computer-driven approach.

Phone surveying is the best choice for relatively short surveys of the general population. Response rates in phone surveys traditionally used to be high—often above 80%—because few individuals would hang up on a polite caller or refuse to stop answering questions (at least within the first 30 minutes or so). However, the refusal rate in phone interviews is rising, probably as a result of a dislike of telemarketing, the use of answering machines, and caller ID that helps to screen out unknown callers (Dillman, 2000). For example, the response rate to the University of Michigan's annual Survey of Consumer Attitudes has declined from 77% in 1979 to less than 60% in 2003 (Curtin, Presser, & Singer, 2005).

In-Person Interviews

What is unique to the **in-person interview**, compared with the other survey designs, is the face-to-face social interaction between the interviewer and respondent. If money is no object, in-person interviewing is often the best survey design.

In-person interviewing has several advantages. Response rates are higher than with any other survey design. Questionnaires can be much longer than with mailed or phone surveys; the questionnaire can be complex, with both open-ended and closed-ended questions and frequent branching patterns; the order in which questions are read and answered can be controlled by the interviewer; the physical and social circumstances of the interview can be monitored; and respondents' interpretations of questions can be probed and clarified.

As with phone interviewing, computers can be used to increase control of the in-person interview. In a computer-assisted personal interviewing (CAPI) project, interviewers carry a laptop computer that is programmed to display the interview questions and to process the responses that the interviewer types in, as well as to check that these responses fall within allowed ranges (Tourangeau, 2004). Interviewers seem to like CAPI, and the quality of data obtained this way is at least as good as data from a noncomputerized interview (Shepherd, Hill, Bristor, & Montalvan, 1996). A CAPI approach also makes it easier for the researcher to develop skip patterns and experiment with different types of questions for different respondents without increasing the risk of interviewer mistakes (Couper et al., 1998).

There are several special hazards due to the presence of the interviewer. Every respondent should have the same interview experience; that is, he or she should be asked the same questions in the same way by the same type of person, who should react similarly to the answers. Therein lies the researcher's challenge—to plan an interview process that will be personal and engaging, yet consistent and nonreactive (and to hire interviewers who can carry out this plan). Careful training and supervision are essential because small differences in intonation or emphasis on particular words can alter respondents' interpretations of question meanings (Peterson, 2000). Without a personalized approach, the rate of response will be lower and answers will be less thoughtful and potentially less valid. Without a consistent approach, information obtained from different respondents will not be comparable, and will thus be less reliable and less valid.

The presence of an interviewer may make it more difficult for respondents to give honest answers to questions about sensitive personal matters. CAPI is valued for this reason, since respondents can enter their answers directly into the laptop without the interviewer knowing what their response is. Alternatively, interviewers can hand respondents a separate self-administered questionnaire containing the more sensitive questions. After answering these questions, the respondent then seals the separate questionnaire in an envelope so that the interviewer does not know the answers.

The degree of rapport becomes a special challenge when survey questions concern issues related to such demographic characteristics as race or gender (Groves, 1989). If the interviewer and respondent are similar on these characteristics, the responses to these questions may differ from those that would be given if the interviewer and respondent differ on these characteristics.

Maximizing Response to Interviews

Several factors affect the response rate in interview studies. Contact rates tend to be lower in central cities, in part because of difficulties in finding people at home and gaining access to high-rise apartments, and in part because of interviewer reluctance to visit some areas at night, when people are more likely to be home (Fowler, 1988). Households with young children or elderly adults tend to be easier to contact, whereas single-person households are more difficult to reach (Groves & Couper, 1998).

Web Surveys

The Internet has created an entirely new mode of survey research: the Web-based survey. It is not yet possible to survey a representative sample of the U.S. population on the Web, since about 40% of American households are not connected to the Internet. Households without Internet access tend to be older and poorer than those who are connected (Tourangeau, 2004). However, many specific populations have very high rates of Internet use, making Internet-based surveys of groups such as professionals, middle-class communities, and, of course, college students a viable alternative to other survey methods. Due to the Internet's global reach, Web surveys also make it possible to conduct large, international surveys, although problems of representativeness are multiplied.

Web surveys may be announced with an e-mail message to potential respondents that contains a direct "hotlink" to the survey Web site. If a defined population with known e-mail addresses is to be surveyed, a researcher can send e-mail invitations to a representative sample without difficulty. To ensure that the appropriate people respond to a Web-based survey, researchers may require that respondents enter a personal identification number to gain access to the Web survey (Dillman, 2000). However, lists of unique e-mail addresses for the members of the defined populations generally do not exist outside of organizational settings. Many people have more than one e-mail address, and often there is no apparent link between an e-mail address and the name or location of the person to whom it is assigned. As a result, there is no available method for drawing a random sample of e-mail addresses for people from any general population, even if the focus is only on those with Internet access (Dillman, 2007).

Some Web surveys are instead linked to a Web site that is used by the intended population, and everyone who visits that site is invited to complete the survey. Although this approach can generate a large number of respondents, the resulting sample will necessarily reflect the type of people who visit that Web site and thus be a biased representation of the larger population (Dillman, 2000). Some control over the resulting sample can be maintained by requiring participants to meet certain inclusion criteria (Selm & Jankowski, 2006).

When they are appropriate for a particular population, Web surveys have some unique advantages (Selm & Jankowski, 2006). Questionnaires completed on the Web can elicit more honest reports of illicit behavior and of victimization as compared with phone interviews (Parks, Pardi, & Bradizza, 2006). They are relatively easy to complete, as respondents simply click on response boxes, and the survey can be programmed to move respondents easily through sets of questions, not presenting questions that do not apply to the respondent. Pictures, sounds, and animation can be used as a focus of particular questions, and graphic and typographic variation can be used to enhance visual survey appeal. Definitions of terms can "pop up" when respondents scroll over them (Dillman, 2007). In these ways, a skilled Web programmer can generate a survey layout with many attractive features that make it more likely that respondents will give their answers and have a clear understanding of the question (Smyth, Dillman, Christian, & Stern, 2004). Responses can quickly be checked to make sure they fall within the allowable range. Because answers are recorded directly in the researcher's database, data entry errors are almost eliminated and results can be reported quickly.

Mixed-Mode Surveys

Survey researchers increasingly are combining different survey designs to improve the overall participation rate. **Mixed-mode surveys** allow the strengths of one survey design to compensate for the weaknesses of another and can maximize the likelihood of securing data from different types of respondents (Dillman, 2007; Selm & Jankowski, 2006). For example, a survey may be sent electronically to sample members who have e-mail addresses and mailed to those who do not. Phone reminders may be used to encourage responses to Web or paper surveys, or a letter of introduction may be sent in advance of calls in a phone survey (Guterbock, 2008). Nonrespondents to a mail survey may be interviewed in person or over the phone. An interviewer may use a self-administered questionnaire to present sensitive questions to a respondent.

The mixed-mode approach is not a perfect solution. Respondents to the same questions may give different answers because of the survey mode, rather than because they actually have different opinions. Respondents to phone survey questions tend to endorse more extreme responses to scalar questions (which range from more to less) than respondents to mail or Web surveys (Dillman, 2007). When responses differ by survey mode, there is often no way to know which responses are more accurate (Peterson, 2000). However, the use of the same question structures, response choices, and skip instructions across modes substantially reduces the likelihood of mode effects, as does using a small number of response choices for each question (Dillman, 2000; Dillman & Christian, 2005).

A Comparison of Survey Designs

Which survey design should be used when? Group-administered surveys are similar in most respects to mail surveys, except that they require the unusual circumstance of having access to the sample in a group setting. We therefore do not need to consider this survey design by itself; what applies to mail surveys applies to group-administered survey designs, with the exception of sampling issues. The features of mixed-mode surveys depend on the survey types that are being combined. Thus, we can focus our comparison on the four survey designs that involve the use of a questionnaire with individuals sampled from a larger population: mail surveys, phone surveys, in-person surveys, and electronic surveys. Exhibit 7.7 summarizes the strong and weak points of each design.

The most important consideration is the likely response rate each method will generate. Because the response rates obtained in mail surveys are lower, they are the least preferred survey design from a sampling standpoint. However, researchers may still prefer a mail survey when they have to reach a widely dispersed population and do not have enough

---

EXHIBIT 7.7   Advantages and Disadvantages of Four Survey Designs

Characteristics of Design	Mail Survey	Phone Survey	In-Person Survey	Web Survey
Representative sample				
Opportunity for inclusion is known				
For completely listed populations	High	High	High	Medium
For incompletely listed populations	Medium	Medium	High	Low
Selection within sampling units is controlled				
(e.g., specific family members must respond)	Medium	High	High	Low
Respondents are likely to be located				
If samples are heterogeneous	Medium	High	High	Low
If samples are homogeneous and specialized	High	High	High	High
Questionnaire construction and question design				
Allowable length of questionnaire	Medium	Medium	High	Medium
Ability to include				
Complex questions	Medium	Low	High	High
Open questions	Low	High	High	Medium
Screening questions	Low	High	High	High
Tedious, boring questions	Low	High	High	Low
Ability to control question sequence	Low	High	High	High
Ability to ensure questionnaire completion	Medium	High	High	Low
Distortion of answers				
Odds of avoiding social desirability bias	High	Medium	Low	High
Odds of avoiding interviewer distortion	High	Medium	Low	High
Odds of avoiding contamination by others	Medium	High	Medium	Medium
Administrative goals				
Odds of meeting personnel requirements	High	High	Low	Medium
Odds of implementing quickly	Low	High	Low	High
Odds of keeping costs low	High	Medium	Low	High

Source: Adapted from Dillman (2007). Copyright © 2007 John Wiley & Sons, Inc. Reproduced with permission of John Wiley & Sons, Inc.

financial resources to hire and train an interview staff or to contract with a survey organization that already has an interview staff available in many locations.

Contracting with an established survey research organization for a phone survey is often the best alternative to a mail survey. The persistent follow-up attempts that are necessary to secure an adequate response rate are much easier over the phone than in person. However, the declining rate of response to phone interview calls is reducing the advantages of this method.

In-person surveys are clearly preferable in terms of the possible length and complexity of the questionnaire as well as the researcher's ability to monitor conditions while the questionnaire is being completed. Hesitancy to answer sensitive questions can be reduced by giving respondents a separate sheet to fill out on their own. Although interviewers may distort results, either by changing the wording of questions or by failing to record answers properly, this problem can be lessened by careful training, monitoring, and tape-recording the answers.

The advantages and disadvantages of electronic surveys must be weighed in light of the population that is to be surveyed and capabilities at the time that the survey is to be conducted. At this time, too many people lack Internet connections for general use.

These various points about the different survey designs lead to two general conclusions. First, in-person interviews are the strongest design and generally preferable when sufficient resources and trained interview staff are available; telephone surveys have many of the advantages of in-person interviews at much less cost, but technological changes are making them less effective. Second, the "best" survey design for any particular study must take into account the unique features and goals of the study.

▣ SECONDARY DATA

Secondary data are data that the researcher did not collect to answer the research question that is now of interest; rather, such data were collected by someone else. Generally, secondary data are obtained from publicly available data archives, from another researcher, or even from one's own previous projects that were designed to address some other research question. Many data sets available to social workers have been obtained in survey research projects. Secondary data also may be obtained from social service agencies' administrative data archives.

Analysis of secondary data presents several challenges, ranging from uncertainty about the methods of data collection to the lack of maximum fit between the concepts that the primary study measured and each of the concepts that are the focus of the current investigation. Responsible use of secondary data requires a good understanding of the primary data source. The researcher should be able to answer the following questions (most adapted from Riedel, 2000; Stewart, 1984):

1. What were the agency's goals in collecting the data? If the primary data were obtained in a research project, what were the project's purposes?

2. Who was responsible for data collection, and what were their qualifications? Are they available to answer questions about the data? Each step in the data-collection process should be charted and the personnel involved identified.

3. What data were collected, and what were they intended to measure?

4. When was the information collected?

5. What methods were used for data collection? Copies of the forms used for data collection should be obtained, and how the data were processed by the agency/agencies should be reviewed.

6. How is the information organized (by date, event, etc.)? Are there identifiers that are used to identify the different types of data available on the same case? In what form are the data available (computer tapes, disks, paper files)?

7. How consistent are the data with data available from other sources?

8. What is known about the success of the data-collection effort? How are missing data treated and indicated? What kind of documentation is available?

Answering these questions helps to ensure that the researcher is sufficiently familiar with the data and can help to identify any problems with them.

Researchers who rely on secondary data analysis inevitably make trade-offs between their ability to use a particular data set and the specific hypotheses they can test. If a concept that is critical to a hypothesis was not measured adequately in a secondary data source, the study might have to be abandoned until a more adequate source of data can be found. Alternatively, hypotheses or even the research question may be modified in order to match the analytic possibilities presented by the available data (Riedel, 2000).

Many sources of relevant secondary data are available to social work researchers. The U.S. Bureau of the Census Web site (www.census.gov) provides access to a wide variety of surveys in addition to the Decennial Census. These data sets include *Current Population Survey* (monthly survey of 72,000 households looking at employment and economic status); *National Health Interview Survey* (looks at acute and chronic illness and health-related services); *National Long-Term Care Survey* (data on elderly individuals including demographic characteristics and their ability to perform activities of daily living); and the *Survey of Income and Program Participation* (a series of panel studies of households providing data about source and amount of income, labor force participation, program participation, and program eligibility data) (U.S. Bureau of the Census, 2003). The General Social Survey (GSS) is an annual survey of social and behavioral attitudes that has been conducted since 1972 by the National Opinion Research Center at the University of Chicago. We have included a data set from the 2006 GSS on the study site. Additional information is available on the GSS Web site (www.norc.org/GSS+Website). The Inter-University Consortium for Political and Social Research at the University of Michigan (www.icpsr.umich.edu) provides access to a large number of survey data sets that are of interest to social work researchers and students.

🔲 SURVEY RESEARCH DESIGN IN A DIVERSE SOCIETY

Diversity and the impact of differences in shared belief systems must be considered in designing questions, constructing questionnaires, and choosing a data-collection method. When developing individual questions, you need to be careful about your choice of language; when constructing the questionnaire, you need to ensure that the format provides the same meaning for respondents; when deciding on a data-collection method, particularly interviewing, you may find that responses to questions are affected by interviewer-respondent characteristics.

To have valid information, all survey respondents should attach the same meaning to a question, and therefore you should ensure that the question has the same meaning across different population subgroups. Although it is important that the wording be appropriate for different groups, it is also necessary to show that the concept being examined is equivalent across groups—that questions adequately reflect group values, traditions, and beliefs (Marin & Marin, 1991). For example, the wording of a question about *family* and the available response categories would need to account for cultural differences in both the boundaries used to establish membership in a family and the expectations and obligations of family members (Luna et al., 1996).

In Chapter 3, we addressed the issue of measurement equivalence with a particular focus on methods to evaluate the equivalence of scales. Measures should capture not only universal definitions of the concept but also group-specific concerns and issues (Stewart & Nápoles-Springer, 2000). We return to some of the methods described in this chapter to illustrate how researchers examine the meaning of concepts, questions, and words and use what they learn to revise questions and instruments.

Nápoles-Springer, Santoyo-Olsson, O'Brien, and Stewart (2006) describe the process of using cognitive interviews, behavioral coding, and content analysis of the interviewer-respondent interaction to improve the wording and format of a health questionnaire. Their cognitive interview included probes about the meaning of specific words, whether some questions were redundant, what respondents were thinking as they heard and answered questions, whether questions were offensive, and whether the items were culturally appropriate. Behavior coding of tapes and transcripts was used to assess the interview process. They found that interviewers accidentally or purposefully skipped questions, reacted to responses, or changed the meaning of questions; while respondents did not understand some questions, gave responses not offered on a scale, and avoided answering questions directly by telling irrelevant stories. Whites, African Americans, Latinos interviewed in English, and Latinos interviewed in Spanish interpreted words differently, so the researchers had to provide different wording for each group.

O'Brien (1993) used focus groups to design his survey of social relationships and health behavior among gay and bisexual men at risk for AIDS. In part, the groups were conducted to "learn the language the men used to discuss their private emotional and sexual experiences" (p. 106).

Translating Instruments

English is not the first language of some respondents, and many would prefer to use their native language as they do in their daily lives (Marin & Marin, 1991). Translating questions creates an additional challenge to ensure that the questions have the same meaning.

In translating instruments, researchers want to produce questions that mean the same across different language instruments, rather than having instruments that are simply literal translations of each other. Five dimensions that should be evaluated to achieve this goal include the following:

1. *Content equivalence.* The content of each item is relevant to the phenomena of each culture being studied.

2. *Semantic equivalence.* The meaning of each item is the same in each culture after translation into the language and idiom of each culture.

3. *Technical equivalence.* The method of assessment (e.g., pencil and paper, interview) is comparable in each culture with respect to the data that it yields.

4. *Criterion equivalence.* The interpretation of the measurement of the variable remains the same when compared with the norm for each culture studied.

5. *Conceptual equivalence.* The instrument is measuring the same theoretical construct in each culture. (Flaherty et al., 1976, p. 258)

Chavez, Matías-Carrelo, Barrio, and Canino (2007) used a complex process to achieve content, semantic, and technical equivalence in their efforts to adapt a Youth Quality of Life scale for Latinos. The instrument included such domains as sense of self, social relationships, environment, and general quality of life, as well as contextual and behavioral items. They used an iterative process known as **decentering**, which means that both the original and the translated instruments are modified to increase their equivalence (Chavez et al., 2007). The original English and Spanish versions were reviewed by a bilingual committee composed of clinicians and researchers from Puerto Rico and then a multinational bilingual committee for such changes as wording, syntax, and colloquial use. This revised version was then assessed by 10 focus groups: 5 in Puerto Rico and 5 in Los Angeles. These groups included adolescents, parents, and clinicians. The focus groups began with discussions of "quality of life," the meaning of each domain, the meaning and relevance of each item, and the format of the instrument, rating scales, and instructions. Their comments were reviewed by the bilingual committee, who modified items based on the focus group comments; these changes were sent to the multilingual committee, who made further modifications, found universal Spanish equivalents where possible, or integrated multiple words to reflect differences in Mexican American and Puerto Rican cultures.

Chavez et al. (2007) believed that content equivalence was achieved through the reviews and evaluations of content by the two expert committees. Semantic equivalence was achieved through the translation and retranslation efforts. Technical, criterion, and conceptual equivalence would ultimately require data collection.

Other researchers use less involved methods to translate concepts. In a survey of Russian-speaking elderly, Tran, Khatutsky, Aroian, Balsam, and Conway (2000) used a male and a female translator to modify a survey. The modifications were reviewed in a focus group by bilingual health experts. To develop an instrument to be used with a group of Cuban Americans, Moreno (2003) had the instrument translated into Spanish and then translated back into English. After modifications were made, the newly translated version was pilot tested, accompanied by an interview with respondents.

Another challenge arises when there are regional or national differences in a spoken language. Marin and Marin (1991) offer these suggestions to deal with regional variations for Hispanics, but in many ways these suggestions are generalizable when a particular language is used in many different countries:

1. Use all appropriate variations of a word in a self-administered questionnaire.

2. Target vocabulary variations to each subgroup. When there are subgroups, alter the wording to conform to the vocabulary of that subgroup.

3. Avoid colloquialisms. Colloquialisms may differ from place to place and add to the confusion of a word's meaning.

4. Use alternate questions. (pp. 85–86)

Interviewer-Respondent Characteristics

As we noted earlier, rapport may depend on the interaction of interviewer-respondent characteristics; responses may differ when there is a similarity in characteristics versus when characteristics differ. There is a greater tendency for respondents to give socially desirable responses on sensitive topics. A White respondent might not disclose feelings of racial prejudice to an African American interviewer that he or she would admit to a White interviewer. Respondents were more likely to express support for gender equality and women's issues when the interviewer was a female than when the interviewer was a male (Huddy et al., 1997).

IMPLICATIONS FOR EVIDENCE-BASED PRACTICE

The survey research designs we have described in this chapter are typically not used to test the effectiveness of a particular intervention, although the methods described in this chapter are relevant to data gathering for any of the quantitative designs. Survey research designs can be used to evaluate the impact of social policies, and these designs often provide critical information about the need, availability, and utilization of various services.

In Chapter 2, we distinguished between cross-sectional and longitudinal designs. In a cross-sectional survey, data are collected at a single time point. Depending on the research question, it is possible to use a cross-sectional design to determine whether a program had an effect on participants. For example, one of the desired outcomes of the Women, Infants, and Children program (WIC) is the baby's birth weight. You can survey participants in WIC to find their children's birth weights and compare their responses with those of eligible nonparticipants to determine whether the program made a difference. Statistical controls enable you to evaluate program impact while holding other variables constant. Panel designs provide additional evidence that a program may have had an effect. Because data are collected over time with the same respondents, it is possible to see the impact of a program if the participation occurs during the course of the panel. Therefore, longitudinal survey research can provide useful evidence.

Another use of survey research for evidence-based practice is that it provides information about the use or lack of use of various programs. Survey research can be used to address important questions such as these: What is the prevalence of a particular status or condition? Are services being used? What are the barriers to service use? What characteristics distinguish between those who use and those who do not use a service? Although these questions do not address specifically the effectiveness of a particular intervention or program, these data can be used to improve treatment delivery (Clark, Power, Le Fauve, & Lopez, 2008).

ETHICAL ISSUES IN SURVEY RESEARCH

Survey research designs usually pose fewer ethical dilemmas than do experimental or field research designs. Potential respondents can easily decline to participate, and a cover letter or introductory statement that identifies the sponsors of and motivations for the survey gives them the information required to make this decision. The data-collection methods are quite obvious in a survey, so little is concealed from the respondents.

If the survey could possibly have any harmful effects for the respondents, these should be disclosed fully in the cover letter or introductory statement. The procedures used to reduce such effects should also be delineated, including how the researcher will keep interviews confidential or anonymous. Surveys that attempt to measure sensitive subject matter should have other protections in place. When asking respondents to recall sensitive topics, there is the possibility of causing respondents emotional harm. Respondents might be offered a phone number they can call if they are emotionally upset.

Many surveys include some essential questions that might in some way prove damaging to the subjects if their answers were disclosed. To prevent any possibility of harm to subjects due to disclosure of such information, it is critical to preserve subject confidentiality. Nobody but research personnel should have access to information that could be used to link respondents to their responses, and even that access should be limited to what is necessary for specific research purposes. Questionnaires should only have numbers to identify respondents; the researcher should keep the names that correspond to these numbers in a safe, private location, unavailable to staff and others who might otherwise come across them. Follow-up mailings or contact attempts that require linking the ID numbers with names and addresses should be carried out by trustworthy assistants under close supervision. If an electronic survey is used, encryption technology should be used to make information provided over the Internet secure from unauthorized persons.

Not many surveys can provide true **anonymity** so that no identifying information is ever recorded to link respondents with their responses. The main problem with anonymous surveys is that they preclude follow-up attempts to encourage participation by initial nonrespondents, and they prevent panel designs, which measure change through repeated surveys of the same individuals. In-person surveys rarely can be anonymous because an interviewer must in almost all cases know the name and address of the interviewee. However, phone surveys can safely be completely anonymous. When no future follow-up is desired, group-administered surveys also can be anonymous. To provide anonymity in a mail survey, the researcher should omit identifying codes from the questionnaire and could include a self-addressed, stamped postcard so the respondent can notify the researcher that the questionnaire has been returned without creating any linkage to the questionnaire itself (Mangione, 1995, p. 69).

🔲 CONCLUSION

Survey research is an exceptionally efficient and productive method for investigating a wide array of social research questions. In addition to the potential benefits for social science, considerations of time and expense frequently make a survey the preferred data-collection method. One or more of the survey designs reviewed in this chapter can be applied to almost any research question. Surveys are one of the most popular research methods in social work. As use of the Internet increases, survey research should become even more efficient and popular.

The relative ease of conducting at least some types of survey research leads many people to imagine that no particular training or systematic procedures are required. Nothing could be further from the truth. But as a result of this widespread misconception, you will encounter a great many nearly worthless survey results. You must be prepared to examine carefully the procedures used in any survey before accepting its findings as credible. And, if you decide to conduct a survey, you must be prepared to invest the time and effort required by proper procedures.

KEY TERMS

Acquiescence bias	Interview schedule
Anonymity	Mail survey
Behavior coding	Matrix questions
Closed-ended question	Mixed-mode surveys
Cognitive interview	Open-ended question
Confidentiality	Phone survey
Context effects	Pilot study
Contingency questions	Pretest
Cover letter	Questionnaire
Decentering	Random digit dialing
Double-barreled questions	Response set
Fence-sitters	Secondary data
Filter question	Skip patterns
Floaters	Social desirability
Group-administered survey	Survey research
In-person interview	Telescoping effect

HIGHLIGHTS

• Surveys are the most popular form of social research because of their versatility, efficiency, and generalizability. Many survey data sets, like the Survey of Income and Program Participation or the General Social Survey, are available for social work researchers and students.

• Survey designs must minimize the risk of errors of observation (measurement error) and errors of nonobservation (errors due to inadequate coverage, sampling error, and nonresponse). The likelihood of both types of error varies with the survey goals.

• A survey questionnaire or interview schedule should be designed as an integrated whole, with each question and section serving some clear purpose and complementing the others.

• Questions must be worded carefully to avoid confusing respondents, encouraging a less-than-honest response, or triggering biases. The wording of questions should have the same meaning to all respondents regardless of race, ethnicity, gender, age, or class.

• Inclusion of *"Don't know"* choices and neutral responses may help, but the presence of such options also affects the distribution of answers. Open-ended questions can be used to determine the meaning that respondents attach to their answers. Answers to any survey questions may be affected by the questions that precede them in a questionnaire or interview schedule.

• Questions can be tested and improved through review by experts, focus group discussions, cognitive interviews, interpretive questions, and pilot testing. Every questionnaire and interview schedule should be pretested on a small sample that is like the sample to be surveyed.

• The cover letter for a mailed questionnaire should be credible, personalized, interesting, and responsible.

- Response rates in mailed surveys are typically well below 70% unless multiple mailings are made to nonrespondents and the questionnaire and cover letter are attractive, interesting, and carefully planned. Response rates for group-administered surveys are usually much higher.

- Phone interviews using random digit dialing allow fast turnaround and efficient sampling. Multiple callbacks are often required and the rate of nonresponse to phone interviews is rising.

- In-person interviews have several advantages over other types of surveys: They allow longer and more complex interview schedules, monitoring of the conditions when the questions are answered, probing for respondents' understanding of the questions, and high response rates. However, the interviewer must balance the need to establish rapport with the respondent with the importance of maintaining control over the delivery of the interview questions.

- Electronic surveys may be e-mailed or posted on the Web. Interactive voice-response systems using the telephone are another option. At this time, use of the Internet is not sufficiently widespread to allow e-mail or Web surveys of the general population, but these approaches can be fast and efficient for populations with high rates of computer use.

- The decision to use a particular survey design must take into account the unique features and goals of the study. In general, in-person interviews are the strongest but most expensive survey design.

- For survey data to be valid, the wording of questions should convey the same meaning to different population groups. This may require translating and retranslating questions.

- Most survey research poses few ethical problems because respondents are able to decline to participate—an option that should be stated clearly in the cover letter or introductory statement. Special care must be taken when questionnaires are administered in group settings (to "captive audiences") and when sensitive personal questions are to be asked; subject confidentiality should always be preserved.

DISCUSSION QUESTIONS

1. Why is survey research popular among social work researchers and social service agencies? Although popular, survey research is at risk for error. What are the two potential errors common in survey research? How can the researcher minimize the risk of error?

2. Design a survey experiment to determine the effect of phrasing a question or its response choices in different ways. Check recent issues of a local newspaper for a question used in a survey of attitudes about some social policy. Propose some hypothesis about how the wording of the question or its response choices might have influenced the answers people gave and devise an alternative that differs only in this respect. Distribute these questionnaires to a large class (after your instructor makes the necessary arrangements) to test your hypothesis.

3. Thinking about the primary benefits and disadvantages of each of the five basic survey designs, which would you choose if you were interested in learning more about the caregiver burden experienced by parents raising young children below the age of 6? How would you try to ensure sample representativeness? What steps would you take to maximize the rate of response?

CRITIQUING RESEARCH

1. Develop 10 survey questions about beliefs of social work students about poverty. Did you use open- or closed-ended questions or both? What demographic information did you query? Did you attend to attractiveness? Is the instrument user-friendly?

2. After putting the survey you have developed for Question 1 away for several days, review the questions for the following: confusing phrasing, vague language, double negatives, double-barreled questions, jargon, and leading questions. Once you have revised your survey instrument, pilot it with your classmates. Ask for their critical feedback.

3. Examine an existing instrument measuring beliefs about attitudes toward poverty. Would you consider using this instrument for your own research? Why or why not? How does the published instrument compare with yours? Is it measuring the same concept?

MAKING RESEARCH ETHICAL

1. How can researchers ameliorate the negative consequences that responding to a survey on experiences with trauma may have? What responsibility do researchers have in providing respondents safety should they need it? Write a short statement in response to each question.

DEVELOPING A RESEARCH PROPOSAL

These questions apply to survey research as well as data collection in group and single-subject designs.

1. How will you gather the data? What specific data-collection method will you use (e.g., mail, telephone interview, or self-administered)?

2. Write questions for a one-page questionnaire that relate to your proposed research question. The questions should operationalize the variables on which you are focused.

3. Conduct a pretest of the questionnaire by conducting cognitive interviews with several respondents. For example, if you have closed-ended questions, ask the respondents what they meant by each response or what came to mind when they were asked each question.

4. Polish up the organization and layout of the questionnaire following the guidelines in the chapter.

5. List the relative advantages and disadvantages to the way you will collect the data.

6. Develop appropriate procedures for the protection of human subjects in your study. Include a cover letter directed to the appropriate population that contains relevant statements about research ethics.

To assist you in completing the Web exercises below and to gain a better understanding of the chapter's contents, please access the study site at http://www.sagepub.com/fswrstudy where you will find the Web exercises reproduced with suggested links, along with self-quizzes, e-flash cards, interactive exercises, journal articles, and other valuable resources.

WEB EXERCISES

1. Go to the Research Triangle Institute Web site (http://www.rti.org); click on Tools and Methods, then Surveys, and then Survey Design and Development. Read about their methods for computer-assisted interviewing (under Survey Methods) and their cognitive laboratory methods for refining questions (under Usability Testing). What does this add to the treatment of these topics in this chapter?

2. Go to the Question Bank Web site (http://qb.soc.surrey.ac.uk/docs/home.htm). Go to the "Surveys" link and then click on one of the listed surveys or survey sections that interest you. Review 10 questions used in the survey, and critique them in terms of the principles for question writing that you have learned. Do you find any question features that might be attributed to the use of British English? How might you change those features?

CHAPTER 8

Qualitative Methods

Observing, Participating, Listening

What Are Qualitative Methods?
  Case Study: Making Gray Gold

Participant Observation
  Choosing a Role
      Complete Observation
      Participation and
        Observation
      Covert Participation
  Entering the Field
  *Developing and Maintaining
      Relationships*
  Sampling People and Events
  Taking Notes
  *Managing the Personal
      Dimensions*
  Systematic Observation

Intensive Interviewing
  *Establishing and Maintaining a
      Partnership*

  *Asking Questions and Recording
      Answers*

Focus Groups
Photovoice
**Qualitative Research
    in a Diverse Society**
**Implications for Evidence-Based
    Practice**
Ethical Issues in Qualitative Research
Conclusion
Key Terms
Highlights
Discussion Questions
Critiquing Research
Making Research Ethical
Developing a Research Proposal
Web Exercises

"You have to look into a patient's eyes as much as you can and learn to get the signals from there." This suggestion was made by a nurse explaining to future nursing home assistants how they were to deal with a dying patient. One of those future assistants, Timothy Diamond (1992), was also a researcher intent on studying work in nursing homes. For us, the statement he recorded has a dual purpose: It exemplifies qualitative methods, in which we learn by observing as we participate in a natural setting; it also reminds us that some features of the social world are ill-suited to investigation with experiments or surveys.

But you will also learn that qualitative research is much more than just doing what comes naturally in social situations. Qualitative researchers must keenly observe, take notes systematically, question respondents strategically, and prepare to spend more time and invest more of their whole selves than often occurs with experiments or surveys. Moreover, if we are to have any confidence in the validity of a qualitative study's conclusions, each element of its design must be reviewed as carefully as we would review the elements of an experiment, single subject design, or survey.

The chapter begins with an overview of the major features of qualitative research. The next section discusses participant observation research, which is the most distinctive qualitative method, and reviews the stages of research using participant observation. We discuss the issues involved in intensive interviewing before briefly explaining focus groups, an increasingly popular qualitative method. The last section covers ethical issues that are of concern in any type of qualitative research project. By the chapter's end, you should appreciate the hard work required to translate "doing what comes naturally" into systematic research and be able to recognize strong and weak points in qualitative studies.

WHAT ARE QUALITATIVE METHODS?

Qualitative methods refer to several distinctive research designs including **participant observation**, **intensive interviewing**, and **focus groups**. Although these qualitative designs differ in many respects, they share several features that distinguish them from experimental group, single-subject, and survey research designs (Denzin & Lincoln, 1994; Maxwell, 1996; Wolcott, 1995):

A collection primarily of qualitative rather than quantitative data. Any research design may collect both qualitative and quantitative data, but qualitative methods emphasize observations about natural behavior and artifacts that capture social life as it is experienced by the participants rather than in categories predetermined by the researcher.

Exploratory research questions, with a commitment to inductive reasoning. Qualitative researchers typically begin their projects seeking not to test hypotheses but to discover what people think and how and why they act in some social setting. Only after many observations do qualitative researchers try to develop general principles to account for their observations.

A focus on previously unstudied processes and unanticipated phenomena. Previously unstudied attitudes and actions cannot adequately be understood with a structured set of questions or within a highly controlled experiment. Therefore, qualitative methods have their greatest appeal when we need to explore new issues, investigate hard-to-study groups, or determine the meaning people give to their lives and actions.

An orientation to social context, to the interconnections between social phenomena rather than to their discrete features. The context of concern may be a program or organization, a case, or a broader social context.

A focus on human subjectivity, on the meanings that participants attach to events and that people give to their lives. "Through life stories, people 'account for their lives.' . . . The themes people create are the means by which they interpret and evaluate their life experiences and attempt to integrate these experiences to form a self-concept" (Kaufman, 1986, pp. 24–25).

A focus on the events leading up to a particular event or outcome instead of general causal explanations. With its focus on particular actors and situations and the processes that connect them, qualitative research tends to identify causes as particular events embedded within an unfolding, interconnected action sequence (Maxwell, 1996). The language of variables and hypotheses appears only rarely in the qualitative literature.

Reflexive research design. The design develops as the research progresses:

> Each component of the design may need to be reconsidered or modified in response to new developments or to changes in some other component. . . . The activities of collecting and analyzing data, developing and modifying theory, elaborating or refocusing the research questions, and identifying and eliminating validity threats are usually all going on more or less simultaneously, each influencing all of the others. (Maxwell, 1996, pp. 2–3)

Sensitivity to the subjective role of the researcher. Little pretense is made of achieving an objective perspective on social phenomena.

Case Study: Making Gray Gold

You can get a better feel for qualitative methods by reading the following excerpts from Timothy Diamond's (1992) book, *Making Gray Gold*, about nursing homes and reasoning inductively from his observations. To conduct this study, Diamond became a nursing home assistant. In his own words,

> First I went to school for six months in 1982, two evenings a week and all day Saturdays, to obtain the certificate the state required [to work in a nursing home]. Then, after weeks of searching

Participant observation A qualitative method for gathering data that involves developing a sustained relationship with people while they go about their normal activities.

Intensive interviewing A qualitative method that involves open-ended relatively unstructured questioning in which the interviewer seeks in-depth information on the interviewee's feelings, experiences, and perceptions (Lofland & Lofland, 1984).

Focus groups A qualitative method that involves unstructured group interviews in which the focus group leader actively encourages discussion among participants on the topics of interest.

for jobs, I worked in three different nursing homes in Chicago for periods of three to four months each. (p. 5)

As this excerpt indicates, Diamond's research involved becoming a participant in the social setting that was the object of his study. Diamond spent more than 1 year gathering data as he worked full-time as an aide.

Diamond (1992) also describes the development of his research questions. His curiosity about health care for older people was piqued when he happened to become acquainted with Ina Williams and Aileen Crawford in a coffee shop across the street from the nursing home where they worked as assistants. Diamond began to wonder:

How does the work of caretaking become defined and get reproduced day in and day out as a business? . . . How, in other words, does the everyday world of Ina and Aileen and their co-workers, and that of the people they tend, get turned into a system in which gray can be written about in financial journals as producing gold, a classic metaphor for money? What is the process of making gray gold? (p. 5)

With these exploratory research questions in mind, Diamond (1992) explains why he chose participant observation as his research method: "I wanted to collect stories and to experience situations like those Ina and Aileen had begun to describe. I decided that . . . I would go inside to experience the work myself" (p. 5).

The choice of participant observation precluded random sampling of cases, but Diamond (1992) did not ignore the need to generalize his findings. He went to considerable lengths to include three nursing homes that would represent a range of caregiving arrangements:

These [nursing] homes were situated in widely different neighborhoods of the city. In one of them residents paid for their own care, often with initial help from Medicare. In the other two, most of the residents were supported by Medicaid. . . . In the course of writing, I visited many homes across the United States to validate my observations and to update them in instances where regulatory changes had been instituted. (p. 6)

The data in Diamond's study were notes on the activities of the people as he observed and interacted with them. He did not use structured questionnaires and other formal data-collection instruments, so his data are primarily qualitative rather than quantitative.

As for his method, it was inductive. First he gathered data. Then, as data collection continued, Diamond (1992) figured out how to interpret the data—how to make sense of the social situations he was studying. His analytic categories ultimately came not from social theory but from the categories by which people described one another and made sense of their social world. These categories seem to have broad applicability, suggesting the generalizability of the researcher's findings. Central to his case study was creating a **thick description** of the setting being studied; a thick description provides a sense of what it is like to experience that setting from the standpoint of the natural actors in that setting (Geertz, 1973).

To summarize, Diamond's (1992) research began with an exploratory question (to find out what was going on) and proceeded inductively throughout, developing general concepts to make sense of specific observations. Although Diamond, a White man, was something of an outsider in a setting dominated by women of color, he was able to share many participants' experiences and perspectives. His connecting sequences of events enabled him to construct plausible explanations about what seemed to be a typical group. He thus used qualitative research to explore human experiences in depth, carefully analyzing the social contexts in which they occur.

▣ PARTICIPANT OBSERVATION

Participant observation is a method in which natural social processes are studied as they happen in their natural setting and are left relatively undisturbed. It is a means for seeing the social world as the research subjects see it, in its totality, and for understanding subjects' interpretations of that world (Wolcott, 1995). By observing people and interacting with them in the course of their normal activities, participant observers seek to avoid the artificiality of experimental designs and the unnatural structured questioning of survey research (Koegel, 1987). This method encourages consideration of the context in which social interaction occurs, of the complex and interconnected nature of social relations, and of the sequencing of events (Bogdewic, 1999).

The term *participant observer* actually represents a continuum of roles (see Exhibit 8.1), ranging from being a complete observer who does not participate in group activities and is publicly defined as a researcher, to being a covert participant, who acts just like other group members and does not disclose his or her research role. Many field researchers develop a role between these extremes, publicly acknowledging being a researcher, but nonetheless participating in group activities.

Choosing a Role

The first concern of all participant observers is to decide what balance to strike between observing and participating and whether to reveal their role as researchers. These decisions must take into account the specifics of the social situation being studied, the researcher's own background and personality, the larger sociopolitical context, and ethical concerns. Which balance of participating and observing is most appropriate may change during a particular study.

Complete Observation

In **complete observation**, researchers try to see things as they happen without actively participating in these events. Of course, the researcher's very presence as an observer alters

EXHIBIT 8.1	**The Observational Continuum**

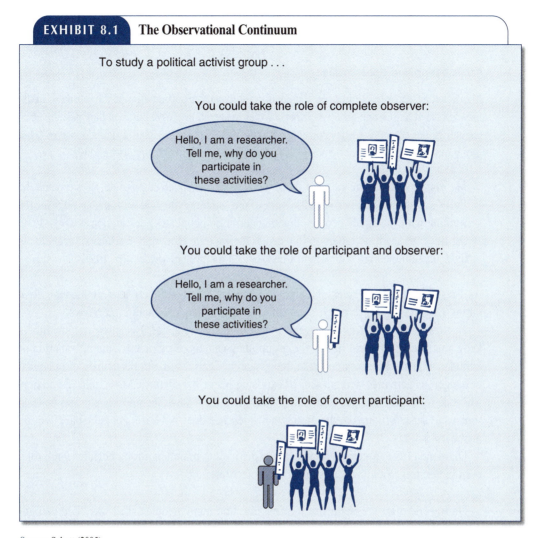

Source: Schutt (2005).

the social situation being observed; this is the problem of **reactive effects.** It is not "natural" in most social situations for someone to record observations for research, so individuals may alter their behavior. In social settings involving many people, the complete observer is unlikely to have much effect on social processes. However, when the social setting involves few people and observing is unlike the usual activities in the setting, or when the observer differs in obvious respects from the participants, the complete observer is more likely to have an impact. Karen Lyman (1994) notes in her study of staff and patients in Alzheimer's day-care centers that some staff monitored their speech:

Some workers displayed frustration over the heads of clients (eyes rolling, sighs) or made humorous comments to clients about their personal quirks, clearly intended for me as the observer. . . . At one site a program aide caught himself midsentence: "They're all cra—. . . ." (p. 166)

Participation and Observation

Many field researchers adopt a role that involves some active participation in the setting. Usually they inform at least some group members of their research interests, but then they participate in enough group activities to develop rapport with members and to gain a direct sense of what group members experience. Lyman (1994) described her efforts at rapport-building:

> My role was to become a part of these social worlds as much as possible, to overcome the status of outsider. I helped with the work of day care: serving and cleaning up after meals, walking with "agitated" people, directing confused people to a destination. I worked "on the floor" to assist one short-staffed center during a flu epidemic in which several clients died, including a man with whom I had danced the previous week. (p. 165)

As a result of her involvement, all eight program directors and their staff were cooperative during Lyman's (1994) research, even offering unsolicited and candid interviews.

Participating and observing have two clear ethical advantages: Because group members know the researcher's real role in the group, they can choose to keep some information or attitudes hidden. By the same token, the researcher can decline to participate in unethical or dangerous activities without fear of exposing his or her identity. Most field researchers who opt for disclosure get the feeling that, after they have become known and at least somewhat trusted figures in the group, their presence does not have any palpable effect on members' actions.

Diamond (1992) describes how it can be difficult to maintain a fully open research role, even in a setting without these special characteristics:

> During and after the fieldwork the first question many people asked was "Did you tell them?" . . . I had initially hoped to disclose at every phase of the project my dual objective of working as a nursing assistant and writing about these experiences. In some instances it was possible to disclose this dual purpose, in others it was not. I told many nursing assistants and people who lived in the homes that I was both working and investigating. I told some of my nursing supervisors and some administrators. . . . The short answer is that as the study proceeded it was forced increasingly to become a piece of undercover research. (pp. 7–8)

Even when researchers maintain a public identity as researchers, ethical dilemmas arising from participation in the lives of their research subjects do not go away. In fact, social workers conducting qualitative research may obtain information that suggests some clinical intervention may be warranted to improve the life or health of a research subject, and then they must decide whether taking action would be consistent with research guidelines. When Kayser-Jones and Koenig (1994) found that one of their elderly demented nursing home patients seemed to be dying from an untreated illness, they encouraged a nurse to override the wishes of the family to avoid any "heroic" measures and convinced the doctor on call to begin intravenous fluids.

Experienced participant observers try to lessen some of the problems of identity disclosure by evaluating both their effect on others in the setting and the effect of others on the observers, writing about these effects throughout the time they are in the field and while they analyze their data. They also are sure while in the field to preserve some physical space and regular time when they can concentrate on their research and schedule occasional meetings with other researchers to review the fieldwork.

Covert Participation

To lessen the potential for reactive effects and to gain entry to otherwise inaccessible settings, some field researchers have adopted the role of **covert participant**, keeping their research secret and trying their best to act like other participants in a social setting or group. Humphreys (1970) served as a "watch queen" so that he could learn about men engaging in homosexual acts in a public restroom. Goffman (1961) worked as a state hospital assistant while studying the treatment of psychiatric patients.

The researcher's covert behavior lessens some of the reactive effects, but there are other problems. The researcher must write notes based solely on memory and must do so at times when it is natural to be away from group members. Covert participants cannot ask questions that will arouse suspicion, so they often have trouble clarifying the meaning of other participants' attitudes or actions. The role is difficult to play, and the researchers' spontaneous reactions to every event are unlikely to be consistent with those of the regular participants, thereby raising suspicion that the researchers are not "one-of-us" (Mitchell, 1993). Diamond (1992), though an acknowledged researcher in the nursing home, found that simply disclosing the fact that he did not work another job to make ends meet set him apart from other nursing assistants:

> "There's one thing I learned when I came to the States," [said a Haitian nursing assistant]. "Here you can't make it on just one job." She tilted her head, looked at me curiously, then asked, "You know, Tim, there's just one thing I don't understand about you. How do you make it on just one job?" (pp. 47–48)

Entering the Field

Entering the field, the setting under investigation, is a critical stage in a participant observation project. Before entering the field, a researcher must review his or her personal stance toward the people and problems likely to be encountered. Researchers must learn in advance how participants dress and what their typical activities are so as to avoid being caught completely unprepared. For his study, Diamond (1992) tried to enter a nursing home twice, first without finding out about necessary qualifications:

My first job interview. . . . The administrator of the home had agreed to see me on [the recommendation of two current assistants]. [T]he administrator . . . probed suspiciously, "Now why would a white guy want to work for these kinds of wages?" . . . He continued without pause, "Besides, I couldn't hire you if I wanted to. You're not certified." That, he quickly concluded, was the end of our interview, and he showed me to the door. (pp. 8–9)

After taking a course and receiving his certificate, Diamond (1992) was able to enter the role of nursing assistant as others did.

When participant observing involves public figures or organizations that are used to publicity, a more direct approach may secure entry into the field. Dorothy and David Counts (1996) simply wrote a letter to the married couple who led the Escapees RV Club describing their project and asking for permission to work with members. After a warm welcome from the leaders, the Countses were able to meet with Escapees at regular park gatherings and distribute questionnaires. They received few refusals, attributing this high rate of subject cooperation to members' desires to increase understanding of and appreciation for their life-style. Other groups have other motivations, but in every case some consideration of these potential motives in advance should help smooth entry into the field.

In short, field researchers must be very sensitive to the impression they make and the ties they establish when entering the field. This stage lays the groundwork for collecting data from people who have different perspectives and for developing relationships that the researcher can use to surmount the problems in data collection that inevitably arise in the field. Researchers should be ready with a rationale for their participation and some sense of the potential benefits to participants. Discussion about these issues with key participants or gatekeepers should be honest and should identify what the participants expect from the research, without necessarily going into detail about the researcher's hypotheses or research questions (Rossman & Rallis, 1998).

Developing and Maintaining Relationships

Researchers must be careful to manage their relationships in the research setting so they can continue to observe and interview diverse members of the social setting throughout the long period typical of participant observation (Maxwell, 1996). Interaction early in the research process is particularly sensitive because participants do not know the researcher and the researcher does not know the routines. Kahana, Kahana, and Riley (1988) give some specific advice for those studying institutional settings for the aged:

Prior to implementation of the project, it is useful for the research team to spend some time in the facility, familiarizing themselves with the staff and with the physical and social environment and becoming acceptable additions to the institutional setting. (p. 200)

Experienced participant observers have developed some sound advice for others seeking to maintain relationships in the field (Bogdewic, 1999; Rossman & Rallis, 1998; Whyte, 1955; Wolcott, 1995). Develop a plausible explanation about yourself and the study. It is important to identify and maintain the support of key individuals. Do not be arrogant, showing off your expertise, and do not be too aggressive in questioning others. Do not fake you social similarity with your subjects; they recognize the differences and limit self-disclosure. Finally, avoid giving or receiving money or tangible gifts.

Sampling People and Events

Sampling decisions in qualitative research are guided by the need to study intensively the people, places, or phenomena of interest. Most qualitative researchers limit their focus to just one or a few sites, programs, or specific types of people so they can focus all their attention on the social dynamics of those settings or the activities and attitudes of these people. Sampling is still important as the sample must be appropriate and adequate for the study, even if it is not representative. The qualitative researcher may select one or more "critical cases" that are unusually rich in information pertaining to the research question, "typical cases" precisely because they are judged to be typical, or "deviant cases" that provide a useful contrast (Kuzel, 1999). Within a research site, plans may be made to sample different settings, people, events, and artifacts (see Exhibit 8.2).

Studying more than one case or setting almost always strengthens the causal conclusions and makes the findings more generalizable (King, Keohane, & Verba, 1994). Diamond (1992) worked in three different Chicago nursing homes "in widely different neighborhoods" and with different fractions of residents supported by Medicaid. He then "visited many homes across the United States to validate [his] observations" (p. 5). Wallace (1994) encourages "efforts to include all kinds of people—African-Americans, Hispanics, males, females, rich and poor" to provide a more complete experience of aging in life history interview research (pp. 143–144).

Other approaches to sampling in field research are more systematic. Purposive sampling can be used to identify opinion leaders and representatives of different roles. With snowball sampling, field researchers learn from participants about who represents different subgroups in a setting. Quota sampling also may be employed to ensure the representation of particular categories of participants. **Theoretical sampling** (see Exhibit 8.3) is a systematic approach used when field researchers focus on particular processes that seem to be important and select new settings or individuals that permit comparisons to check their perceptions (Ragin, 1994).

Sampling in qualitative studies can lead to bias. For example, a nonrandom sample of elderly persons in institutional settings can be biased by staff motivation to suggest residents who will present the institution in a particular light or simply by staff lack of reliable knowledge about residents' diagnosis, tenure, or other characteristics that are important in the researcher's sampling strategy (Kahana et al., 1988).

EXHIBIT 8.2	Sampling Plan for a Participant Observation Project in Schools

Type of Information to Be Obtained

Information Source	Collegiality	Goals and Community	Action Expectations	Knowledge Orientation	Base
SETTINGS:					
Public places (halls, main offices)	X	X	X	X	X
Teachers' lounge	X	X		X	X
Classrooms		X	X	X	X
Meeting rooms			X	X	
Gymnasium or locker room		X			
EVENTS:					
Faulty meetings	X		X		X
Lunch hour	X				X
Teaching		X	X	X	X
PEOPLE:					
Principal		X	X	X	X
Teachers	X	X	X	X	X
Students		X	X	X	
ARTIFACTS:					
Newspapers		X	X		X
Decorations		X			

Source: Adapted from Marshall & Rossman (1999, pp. 75–76).

Taking Notes

Notes are the primary means of recording participant observation data (Emerson, Fretz, & Shaw, 1995). Many field researchers jot down partial notes while observing and then retreat

EXHIBIT 8.3 **Theoretical Sampling**

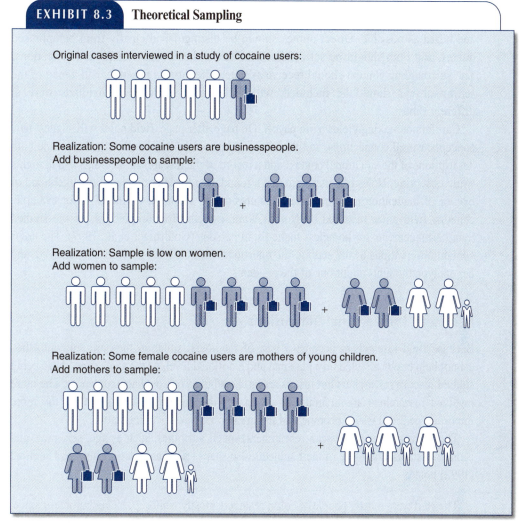

Original cases interviewed in a study of cocaine users:

Realization: Some cocaine users are businesspeople.
Add businesspeople to sample:

Realization: Sample is low on women.
Add women to sample:

Realization: Some female cocaine users are mothers of young children.
Add mothers to sample:

Source: Schutt (2005).

to their computers to write up more complete notes on a daily basis. The computerized text can then be inspected and organized after it is printed out, or it can be marked up and organized for analysis using one of several computer programs designed especially for the task, as it is too disruptive to try to be more comprehensive. Some researchers will also maintain a daily log in which each day's activities are recorded (Bogdewic, 1999). Diamond (1992) described his note-taking process:

> While I was getting to know nursing assistants and residents and experiencing aspects of their daily routines, I would surreptitiously take notes on scraps of paper, in the bathroom or otherwise out of sight, jotting down what someone had said or done. (pp. 6–7)

Usually, writing up notes takes much longer—at least three times longer—than the observing did. Field notes must be as complete, detailed, and true to what was observed and heard as possible. Direct quotes should be distinguished clearly from paraphrased quotes, and both should be set off from the researcher's observations and reflections. The surrounding context should receive as much attention as possible, and a map of the setting always should be included, with indications of where individuals were at different times.

Careful note-taking yields a big payoff. On page after page, field notes will suggest new concepts, causal connections, and theoretical propositions. Notes also should include both descriptions of the situational context and a record of the researchers' feelings and thoughts while observing. Notes like these provide a foundation for later review of the likelihood of bias or of inattention to some salient features of the situation. Exhibit 8.4, for example, contains field notes recorded by Norma Ware, a medical anthropologist, as she studied living arrangements for homeless mentally ill persons (Goldfinger et al., 1997). The notes contain observations of the setting, the questions she asked, the answers she received, and her analytic thoughts about one of the residents.

Managing the Personal Dimensions

Because field researchers become a part of the social situation they are studying, they cannot help but be affected on a personal and emotional level. At the same time, those being studied react to researchers not just as researchers but as personal acquaintances. The more involved researchers are in multiple aspects of the ongoing social situation, the more important personal issues become and the greater the risk of "going native."

The correspondence between researchers' social attributes, such as age, sex, race, and economic status, and those of their subjects also shapes personal relationships, as Diamond (1992) noted:

The staff were mostly people of color, residents mostly white. . . . Never before, or since, have I been so acutely aware of being a white American man. At first the people who lived in the homes stared at me, then some approached to get a closer look, saying that I reminded them of a nephew, a son, a grandson, a brother, a doctor. This behavior made more sense as time went on: except for the few male residents and occasional visitors, I was the only white man many would see from one end of the month to the next. (p. 39)

There is no formula for successfully managing the personal dimension of field research. It is much more art than science, and it flows more from the researcher's own personality and natural approach to other people than from formal training. Beginning field researchers often neglect to consider how they will manage personal relationships when they plan and carry out their projects. Then they suddenly find themselves doing something they do not believe they should, just to stay in the good graces of research

EXHIBIT 8.4	Field Notes From the Evolving Consumer Household (ECH)

I arrive around 4:30 p.m. and walk into a conversation between Jim and somebody else as to what color jeans he should buy. There is quite a lot of joking going on between Jim and Susan. I go out to the kitchen and find Dick about to take his dinner out to the picnic table to eat (his idea?) so I go ask if I can join him. He says yes. In the course of the conversation, I find out that he works 3 days a week in the "prevoc" program at the local day program, Food Services branch, for which he gets $10 per week. Does he think the living situation will work out? Yes. All they need is a plan for things like when somebody buys something and then everybody else uses it. Like he bought a gallon of milk and it was gone in two days because everyone was using it for their coffee. I ask if he's gone back to the shelter to visit and he says "No. I was glad to get out of there." He came to the [ECH] from [a shelter] through homeless outreach [a Department of Mental Health Program]. Had been at [the shelter] since January. Affirms that [the ECH] is a better place to live than the shelter. Why? Because you have your own room and privacy and stuff. How have people been getting along with each other? He says, "Fine."

I return to the living room and sit down on the couch with Jim and Susan. Susan teases Jim and he jokes back. Susan is eating a TV dinner with M and M's for dessert. There is joking about working off the calories from the M and M's by doing sit-ups, which she proceeds to demonstrate. This leads to a conversation about exercise during which Jim declares his intention to get back into exercise by doing sports, like basketball.

Jim seems to have his mind on pulling himself together, which he characterizes as "getting my old self back." When I ask him what he's been doing since I saw him last, he says, "Working on my appearance." And in fact, he has had a haircut, a shave, and washed his clothes. When I ask him what his old self was like, he says, "you mean before I lost everything?" I learn that he used to work two jobs, had "a family" and was "into religion." This seems to have been when he was quite young, around eighteen. He tells me he was on the street for 7–8 years, from 1978–1985, drinking the whole time. I ask him whether he thinks living at [the ECH] will help him to get his "old self back" and he says that it will "help motivate me." I observe that he seems pretty motivated already. He says yes, "but this will motivate me more."

Jim has a warm personality, likes to joke and laugh. He also speaks up—in meetings he is among the first to say what he thinks and he talks among the most. His "team" relationship with Bill is also important to him—"me and Bill, we work together."

Source: Norma Ware, PhD, Department of Psychiatry, Harvard Medical School, unpublished ethnographic notes (1991).

subjects, or juggling the emotions resulting from conflict with the group. Whyte (1955) offers the following guidelines:

- Take the time to consider how you want to relate to your potential subjects as people.

- Speculate about what personal problems might arise and how you will respond to them.

- Keep in touch with other researchers and personal friends outside the research setting.

- Maintain standards of conduct that make you comfortable as a person and that respect the integrity of your subjects.

Systematic Observation

We would be remiss if we failed to note that observations can be made in a more systematic, quantitative design that allows systematic comparisons and more confident generalizations. A research study using **systematic observation** develops a standard form on which to record variation within the observed setting in terms of the variables of interest. Such variables might include the frequency of some behavior(s), the particular people observed, and environmental conditions.

Shapiro and Mangelsdorf (1994) used systematic observation and surveys to look for factors related to the parenting abilities of adolescent mothers. Participants first completed the survey, which consisted of a variety of measures, such as self-efficacy, life events, self-concept, and life stress, as well as demographic information. The participants were then videotaped engaging in three parenting activities: feeding, unstructured play, and structured play. Coders viewed the videotapes and, using standardized scales, rated the adolescent mothers on their parental sensitivity, expressiveness with the child, positive regard, negative regard, and caretaking ability, and the extent to which the adolescents permitted their child autonomy, as well as child responsiveness to the interaction.

回 INTENSIVE INTERVIEWING

Qualitative researchers can employ intensive or depth interviewing exclusively, without systematic observation of respondents in their natural setting or as part of their participant-observation design. Unlike the more structured interviewing that may be used in survey research, intensive interviewing relies on open-ended questions. Qualitative researchers do not presume to know the range of answers that respondents might give and seek to hear these answers in the respondents' own words. Rather than asking standard questions in a fixed order, intensive interviewers allow the specific content and order of questions to vary from one interviewee to another.

What distinguishes intensive interviewing from less structured forms of questioning is consistency and thoroughness. The goal is to develop a comprehensive picture of the interviewee's background, attitudes, and actions in his or her own terms; to "listen to people as they describe how they understand the worlds in which they live and work" (Rubin & Rubin, 1995, p. 3). For example, Kaufman (1986) sought through intensive interviewing to learn how old people cope with change. She wanted to hear the words of the elderly themselves, for "the voices of individual old people can tell us much about the experience of being old" (p. 6).

Intensive interview studies do not reveal as directly as does participant observation the social context in which action is taken and opinions are formed. Like participant observation studies, intensive interviewing engages researchers actively with subjects. The researchers must listen to lengthy explanations, ask follow-up questions tailored to the preceding answers, and seek to learn about interrelated belief systems or personal approaches to things, rather than measure a limited set of variables. As a result, intensive interviews are often much longer than standardized interviews, sometimes as long as 15 hours, conducted in several different sessions. The intensive interview is more like a conversation between partners than between a researcher and a subject (Kaufman, 1986). Intensive interviewers actively try to probe understandings and engage interviewees in a dialogue about what they mean by their comments.

Random selection is rarely used to select respondents for intensive interviews, but the selection method still must be carefully considered. Researchers try to select interviewees who are knowledgeable about the subject of the interview, who are open to talking, and who represent the range of perspectives (Rubin & Rubin, 1995). Selection of new interviewees should continue, if possible, at least until the **saturation point** is reached, the point when new interviews seem to yield little additional information.

Establishing and Maintaining a Partnership

Because intensive interviewing does not engage researchers as participants in subjects' daily affairs, the problems of entering the field are much reduced. However, the logistics of arranging long periods for personal interviews can still be pretty complicated. It also is important to establish rapport with subjects by considering in advance how they will react to the interview arrangements and by developing an approach that does not violate their standards for social behavior. Interviewees should be treated with respect, as knowledgeable partners whose time is valued (that means you should avoid coming late for appointments). A commitment to confidentiality should be stated and honored (Rubin & Rubin, 1995).

In the first few minutes of the interview, the goal is to show interest in the interviewee and to explain clearly the purpose of the interview (Kvale, 1996). During the interview, the interviewer should maintain an appropriate distance from the interviewee, one that does not violate cultural norms, and the interviewer should maintain eye contact and not engage in distracting behavior. An appropriate pace is also important; pause to allow the interviewee to reflect, elaborate, and generally not feel rushed (Gordon, 1992). When an interview covers emotional or otherwise stressful topics, the interviewer should give the interviewee an opportunity to unwind at the interview's end (Rubin & Rubin, 1995).

Asking Questions and Recording Answers

Intensive interviewers must plan their main questions around an outline of the interview topic. The questions should generally be short and to the point. More details can be elicited through nondirective probes such as "Can you tell me more about that?" or "uh-huh," echoing the respondent's comment, or just maintaining a moment of silence. Follow-up questions should be tailored to answers to the main questions. Interviewers should strategize throughout an interview about how best to achieve their objectives while taking into account interviewees' answers. They must also be sensitive to the ways in which they shape the answers by their words, style of questioning, and personal characteristics.

It is the combination of personal characteristics and expectations of the interviewer, the attitudes toward aging that he or she indicates, and the conceptual grounding of the questions themselves that influence the topics informants choose to express and expand on, as well as the topics they omit from discussion entirely (Kaufman, 1994, p. 128).

Habits of the Heart, by Bellah, Madsen, Sullivan, Swidler, and Tipton (1985), provides a useful illustration:

[Coinvestigator Steven] Tipton, in interviewing Margaret Oldham [a pseudonym], tried to discover at what point she would take responsibility for another human being:

Q: So what are you responsible for?

A: I'm responsible for my acts and for what I do.

Q: Does that mean you're responsible for others, too?

A: No.

Q: Are you your sister's keeper?

A: No.

Q: Your brother's keeper?

A: No.

Q: Are you responsible for your husband?

A: I'm not. He makes his own decisions. He is his own person. He acts his own acts. I can agree with them, or I can disagree with them. If I ever find them nauseous enough, I have a responsibility to leave and not deal with it any more.

Q: What about children?

A: I . . . I would say I have a legal responsibility for them, but in a sense I think they in turn are responsible for their own acts. (p. 304)

Do you see how the interviewer actively encouraged the subject to explain what she meant by "responsibility." This sort of active questioning undoubtedly did a better job of clarifying the respondent's concept of responsibility than a fixed set of questions would have.

Tape recorders are commonly used to record intensive interviews. Tape-recording does not inhibit most interviewees, and, in fact, tape recorders are routinely ignored. Occasionally a respondent is concerned with his or her public image and may speak "for the tape recorder," but such individuals are unlikely to speak frankly in any research interview. In any case, constant note-taking during an interview prevents adequate displays of interest and is distracting. If the tape recorder is inhibiting the interview, you can turn it off.

▣ FOCUS GROUPS

Focus groups are groups of unrelated individuals that are formed by a researcher and then led in group discussion of a topic for 1 to 2 hours. The researcher asks specific questions and guides the discussion to ensure that group members address these questions, but the resulting information is qualitative and relatively unstructured. Focus groups do not involve representative samples; instead, a few individuals who have the time to participate, have some knowledge pertinent to the focus group topic, and share key characteristics with the target population are recruited for the group.

Most focus groups involve 7 to 10 people, a number that facilitates discussion by all in attendance. Participants usually do not know one another, although some studies in organized settings may include friends or coworkers. Homogeneous groups may be more convivial and willing to share feelings, but heterogeneous groups may stimulate more ideas (Brown, 1999). Of course, the characteristics of individuals that determine their inclusion are based on the researcher's conception of the target population for the study.

Focus group leaders must begin the discussion by creating the expectation that all will participate and that the researcher will not favor any particular perspective or participant. The researcher, or group moderator, uses an interview guide, but the dynamics of group discussion often require changes in the order and manner in which different topics are addressed (Brown, 1999). No formal procedure exists for determining the generalizability of focus group answers, but the careful researcher should conduct at least several focus groups on the same topic and check for consistency in the findings. Some focus group experts suggest conducting enough focus groups to reach the point of "saturation," when an additional focus group adds little new information to that which already has been generated (Brown, 1999).

Ingersoll-Dayton, Neal, Ha, and Hammer (2003) provide a good example of how focus groups can offer unexpected responses that produce new knowledge. Their groups focused on caregiving and work, and caregiving and family responsibilities, but participants initiated a discussion of sibling relationships and caregiving in 16 of 17 focus groups. Focusing on these responses, the researchers concluded that

> by examining caregiving from a collaborative perspective, this study revealed caregiving as a dynamic process. In fact, we found that sibling caregivers consciously switched from primary to secondary roles on a regular basis. As illustrated by the two sisters who planned to take turns caring for their dying father, siblings may purposefully vary their caregiving responsibilities. . . . Another important discovery is that aging parents can facilitate collaboration among adult siblings. . . . Our study shows how older parents can help their children cooperate by providing the same information or instructions to all of them. In so doing, siblings can concentrate their efforts on a similar goal rather than feeling confused and conflicted when parents provide contradictory instructions to different children. (p. 63)

Focus group methods share with other field research techniques an emphasis on discovering unanticipated findings and exploring hidden meanings. Although they do not provide a means for developing reliable, generalizable results (the traditional strong suits of survey research), focus groups can be an indispensable aid for research studies, such as to develop hypotheses and test survey questions, or for social work practice, such as for needs assessment or to quickly assess the range of opinion about an issue.

▣ PHOTOVOICE

For about 150 years, people have been creating a record of the social world with photographs. This creates the possibility of observing the social world through photographs and of interpreting the resulting images as "text." For the most part, such visual imagery has captured social reality from the eyes of the researchers and therefore was being constructed by the researchers' interests and not from the perspective of the participants. **Photovoice** builds on this history, but like other qualitative methods, it is designed to preserve the voice of the respondents. Photovoice allows the participants to construct their social reality.

Wang and Burris (1997) describe Photovoice as a method to enable people to "identify, represent, and enhance their community through a specific photographic technique" (p. 369). Therefore, Photovoice is a form of participatory research that can be used for community needs assessment (Wang & Burris, 1997; Baker & Wang, 2006). The goals of Photovoice are to

1. Enable people to record and reflect on their community's strengths and concerns;

2. Promote critical dialogue and knowledge about personal and community issues through large and small group discussions of photographs; and

3. Reach policy makers (Wang & Burris, 1997, p. 369).

Photovoice includes the visual images provided by the photographs and is accompanied by narratives provided by the participants. Cameras are distributed to participants who share something in common, such as a social condition like homelessness or living in a particular community. There is a group facilitator who trains the group members in using the cameras, serves as a resource for information, and enables the group to work together. The participants actively engage in the analysis of the photographs, choosing representative pictures, discussing their meaning, and developing themes and patterns.

Rosen, Smith, Goodkind, and Davis-Jones (2006) used Photovoice to learn about the struggles and survival strategies as well as the service needs and barriers to remaining abstinent of 10 methadone clients over the age of 50. The project included a training session and 8 weekly 2-hour group sessions, as well as brief individual interviews before each session. During the first 6 weeks, the discussions were centered on these questions: What are we seeing? What is happening? Why does this go on? How do you feel about this? The group sessions were also used by the participants to decide on a weekly theme about which they would take pictures during the week. The two remaining sessions were used for the participants to select the photographs that they felt most accurately represented their concerns, to tell stories about what the photographs meant, and to identify the themes they felt relevant. The findings, presented by the participants to the staff of the treatment setting at a staff in-service, included the following:

- Barriers to abstinence from illegal drug use included negative influences of family and friends, neighborhood crime and violence, and transportation problems.

- Caregiving responsibilities for family members and grandchildren provided motivation to abstain from drug use.

- Methadone maintenance had a positive impact on their lives.

You can see how Photovoice can be a way to see and hear the voice of people. Photovoice has been used to explore social issues with such diverse groups as Latino adolescents in rural North Carolina (Steng et al., 2004), parenting adolescents (Stevens, 2006), chronically mentally ill (Thompson et al., 2008), chronic pain in older adults (Baker & Wang, 2006), and employment-seeking behavior of people with HIV/AIDS (Hergenrather, Rhodes, & Clark, 2006). Molloy (2007) suggests that this process is consistent with the empowerment tradition in social work because it brings groups together and enables them to move to social action through their participation in the process.

▣ QUALITATIVE RESEARCH IN A DIVERSE SOCIETY

Qualitative research studies can enhance quantitative studies. We have described in Chapters 3 and 7 the need to make questions and measures culturally equivalent. To do so requires the use of qualitative data-collection techniques such as intensive interviewing (e.g., cognitive interviewing), observing or listening (behavioral coding), and focus groups. These strategies are designed to improve the validity of the measures used in quantitative studies and, therefore, enhance the validity of the findings.

But qualitative studies go beyond just improving quantitative studies. Kagawa-Singer (2000) and Nápoles-Springer and Stewart (2006) suggest that health disparities and health care research have been too focused on the values and practices of European Americans. A narrow approach to culture discounts how those with different worldviews define problems and precludes identifying alternative methods to deliver services that might be more effective. Therefore, a broader framework that encompasses both universal factors and cultural factors can improve outcomes for diverse and underserved populations (Kagawa-Singer, 2000; Nápoles-Springer & Stewart, 2006). Similar arguments can be made about different fields, such as mental health, aging, or child welfare.

This view of the virtues of qualitative methods has a philosophical foundation. Researchers who rely on quantitative methods most often adhere to a "positivist" philosophy that seeks to find universal rules about the social world. This philosophy does not account for cultural differences, and so positivist research strategies and findings have been criticized as monocultural and Eurocentric (Kagawa-Singer, 2000; Stanfield, 1999) and gender focused (Griffin & Phoenix, 1994). The criticism is that what the researchers deem as neutral and objective is not, because the research is guided by their worldviews (Stanfield, 1999). Qualitative research allows researchers to obtain a richer and more intimate view of the social world than more structured methods. Qualitative methods provide a greater voice to the people being studied than do the rigid structures imposed by quantitative methods. Qualitative methods are therefore useful for research with diverse population groups as they focus on the meaning and interpretations ascribed to behavior and not just the behavior alone.

▣ IMPLICATIONS FOR EVIDENCE-BASED PRACTICE

There is general agreement that qualitative methods can and do provide useful research findings about practice effectiveness. As we have said in previous chapters, evidence-based practice involves integrating the best available research evidence with clinical expertise and client values and *not* just the application of empirically supported interventions (Gambrill, 2006). This means that the best research evidence needs to be integrated with information about the client learned during the course of treatment and a client's characteristics, such as the way problems may be defined by the client or how they present to the social worker, developmental and life stage, social and cultural factors, family factors, environmental factors such as stressors, and personal preferences (American Psychological Association, 2006). Qualitative methods are useful in shedding light on what is the most appropriate practice for a particular client, given a particular situation, and given the context in which it is used (Plath, 2006).

There are various ways in which qualitative methods inform practice:

• *Qualitative methods can be used to assess the design and delivery of services.* For example, Anderson-Butcher, Khairallah, and Race-Bigelow (2004) recognized that, although much of the effort around welfare reform involved strategies and interventions designed to get TANF recipients to work, there were few interventions to support recipients over the long term. To understand how participation in a support group impacted group participants, nine participants were interviewed with open-ended, nondirective questions. Anderson-Butcher et al. learned that what made a group successful included structural considerations (e.g., babysitting), facilitator characteristics (e.g., being a mediator), and group composition as well as the benefits for participants and their families.

• *Qualitative methods are useful in uncovering the process and nature of service delivery.* For example, although there is evidence to support Assertive Community Treatment (ACT) as a treatment approach with the chronically mentally ill, it has been criticized for being coercive and paternalistic in getting clients to adhere to treatment (Angell, Mahoney, & Martinez, 2006). To examine whether there was a coercive nature to

ACT, Angell et al. identified an urban program and a rural program, observed 14 providers in interactions with clients, and subsequently conducted open-ended interviews with each of the participants. Through their study, they learned how ACT providers construct problems of nonadherence, how they promote adherence in their clients, and under what conditions the strategies vary.

• *Qualitative methods can clarify clients' perceptions of interventions.* Singer (2005) asked this question: How do clients make sense of the experience of therapy (p. 269)? Singer asked clients to write weekly case notes following a question guide, conducted taped interviews, and reviewed her own notes during the data-collection period to understand the role of the client-therapist relationship in achieving outcomes.

• *These methods can help social workers understand why people in need of services do not seek help.* Lindsey et al. (2006) wanted to learn about help-seeking behaviors and depression among African American adolescent boys. They conducted interviews with 18 urban youth recruited from community mental health centers and after-school programs. Those in treatment had family members and school personnel who noted their depressive symptoms and facilitated their access to mental health services, whereas those youth not in treatment had family members who argued against seeking professional help.

The need to establish credible evidence should not be an argument for or against qualitative methods. Evidence-based practice includes anything that provides systematically collected information to inform social work practice (Pollio, 2006). Yet, some fear that the experimental methods we have described up to this point will become the only acceptable research paradigm for securing evidence about best practices. At the extreme, Denzin (2005) suggests that "the evidence-based experimental science movement, with accompanying federal legislation, threatens to deny advances in critical qualitative inquiry, including rigorous criticisms of positivist research" (pp. 109–110). Broader recognition of the value of qualitative methods will help social work practitioners avoid such a one-sided perspective on research.

ETHICAL ISSUES IN QUALITATIVE RESEARCH

Qualitative research can raise some complex ethical issues. No matter how hard the field researcher strives to study the social world naturally, leaving no traces, the act of research imposes something "unnatural" on the situation. It is up to the researcher to identify and take responsibility for the consequences of her or his involvement. Four main ethical issues arise:

• *Voluntary participation.* Ensuring that subjects are participating in a study voluntarily is not often a problem with intensive interviewing and focus group research, but it is often a point of contention in participant observation studies. Erikson (1967) argues that covert participation is, by its very nature, unethical and should not be allowed except in public settings. Covert researchers cannot anticipate the unintended consequences of their actions for research subjects. Few researchers or institutional review boards are willing to condone covert participation because it offers no way to ensure that participation by the subjects is voluntary. Even when the researcher's role is more open, interpreting the standard of voluntary participation still can be difficult. However, much field research would be impossible if the participant observer was required to request permission of everyone having some contact, no matter how minimal, with a group or setting being observed. And should the requirement of voluntary participation apply equally to every member of an organization being observed? What if the manager consents, the workers are ambivalent, and the union says no? Requiring everyone's consent would limit participant observation research to only settings without serious conflicts of interest.

- *Subject well-being.* Before beginning a new project, every field researcher should consider carefully how to avoid harm to subjects. It is not possible to avoid every theoretical possibility of harm nor to be sure that any project will cause no adverse consequences whatsoever to any individual. Direct harm to the reputations or feelings of particular individuals is what researchers must carefully avoid. It will be difficult for others to counter the interpretations offered by participant observers since findings are not verifiable and the contextual nature of the research makes it more difficult to replicate the study (Herrera, 2003). Maintaining the confidentiality of research subjects will be critical to avoiding harm to subjects. Participant observers must also avoid adversely affecting the course of events while engaged in a setting. These problems are rare in intensive interviewing and focus groups, but even there, researchers should try to identify negative feelings and help distressed subjects cope with their feelings through debriefing or referrals for professional help.

- *Identity disclosure.* Current ethical standards require informed consent of research subjects, and most would argue that this standard cannot be met in any meaningful way if researchers do not disclose fully their identity. Some complete observers may become so wrapped up in the role they are playing that they adopt not just the mannerisms but also the perspectives and goals of the regular participants and, by doing so, abandon research goals and cease to evaluate critically what they are observing. But how much disclosure about the study is necessary and how hard should researchers try to make sure that their research purposes are understood? In field research on Codependents Anonymous, Irvine (1998) found that the emphasis on anonymity and the expectations for group discussion made it difficult to disclose her identity. Less-educated subjects may not readily comprehend what a researcher is or be able to weigh the possible consequences of the research for themselves. Should researchers inform subjects if the study's interests and foci change while it is in progress? Can a balance be struck between the disclosure of critical facts and a coherent research strategy?

- *Confidentiality.* Field researchers normally use fictitious names for the characters in their reports, but doing so does not always guarantee confidentiality to their research subjects. Individuals in the setting studied may be able to identify those whose actions are described and may thus become privy to some knowledge about their colleagues or neighbors that had formerly been kept from them. Researchers should thus make every effort to expunge possible identifying material from published information and to alter unimportant aspects of a description when necessary to prevent identity disclosure. In any case, no field research project should begin if some participants clearly will suffer serious harm by being identified in project publications.

Online research and Photovoice add unique twists to these ethical issues. The large number of discussion groups and bulletin boards on the Internet has stimulated much research. Such research can violate the principles of voluntary participation and identity disclosure when researchers participate in discussions and record and analyze text but do not identify themselves as researchers (Jesnadum, 2000).

With Photovoice, the research participants are actively involved in gathering data as they take photos to address different topics. As part of the informed consent process, participants should be told that the researchers are legally required to report to legal authorities photos revealing child or elder abuse or the likely prospect of harm to participants themselves or to others. Participants might need to be discouraged from taking identifiable pictures of people, and if they do, then they will need to learn about methods to obtain consent prior to taking the pictures. The participant should also know that the researcher legally owns the photographs, though part of the Photovoice process is that the researcher and the participants decide jointly which photographs to make public; nonetheless, ownership and publishing of the photos may become a source of conflict.

These ethical issues cannot be evaluated independently. The final decision to proceed must be made after weighing the relative benefits and risks to participants. Except for studies involving covert participation, few qualitative research projects will be barred by consideration of these ethical issues. The more important concern for researchers is to identify the ethically troublesome aspects of their proposed research and resolve them before the project begins and to act on new ethical issues as they come up during the project. Combining methods is often the best strategy.

▣ CONCLUSION

Qualitative research allows the careful investigator to obtain a richer and more intimate view of the social world than would be possible with more structured methods. It is not hard to understand why so many qualitative studies have become classics in the sociological literature. And the emphases in qualitative research on inductive reasoning and incremental understanding help to stimulate and inform other research approaches. Exploratory research to chart the dimensions of previously unstudied social settings and intensive investigations of the subjective meanings that motivate individual action are particularly well-served by the techniques of participant observation, intensive interviewing, and focus groups.

The characteristics that make qualitative research techniques so appealing restrict their use to a limited set of research problems. It is not possible to draw representative samples for study using participant observation, and for this reason the generalizability of any particular field study's results cannot really be known. Only the accumulation of findings from numerous qualitative studies permits confident generalization, but here again the time and effort required to collect and analyze the data make it unlikely that many field research studies will be replicated.

Even when qualitative researchers make more of an effort to replicate key studies, the need to develop and ground explanations inductively in the observations made in a particular setting hamper comparison of findings. Measurement reliability is thereby hindered, as are systematic tests for the validity of key indicators and formal tests for causal connections.

In the final analysis, qualitative research involves a mode of thinking and investigating different from that used in experimental and survey research. Both approaches can help social scientists learn about the social world; the proficient researcher must be ready to use either. Qualitative data are often supplemented with counts of characteristics or activities. And as you have already seen, quantitative data are often enriched with written comments and observations, and focus groups have become a common tool of survey researchers seeking to develop their questionnaires. Thus the distinction between qualitative and quantitative research techniques is not always clear-cut, and combining methods is often a good idea.

KEY TERMS

Covert participation	Reactive effects
Focus groups	Saturation point
Intensive interviewing	Systematic observation
Participant observation	Theoretical sampling
Photovoice	Thick description

HIGHLIGHTS

• Qualitative methods are most useful in exploring new issues, investigating hard-to-study groups, and determining the meaning people give to their lives and actions. In addition, most social research projects can be improved in some respects by taking advantage of qualitative techniques.

• Qualitative researchers tend to develop ideas inductively, try to understand the social context and sequential nature of attitudes and actions, and explore the subjective meanings that participants attach to events. They rely primarily on participant observation, intensive interviewing, and focus groups.

• Participant observers may adopt one of several roles for a particular research project. Each role represents a different balance between observing and participating. Many field researchers prefer a moderate role, participating as well as observing in a group, but acknowledging publicly the researcher role. Such a role avoids ethical issues posed by covert participating while still allowing the insights into the social world derived from participating directly in it. The role that the participant observer chooses should be based on an evaluation of the problems likely to arise from reactive effects and the ethical dilemmas of covert participating.

- Systematic observation techniques quantify the observational process to allow more systematic comparison between cases and greater generalizability.

- Field researchers must develop strategies for entering the field, developing and maintaining relations in the field, sampling, and recording and analyzing data. Selection of sites or other units to study may reflect an emphasis on typical cases, deviant cases, or critical cases that can provide more information than others. Sampling techniques commonly used within sites or in selecting interviewees in field research include theoretical sampling, purposive sampling, snowball sampling, quota sampling, and, in special circumstances, random selection.

- Recording and analyzing notes is a crucial step in field research. Jottings are used as brief reminders about events in the field, while daily logs are useful to chronicle the researcher's activities. Detailed field notes should be recorded and analyzed daily. Analysis of the notes can guide refinement of methods used in the field and of the concepts, indicators, and models developed to explain what has been observed.

- Intensive interviews involve open-ended questions and follow-up probes, with specific question content and order varying from one interview to another. Intensive interviews can supplement participant observation data.

- Focus groups use elements of participant observation and intensive interviewing. They can increase the validity of attitude measurement by revealing what people say when presenting their opinions in a group context, instead of the artificial one-on-one interview setting.

- Four main ethical issues in field research that should be given particular attention concern voluntary participation, subject well-being, identity disclosure, and confidentiality.

DISCUSSION QUESTIONS

1. Define and describe participant observation, intensive interviewing, and focus groups. What features do these research designs share? How are they different?

2. Discuss the relative merits of complete observation, participant observation, and covert participation. What are the ethical considerations inherent in each?

3. Compare and contrast intensive interviewing with interviews used in survey research. Under what circumstances might you choose intensive interviewing techniques? What are the potential difficulties of using this type of research?

CRITIQUING RESEARCH

1. Read and summarize one of the qualitative studies on the student Web site (http://www.sagepub.com/fswrstudy). Review and critique the study using the article review questions presented in Appendix B. What questions are answered by the study? What questions are raised for further investigation?

MAKING RESEARCH ETHICAL

1. In journalism, paying for information is a "cardinal sin" because journalists are "indoctrinated" with the notion that they are observers. They are trained to report on situations but not to influence a situation. This is what many scholars believe a researcher's role should be. Does paying for information unduly influence the truthfulness of the information being sought? Do you believe some people will say anything to earn money? What are your thoughts on paying for information? What if you were investigating the problems faced by families living below the poverty level and, during an interview, you noticed that the family refrigerator and cupboards were empty and the baby was crying from hunger? What is the ethical reaction? If you believe the most ethical response would be to provide food or money for food, is it fair that there is another family next door in the same condition that did not happen to be on your interview list? How should gratuities be handled?

2. Should any requirements be imposed on researchers who seek to study other cultures in order to ensure that procedures are appropriate and interpretations are culturally sensitive? What practices would you suggest for cross-cultural researchers in order to ensure that ethical guidelines are followed? (Consider the wording of consent forms and the procedures for gaining voluntary cooperation.)

3. Discuss the ethical issues you would face in creating a focus group consisting of agency clients. Develop a written statement to recruit participants.

DEVELOPING A RESEARCH PROPOSAL

Choose either to conduct a qualitative study or to add a qualitative component to your proposed study. Pick the method that seems most likely to help answer the research question for the overall project.

1. For a participant observation component, propose an observational plan that would answer your research question. Present in your proposal the following information about your plan:
    a. Choose a site and justify its selection in terms of its likely value for the research.
    b. Choose a role along the participant-observation continuum and justify your choice.
    c. Describe access procedures and note any likely problems.
    d. Discuss how you will develop and maintain relations in the site.
    e. Review any sampling issues.
    f. Present an overview of the way in which you will analyze the data you collect.

2. For an intensive interview component, propose a focus for the intensive interviews that you believe will add the most to your research question. Present in your proposal the following information about your plan:
    a. Present and justify a method for selecting individuals to interview.
    b. Write out several introductory biographical questions and five "grand tour" questions for your interview schedule.

c. List different probes you may use.

d. Present and justify at least two follow-up questions for one of your grand tour questions.

To assist you in completing the Web exercises below and to gain a better under-standing of the chapter's contents, please access the study site at http://www.sagepub .com/fswrstudy where you will find the Web exercises reproduced with suggested links, along with self-quizzes, e-flash cards, interactive exercises, journal articles, and other valuable resources.

WEB EXERCISES

1. Go to the Social Science Information Gateway (SOSIG; at http://sosig.esrc.bris.ac .uk). Choose Research Tools and Methods and then Qualitative Methods. Now choose three or four interesting sites to find out more about field research. Explore the sites to find out what information they provide regarding field research, what kinds of projects are being done that involve field research, and the purposes for which specific field research methods are being used.

2. You have been asked to do field research on the World Wide Web's impact on the socialization of children in today's world. The first part of the project involves your writing a compare-and-contrast report on the differences between how you and your generation were socialized as children and the way children today are being socialized. Collect your data by surfing the Web "as if you were a kid." Using any of the major search engines, explore the Web within the Kids or Children subject heading, keeping field notes on what you observe. Write a brief report based on the data you have collected. How has the Web affected child socialization in comparison with when you were a child?

CHAPTER 9

Qualitative Data Analysis

Features of Qualitative Data Analysis
  Qualitative Data Analysis as an Art
  Qualitative Compared With
    Quantitative Data Analysis

Techniques of Qualitative Data Analysis
  Documentation
  Conceptualization, Coding, and
    Categorizing
  Examining Relationships and
    Displaying Data
  Authenticating Conclusions
  Reflexivity

Alternatives in Qualitative
  Data Analysis
  Ethnography
  Qualitative Comparative Analysis

Narrative Analysis
Grounded Theory

Computer-Assisted Qualitative
  Data Analysis

Content Analysis

Ethics in Qualitative Data Analysis

Conclusion

Key Terms

Highlights

Discussion Questions

Critiquing Research

Making Research Ethical

Developing a Research Proposal

Web Exercises

*I was at lunch standing in line and he [another male student] came up
to my face and started saying stuff and then he pushed me. I said . . .
I'm cool with you, I'm your friend and then he push[ed] me again and
[started] calling me names. I told him to stop pushing me and then he
push[ed] me hard and said something about my mom. And then he hit
me, and I hit him back. After he fell I started kicking him.*

—Morrill, Yalda, Adelman, Musheno, & Bejarano, 2000, p. 521

This statement was by a student writing an in-class essay about conflicts in which he had participated. But then, you already knew that such conflicts are common in many high schools, so perhaps it will be reassuring to know that this statement was elicited by a team of social scientists who were studying conflicts in high schools to better understand their origins and to inform prevention policies.

Does it surprise you that the text excerpt above is data used in a qualitative research project? The first difference between qualitative and quantitative data analysis is that the data to be analyzed are text rather than numbers, at least when the analysis first begins. In this chapter, we present the features that most qualitative data analyses share. You will learn that there is no one way to analyze textual data. We discuss some of the different types of qualitative data analysis before focusing on content analysis, an approach to analyzing text that relies on quantitative techniques. We illustrate how computer programs are used for qualitative data analysis and how they blur the distinctions between quantitative and qualitative approaches to textual analysis.

▣ FEATURES OF QUALITATIVE DATA ANALYSIS

The distinctive features of qualitative data collection methods are also reflected in the methods used to analyze the data. The focus on text, on qualitative data rather than on numbers, is the most important feature of qualitative analysis. The "texts" that qualitative researchers analyze are most often transcripts of interviews or notes from participant observation sessions, but text can also refer to pictures or images that the researcher examines.

What can the qualitative data analyst learn from a text? Here qualitative analysts may have two different goals. Some view analysis of a text as a way to understand what participants really thought, felt, or did in some situation or at some point in time. The text becomes a way to get "behind the numbers" that are recorded in a quantitative analysis to see the richness of real social experience. Other qualitative researchers have adopted a hermeneutic perspective on texts—that is, a perspective that views text as an interpretation that can never be judged true or false. The text is only one possible interpretation among many (Patton, 2002).

One of the important differences between qualitative and quantitative data analysis is in the priority given to the views of the researcher and to those of the subjects of the research. Qualitative data analysts seek to describe their textual data in ways that capture the setting or people who produced this text in their own terms, rather than in terms of predefined measures and hypotheses. What this means is that qualitative data analysis tends to be inductive—drawing from their data, analysts identify important categories in the data, as well as patterns and relationships, through a process of discovery. There are often no predefined measures or hypotheses.

Good qualitative data analyses are also distinguished by their focus on the interrelated aspects of the setting or group, or person, under investigation; the focus is on the case as a whole rather than breaking the whole into separate parts. The whole is understood to be greater than the sum of its parts, and so the social context of events, thoughts, and actions becomes essential for interpretation. Within this framework, it does not really make sense to focus on two variables out of an interacting set of influences and test the relationship between just those two.

Qualitative data analysis is an iterative and reflexive process that begins as data are being collected rather than after data collection has ceased (Stake, 1995). Next to the field notes or interview transcripts, the qualitative analyst jots down ideas about the meaning of the text and how it might relate to other issues. This process of reading through the data and interpreting them continues throughout the project. The analyst adjusts the data-collection process when it begins to appear that additional concepts need to be investigated or new relationships explored. This process is termed **progressive focusing** (Parlett & Hamilton, 1976).

Progressive focusing The process by which a qualitative analyst interacts with the data and gradually refines his or her focus.

In the 1970s, Anderson (2007) was interested in how people organized themselves and how this resulted in a local system of social stratification. He conducted an ethnographic study of life at Jelly's Bar, a street corner bar, where he observed 55 African American men. In his memoir about this study, Anderson describes the progressive focusing process:

> Throughout the study, I also wrote conceptual memos to myself to help sort out my findings. Usually no more than a page long, they represented theoretical insights that emerged from my engagement with the data in my field notes. As I gained tenable hypotheses and propositions, I began to listen and observe selectively focusing on those events that I thought might bring me alive to my research interests and concerns. This method of dealing with the information I was receiving amounted to a kind of dialogue with the data, sifting out ideas, weighing new notions against the reality with which I was faced there on the streets and back at my desk. (p. 51)

Qualitative Data Analysis as an Art

If you find yourself longing for the certainty of predefined measures and deductively derived hypotheses, you are beginning to understand the difference between setting out to analyze data quantitatively and planning to do so with a qualitative approach in mind. The process of qualitative data analysis is even described by some as involving as much "art" as science—as a "dance," in the words of Miller and Crabtree (1999, p. 139). The "dance" of qualitative data analysis is represented in Exhibit 9.1, which captures the alternation between immersion in the text to identify meanings and editing the text to create categories and codes. The process involves three different modes of reading the text:

EXHIBIT 9.1	**Dance of Qualitative Analysis**

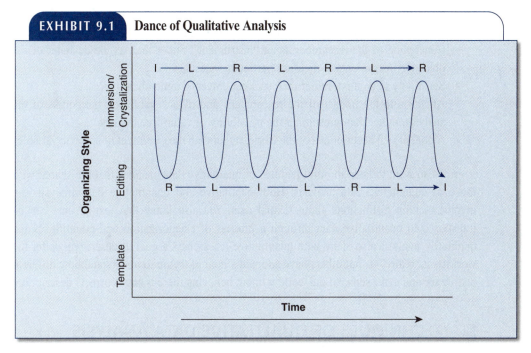

Source: Miller & Crabtree (1999, p. 139, Figure 7.1). Based on Addison (1999).

1. When the researcher reads the text *literally* (L in Exhibit 9.1), the focus is on its literal content and form, so the text "leads" the dance.

2. When the researcher reads the text *reflexively* (R), the researcher focuses on how his or her own orientation shapes interpretations and focus. Now, the researcher leads the dance.

3. When the researcher reads the text *interpretively* (I), the researcher tries to construct his or her own interpretation of what the text means.

In this way, analyzing text involves both inductive and deductive processes: The researcher generates concepts and linkages between them based on reading the text and also checks the text to see whether the concepts and interpretations are reflected in it.

Qualitative Compared With Quantitative Data Analysis

With these points in mind, let's review the ways in which qualitative data analysis differs from quantitative analysis (Denzin & Lincoln, 2000; Patton, 2002):

- A focus on meanings, rather than on quantifiable phenomena
- Collection of many data on a few cases, rather than few data on many cases

- Study in depth and detail without predetermined categories or directions, rather than emphasis on analyses and categories determined in advance
- Conception of the researcher as an "instrument," rather than as the designer of the objective instruments to measure particular variables
- Sensitivity to context, rather than seeking universal generalizations
- Attention to the impact of the researcher's and others' values on the course of the analysis, rather than presuming the possibility of value-free inquiry
- A goal of rich descriptions of the world, rather than measurement of specific variables

You also want to keep in mind features of qualitative data analysis that are shared with those of quantitative data analysis. Both qualitative and quantitative data analysis can involve making distinctions about textual data. You also know that textual data can be transposed to quantitative data through a process of categorization and counting. Some qualitative analysts also share with quantitative researchers a goal of describing better the world as it "really" is, but others have adopted a goal of trying to understand how different people see and make sense of the world without believing there is any "correct" description.

TECHNIQUES OF QUALITATIVE DATA ANALYSIS

The following phases are shared by most approaches to qualitative data analysis:

1. Documentation of the data and the process of data collection

2. Organization/categorization of the data into concepts

3. Connection of the data to show how one concept may influence another

4. Corroboration/legitimization by evaluating alternative explanations and disconfirming evidence and searching for negative cases

5. Representing the account (reporting the findings)

The analysis of qualitative research notes begins in the field at the time of observation, interviewing, or both, as the researcher identifies problems and concepts that appear likely to help in understanding the situation. Simply reading the notes or transcripts is an important step in the analytic process. Researchers should make frequent notes in the margins to identify important statements and to propose ways of coding the data.

An interim stage may consist of listing the concepts reflected in the notes and diagramming the relationships among concepts (Maxwell, 1996). In a large project, weekly team meetings are an important part of this process. Miller (1999) described this process in her study of neighborhood police officers. Her research team met to go over their field notes and resolve points of confusion, as well as to dialogue with other skilled researchers who helped to identify emerging concepts:

The fieldwork team met weekly to talk about situations that were unclear and to troubleshoot any problems. We also made use of peer-debriefing techniques. Here, multiple colleagues, who were familiar with qualitative data analysis but not involved in our research, participated in preliminary analysis of our findings. (p. 233)

This process continues throughout the project and should assist in refining concepts during the report-writing phase, long after data collection has ceased.

Documentation

The data for a qualitative study most often are notes jotted down in the field or during an interview—from which the original comments, observations, and feelings are reconstructed—or text transcribed from audiotapes. "The basic data are these observations and conversations, the actual words of people reproduced to the best of my ability from the field notes" (Diamond, 1992, p. 7). What to do with all this material? Many field research projects have slowed to a halt because a novice researcher becomes overwhelmed by the quantity of information that has been collected. A 1-hour interview can generate 20 to 25 pages of single-spaced text (Kvale, 1996). Analysis is less daunting, however, if the process is broken into smaller steps.

The first formal analytical step is documentation. The various contacts, interviews, written documents, and whatever it was that preserves a record of what happened all need to be saved and listed. Documentation is critical to qualitative research for several reasons: It is essential for keeping track of what will be a rapidly growing volume of notes, tapes, and documents; it provides a way of developing an outline for the analytic process; and it encourages ongoing conceptualizing and strategizing about the text.

Conceptualization, Coding, and Categorizing

Identifying and refining important concepts is a key part of the iterative process of qualitative research. Sometimes conceptualization begins with a simple observation that is interpreted directly, "pulled apart," and then put back together more meaningfully. Stake (1995) provides an example about a student in a school he studied:

When Adam ran a pushbroom into the feet of the children nearby, I jumped to conclusions about his interactions with other children: aggressive, teasing, arresting. Of course, just a few minutes earlier I had seen him block the children climbing the steps in a similar moment of smiling bombast. So I was aggregating, and testing my unrealized hypotheses about what kind of kid he was, not postponing my interpreting. . . . My disposition was to keep my eyes on him. (p. 74)

More often, analytic insights are tested against new observations, the initial statement of problems and concepts is refined, the researcher then collects more data and interacts with it again, and the process continues. Anderson (2007) recounts how his conceptualization of social stratification at Jelly's Bar developed over a long period of time:

> I could see the social pyramid, how certain guys would group themselves and say in effect, "I'm here and you're there." . . . I made sense of these "crowds" as the "respectables," the "non-respectables," and the "near-respectables." . . . Inside, such non-respectables might sit on the crates, but if a respectable came along and wanted to sit there, the lower status person would have to move. (pp. 42–43)

But this initial conceptualization changed with experience, as Anderson (2007) realized that the participants used other terms to differentiate social status: "winehead," "hoodlum," and "regular" (p. 46). What did they mean by these terms? "The regulars basically valued 'decency.' They associated decency with conventionality but also with 'working for a living,' or having a 'visible means of support'" (p. 47). In this way, Anderson progressively refined his concept as he gained experience in the setting.

Examining Relationships and Displaying Data

Examining relationships is the centerpiece of the analytic process because it allows the researcher to move from simple description of the people and settings to explanations of why things happened as they did with those people in that setting. The process of examining relationships can be captured in a **matrix** that shows how different concepts are connected or perhaps what causes are linked with what effects.

Exhibit 9.2 displays a matrix used to capture the relationship between the extent to which stakeholders in a new program had something important at stake in the program and the

EXHIBIT 9.2	Coding Form for Relationships: Stakeholders' Stakes	
Estimate of Various Stakeholders' Inclination Toward the Program		
How high are the stakes for various primary stakeholders?	Favorable	Neutral or Unknown	Antagonistic
High			
Moderate			
Low			

Source: Patton (2002, p. 472).

Note: Construct illustrative case studies for each cell based on fieldwork.

researcher's estimate of their favorability toward the program. Each cell of the matrix was to be filled in with a summary of an illustrative case study. In other matrix analyses, quotes might be included in the cells to represent the opinions of these different stakeholders, or the number of cases of each type might appear in the cells. The possibilities are almost endless. Keeping this approach in mind will generate many fruitful ideas for structuring a qualitative data analysis.

The simple relationships that are identified with a matrix like that shown in Exhibit 9.2 can be examined and then extended to create a more complex causal model (see Exhibit 9.3). Such a model represents the multiple relationships among the constructs identified in a qualitative analysis as important for explaining some outcome. A great deal of analysis must precede the construction of such a model, with careful attention to the identification of important variables and the evidence that suggests connections between them.

Authenticating Conclusions

No set standards exist for evaluating the validity or "authenticity" of conclusions in a qualitative study, but the need to consider carefully the evidence and methods on which conclusions are based

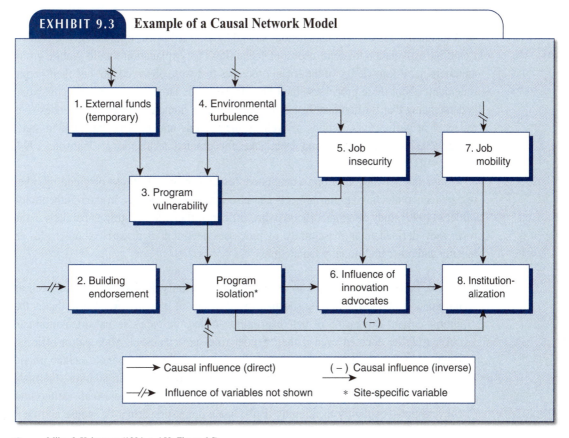

EXHIBIT 9.3 **Example of a Causal Network Model**

Source: Miles & Huberman (1994, p. 159, Figure 6.5).

is just as great as with other types of research. Individual items of information can be assessed in terms of at least three criteria (Becker, 1958):

- *How credible was the informant?* Were statements made by someone with whom the researcher had a relationship of trust or by someone the researcher had just met? Did the informant have reason to lie? If the statements do not seem to be trustworthy as indicators of actual events, can they be used at least to help understand the informant's perspective?

- *Were statements made in response to the researcher's questions or were they spontaneous?* Spontaneous statements are more likely to indicate what would have been said had the researcher not been present.

- *How does the presence or absence of the researcher or the researcher's informant influence the actions and statements of other group members?* Reactivity to being observed can never be ruled out as a possible explanation for some directly observed social phenomenon. However, if the researcher carefully compares what the informant says goes on when the researcher is not present, what the researcher observes directly, and what other group members say about their normal practices, the extent of reactivity can be assessed to some extent.

A qualitative researcher's conclusions should be assessed by his or her ability to provide a credible explanation for some aspect of social life. That explanation should capture group members' **tacit knowledge** of the social processes that were observed, not just their verbal statements about these processes. Tacit knowledge—"the largely unarticulated, contextual understanding that is often manifested in nods, silences, humor, and naughty nuances"—is reflected in participants' actions as well as their words and in what they fail to state, but nonetheless feel deeply and even take for granted (Altheide & Johnson, 1994, pp. 492–493).

Comparing conclusions from a qualitative research project to those obtained by other researchers conducting similar projects can also increase confidence in their authenticity. Miller's (1999) study of neighborhood police officers (NPOs) found striking parallels in the ways they defined their masculinity to processes reported in research about males in nursing and other traditionally female jobs:

> In part, male NPOs construct an exaggerated masculinity so that they are not seen as feminine as they carry out the social-work functions of policing. Related to this is the almost defiant expression of heterosexuality, so that the men's sexual orientation can never truly be doubted even if their gender roles are contested. Male patrol officers' language—such as their use of terms like "pansy police" to connote neighborhood police officers—served to affirm their own heterosexuality. . . . In addition, the male officers, but not the women, deliberately wove their heterosexual status into conversations, explicitly mentioning their female domestic partner or spouse and their

children. This finding is consistent with research conducted in the occupational field. The studies reveal that men in female dominated occupations, such as teachers, librarians, and pediatricians, over-reference their heterosexual status to ensure that others will not think they are gay. (p. 222)

Reflexivity

Confidence in the conclusions from a field research study is also strengthened by an honest and informative account about how the researcher interacted with subjects in the field, what problems he or she encountered, and how these problems were or were not resolved. Such a "natural history" of the development of the evidence, termed reflexivity, enables others to evaluate the findings. Such an account is important, first and foremost, because of the evolving and variable nature of field research: To an important extent, the researcher "makes up" the method in the context of a particular investigation, rather than applying standard procedures that are specified before the investigation begins.

Qualitative data analysts, more often than quantitative researchers, display real sensitivity to how a social situation or process is interpreted from a particular background and set of values and not simply from the situation (Altheide & Johnson, 1994). Researchers are only human, after all, and must rely on their own senses and process all information through their own minds. By reporting how and why they think they did what they did, they can help others determine whether or how the researchers' perspectives influenced their conclusions. "There should be clear 'tracks' indicating the attempt [to show the hand of the ethnographer] has been made" (Altheide & Johnson, 1994, p. 493).

Anderson (2007) illustrates the type of "tracks" that an ethnographer makes as well as how he can describe those tracks. After starting to observe at Jelly's, Anderson's "tracks" led to Herman:

> After spending a couple of weeks at Jelly's I met Herman and I felt that our meeting marked a big achievement. We would come to know each other well. . . . something of an informal leader at Jelly's . . . We were becoming friends . . . He seemed to genuinely like me, and he was one person I could feel comfortable with. (p. 37)

So we learn that Anderson's (2007) observations were to be shaped, in part, by Herman's perspective. We also learn that Anderson was debriefed and questioned by his fellow students and friends at the University of Chicago and that their questions outside the bar helped to shape his analysis: "By relating my experiences to my fellow students, I began to develop a coherent perspective, or a 'story' of the place which complemented the accounts that I had detailed in my accumulating field notes" (p. 37). In this way, the outcome of Anderson's analysis of qualitative data resulted, in part, from the way in which he "played his role" as a researcher and participant, not just from the setting itself.

▣ ALTERNATIVES IN QUALITATIVE DATA ANALYSIS

The qualitative data analyst can choose from many interesting alternative approaches. Of course, the research question under investigation should shape the selection of an analytic approach, but the researcher's preferences and experiences inevitably also will have an important influence on the method chosen. The alternative approaches presented here, traditional ethnography, qualitative comparative analysis, narrative analysis, and grounded theory, give you a good sense of the different possibilities, but be forewarned that these four were selected from a long and growing list (Patton, 2002).

Ethnography

Ethnography is the study of a culture or cultures that some group of people share (Van Maanen, 1995). As a method, it usually is meant to refer to the process of participant observation by a single investigator who immerses himself or herself in the group for a long period of time (often 1 or more years). But there are no particular methodological techniques associated with ethnography, other than just "being there." The analytic process relies on the thoroughness and insight of the researcher to "tell us like it is" in the setting as he or she experienced it.

Code of the Street, Elijah Anderson's (1999) award-winning study of Philadelphia's inner city, captures the flavor of this approach:

> My primary aim in this work is to render ethnographically the social and cultural dynamics of the interpersonal violence that is currently undermining the quality of life of too many urban neighborhoods. . . . How do the people of the setting perceive their situation? What assumptions do they bring to their decision making? (pp. 10–11)

Like most traditional ethnographers, Anderson (1999) describes his concern with being "as objective as possible" and using his training as other ethnographers do, "to look for and to recognize underlying assumptions, their own and those of their subjects, and to try to override the former and uncover the latter" (p. 11).

From analysis of the data obtained in these ways, a rich description emerges of life in the inner city. Although we often do not "hear" the residents speak, we feel the community's pain in Anderson's (1999) description of "the aftermath of death":

> When a young life is cut down, almost everyone goes into mourning. The first thing that happens is that a crowd gathers about the site of the shooting or the incident. The police then arrive, drawing more of a crowd. Since such a death often occurs close to the victim's house, his mother or his close relatives and friends may be on the scene of the killing. When they arrive, the women and girls often wail and moan, crying out their grief for all to hear, while the young men simply look on, in studied silence. . . . Soon the ambulance arrives. (p. 138)

Anderson (1999) uses these descriptions as a foundation on which he develops the key concepts in his analysis, such as "code of the street":

> The "code of the street" is not the goal or product of any individual's actions but is the fabric of everyday life, a vivid and pressing milieu within which all local residents must shape their personal routines, income strategies, and orientations to schooling, as well as their mating, parenting, and neighbor relations. (p. 326)

This rich ethnographic tradition is being abandoned by some qualitative data analysts, however. Many have become skeptical of the ability of social scientists to perceive the social world in a way that is not distorted by their own subjective biases or to receive impressions from the actors in that social world that are not altered by the fact of being studied (Van Maanen, 2002). As a result, both specific techniques and alternative approaches to qualitative data analysis have proliferated.

Qualitative Comparative Analysis

Cress and Snow (2000) asked a series of specific questions about social movement outcomes in their study of homeless social movement organizations (SMOs). They collected qualitative data about 15 SMOs in eight cities. A content analysis of newspaper articles indicated that these cities represented a range of outcomes, and the SMOs within them were also relatively accessible to Cress and Snow due to prior contacts. In each of these cities, Cress and Snow used a snowball sampling strategy to identify the homeless SMOs and the various supporters, antagonists, and significant organizational bystanders with whom they interacted. They then gathered information from representatives of these organizations, including churches, other activist organizations, police departments, mayors' offices, service providers, federal agencies, and, of course, the SMOs.

To answer their research questions, Cress and Snow (2000) needed to operationalize each of the various conditions that they believed might affect movement outcomes, using coding procedures that were much more systematic than those often employed in qualitative research. For example, Cress and Snow defined sympathetic allies operationally as

> the presence of one or more city council members who were supportive of local homeless mobilization. This was demonstrated by attending homeless SMO meetings and rallies and by taking initiatives to city agencies on behalf of the SMO. (Seven of the 15 SMOs had such allies.) (p. 1078)

Cress and Snow (2000) also chose a structured method of analysis, **qualitative comparative analysis**, to assess how the various conditions influenced SMO outcomes. This procedure identifies the combination of factors that had to be present across multiple cases to produce a particular outcome (Ragin, 1987). Cress and Snow explain why this strategy was appropriate for their analysis:

[Qualitative comparative analysis] is conjunctural in its logic, examining the various ways in which specified factors interact and combine with one another to yield particular outcomes. This increases the prospect of discerning diversity and identifying different pathways that lead to an outcome of interest and thus makes this mode of analysis especially applicable to situations with complex patterns of interaction among the specified conditions. (p. 1079)

Exhibit 9.4 summarizes the results of much of Cress and Snow's (2000) analysis. It shows that homeless SMOs that were coded as organizationally viable and that used disruptive tactics, had sympathetic political allies, and presented a coherent diagnosis and program in response to the problem they were protesting were likely to achieve all four valued outcomes: representation, resources, protection of basic rights, and some form of tangible relief. Some other combinations of the conditions were associated with the increased likelihood of achieving some valued outcomes, but most of these alternatives had positive effects less frequently.

EXHIBIT 9.4	Multiple Pathways to Outcomes and Level of Impact	
Pathways	Outcomes	Impact
1. VIABLE * DISRUPT * ALLIES * DIAG * PROG	Representation, Resources, Rights, and Relief	Very strong
2. VIABLE * disrupt * CITY * DIAG * PROG	Representation and Rights	Strong
3. VIABLE * ALLIES * CITY * DIAG * PROG	Resources and Relief	Moderate
4. viable * DISRUPT * allies * diag * PROG	Relief	Weak
5. viable * allies * city * diag * PROG	Relief	Weak
6. viable * disrupt * ALLIES * CITY * diag * prog	Resources	Weak

Source: Cress & Snow (2000, p.1097, Table 6).
Note: Uppercase letters indicate the presence of a condition and lowercase letters indicate the absence of a condition. Conditions not in the equation are considered irrelevant. Multiplication signs (*) are read as "and."

The qualitative textual data on which the codes were based indicate how particular combinations of conditions exerted their influence. For example, one set of conditions that increased the likelihood of achieving increased protection of basic rights for homeless people included avoiding disruptive tactics in cities that were more responsive to the SMOs. Cress and Snow (2000) use a quote from a local SMO leader to explain this process:

We were going to set up a picket, but then we got calls from two people who were the co-chairs of the Board of Directors. They have like 200 restaurants. And they said, "Hey, we're not bad guys, can we sit down and talk?" We had been set on picketing. . . . Then we got to thinking, wouldn't it be better . . . if they co-drafted those things [rights guidelines] with us? So that's what we asked them to do. We had a work meeting, and we hammered out the guidelines. (p. 1089)

Narrative Analysis

Narrative "displays the goals and intentions of human actors; it makes individuals, cultures, societies, and historical epochs comprehensible as wholes" (Richardson, 1995, p. 200). **Narrative analysis** focuses on "the story itself" and seeks to preserve the integrity of personal biographies or a series of events that cannot adequately be understood in terms of their discrete elements (Riessman, 2002). The coding for a narrative analysis is typical of the narratives as a whole, rather than of the different elements within them. The coding strategy revolves around reading the stories and classifying them into general patterns.

For example, Lietz (2006, 2007) conducted in-depth interviews with six families who were at high risk of poor family functioning yet were functioning quite well, which she labeled as "resilience." She wanted to uncover the meaning of resilience from the stories these families told her. She identified five stages of reactions to difficulties that included survival, adaptation, acceptance, growing stronger, and helping others that families experienced, but she also learned that families could progress back and forth in these stages. In addition to these five stages, she found that there were 10 strengths that families relied on and that different strengths were associated with different stages.

Lietz (2007) defines survival as "a time at which these families took one day at a time just trying to figure out how to keep the family going" (p. 148). She describes an interview with parents whose son was diagnosed with leukemia:

The tough things in life hadn't hit us until really our daughter was a little bit older . . . but I think our son's the real kicker. That was real hard . . . it was touch and go on whether he was going to live. He had a bad case. . . . When I think about my son's thing . . . I learned how to get through life one day at a time. It was like, okay, well tomorrow we are going for treatment. Am I going to worry about this all night about what could of happened or can I go and get this done? (p. 149)

Lietz (2007) summarizes her classification of the steps of family resilience and their relationship with specific family strengths in a table. How does such an analysis contribute to our understanding of family resilience? Much of the literature has suggested that the more risks a family faces, the poorer the functioning; therefore, social work interventions have often focused on reducing risk factors (Lietz, 2007). But Lietz concludes that these findings suggest that teaching families to maximize their strengths and build new strengths may be an effective model of intervention.

Grounded Theory

Theory development occurs continually in qualitative data analysis (Coffey & Atkinson, 1996). The goal of many qualitative researchers is to create **grounded theory**—that is, to inductively build a systematic theory that is "grounded" in, or based on, the observations. The observations are summarized into conceptual categories, which are tested directly in the research setting with more observations. Over time, as the conceptual categories are refined and linked, a theory evolves (Glaser & Strauss, 1967; Huberman & Miles, 1994).

As observation, interviewing, and reflection continue, researchers refine their definitions of problems and concepts and select indicators. They can then check the frequency and distribution of phenomena: How many people made a particular type of comment? How often did social interaction lead to arguments? Social system models may then be developed, which specify the relationships among different phenomena. These models are modified as researchers gain experience in the setting. For the final analysis, the researchers check their models carefully against their notes and make a concerted attempt to discover negative evidence that might suggest the model is incorrect.

🔲 COMPUTER-ASSISTED QUALITATIVE DATA ANALYSIS

The analysis process can be enhanced in various ways by using a computer. Programs designed for qualitative data can speed up the analysis process, make it easier for researchers to experiment with different codes, test different hypotheses about relationships, and facilitate diagrams of emerging theories and preparation of research reports (Coffey & Atkinson, 1996; Richards & Richards, 1994). The steps involved in **computer-assisted qualitative data analysis** parallel those used traditionally to analyze such text as notes, documents, or interview transcripts: preparation, coding, analysis, and reporting. We use two of the most popular programs to illustrate these steps: HyperRESEARCH and QSR NVivo.

Text preparation begins with typing or scanning text in a word processor or, with NVivo, directly into the program's rich text editor. NVivo will create or import a rich text file. HyperRESEARCH requires that your text be saved as a text file (as ASCII in most word processing programs) before you transfer it into the analysis program. HyperRESEARCH expects your text data to be stored in separate files corresponding to each unique case, such as an interview with one subject.

Coding the text involves categorizing particular text segments. This is the foundation of much qualitative analysis. Either program allows you to assign a code to any segment of text (in HyperRESEARCH, you click on the first and last words to select text; in NVivo, you drag through the characters to select them). You can make up codes as you go through a document and assign codes that you have already developed to text segments. Exhibits 9.5a and 9.5b show the screens that appear in the two programs at the coding stage when a particular text segment is being labeled. You can also have the programs "autocode" text by identifying a word or phrase that should always receive the same code or, in NVivo, by coding each section identified by the style of the rich text document—for example, each question or speaker (of course, you should carefully check the results of autocoding). Both programs also let you examine the coded text "in context"—embedded in its place in the original document.

In qualitative data analysis, coding is not a one-time-only or one-code-only procedure. Both HyperRESEARCH and NVivo allow you to be inductive and holistic in your coding: You can revise codes as you go along, assign multiple codes to text segments, and link your own comments (memos) to text segments. In NVivo, you can work "live" with the coded text to alter coding or create new, more subtle categories. You can also place hyperlinks to other documents in the project or any multimedia files outside it.

Analysis focuses on reviewing cases or text segments with similar codes and examining relationships among different codes. You may decide to combine codes into larger concepts. You may specify additional codes to capture more fully the variation among cases. You can test hypotheses about relationships among codes. In HyperRESEARCH, you can specify combinations of codes that identify cases that you want to examine. NVivo allows the development of an indexing system to facilitate thinking about the relationships among

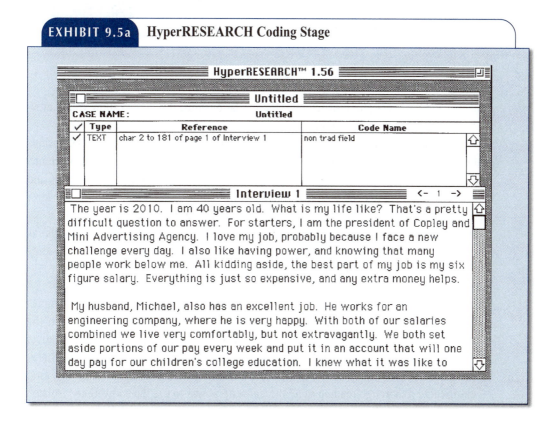

EXHIBIT 9.5a   HyperRESEARCH Coding Stage

EXHIBIT 9.5b   **Coding Stage in NVivo**

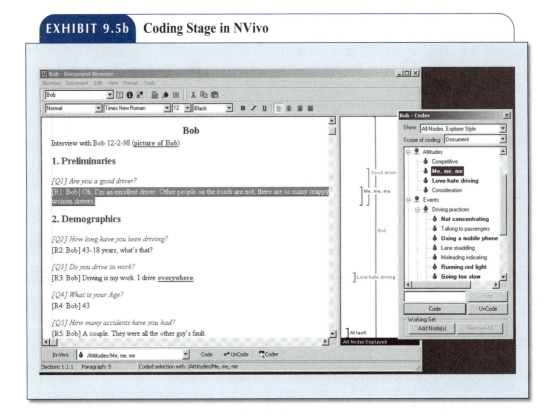

concepts and the overarching structure of these relationships. It will also allow you to draw more free-form models (see Exhibit 9.6).

Reports from both programs can include text to illustrate the cases, codes, and relationships that you specify. You can also generate counts of code frequencies and then import these counts into a statistical program for quantitative analysis. However, the many types of analyses and reports that can be developed with qualitative analysis software do not lessen the need for a careful evaluation of the quality of the data on which conclusions are based.

In reality, using a qualitative data analysis computer program is not always as straightforward as it appears. Decker and Van Winkle (1996) describe the difficulty they faced in using a computer program to identify instances of the concept of drug sales:

The software we used is essentially a text retrieval package. . . . One of the dilemmas faced in the use of such software is whether to employ a coding scheme within the interviews or simply to leave them as unmarked text. We chose the first alternative, embedding conceptual tags at the appropriate points in the text. An example illustrates this process. One of the activities we were concerned with was drug sales. Our first chore (after a thorough reading of all the transcripts) was to use the software to "isolate"

EXHIBIT 9.6   **A Free-Form Model in NVivo**

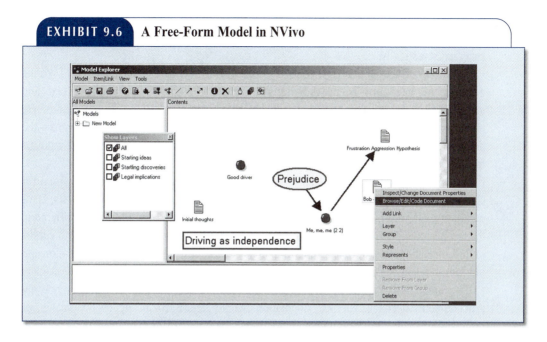

all of the transcript sections dealing with drug sales. One way to do this would be to search the transcripts for every instance in which the word "drugs" was used. However, such a strategy would have the disadvantages of providing information of too general a character while often missing important statements about drugs. Searching on the word "drugs" would have produced a file including every time the word was used, whether it was in reference to drug sales, drug use, or drug availability, clearly more information than we were interested in. However, such a search would have failed to find all of the slang used to refer to drugs ("boy" for heroin, "Casper" for crack cocaine) as well as the more common descriptions of drugs, especially rock or crack cocaine. (pp. 53–54)

Decker and Van Winkle (1996) solved this problem by parenthetically inserting conceptual tags in the text whenever talk of drug sales was found. This process allowed them to examine all of the statements made by gang members about a single concept (drug sales). As you can imagine, however, this still left the researchers with many pages of transcript material to analyze.

▣ CONTENT ANALYSIS

Content analysis is "the systematic, objective, quantitative analysis of message characteristics" (Neuendorf, 2002, p. 1). The goal of content analysis is to develop inferences from text (Weber, 1985). You can think of a content analysis as a survey of some documents or other records of prior communication. In fact, a content analysis is a survey designed with fixed-choice responses so that it produces quantitative data that can be analyzed statistically.

As a form of textual analysis, content analysis is like qualitative data analysis. Like the methods we have just been studying, it involves coding and categorizing text and identifying relationships among constructs identified in the text. However, as a quantitative procedure, content analysis overlaps with qualitative data analysis only at the margins—the points where qualitative analysis takes on quantitative features or where content analysis focuses on qualitative features of the text.

Tichon and Shapiro's (2003) analysis of e-mail postings to an online support group for children whose siblings have special needs highlights both aspects of content analysis. Their qualitative analyses involved describing e-mail topics, the types of social support offered in the e-mails, and patterns of self-disclosure. The quantitative analysis provided both counts of different categories of topics, support, and patterns of self-disclosure and the relationship of types of social support to patterns of self-disclosure.

The units that are surveyed in a content analysis can include newspapers, journal articles, court decisions, books, videotapes, themes expressed in agency documents, or propositions made in different statements. Words or other features of these units are then coded to measure the variables involved in the research question. The content analysis proceeds through several stages (Weber, 1985):

• Identify a population of documents or other textual sources for study. This population should be selected so that it is appropriate to the research question of interest. Perhaps the population will be all newspapers published in the United States, all agency annual reports, all U.S. Supreme Court decisions, or all articles in a particular journal.

• Determine the units of analysis. These could be items such as newspaper articles, court decisions, research articles, or case records.

• Select a sample of units from the population. The simplest strategy might be a simple random sample of documents. However, a stratified sample might be needed to ensure adequate representation of community newspapers in large and small cities. Sampling may be purposive, such as the use of 3 consecutive months of e-mail postings by Tichon and Shapiro (2003).

• Design coding procedures for the variables to be measured. This requires deciding what unit of text to code, such as words, sentences, themes, or paragraphs. Then the categories into which the text units are to be coded must be defined. These categories may be broad, such as *client goal,* or narrow, such as *client improves behavior.*

• Test and refine the coding procedures. Clear instructions and careful training of coders are essential.

• Base statistical analyses on counting occurrences of particular words, themes, or phrases, and test relations between different variables. These analyses would use some of the statistics introduced in Chapter 11, including frequency distributions, measures of central tendency and variation, crosstabulations, and correlation analysis.

Developing reliable and valid coding procedures is not an easy task. The meaning of words and phrases is often ambiguous. As a result, coding procedures cannot simply categorize and count words; text segments in which the words are embedded must also be inspected before codes are finalized. Because different coders may perceive different meanings in the same text segments, explicit coding rules are required to ensure coding consistency. Special dictionaries can be developed to keep track of how the categories of interest are defined in the study (Weber, 1985).

After coding procedures are developed, their reliability should be assessed by comparing different coders' codes for the same variables. The criteria for judging qualitative content analyses of text require the same standards of reliability and validity used for quantitative data.

ETHICS IN QUALITATIVE DATA ANALYSIS

The qualitative data analyst is never far from ethical issues and dilemmas. Throughout the analytic process, the analyst must consider how the findings will be used and how participants in the setting will react. Miles and Huberman (1994) suggest several specific questions that should be kept in mind:

- *Privacy, confidentiality, and anonymity.* It can be difficult to present a rich description in a case study while not identifying the setting. It can be easy for participants in the study to identify each other in a qualitative description even if outsiders cannot. Qualitative researchers should negotiate with participants early in the study about the approach that will be taken to protecting privacy and maintaining confidentiality. Selected participants should also be asked to review reports or other products before their public release in order to gauge the extent to which they feel privacy has been appropriately preserved.

- *Intervention and advocacy.* What do I do when I see harmful, illegal, or wrongful behavior on the part of others during a study? Should I speak for anyone's interests besides my own? If so, whose interests do I advocate? Maintaining what is called "guilty knowledge" may force the researcher to suppress some parts of the analysis so as not to disclose the wrongful behavior, but presenting "what really happened" in a report may prevent ongoing access and violate understandings with participants.

- *Research integrity and quality.* Real analyses have real consequences, so you owe it to yourself and those you study to adhere strictly to the analysis methods that you believe will produce authentic, valid conclusions.

- *Ownership of data and conclusions.* Who owns my field notes and analyses: me, my organization, or my funders? Once my reports are written, who controls their diffusion? Of course, these concerns arise in any social research project, but the intimate involvement of the qualitative researcher with participants in the setting studied makes conflicts of interest between different stakeholders much more difficult to resolve.

• *Use and misuse of results.* Do I have an obligation to help my findings be used appropriately? What if they are used harmfully or wrongly? It is prudent to develop understandings early in the project with all major stakeholders that specify what actions will be taken to encourage appropriate use of project results and to respond to what is considered misuse of these results.

▣ CONCLUSION

The variety of approaches to qualitative data analysis makes it difficult to provide a consistent set of criteria for interpreting their quality. Denzin's (2002) interpretive criteria are a good place to start. Denzin suggests that, at the conclusion of their analyses, qualitative data analysts ask the following questions about the materials they have produced. Reviewing several of them serves as a fitting summary for our understanding of the qualitative analysis process.

• Do they illuminate the phenomenon as lived experience? In other words, do the materials bring the setting alive in terms of the people in that setting?

• Are they based on thickly contextualized materials? We should expect thick descriptions that encompass the social setting studied.

• Are they historically and relationally grounded? There must be a sense of the passage of time between events and the presence of relationships between social actors.

• Are they processual and interactional? The researcher must have described the research process and his or her interactions within the setting.

• Do they engulf what is known about the phenomenon? This includes situating the analysis in the context of prior research and also acknowledging the researcher's own orientation on starting the investigation.

When an analysis of qualitative data is judged as successful in terms of these criteria, we can conclude that the goal of authenticity has been achieved.

In contrast, the criteria for judging quantitative content analyses of text are the same standards of validity applied to data collected with other quantitative methods. We must review the sampling approach, the reliability and validity of the measures, and the controls used to strengthen any causal conclusions. But you have seen in this chapter that there is no sharp demarcation between what is considered a qualitative or a quantitative analysis. As a research methodologist, you must be ready to use both types of techniques, evaluate research findings in terms of both sets of criteria, and mix and match the methods as required by the research problem to be investigated and the setting in which it is to be studied.

Computer-assisted qualitative data analysis
Content analysis
Ethnography
Grounded theory
Matrix

Narrative analysis
Progressive focusing
Qualitative comparative analysis
Tacit knowledge

HIGHLIGHTS

- Qualitative data analysts are guided by an *emic* focus of representing people in the setting on their own terms, rather than by an *etic* focus on the researcher's terms.

- Case studies use thick description and other qualitative techniques to provide the whole picture of a setting or group.

- Ethnographers attempt to understand the culture of a group.

- Narrative analysis attempts to understand a life or a series of events as they have unfolded, in a meaningful progression.

- Grounded theory connotes a general explanation that develops in interaction with the data and is continually tested and refined as data collection continues.

- Special computer software can be used for the analysis of qualitative, textual, and pictorial data. Users can record their notes, categorize observations, specify links between categories, and count occurrences.

- Content analysis is a tool for systematic quantitative analysis of documents and other textual data. It requires careful testing and control of coding procedures to achieve reliable measures.

DISCUSSION QUESTIONS

1. Describe the differences between quantitative and qualitative data analysis. What are the important guidelines to consider when analyzing qualitative data? Discuss the different modes of reading the text.

2. Identify and describe the five phases of qualitative data analysis. Discuss the importance of developing a matrix for coding the data.

3. What criteria should be used to evaluate a qualitative study's authenticity?

4. Compare and contrast traditional ethnography, qualitative comparative analysis, narrative analysis, and grounded theory. What are the advantages and disadvantages of these approaches?

5. What are the advantages and disadvantages of using computer-assisted qualitative data analysis?

6. What are the similarities and differences between content analysis and qualitative data analysis? Under what circumstances would you choose one mode of analysis over the other? Why?

7. Identify a social issue that is currently a "hot topic" nationally. Conduct a content analysis of the coverage of this issue on Internet discussion message boards. What is your unit of analysis? Randomly sample these messages. What are the dominant themes? Evaluate these themes statistically.

8. Examine a qualitative study from a social work journal (e.g., *Affilia*). What techniques did the author employ to analyze the data? Critique the study with regard to the researcher's ability to authenticate the conclusions.

CRITIQUING RESEARCH

1. Read the text of one of the qualitative studies posted on the study site (http://www .sagepub.com/fswrstudy) and evaluate its conclusions for authenticity, using the criteria in this chapter.

2. Review one of the articles on the study site (http://www.sagepub.com/fswrstudy) that uses qualitative methods. Describe the data that were collected, and identify the steps used in the analysis. What type of qualitative analysis was this? How confident are you in the conclusions given the methods of analysis used?

MAKING RESEARCH ETHICAL

1. Stake (1995) described behaviors of high school students that seemed likely to provoke violence in others. Should he have intervened directly to prevent escalation of conflicts? Should he have informed the school principal? What ethical guideline about intervention to prevent likely harm to others would you recommend?

2. In an innovative study of American Indian reservations, Bachman (1992) found high rates of homicide. She reported this and other important and troubling findings in her book, *Death and Violence on the Reservation*. In your opinion, does a researcher have an ethical obligation to urge government officials or others to take action in response to social problems that he or she has identified? Why or why not?

DEVELOPING A RESEARCH PROPOSAL

1. Which qualitative data analysis alternative is most appropriate for the qualitative data you proposed to collect for your project? Using this approach, develop a strategy for using the techniques of qualitative data analysis to analyze your textual data.

To assist you in completing the Web exercises below and to gain a better understanding of the chapter's contents, please access the study site at http://www.sagepub .com/fswrstudy where you will find the Web exercises reproduced with suggested links, along with self-quizzes, e-flash cards, interactive exercises, journal articles, and other valuable resources.

WEB EXERCISES

1. The Qualitative Report is an online journal about qualitative research. Inspect the table of contents for a recent issue (at http://www.nova.edu/ssss/QR/index.html). Read one of the articles about issues pertaining to elders, and write a brief article review.

2. Become a qualitative explorer! Go to the list of qualitative research Web sites and see what you can find that enriches your understanding of qualitative research (www.qualitativeresearch.uga .edu/QualPage). Be careful to avoid textual data overload.

CHAPTER 10

Evaluation Research

Evaluation Basics

Describing the Program: The Logic Model

Questions for Evaluation Research
 Needs Assessment
 Process Evaluation
 Outcome Evaluation
 Efficiency Analysis

Design Considerations
 Black Box or Program Theory?
 Researcher or Stakeholder
  Orientation?
 Quantitative or Qualitative Methods?
 Simple or Complex Outcomes?

**Implications for
 Evidence-Based Practice**
 C2-SPECTR

**Evaluation Research in a Diverse
 Society**

Ethical Considerations

Conclusion

Key Terms

Highlights

Discussion Questions

Critiquing Research

Making Research Ethical

Developing a Research Proposal

Web Exercises

What is evaluation research? Evaluation research is not a method of data collection, like survey research or experiments, nor is it a unique component of research designs, like sampling or measurement. Instead, evaluation research (or program evaluation) utilizes the tools and processes of research for a distinctive purpose: to investigate social programs such as substance abuse treatment programs, welfare programs, mental health programs, or employment and training programs. For each evaluation project, the researcher (or evaluator) must select a research design, sample, and method of data collection that are useful for answering the particular questions posed and appropriate for the particular program investigated. So you can see why this chapter comes after those on measurement, sampling, and research designs, for when you review or plan evaluation research, you have to think about the research process as a whole and how different parts of that process can best be combined.

In this chapter, we describe the distinctive features of evaluation research. You will learn a different vocabulary to understand agency-related processes and to integrate these into a model to describe these processes. We then turn to the kinds of questions often asked in an evaluation and the design alternatives to address these questions.

▣ EVALUATION BASICS

Exhibit 10.1 illustrates the process of evaluation research as a simple systems model. First, clients, customers, students, or some other persons or units enter the program as **inputs**. In addition to clients, social programs require other inputs such as staff and resources such as money, supplies, and equipment. Clients or consumers then participate in a set of activities that constitute the **program process**. It is these activities that are designed to have some impact on the client.

The direct product of the program's service delivery process is its **output**. Program outputs may include clients served, case managers trained, food parcels delivered, or child abuse reports investigated. The program outputs primarily serve to indicate that the program is operating. Program **outcomes** indicate the impact of the program on the recipients of the activities. Any social program is likely to have multiple outcomes, some intended and some unintended.

EXHIBIT 10.1   **A Model of Evaluation**

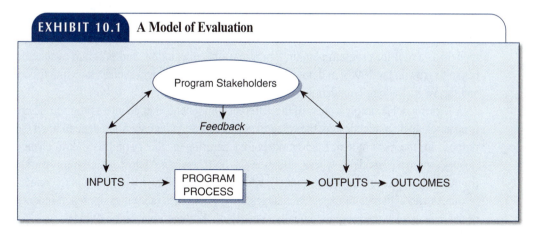

Source: Adapted from Martin & Kettner (1996).

A distinctive feature of evaluation research is that variation in both outputs and outcomes influence the inputs to the program through a **feedback** process (see Exhibit 10.1). Weiss (1972, 1998) suggests that this feedback can identify factors that lead to a successful program. In a successful program, the inputs (resources) are sufficient and appropriate to carry out the specific activities of the program, which set into motion a causal process (based on some practice theory) resulting in the desired outcome. Programs may fail to achieve their desired outcomes for different reasons. The inputs may not be sufficient to carry out the program activities (input failure); the inputs may be sufficient, but the actual activities may be incomplete, insufficient, or poorly designed so that they do not set into motion the causal process (program failure); or the inputs may be sufficient, and the program activities appropriate, but the causal process may not produce the desired outcomes (theory failure or wrong theory).

Inputs Resources, raw materials, clients, and staff that go into a program.

Program process The complete treatment or service delivered by the program.

Outputs The services delivered or new products produced by the program process.

Outcomes The impact of the program process on the cases processed.

Feedback Information about service delivery system outputs, outcomes, or operations that is available to any program inputs.

Stakeholders Individuals and groups who have some basis of concern with the program.

Evaluation research also broadens this loop to include connections to parties outside of the program. The evaluation process as a whole and feedback in particular can be understood only in relation to the interests and perspectives of program stakeholders. **Stakeholders** are those individuals and groups who have some interest in the program. They might be clients, staff, managers, funders, or the public, and each has an interest in the outcome of any program evaluation.

DESCRIBING THE PROGRAM: THE LOGIC MODEL

How can we put all these pieces of a program together and summarize it in an easy fashion? One increasingly popular method is to develop a **logic model**—a schematic representation of the various components that make up a social service program. The popularity of logic models as a tool for program planning, program implementation, and program evaluation began to grow in the 1990s, and now they are often used by funders such as the United Way and the W. K. Kellogg Foundation.

A logic model is simply a chart of the different components that go into a program. There is no single logic model design; the categories you choose to include often depend upon the purpose for the logic model. Logic models may describe (a) theory and its link to change (theory approach model), where attention is on "how and why" a program works; (b) outcomes (outcome approach model), where the focus of the logic model is to connect resources and activities to expected changes; or (c) activities (activities approach model), or describing what the program actually does (W. K. Kellogg Foundation, 2004).

Exhibit 10.2 presents a logic model of a partial hospitalization program to treat children with psychiatric problems. These programs often provide therapeutic services and educational

EXHIBIT 10.2   Program Logic Model: Partial Hospitalization Program

Problem: Inability to function independently in the community

For Whom	Assumptions	Inputs	Activities	Outputs	Outcomes
Children age 6 to 12 living in the county who display moderate to severe psychiatric disorders and are at risk of inpatient hospitalization	The inability to function independently in the community is due to a. Increased psychiatric symptoms b. Lack of anger management skills c. Behavioral problems d. Lack of problem-solving skills e. Lack of communication skills f. Poor coping skills g. Low self-esteem h. Parental lack of knowledge	3 MSW-level therapists 1 Child psychiatrist 1 Nurse M.Ed. in special education Space Chairs, desks Educational materials Computers Money	Assessment Treatment planning Individual counseling Group therapy Family meetings Team meetings Discharge planning Discharge Educational classes	Intermediate: Number of assessments completed per month Number of hours of individual counseling provided per month Number of group therapy sessions held per month Number of hours of family meetings Number of team meetings Number of hours of discharge planning Number of discharges	Intermediate: 1. Reduction in psychiatric symptoms 2. Increased anger management skills 3. Fewer behavioral 4. problems Improved problem-solving skills 5. Improved communication skills 6. Improved coping skills 7. Increased self-esteem 8. Increase in parents' knowledge about diagnosis and symptoms
	Treatment Model: Multiple interventions including cognitive behavioral therapy and medication management			Service Completion: Child attends 80% of individual and group counseling sessions and family attends all family meetings.	Final: Child can function independently in school, home, and community.

Source: Engel & Schutt (2008).

classes designed to enable children to remain in the community (Kotsopoulos, Walker, Beggs, & Jones, 1996; Whitelaw & Perez, 1987).

The first component of a logic model is to identify the *social problem.* Programs are designed to address a social condition deemed undesirable or to enhance desirable conditions. The actual program may not address the entire social problem but an aspect of the problem. In this example, the social problem is that children with moderate or severe psychiatric disorders have difficulty functioning in the community and therefore are at risk of placement in a full-time hospital environment.

The next step is to identify the **target population**—the "for whom" column. The evaluator identifies the criteria used to define an appropriate recipient of the service. There are a wide range of possible criteria to describe the target population, such as age-group, geographic residence, or status. In this example, the target population has been defined by age (6 to 12), residence (county), and the presence of severe psychiatric disorders.

Because programs are designed to impact social conditions, the program design is based on both assumptions about the causes of the social condition and an appropriate intervention method. This suggests that two agencies may address the same social condition, but each may design different programs with different expected outcomes. In Exhibit 10.2, the program providers believe that the risk of institutionalization is due to several different problems, including the failure to control psychiatric symptoms, problems in anger management, behavioral problems, the lack of coping and communication skills, poor self-esteem, and the lack of parental knowledge. Based on practice research, they believe that the best treatment incorporates both cognitive behavioral therapy and medication management.

The next component of the logic model is to detail the *inputs* required to run the program. The logic model description of inputs is specific, identifying, for example, the type of staff, their number, and their expertise. Inputs also include material resources such as equipment or space.

The evaluator identifies the specific *activities* (the program processes) that comprise the program. Activities include actions taken directly with the client, such as assessment, counseling, or family meetings and activities that may not directly involve the client but are necessary for the program, such as treatment planning or team meetings.

Programs produce two types of *outputs:* (1) intermediate outputs reflecting units of service; and (2) final outputs called service completions (Martin & Kettner, 1996). Units of service describe activities undertaken by the program staff; such units of service are often described in terms of frequency or number, time or duration, or tangible good. Service units are often found on staff reporting forms. For example, the output of an individual counseling session might be described as the number of individual counseling sessions, the amount of time spent in providing counseling, or the number of counseling sessions lasting a certain amount of time. Units of service reflect the aggregation of activities completed with clients during a specific time period.

Service completions refer to the agency's definition of a client who has received the "full package of services," as opposed to someone who began the program but dropped out prematurely (Martin & Kettner, 1996). Service completions are often defined as encompassing a mix of services: For example, clients in the partial hospitalization program have completed the full range of services if they attended 80% of their assigned groups, participated in 80% of their scheduled individual counseling sessions, and attended all meetings with their families. Another way of defining a service completion is by using some measure of time. In the partial hospitalization program, client reviews are done every 30 days; if it made sense to the agency administrator, a service completion might have been defined as this unit of time.

Defining a service completion is particularly important for evaluations that examine program impact on the clients. A client should have the "full dose" of activities if improvements are to occur, or else why provide the various activities? This is similar to the warning your doctor gives you when prescribing an antibiotic for an ear infection, namely that if you do not take the antibiotic for the full 12 days, you will not get better. When evaluators do studies of client change, they want to include only those persons who have received the full mix of program activities.

The last category on the logic model identifies the program's expected outcomes. These are the kinds of changes in a client that are expected to occur as the result of the program. There are intermediate outcomes and final or ultimate outcomes. *Intermediate outcomes* are the changes in the client that are necessary before the final or *ultimate outcome* might occur, such as increased anger management skills, fewer behavioral problems, or improved problem-solving skills. If the program assumptions are correct about why the child cannot function independently in the community, and if the intermediate outcomes are achieved, the ultimate outcome of the child functioning independently in school, home, and the community should be more likely.

You might notice that there is a relationship between the assumptions about the factors related to the social problem and the intermediate and final outcomes. The activities in the program are intended to improve upon each of the areas identified in the assumptions. So the intermediate outcomes reflect the desired changes in each of these areas. In the example, one problem is increased psychiatric symptoms; therefore, the intermediate outcome is a reduction in psychiatric symptoms. Each of the factors listed in the assumptions has a parallel intermediate outcome. The same is true with the overall social problem; if the problem is the inability of children to function independently in the community, then the ultimate outcome is that this is no longer a problem; rather, the child can function independently.

This symmetry also occurs with activities and intermediate outputs as each activity has a measure of service. In the partial hospitalization program, service activity was measured using a count or frequency of activity. If it was important, the evaluator might have used a measure of time, such as the number of hours spent completing assessments each month. And remember, this count (or length of time) is how many times (or how much time) the staff person spent on the activity with all clients in that month and not how much time the client spent on each activity.

As you can see, a logic model succinctly summarizes a great deal of information about the program. After completing the logic model, the evaluator, and often stakeholders, should have a better understanding about the logic underlying the program.

🔲 QUESTIONS FOR EVALUATION RESEARCH

Evaluation projects can focus on a variety of questions related to the operation of social programs and the impact they have:

- Is the program needed?

- How does the program operate?

- What is the program's impact?

- How efficient is the program?

You can see how a logic model is helpful because it provides detail for these questions. If you wanted to measure program activities, the outputs column provides measures. If you are interested in the program's impact, then the intermediate and final outcomes can serve as a guide. The specific methods used in an evaluation research project depend in part on the particular question of interest.

Needs Assessment

Is a new program needed or is an old one still required? Is there a need at all? A **needs assessment** attempts to answer this question with systematic, credible evidence. Need may be identified and enumerated by social indicators, such as the poverty rate or school drop-out rate; by interviews with local experts, such as mental health providers; by surveys of community residents or service providers; by using structured groups, such as focus groups with community residents; or by taking a resource inventory of available services and service capacity, such as is often done by a local United Way (McKillip, 1987). The evaluation will enumerate need, whereas the assessment of need and subsequent priorities will depend ultimately on the final judgment of key stakeholders.

Evaluators must determine whose definitions or perceptions should be used to describe the level of need. The decision from whom to collect data is crucial as different stakeholders will have different perceptions. You can imagine, for instance, that students would describe their needs differently than if professors were asked to comment on students' needs. A good evaluator will do his or her best to capture different perspectives on need and then to help others make sense of the results.

A wonderful little tale reveals the importance of thinking creatively about what people "need":

> The manager of a 20-story office building had received many complaints about the slowness of the elevators. He hired an engineering consultant to propose a solution. The consultant measured traffic flow and elevator features and proposed replacing the old elevators with new ones, which could shave 20 seconds off the average waiting time. The only problem: it cost $100,000. A second consultant proposed adding 2 additional

elevators, for a total wait time reduction of 35 seconds and a cost of $150,000. Neither alternative was affordable. A third consultant was brought in. He looked around for a few days and announced that the problem was not really the waiting times, but boredom. For a cost of less than $1000, the manager had large mirrors installed next to the elevators so people could primp and observe themselves while waiting for an elevator. The result: no more complaints. Problem solved. (Witkin & Altschuld, 1995, p. 38)

Process Evaluation

What actually happens in a social program? The purpose of a **process evaluation** is to investigate how the program is operating. Process evaluations are completed to answer a variety of different questions related to the operation of a particular program. One question concerns program coverage: Is the program serving its target population? Other questions focus on service delivery: Has the program been implemented as designed? What are the outputs of various program activities? In the past, process evaluations were the primary response to funders who wanted to know whether the agency had actually carried out its planned activities. Increasingly, process evaluations are conducted to identify specific activities that produced program outcomes as well as to determine client satisfaction with the program activities.

Formative evaluation may be used instead of process evaluation when the evaluation findings are used to help shape and refine the program (Rossi & Freeman, 1989). Formative evaluation procedures that are incorporated into the initial development of the service program can specify the treatment process and lead to changes in recruitment procedures, program delivery, or measurement tools (Patton, 2002).

Process evaluation can employ a wide range of indicators. Program coverage can be monitored through program records, participant surveys, community surveys, or comparisons of people using the program, people who drop out of the program, and people who are ineligible for the program.

Service delivery can be monitored through service records completed by program staff, a management information system maintained by program administrators, or reports by program recipients (Rossi & Freeman, 1989). Service delivery can also be reviewed through the use of a flowchart to describe program activities. The flowchart typically includes program activities; decision points where, based on the decision, a client may receive a different set of activities; and points at which documentation is necessary. Flowcharts are used to answer questions such as these: Are all necessary activities present in the program or are there missing activities? Is there duplication of service effort? How long does it take for a client to go through the entire process? How long does it take for a client to go from initial intake to assessment to intervention?

Increasingly, both program providers and those funding programs are interested in client satisfaction with program processes. A well-designed client satisfaction survey focused on the specific operation of the program can provide useful information about how to improve the program. Martin and Kettner (1996) suggest that rather than using global measures of satisfaction, providers should include questions that focus on particular dimensions of interest to the agency, such as the accessibility of services, courtesy of staff, timeliness of services, competency of practitioners, staff attitudes toward the client, or the appearance of the facilities, staff, and program materials.

Qualitative methods are often a key component of process evaluation studies because they can be used to elucidate and understand internal program dynamics—even those that were not anticipated (Patton, 2002; Posavac & Carey, 1997). Qualitative researchers may develop detailed descriptions of how program participants engage with each other, how the program experience varies for different people, and how the program changes and evolves over time.

Outcome Evaluation

Did the program work? Did the intervention have the intended result? These are the core questions of evaluation research, and this part of the research is called **outcome evaluation** (sometimes called impact or summative evaluation). Formally speaking, outcome evaluation compares what happened after a program with what would have happened had there been no program.

Think of the program as the independent variable and the result it seeks as a dependent variable. For instance, the partial hospitalization program described earlier (independent variable) is designed to enable adolescents to remain in the community (dependent variable). We would expect fewer instances of institutionalization for program participants than for those persons who do not participate in the program. In a more elaborate study, we might have multiple values of the independent variable; for instance, we might look at "no program," "partial hospitalization program," and "other treatment program" conditions, and compare the results of each.

As in other areas of research, an experimental design is the preferred method for maximizing internal validity—that is, for making sure your causal claims about program impact are justified. The goal is to achieve a fair, unbiased test of the program itself so that the judgment about the program's impact is not influenced by differences between the types of people who are in the different groups. Drake, McHugo, Becker, Anthony, and Clark (1996) used a *Pretest-Posttest Comparison Group Design* to evaluate the impact of two different approaches to providing employment services for people diagnosed with severe mental disorders (see Exhibit 10.3). Participants were randomly assigned into two groups; one group received group skills training (GST), emphasizing preemployment skills training and separate agencies to provide vocational and mental health services, while the second group received individual placement and support (IPS), providing vocational and mental health services in a single program and placing people directly into jobs without preemployment skills training. Both groups received a pretest and a posttest.

While experimental designs provide the best evidence of the impact of the program, they are often not feasible for an agency. Designing a true experimental design can be a difficult goal to achieve because the usual practice in social programs is to let people decide for

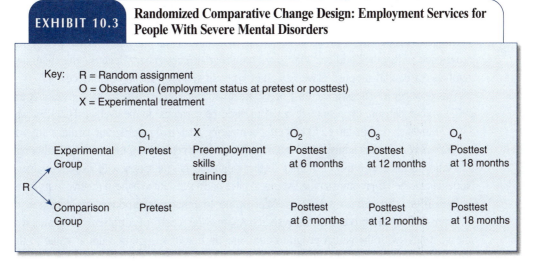

| EXHIBIT 10.3 | Randomized Comparative Change Design: Employment Services for People With Severe Mental Disorders |

Key: R = Random assignment
      O = Observation (employment status at pretest or posttest)
      X = Experimental treatment

Source: Drake, McHugo, Becker, Anthony, & Clark (1996).

themselves whether they want to enter a program and to establish eligibility criteria that ensure that people who enter the program are different from those who do not (Boruch, 1997). Therefore program outcomes are often evaluated with other methods, such as quasi-experimental designs, nonexperimental designs (for example, the One Group Pretest-Posttest Design), surveys, single-subject designs (e.g., A-B design), or qualitative designs.

Efficiency Analysis

Whatever the program's benefits, are they sufficient to offset the program's costs? Are the funders getting their money's worth? These efficiency questions can be the primary reason that funders require evaluation of the programs they fund. As a result, **efficiency analysis**, which compares program effects with costs, is often a necessary component of an evaluation research project. Two types of efficiency analysis are cost-benefit analysis and cost-effectiveness analysis.

A **cost-benefit analysis** involves comparing the specific costs and benefits of the program. The analyst must identify the particular costs and benefits to be evaluated; this, in turn, requires the analyst to identify whose perspective will be used in order to determine what can be considered a benefit and a cost. Program clients will have a different perspective on these issues than do program staff. As a student, you are likely to list different costs and benefits of attending school than would the university administration. Your *costs* include things like tuition and fees which are *benefits* for the university.

Once potential costs and benefits have been identified, they must be measured. Costs and benefits must be translated into a common monetary unit in order to make a comparison. The challenge is estimating the dollar value of how clients benefit from the program.

Sacks, McKendrick, DeLeon, French, and McCollister's (2002) study of therapeutic communities (TCs) provides a clear illustration. A "therapeutic community" is a method for treating substance abuse in which abusers participate in an intensive, structured living experience with other addicts who are attempting to stay sober. Because the treatment involves residential support as well as other types of services, it can be quite costly.

Was it worth it? The average cost of TC treatment for a client was $20,361 (Sacks et al., 2002). In comparison, the economic benefit (based on earnings) to the average TC client was $305,273, which declined to $273,698 after comparing post- and preprogram earnings but was still $253,337 even after adjustment for costs. The resulting benefit-cost ratio was 13:1, although this ratio declined to only 5.2:1 after further adjustments (for cases with extreme values). Nonetheless, the TC program studied seems to have had a substantial benefit relative to its costs.

It is often difficult to assign a dollar value to outcomes produced in social work programs. **Cost-effectiveness analysis** compares the costs of different programs (or interventions) with the actual program outcomes in lieu of assigning a dollar value to the outcomes. In these comparisons the program costs are calculated, whereas the benefits are listed and not assigned a cash value.

A study by Essock, Frisman, and Kontos (1998) illustrates the use of cost-effectiveness analysis in a program for persons with mental disorders. They compared the costs and benefits of assertive community multidisciplinary treatment teams (ACT) providing 24-hour coverage to standard case managers (SCM) providing treatment or referral. Over an 18-month period, ACT clients reported a higher quality of life that included enhanced personal safety, more leisure activities, an improved living situation, more frequent contact with friends, and more days spent in the community. The actual cost of the program to the state department of mental health, the state overall, or society did not differ significantly for ACT and SCM, though in each category the ACT program was slightly cheaper. Therefore, at about the same cost, the ACT program produced more desirable outcomes.

🔲 DESIGN CONSIDERATIONS

Once we have decided on the focus of the evaluation, there are still important decisions to be made about how to design the specific evaluation project. These include the following questions:

- Black box or program theory: Do we care how the program gets results?

- Researcher or stakeholder orientation: Whose goals matter most?

- Quantitative or qualitative methods: Which methods provide the best answers?

- Simple or complex outcomes: How complicated should the findings be?

Black Box or Program Theory?

The "meat and potatoes" of most evaluation research involves determining whether a program has the intended effect. If the effect occurred, the program "worked"; if the effect did not occur, then, some would say, the program should be abandoned or redesigned. In this approach, the process by which a program has an effect on outcomes is often treated as a **black box**—that is, the focus of the evaluation researcher is on whether cases seem to have changed as a result of their exposure to the program between the time they entered the program as inputs and when they exited the program as outputs (Chen, 1990). The assumption is that evaluation research requires only the test of a simple input-output model (see Exhibit 10.1). There may be no attempt to open the black box of the program process.

However, there is good reason to open the black box and investigate how the process works or does not work. Korr and Joseph (1996) found that a demonstration case management program for homeless, mentally ill persons implemented at two different sites resulted in vastly different outcomes. The goals of the program were to identify and place clients in independent living situations and then help the clients maintain their independence. At Site 1, two-thirds of clients in the experimental group were housed after 6 months compared with 34% of the control group, whereas at Site 2, 53% of the experimental group and 66% of the control group were housed after 6 months.

Why the contradictory findings? The investigators reviewed the client, organizational, and community context and found that there were differences that explained the contradictory outcomes. Most clients at the first site had been evicted from single resident occupancy rooms (SROs) and apartments, while most clients at the second site had lived with family or in board and care homes and were homeless because of family disputes. Although this was an interesting finding, it did not fully explain the differences. It turns out that the available housing also differed by site. Site 1 was located in a neighborhood with most of the city's single room occupancy housing, while Site 2 had very few to no single room occupancy alternatives but many board and care facilities. Because the ACT staff members at Site 2 were trying to follow the intervention's guidelines, the effort to place their clients in SROs may have been contrary to the participants' wishes.

If an investigation of program process is conducted, a program theory may be developed. A program theory describes what has been learned about how the program has its effect. When a researcher has sufficient knowledge before the investigation begins, outlining a program theory can help to guide the investigation of program process in the most productive directions. This is termed a **theory-driven evaluation**.

A program theory specifies how the program is expected to operate and identifies which program elements are operational (Chen, 1990). In addition, a program theory specifies how a program is to produce its effects and so improves understanding of the relationship between the independent variable (the program) and the dependent variable (the outcome or outcomes). Future investigations of housing programs for homeless persons with mental illness may be able to test the program theory that Korr and Joseph (1996) developed.

Researcher or Stakeholder Orientation?

Whose prescriptions specify how the program should operate, what outcomes it should try to achieve, or who it should serve? Most social work research assumes that the researcher specifies the research questions, the applicable theory or theories, and the outcomes to be investigated. Social work research results are most often reported in a professional journal or at professional conferences where scientific standards determine how the research is received. In evaluation research, however, the research question is often set by the program sponsors or a funding agency that is responsible for reviewing the program. It is to these authorities that research findings are reported.

Should evaluation researchers insist on designing the evaluation project and specifying its goals, or should they accept the suggestions and adopt the goals of the funding agency? What role should the preferences of program staff or clients play? The different answers that various evaluation researchers have given to these questions are reflected in different approaches to evaluation (Chen, 1990).

Stakeholder approaches encourage researchers to be responsive to program stakeholders. Issues for study are to be based on the views of people involved with the program, and reports are to be made to program participants (Shadish, Cook, & Leviton, 1991). The program theory is developed by the researcher to clarify and develop the key stakeholders' theory of the program (Shadish et al., 1991). In *stakeholder participatory research,* stakeholders are engaged with the researchers as co-researchers and help to design, conduct, and report the research (Rossi & Freeman, 1989).

Balaswamy and Dabelko (2002) used the stakeholder participatory research approach to conduct a community-wide needs assessment of elderly residents. Stakeholders were identified by the agency initiating the project and were defined as "people with a vested interest in improving, protecting, and developing services for the community elders" (p. 60). An oversight committee was formed and included "aging service providers, funders, the city administrator, agency board members, research sponsors, administrator and faculty from local educational institution, seniors, community residents, administrators from private corporations, private non-profit funding organizations, and administrators from other social service agencies" (p. 60). This committee provided input and feedback on every phase of the needs assessment, including establishing goals and objectives, developing the needs assessment tool, sampling issues, data collection methods and actual data collection, and data analysis and dissemination. Because the stakeholders had been a part of the entire evaluation, the findings were used even when they were unexpected and negative. The oversight committee even created subcommittees to follow up on the use of the information by the community.

Social science approaches emphasize the importance of researcher expertise and maintenance of some autonomy in order to develop the most trustworthy, unbiased program evaluation. It is assumed that "evaluators cannot passively accept the values and views of the other stakeholders" (Chen, 1990, p. 78). Evaluators who adopt this approach derive a program theory from information they obtain on how the program operates and extant social science theory and knowledge, not from the views of stakeholders.

Of course, there are disadvantages to both stakeholder and social science approaches to program evaluation. If stakeholders are ignored, researchers may find that participants are uncooperative, that their reports are unused, and that the next project remains unfunded.

However, if social science procedures are neglected, standards of evidence will be compromised, conclusions about program effects will likely be invalid, and results are unlikely to be generalizable to other settings.

These equally undesirable possibilities have led to several attempts to develop more integrated approaches to evaluation research. **Integrative approaches** attempt to cover issues of concern to both stakeholders and evaluators and to include stakeholders in the group from which guidance is routinely sought (Chen & Rossi, 1987). The emphasis given to either stakeholder or social concerns is expected to vary with the specific project circumstances. Integrative approaches seek to balance the goal of carrying out a project that is responsive to stakeholder concerns with the goal of objective, scientifically trustworthy, and generalizable results. When the research is planned, evaluators are expected to communicate and negotiate regularly with key stakeholders and to take stakeholder concerns into account. Findings from preliminary inquiries are reported back to program decision makers so they can make improvements in the program before it is formally evaluated. When the actual evaluation is conducted, the evaluation research team is expected to operate more autonomously, minimizing intrusions from program stakeholders.

Quantitative or Qualitative Methods?

Evaluation research that attempts to identify the effects of a social program typically is quantitative: Did housing retention improve? Did substance abuse decline? It is fair to say that when there is an interest in comparing outcomes between an experimental and a control group, or tracking change over time in a systematic manner, quantitative methods are favored.

But qualitative methods can add much to quantitative evaluation research studies, including more depth, detail, nuance, and exemplary case studies (Patton, 2002). Perhaps the greatest contribution qualitative methods can make in many evaluation studies is investigating program process—that is, finding out what is "inside the black box." Although it is possible to track service delivery with such quantitative measures as contact hours of staff and frequency of complaints, finding out what is happening to clients and how clients experience the program can often best be accomplished by observing program activities and interviewing staff and clients intensively. For example, Patton (2002) describes a study in which process analysis in an evaluation of a prenatal clinic's outreach program led to program changes. The process analysis revealed that the outreach workers were spending much time responding to immediate problems, such as needs for rat control, protection from violence, and access to English classes. As a result, the outreach workers were recruiting fewer community residents for the prenatal clinic. New training and recruitment strategies were adopted to lessen this deviation from program goals.

Another good reason for using qualitative methods in evaluation research is the importance of learning how different individuals react to the treatment. For example, a quantitative evaluation of participant reactions to an adult basic skills program for new immigrants relied heavily on the participants' initial statements of their goals. However, qualitative interviews revealed that most new immigrants lacked sufficient experience in

America to set meaningful goals; their initial goal statements simply reflected their eagerness to agree with their counselors' suggestions (Patton, 2002).

Qualitative methods can also help in understanding how social programs actually operate. Complex social programs have many different features, and it is not always clear whether it is the combination of those features or some particular features that are responsible for the program's effect—or for the absence of an effect.

Simple or Complex Outcomes?

It is unlikely that a program will have only one outcome. How many outcomes are anticipated? Might there be some unintended outcomes? Which are the direct consequences of program action and which are indirect effects that occur as a result of the direct effects (Mohr, 1992)? Do the longer-term outcomes follow directly from the immediate program outputs? Does the intermediate outcome (the increase in test scores at the end of the preparation course) result in the desired final outcome (increased rates of college admission)? Due to these and other possibilities, the selection of outcome measures is a critical step in evaluation research.

Most evaluation researchers attempt to measure multiple outcomes (Mohr, 1992). The result usually is a much more realistic, and richer, understanding of program impact. Some of the multiple outcomes measured in the evaluation of Project New Hope appear in Exhibit 10.4. Project New Hope was designed to answer the following critical policy question: If low-income adults are given a job at a sufficient wage, above the poverty level, with child care and health care assured, what will be the long-term impact on the adults and their children (Miller, Huston, Duncan, McLoyd, & Weisner, 2008)? Participants randomly assigned to the experimental group were offered a job involving work for 30 hours a week, earnings supplements, subsidized child care, and low-cost health care benefits for 3 years. What were the long-term outcomes 5 years after leaving the program? While there had been initial gains in employment and income and reductions in poverty, 5 years after the program had ended, these gains had disappeared. There were no differences between the experimental group and control group in any measure of parents' well-being. But there were some positive effects for their children: Children were more likely to participate in structured activities, had fewer reports of poor grades, being placed in special education, or repeating a grade, and were more engaged in school activities. In comparison with the control group, teachers and parents ranked the youth, especially boys, as better behaved, and the boys had higher reading scores. Finally, youth were more likely to have worked and were more optimistic about work in the future.

So did the New Hope program "work"? Clearly it did not live up to initial expectations, but it certainly showed that social interventions can have some benefits. The long and short of it is that a collection of multiple outcomes gave a better picture of program impact.

In a sense, all of these design choices hinge on what your real goals are in doing the project and how able you will be to achieve those goals. Not every agency really wants to know whether its programs work, especially if the answer is no. Dealing with such issues,

EXHIBIT 10.4	Outcomes in Project New Hope: Year 8

Parents	New Hope	Control Group
Percentage of quarters employed	56.3	54.2
Average annual earnings	11,319	11,031
Average income	13,595	13,285
Below poverty	63.1	67.1
Material hardship	.17	.17
Financial worry	2.52	2.45
Physical health	3.20	3.22
General stress	2.62	2.56
Depression	17.36	17.33
Hope	2.92	2.94
Children	New Hope	Control Group
Structured activities*	2.40	2.30
Reading score	93.31	91.86
Reading score boys*	93.35	90.98
Negative school progress	.22	.25
School engagement*	3.86	3.71
Social behavior*	3.84	3.77
Cynicism about work*	2.49	2.56
Pessimism about future employment	1.98	2.07
Employment and career preparation*	2.35	2.26

* Statistically significant difference

Source: Adapted from Miller, Huston, Duncan, McLoyd, & Weisner (2008).

and the choices they require, is part of what makes evaluation research both scientifically and politically fascinating.

IMPLICATIONS FOR EVIDENCE-BASED PRACTICE

Evaluation research is connected to specific social work programs; as a result, you can learn lessons from the various evaluative questions that might apply to your own agency settings. Even more important, when an agency is engaged in ongoing evaluation to monitor program outcomes, the agency can adjust services or activities when the outcomes do not appear to be successful. Logic modeling and in-depth evaluations are two activities that enable agencies to integrate evidence-based practice (Whittaker et al., 2006).

As we described earlier, when an agency completes a logic model of one or more of its programs, it is deconstructing its program. The logic model provides the basis for an agency asking a variety of evaluation questions: Is the program needed? Are the program assumptions correct? Is the treatment model appropriate? Are the activities implemented correctly with the right kinds of resources? Does the program produce the desired outcomes? The research literature may provide evidence about each of these questions, but this takes us back to our fundamental questions about the evidence—that is, its validity and generalizability. To what extent are the findings from studies about client needs or program assumptions generalizable to the agency's target population? Are the interventions provided in one context generalizable to the agency's context? How valid are the findings about need or program outcome?

In-depth, ongoing program evaluation facilitates the generation of evidence about a program's impacts, as well as understanding what contributes to a program's success. Outcome evaluations provide some level of evidence about the effectiveness of the program for the target population; process evaluation can identify mechanisms of a program's implementation that contribute to the program's success (or lack of success). Including contextual factors into the evaluation process provides insight into the interaction of different systems with the program (Whittaker et al., 2006). In combination, such information is important for decision makers as they seek to ensure that they have the necessary inputs and activities to continue achieving desired client outcomes or as they reevaluate the inputs and activities for a less successful program. Therefore, ongoing monitoring of outcomes is a step toward ensuring that the program design is appropriate for the target population.

C2-SPECTR

As we noted in Chapter 2, the Campbell Collaboration provides systematic reviews of evaluation research studies. Linked to the Campbell Collaboration is the **C2-SPECTR** online archive of evaluation studies in social work, education, and criminal justice (archive available at http://geb9101.gse.upenn.edu). While the archive continues to grow, it may contain only about 1% of the published and unpublished documents in the social sciences (Petrosino, Boruch, Rounding, McDonald, & Chalmers, 2000).

The archive includes studies using experimental and quasi-experimental designs. The archive also includes studies for which the method was not clear, leaving it to users to inspect published or written documents (Petrosino et al., 2000). C2-SPECTR can be used to provide sources for people preparing systematic reviews and for practitioners interested in the effectiveness of a particular intervention with a particular population.

The C2-SPECTR project offers an easy-to-use search engine. As with other data-base searches, you can use keywords, authors, titles, periodicals, year, and the like. The archive returns information such as titles, authors, sources, abstracts, and keywords. The choice of keyword is always important; *homelessness* retrieved 18 studies, whereas *homeless* retrieved 22 studies (C2-SPECTR available at http://geb9101.gse.upenn.edu).

EVALUATION RESEARCH IN A DIVERSE SOCIETY

Throughout this book, we have focused primarily on technical issues relative to our diverse society: Are the measures used reliable and valid for the target group? Is the sample representative? How do we recruit people of color to research studies? Is the question wording appropriate? These technical issues remain as concerns for evaluation research and are addressed elsewhere; in this section, we focus on both broader issues of categorization and ethical challenges with vulnerable participants.

Stanfield (1999) posed this question: "Even if the design and data meet the reliability and validity standards of Campbell and Stanley (1966) or of a particular social scientific or policy-making community, do the data fit the realities of the people it supposedly represents?" (p. 420). He refers to this idea as *relevance validity*. Although Stanfield was speaking about African Americans and people of color, the question is equally relevant for other population groups.

Researchers and agency administrators often define evaluation questions from a perspective that does not necessarily reflect the participants' perspectives. For example, we have argued that a logic model is a particularly useful tool for developing evaluation questions, but often this model is based on the agency's perspectives about a program: The assumptions are the agency's assumptions, the activities are the agency's activities, and the outcomes are those defined by the agency. You can probably begin to wonder whether clients or participants perceive things differently. Engel (1993) once evaluated a program whose intended outcomes were preventing substance abuse and building skills to resist peer pressure among a group of adolescents. Fortunately, he asked the parents of the participants what they saw as the benefits of the program. Not one mentioned anything related to substance abuse; rather, the parents spoke about better school attendance, improved grades, and improved behavior.

A second concern about research in a diverse society involves the process of categorizing clients by their characteristics. Categorizing clients (e.g., by race, gender, sexual orientation, or class) may reflect assumptions about the group's social and cultural characteristics and abilities. Such categorization ignores the heterogeneity within each classification and can result in an inaccurate assessment of a program's impact (Stanfield, 1999).

In research and evaluation, there is a tendency to compare other ethnic groups with Whites, suggesting that the White experience is the baseline to which other groups should aspire—that the majority's experience is what should be appropriate for other population groups (Stanfield, 1999). Similarly, differences between heterosexual participants and gay, lesbian, bisexual, or transgender participants should not be assumed to be deficits (Herek, Kimmel, Amaro, & Melton, 1991; Martin & Meezan, 2003).

This practice results in the application of a deficits model to evaluation; while in social work practice the focus on strengths is becoming more common, it is still emerging in evaluation. For example, needs assessments too often use a deficit model that identifies what are thought to be problems or gaps. A needs assessment that integrates questions to identify the strengths of individuals and the community may lead to different conclusions about "needs," as well as increase the number of options to deal with such needs.

⊡ ETHICAL CONSIDERATIONS

Evaluation research can make a difference in people's lives while it is in progress, as well as after the results are reported. Job opportunities, welfare requirements, housing options, and treatment for substance abuse—each is a potentially important benefit, and an evaluation research project can change both their type and availability. This direct impact on research participants and, potentially, their families heightens the attention that evaluation researchers have to give to human subjects' concerns. Although the particular criteria that are at issue and the decisions that are most ethical vary with the type of evaluation research conducted and the specifics of a particular project, there are always serious ethical as well as political concerns for the evaluation researcher (Boruch, 1997; Dentler, 2002).

Assessing needs and examining the process of treatment delivery have few special ethical dimensions. Cost-benefit analyses also raise few ethical concerns. It is when program impact is the focus that human subjects' considerations multiply. What about assigning persons randomly to receive some social program or benefit? One justification given by evaluation researchers has to do with the scarcity of these resources. If not everyone in the population who is eligible for a program can receive it, due to resource limitations, what could be a fairer way to distribute the program benefits than through a lottery? Random assignment also seems like a reasonable way to allocate potential program benefits when a new program is being tested with only some members of the target recipient population. However, when an ongoing entitlement program is being evaluated and experimental subjects would normally be eligible for program participation, it may not be ethical simply to bar some potential participants from the program. Instead, evaluation researchers may test alternative treatments or provide some alternative benefit while the treatment is being denied.

There are many other ethical challenges in evaluation research:

- Are the risks minimized?
- Are risks reasonable in relation to benefits?
- Is the selection of individuals equitable? (Randomization implies this.)
- Is informed consent given?
- Are the data monitored?
- How can confidentiality be ensured?

Evaluation researchers must consider whether it will be possible to meet each of these criteria long before they even design a study.

Those conducting agency-based program evaluations must be particularly sensitive to ethical issues. Such evaluations are often completed with vulnerable populations, some of whom are using agency programs by choice while others are legally mandated clients. Some of these participants may be marginalized and at risk of discrimination or violence

(Martin & Meezan, 2003). This puts a particular onus on the agency to ensure that clients truly understand how the data are going to be used and participants' rights related to the use of such data.

English (1997) posed the question, "Does informed consent safeguard the interests of disadvantaged and minority target groups?"(p. 51). Gathering data is, first of all, intrusive, and the data-gathering process may have a negative impact on the participants. In addition, the agency may produce information that could lead to some kind of sanction against the participants. English described an interview with a family that in the past had placed a disabled child in an institution, believing it was the right thing to do, but was now having that belief challenged by the interview process. The respondents were extremely distressed by the process. The ethical issue was whether the distress caused by the interview could have been anticipated and been alleviated in some fashion.

The problem of maintaining subject confidentiality is particularly thorny because researchers, in general, are not legally protected from the requirement that they provide evidence requested in legal proceedings, particularly through the process known as "discovery." However, it is important to be aware that several federal statutes have been passed specifically to protect research data about vulnerable populations from legal disclosure requirements.

Part of the problem is that informed consent is linked to the use of the data by the sponsors and that sponsors may not use the data in a way that protects the interests of those providing the information. To protect participants, English (1997) recommends that participants be involved in all stages of the evaluation, including identifying the purposes and information requirements, how data should be obtained, and data analysis, dissemination, and utilization. In this way, the evaluation will not distort the interests of the participants.

Finally, we know that participation must be voluntary. The challenges in agency-based evaluation are to reassure clients that there will be no ramifications for choosing not to participate and to emphasize that there will be no added benefits for clients who do participate. Think about how difficult this might be to a client, given the power differentials between clients and agency providers. You face a similar subtle pressure when a professor hands out a survey in class that the professor intends to use for a journal article; despite the guarantees offered about voluntary participation, it is normal to wonder if failing to complete the survey will somehow impact your grade.

We conclude this discussion on ethics in evaluation by emphasizing one key point: It can be costly to society and potentially harmful to participants to maintain ineffective programs. In the long run, at least, it may be more ethical to conduct an evaluation study than to let the status quo remain in place.

🔲 CONCLUSION

The research methods applied to evaluation research are no different from those covered elsewhere in this text; they can range from qualitative interviews to rigorous randomized designs. For a variety of reasons researchers and evaluators may not be able to use the "best" methods given time, feasibility, and other practical concerns. Nonetheless, to the extent possible, evaluators try to achieve the highest standard possible. The types of practices described in the preceding chapters provide a framework with which the method used in a particular evaluation can be compared.

Hopes for evaluation research are high: Society could benefit from the development of programs that do work well, that accomplish their goals, and that serve people who genuinely need them. At least that is the hope. Unfortunately, there are many obstacles to realizing this hope:

- Because social programs and the people who use them are complex, evaluation research designs can easily miss important outcomes or aspects of the program process.

- Because the many program stakeholders all have an interest in particular results from the evaluation, researchers can be subjected to an unusual level of cross pressures and demands.

- Because the need to include program stakeholders in research decisions may undermine adherence to scientific standards, research designs can be weakened.

- Because some program administrators want to believe their programs really work well, researchers may be pressured to avoid null findings or, if they are not responsive, find their research report ignored. Plenty of well-done evaluation research studies wind up in a recycling bin, or hidden away in a file cabinet.

- Because the primary audiences for evaluation research reports are program administrators, politicians, or members of the public, evaluation findings may need to be overly simplified, distorting the findings. (Posavac & Carey, 1997)

The rewards of evaluation research are often worth the risks, however. Evaluation research can provide social scientists with rare opportunities to study complex social processes, with real consequences, and to contribute to the public good. Although they may face unusual constraints on their research designs, most evaluation projects can result in high-quality analyses and publications in reputable social science journals.

KEY TERMS

Black box
Cost-benefit analysis
Cost-effectiveness analysis
C2-SPECTR
Efficiency analysis
Feedback
Formative evaluation
Inputs
Integrative approach
Logic model
Needs assessment

Outcome
Outcome evaluation
Output
Process evaluation
Program process
Social scientific approach
Stakeholder approach
Stakeholders
Target population
Theory-driven evaluation

HIGHLIGHTS

- Evaluation research is social work research that is conducted to investigate social problems.

- The evaluation process can be modeled as a feedback system with inputs entering the program, which generates outputs and then outcomes, which feed back to program stakeholders and effect program inputs.

- The evaluation process as a whole and the feedback process in particular can be understood only in relation to the interests and perspectives of program stakeholders.

- A logic model provides a schematic representation of the various components that make up a social service program.

- There are four primary types of program evaluation: needs assessment, process evaluation, outcome evaluation, and efficiency analysis.

- The process by which a program has an effect on outcomes is often treated as a "black box," but there is good reason to open the black box and investigate the process by which the program operates and produces, or fails to produce, an effect.

- A program theory may be developed before or after an investigation of program process is completed. It may be either descriptive or prescriptive.

- Qualitative methods are useful in describing the process of program delivery.

- Multiple outcomes are often necessary to understand program effects.

- Evaluation research raises complex ethical issues because it may involve withholding desired social benefits.

DISCUSSION QUESTIONS

1. Choose a social program with which you are familiar and construct a logic model.

2. Select a social program with which you are familiar and list its intended outcomes. What other outcomes might result from the program, both direct and indirect? Try to identify outcomes that would be deemed desirable as well as some that might not be desirable.

3. Review a social work agency's description of one of its primary programs and the objectives it aims to meet. Create a flowchart illustrating the service delivery process. Do you believe that the program design reflects the stated goals? Are necessary activities absent or are activities present that do not appear to contribute to the desired outcomes?

4. Propose an evaluation of a social program you have heard about. Identify a research question you would like to answer about this program, and select a method of investigation. Discuss the strengths and weaknesses of your proposed method.

5. Read and summarize a quantitative research article published in the journal *Evaluation and Program Planning*. Read the article and suggest how qualitative methods might have been added to the research and what benefits these methods might have had for it.

CRITIQUING RESEARCH

1. Evaluate the ethics of one of the studies discussed in this chapter. Which ethical guidelines seem most difficult to adhere to? Where do you think the line should be drawn between not taking any risks at all with research participants and developing valid scientific knowledge?

2. Find a recent article that evaluates a program or an intervention from a social work journal like *Research Practice in Social Work*. Describe its strengths and weaknesses. Do the authors make claims about causality that are supported by their methodology?

MAKING RESEARCH ETHICAL

1. Is it ethical to assign people to receive some social benefit on a random basis? Form two teams and debate the ethics of the New Hope randomized evaluation of employment described in this chapter.

DEVELOPING A RESEARCH PROPOSAL

1. Develop a logic model for a program that might influence the type of attitude or behavior in which you are interested. List the key components of this model.

2. Design a program evaluation to test the efficacy of your program model, using an outcome evaluation approach.

3. Add to your plan a discussion of a program theory for your model. In your methodological plan, indicate whether you will use qualitative or quantitative techniques and simple or complex outcomes.

4. Who are the potential stakeholders for your program? How will you relate to them before, during, and after your evaluation?

> To assist you in completing the Web exercises below and to gain a better understanding of the chapter's contents, please access the study site at http://www.sagepub.com/fswrstudy where you will find the Web exercises reproduced with suggested links, along with self-quizzes, e-flash cards, interactive exercises, journal articles, and other valuable resources.

WEB EXERCISES

1. Describe the resources available for evaluation researchers at these Web sites:
   http://www.wmich.edu/evalctr/ (or) http://www.worldbank.org/oed/

2. You can check out the latest information regarding the D.A.R.E. program (at www.dare.com). What is the current approach? Can you find information on the Web about current research on D.A.R.E.?

CHAPTER 11

Quantitative Data Analysis

Preparing Data for Analysis

Displaying Univariate Distributions
Graphs
Frequency Distributions

Summarizing Univariate Distributions
Measures of Central Tendency
Mode
Median
Mean
Median or Mean?
Measures of Variation
Range
Interquartile Range
Variance
Standard Deviation

Describing Relations Among Variables
Graphing Association
Describing Association
Evaluating Association

Implications for Evidence-Based Practice
Statistical Significance
Choosing a Statistical Test

Ethical Issues: Avoiding Misleading Findings

Conclusion

Key Terms

Highlights

Discussion Questions

Critiquing Research

Making Research Ethical

Developing a Research Proposal

Web Exercises

Statistics is often the word that social work students love to hate. If you are one of these students, we hope in this chapter to help you replace your fear of statistics with an appreciation of them as simply a set of tools with which to summarize and analyze data. Statistics are used to describe clients, agencies, and communities, to monitor practice, and to assess the effectiveness of social work interventions. Data analysis is an integral component of research methods, and it is important that any proposal for quantitative research include a section on the data analysis that will follow data collection. A basic knowledge of statistics is necessary for you to be an informed and critical consumer of research published in professional literature.

This chapter introduces several common statistics in social work research and highlights the factors that must be considered in using and interpreting statistics. Think of it as a review of fundamental social statistics, if you have already studied them, or as an introductory overview, if you have not. We start with a preliminary section in which we outline the process of preparing data for analysis. Next, we review statistical methods to describe the distribution of single variables and the relationships of two variables. We then discuss hypothesis testing and the relationship of statistical significance to causal validity. Along the way, we address ethical issues related to data analysis.

PREPARING DATA FOR ANALYSIS

If you have conducted your own survey or experiment, the information that you have on assorted questionnaires, survey instruments, observational checklists, or tape transcripts needs to be prepared in a format suitable for analyzing data. Generally, this involves a process of assigning a number to a particular response to a question, observation, case record response, or the like. For the most part, this is a straightforward process, but there are pitfalls. We suggest following these steps to prepare the data for analysis:

Assign a unique identifying number. A unique identifying number should be assigned to each form, questionnaire, survey, or transcript, and this identifier should appear on the form. You should include the identifier as a variable in the data. Having an identifier enables you to go back to the original form if you find data entry errors or decide to enter additional information. If you are collecting data from the same people at different points in time, the unique identifier helps you link their responses.

Review the forms. As you review the instruments or questionnaires used to record responses, you may encounter mistakes or unanticipated problems. You need to establish rules that you will follow when you encounter such mistakes. Here are some problems you may encounter:

• Responses that are not clearly indicated. You may find mistakes such as a circle crossing more than one category or an *X* or a check mark falling between responses (see Exhibit 11.1). This presents a dilemma since the respondent has given a response, but because of the ambiguity of what was circled or checked, you are not sure which response to consider correct. Some researchers do not record the information and treat it as missing, whereas others try to discern the intent of the respondent.

• Respondents misreading instructions. Sometimes respondents do not follow instructions about how to respond to a question. They might check responses when they are asked to rank different responses (see Question 4 in Exhibit 11.1), or they may circle multiple answers when they have been asked to choose the best answer.

EXHIBIT 11.1 Unclear Responses

Thanks. This set of questions deals with different feelings and emotions. For each of these questions, please answer for how you felt over the past week by responding yes or no.

In the last week . . .

Yes No 1. Are you basically satisfied with your life?

Now I am going to ask you a couple of questions about your vision and health.

2. Overall, how would you rate your health? Would you say your health is excellent, very good, good, fair, or poor?

    1   Excellent
    2   Very good
    3   Good
    4   Fair
    5   Poor

3. In which category does your annual earned income fall? (Please check)

    ____   Less than $10,000
    ____   10,000–14,999
    ____   15,000–19,999
    ____   20,000–24,999
    ____   25,000–29,999
    ✓   30,000 or more

4. Please rank the top five housing options that are necessary for your agency to provide. Place a "1" by the most necessary option, a "2" by the second most necessary option, a "3" for the third most necessary, a "4" for the fourth most necessary, and a "5" for the fifth most necessary.

    _X_   Homeless shelter
    ____   Emergency rent and utilities financial help
    ____   Transitional/bridge housing
    _X_   Shared with little/none support services
    ____   Subsidized independent living; no on-site services
    _X_   Long-term rental/mortgage assistance
    ____   Shared with on-site support services
    ____   Housing and off-premise D&A use
    _X_   Clean and sober housing program
    ____   Residential hospice
    ____   Skilled nursing facility
    _X_   Personal care home/assisted living
    ____   Other, specify _____

Source: Engel & Schutt (2008).

- Incomplete questionnaires. Some respondents may decide not to complete the entire instrument or may end the interview before it is completed. You have to decide whether to include the responses you have obtained and treat the rest as missing or to consider the entire instrument as missing. There are no hard rules. Your decision may be influenced by your sample size and the number of questions that the respondent failed to answer.

- Unexpected responses. You may get responses that you had not anticipated. For example, you might ask age and get a response like 30½. Decide how you will treat such responses.

Code open-ended questions. There are two types of open-ended questions that are common in structured surveys: (a) when the entire question is left open-ended and (b) where you have *Other (specify)*_____ as a potential response in a list of responses. You will have to develop categories for each type; although the process is similar, it is easier to develop response categories for "*other*" because the responses are likely to be fewer in number, and the most common responses—or at least most anticipated responses—already appear in the questionnaire.

To identify possible response categories, you can rely on your own knowledge of the topic and what are likely response categories. This list, however, is still likely to be insufficient, because if the options had been known, a closed-ended question probably would have been used. First, list the responses; if a respondent provides several answers, separate the responses and treat each as a unique response. One way to list the responses is to write the response on an index card (remember to include the respondent's identification number and the question number). Next, review the responses to see whether patterns begin to emerge; these patterns represent potential response categories for the variable. This should be followed by additional reviews until you are convinced that you have interpreted the responses correctly and the categories are sufficient. Finally, a second opinion should be obtained with at least a subset of responses to establish consistency and accuracy for your conclusions. You can then code additional response categories for the variable.

Create a codebook. A codebook contains the set of instructions used to link a number to a category for a particular variable. This is a record for you to know the values assigned to the response categories for each variable. You may define each variable as you build a data set in a statistical program, or you may create a paper version of your codebook. You should also use the codebook to keep track of any new variables you create as you analyze the data.

Enter the data. There are several common methods of data entry. Research studies using computer-assisted telephone interviews (described in Chapter 7) are designed so that as responses are given, the data are immediately entered into a computer program. Another method is to use optical scan sheets. These are the familiar sheets many of us have used to record responses to standardized tests or to complete class evaluations. Data are coded on the sheets, and then the sheets are read by an optical scanner. A third method is to directly enter the data by hand into a spreadsheet such as Excel or Lotus or into a statistical package such as SPSS or SAS. If the data are entered directly into a statistics program, you have to define the data by identifying each variable and its characteristics. The procedures for doing so vary with the specific statistical or spreadsheet package. Exhibit 11.2 illustrates a variable definition file from SPSS. The information provided for each variable includes the variable name, variable label, labels for each of the variable values, values representing missing data, and the variable's level of measurement (Measure).

EXHIBIT 11.2 **Data Definition File From SPSS**

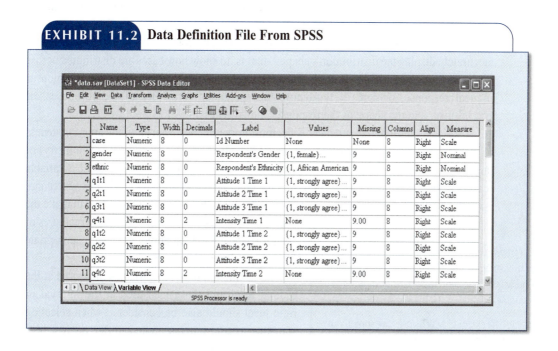

Cleaning the data. After the data are entered, check carefully for errors—a process called **data cleaning**. When using **check coding**, a second person recodes a sample of the forms and then the percentage of agreement on all the items on the forms is computed; if the percentage falls below a preestablished criterion for accuracy, then all forms should be recoded and reevaluated a second time. You should also examine the frequency distribution for every variable to see if there are cases with values that fall outside the range of allowable values for a given variable. When contingency questions are used, you should compute a crosstabulation whereby you compare responses to two variables. (We discuss frequency distributions and crosstabulations in the next sections.) This helps you identify instances in which a respondent should have skipped a question but a response was actually coded. Any mistakes you find can be corrected by going back to the original questionnaire with the corresponding identification number.

▣ DISPLAYING UNIVARIATE DISTRIBUTIONS

The first step in data analysis is usually to display the variation in each variable of interest in what are called *univariate frequency* distributions. For many descriptive purposes, the analysis may go no further. Frequency distributions and graphs of frequency distributions are the two most popular approaches for displaying variation; both allow the analyst to display the distribution of cases across the value categories of a variable. Graphs have the advantage over numerically displayed frequency distributions because they provide a picture that is easier to comprehend. Frequency distributions are preferable when exact numbers of cases with particular values must be reported, and when many distributions must be displayed in a compact form.

No matter which type of display is used, the primary concern of the data analyst is to accurately display the distribution's shape—that is, to show how cases are distributed across the values of the variable. Three important features of the shape include the common or typical response, or **central tendency**; the spread or variability of the responses, or **variability**; and the shape of the responses, or **skewness**.

A variable's level of measurement is the most important determinant of the appropriateness of particular statistics. For example, we cannot talk about the skewness (lack of symmetry) of a variable measured at the nominal level (a qualitative variable). If the values of a variable cannot be ordered from lowest to highest, if the ordering of the variables is arbitrary, we cannot say whether the distribution is symmetric because we could just reorder the values to make the distribution more or less symmetric. Some measures of central tendency and variability are also inappropriate for nominal-level variables.

Central tendency The most common value (for variables measured at the nominal level) or the value around which cases tend to center (for a quantitative variable).

Variability The extent to which cases are spread out through the distribution or clustered in just one location.

Skewness The extent to which cases are clustered more at one or the other end of the distribution of a quantitative variable, rather than in a symmetric pattern around its center. Skew can be positive (a "right skew"), with the number of cases tapering off in the positive direction, or negative (a "left skew"), with the number of cases tapering off in the negative direction.

The distinction between variables measured at the ordinal level and those measured at the interval or ratio level should also be considered when selecting statistics to use, but researchers differ on just how much importance they attach to this distinction. Many researchers think of ordinal variables as imperfectly measured interval-level variables, and believe that, in most circumstances, statistics developed for interval-level variables also provide useful summaries for ordinal-level variables. Other researchers believe that variation in ordinal variables will be distorted by statistics that assume an interval level of measurement.

Graphs

A picture often is worth some immeasurable quantity of words. Graphs can be easy to read, and they highlight a distribution's shape. They are useful for exploring data because they show the full range of variation and identify data anomalies that might require further study. And good, professional-looking graphs can be produced easily with software available for personal computers. While there are many types of graphs, we will discuss bar charts, histograms, and frequency polygons. Each has two axes, the vertical axis (the *y*-axis), which usually represents frequency counts or percentages, and the horizontal axis (the *x*-axis), which displays the values of the variable being graphed. Graphs should have labels to identify the variables and the values, with tick marks showing where each indicated value falls along the axis.

A **bar chart** contains solid bars separated by spaces. It is a good tool for displaying the distribution of variables measured at the nominal level and other discrete categorical variables because there is, in effect, a gap between each of the categories. The bar chart of marital status in Exhibit 11.3 indicates that almost half of adult Americans were married at the time of the survey. Smaller percentages were divorced, separated, widowed, or never married. The most common value in the distribution is married, so this would be the distribution's central tendency. There is a moderate amount of variability in the distribution, because the half who are not married are spread across the categories of widowed, divorced, separated, and never married. Because marital status is not a quantitative variable, the order in which the categories are presented is arbitrary, and skewness is not defined.

Histograms, in which the bars are adjacent, are used to display the distribution of quantitative variables that vary along a continuum that has no necessary gaps. Exhibit 11.4

EXHIBIT 11.3 **Bar Chart of Marital Status**

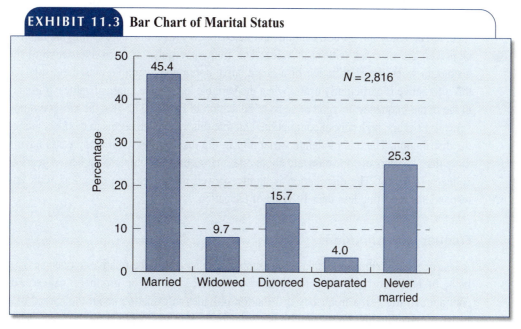

Source: General Social Survey (2000).

Note: Percentages do not add up to 100 due to rounding error.

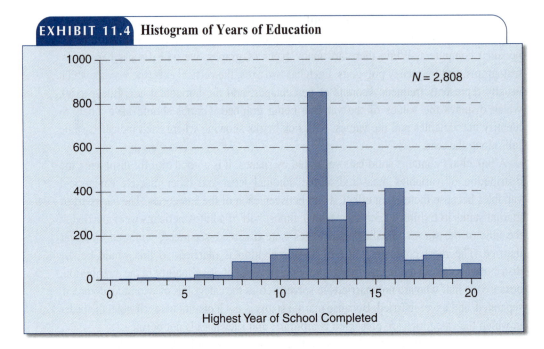

EXHIBIT 11.4 Histogram of Years of Education

Source: General Social Survey (2000).

shows a histogram of years of education. The distribution has a clump of cases centered at 12 years, with the most common value of 12. The distribution is not symmetric because there are more cases just above the central point than below it.

In a **frequency polygon,** a continuous line connects the points representing the number or percentage of cases with each value. The frequency polygon is an alternative to the histogram when the distribution of a quantitative continuous variable must be displayed; this alternative is particularly useful when the variable has a wide range of values. It is easy to see in the frequency polygon of years of education in Exhibit 11.5 that the most common value is 12 years, high school completion, and that this value also seems to be the center of the distribution. There is moderate variability in the distribution, with many cases having more than 12 years of education and about one-quarter having completed at least 4 years of college (16 years). The distribution is highly skewed in the negative direction, with few respondents reporting less than 10 years of education.

Frequency Distributions

A **frequency distribution** displays the number or percentage (the relative frequencies), or both, of cases corresponding to each of a variable's values or group of values. For continuous variables, a frequency distribution provides information about the spread of a variable, providing the lowest and highest categories with valid responses and some sense

EXHIBIT 11.5 **Frequency Polygon of Years of Education**

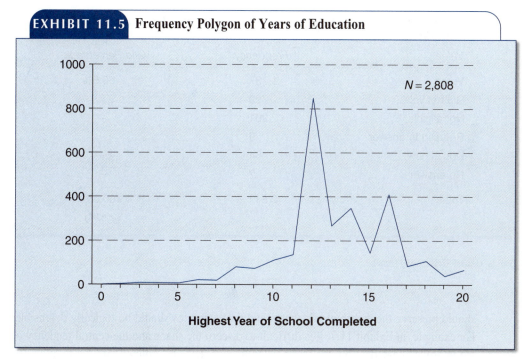

Source: General Social Survey (2000).

of the shape of the responses. The components of the frequency distribution should be clearly labeled, with a title, labels for the values of the variable, a caption identifying whether the distribution includes frequencies, percentages, or both, and perhaps the number of missing cases. If percentages are presented rather than frequencies (sometimes both are included), the total number of cases in the distribution (the base number N) should be indicated.

Constructing and reading frequency distributions for variables with few values is not difficult. The frequency distribution of voting in Exhibit 11.6, for example, shows that 68.5% of the respondents eligible to vote said they voted and that 31.5% reported they did not vote. The total number of respondents to this question was 2,536, although 2,817 actually were interviewed. The rest were ineligible to vote, just refused to answer the question, said they did not know whether they had voted or not, or gave no answer.

Many frequency distributions (and graphs) require grouping of some values after the data are collected. When there are too many values, say 15 or more, it is hard to display the data in a readable table. The distribution of the variable will be clearer or more meaningful if some of the data are grouped together. A frequency distribution of group data is made by combining scores into mutually exclusive and exhaustive categories. The chosen categories

| EXHIBIT 11.6 | Frequency Distribution of Voting in 1996 Presidential Election | |

Value	Frequency	Valid Percentage
Voted	1,737	68.5%
Did not vote	799	31.5
Not eligible	201	–
Refused to answer	9	–
Don't know	64	–
No answer	7	–
Total	2,817	100.0%
		(2,536)

Source: General Social Survey (2000).

should preserve the distribution's shape, and the categories should be logically defensible. For example, in Exhibit 11.7, it is difficult to discern the shape and the central tendency of the ungrouped age data but far easier when the age data are grouped into the familiar 10-year intervals.

While often categories will be the same size, in some cases the most logically defensible categories will vary in size. Grouping years of education (see Exhibit 11.8) as less than 8 (did not finish grade school), 8 to 11 (finished grade school), 12 (graduated high school), 13 to 15 (some college), 16 (graduated college), and 17 or more (some postgraduate education) captures meaningful distinctions in educational distribution and preserves the information that would be important for many analyses.

Combined and compressed frequency displays facilitate the presentation of a large amount of data in a relatively small space. In a **combined frequency display,** the distributions for a set of conceptually similar variables having the same response categories are presented together. Exhibit 11.9 is a combined display reporting the frequency distributions in percentage form for eight variables that indicate the degree to which government should be responsible for a variety of activities. The different variables are identified in the leftmost column and their values are labeled along the top. By looking at the table, you can see quickly that providing for the elderly and assisting low-income college students receive the most support as a government responsibility. A much smaller portion of the American public thinks the government should be responsible for reducing income differences or providing for the unemployed.

Compressed frequency displays can also be used to present crosstabular data and summary statistics more efficiently by eliminating unnecessary percentages (such as those

EXHIBIT 11.7 **Ungrouped and Grouped Age Distributions**

Ungrouped		Grouped	
Age	Percentage	Age (Years)	Percentage
18	0.2	18–19	1.8
19	1.6	20–29	16.9
20	1.4	30–39	21.7
21	1.3	40–49	22.6
22	1.4	50–59	14.5
23	1.7	60–69	9.7
24	1.8	70–79	7.9
25	1.9	80–89	4.8
26	2.1		
27	1.7		99.9
28	1.6		(2,809)
29	2.0		
30	2.2		
31	2.2		
32	2.7		
33	1.6		
34	2.0		
35	2.0		
36	2.2		
37	2.2		
38	2.7		
39	1.9		
40	2.6		
41	2.1		
42	2.6		
43	2.5		
44	2.5		
45	2.5		
46	2.0		
. . .	. . .		

Source: General Social Survey (2000).
Note: Percentages do not add to 100% due to rounding error.

corresponding to the second value of a dichotomous variable) and reducing the need for repetitive labels. Exhibit 11.10 presents a compressed display of agreement with different roles for women. Note that this display presents the number of cases on which the percentages are based.

EXHIBIT 11.8 Years of Education Completed

Years of Education	Percentage	Cumulative Percentage
Less than 8	2.4	2.4
8–11	15.1	17.5
12	29.3	46.8
13–15	28.2	75.0
16	14.0	89.0
17 or more	11.1	100.1
	100.1	
	(2,808)	

Source: General Social Survey (2000).
Note: Percentages do not add to 100% due to rounding error.

EXHIBIT 11.9 Government Responsibilities

Government's Responsibility	Definitely Should Be (%)	Probably Should Be (%)	Probably Should Not Be (%)	Definitely Should Not Be (%)	Total (%)	n
Provide for the elderly	39.8	47.2	10.2	2.8	100	432
Provide jobs for all	0.0	42.8	57.2	0.0	100	423
Assist low-income college students	34.4	51.9	10.4	3.3	100	422
Provide housing to the poor	19.3	46.9	23.9	9.9	100	414
Assist industrial growth	17.1	49.8	24.4	8.8	100	410
Provide for the unemployed	13.5	32.5	33.4	20.7	100	416
Reduce income differences	16.1	29.4	27.7	26.8	100	411
Keep prices under control	24.5	45.3	19.8	10.4	100	424

Source: General Social Survey 1996 Data File (1996).

EXHIBIT 11.10	Appropriate Roles for Women	

Statement	% Agree	n
Women should take care of home not country.	15.4	1,814
Women should work.	82.2	1,837
I would vote for a woman for president.	93.6	1,803
Women are not suited for politics.	23.2	1,747

Source: General Social Survey (2000).

⊡ SUMMARIZING UNIVARIATE DISTRIBUTIONS

Summary statistics are often used to describe particular aspects of the distribution of variables. These statistics facilitate comparisons across variables. In this section, we discuss measures of the typical score known as *central tendency* and measures for scores different from the typical score known as *variability*.

Measures of Central Tendency

Central tendency is usually summarized with one of three statistics: the mode, the median, or the mean. To choose an appropriate measure of central tendency, you must consider a variable's level of measurement, the skewness of a quantitative variable's distribution, and the purpose for which the statistic is used.

Mode

The **mode** is the most frequent value in a distribution. It is also termed the probability average because, being the most frequent value, it is the most probable. For example, if you were to pick a case at random from the distribution of views about government responsibility for the elderly (see Exhibit 11.9, first row), the probability of the case being a *probably should be* would be .47 out of 1, or 47.2%—the most probable value in the distribution. When a variable distribution has one case or interval that occurs more often than others, it is called a *unimodal* distribution.

Sometimes the mode can give a misleading impression of a distribution's central tendency because there are two or more values with an equivalent number of cases. When this happens, the distribution is called *bimodal* (or trimodal, and so on). There is no single mode. Imagine that a particular distribution has two categories, with each having just about the same number of cases, and these are the two most frequent categories. Strictly speaking, the mode would be the one with more cases, although the other frequent category had only slightly fewer cases. When the categories are close to each other, this is not really a problem; it becomes more of a problem when the categories are far apart. For example, the modal age of students at one school of social work is 24 (22%). The percentage at each age drops until 29 and then rises again until reaching the second most common age of 33 (20%). It is useful in this situation to report that the actual age distribution is bimodal.

Another potential problem with the mode is that it might happen to fall far from the main clustering of cases in a distribution. It would be misleading in most circumstances to say simply that the variable's central tendency was whatever the modal value was. In a study of caregivers, the modal response for monthly hours of respite care use was zero because a sizable proportion of caregivers did not use respite care (Cotrell & Engel, 1998). But to say the typical score was zero distorts the typical number of hours reported by those who did use respite care.

Nevertheless, on occasion the mode is appropriate. Most important, the mode is the only measure of central tendency that can be used to characterize the central tendency of variables measured at the nominal level. We cannot say much more about the central tendency of the distribution of marital status in Exhibit 11.3 than that the most common value is married.

Median

The **median** is the value that divides a variable's distribution in half (the 50th percentile). The median is inappropriate for variables measured at the nominal level because their values cannot be put in order and so there is no meaningful middle position. To determine the median, we simply list the variable's values in numerical order and find the value of the case that has an equal number of cases above and below it. If the median point falls between two cases, which happens if the distribution has an even number of cases, the median is defined as the average of the two middle values and is computed by adding the values of the two middle cases and dividing by 2.

The median in a frequency distribution is determined by identifying the value corresponding to a cumulative percentage of 50. Starting at the top of the years of education distribution in Exhibit 11.8, for example, and adding up the percentages, we find that we have reached 46.8% in the 12 years category and then 75.0% in the 13 to 15 years category. The median is therefore 13 to 15 years.

Mean

The **mean** is the arithmetic average of all scores in the distribution. It is computed by adding up the value of all the cases and dividing by the total number of cases, thereby taking into account the value of each case in the distribution:

Mean = Sum of value of cases/number of cases

In algebraic notation, the equation is $\bar{X} = \sum X_i / N.$

For example, to calculate the mean value of eight cases, we add the value of all cases ($\sum X_i$) and divide by the number of cases (N):

$$(28 + 117 + 42 + 10 + 77 + 51 + 64 + 55) / 8 = 444/8 = 55.5$$

Because computing the mean requires adding up the values of the cases, it makes sense to compute a mean only if the values of the cases can be treated as actual quantities—that is, if they reflect an interval or ratio level of measurement, or if they are ordinal and we assume that ordinal measures can be treated as interval. It would make no sense to calculate the mean for a nominal variable such as religion or race.

Median or Mean?

Both the median and the mean are used to summarize the central tendency of quantitative variables, but their suitability for a particular application must be carefully assessed. One consideration is level of measurement; the median and the mean are not appropriate for nominal-level variables. The median is most suited to measure the central tendency of variables measured at the ordinal level, and it can also be used to measure the central tendency of variables measured at the interval and ratio levels. Technically, the mean is only suited to measure central tendency for variables measured at the interval and ratio levels, but as we have already noted, some researchers treat ordinal variables as interval-level.

The shape of a variable's distribution should also be taken into account when deciding whether to use the median or the mean. When a distribution is perfectly symmetric, so that the distribution of values below the median is a mirror image of the distribution of values above the median, the mean and median are the same. But the values of the mean and median are affected differently by skewness, the presence of cases with extreme values on one side of the distribution but not on the other side. Because the median takes into account only the number of cases above and below the median point, not the value of these cases, it is not affected in any way by extreme values. Because the mean is based on adding the value of all the cases, it will be pulled in the direction of exceptionally high (or low) values. The average score on a test for a class of 10 can be easily distorted if one or two students did extremely well relative to everyone else; the median may be a more accurate reflection of the typical score. When the value of the mean is larger than the median, the distribution is skewed in a positive direction, with proportionately more cases with lower than higher values; when the mean is smaller than the median, the distribution is skewed in a negative direction.

The differential impact of skewness on the median and mean is illustrated in Exhibit 11.11. On the first balance beam, the cases (bags) are spread out equally, and the median and the mean are in the same location. On the second and third balance beams, the median corresponds to the value of the middle case, but the mean is pulled toward the value of the one case with an extremely low value.

The single most important influence on the choice of the median or the mean should be the purpose of the statistical summary. If the purpose is to report the middle position in one

EXHIBIT 11.11   **The Mean as a Balance Point**

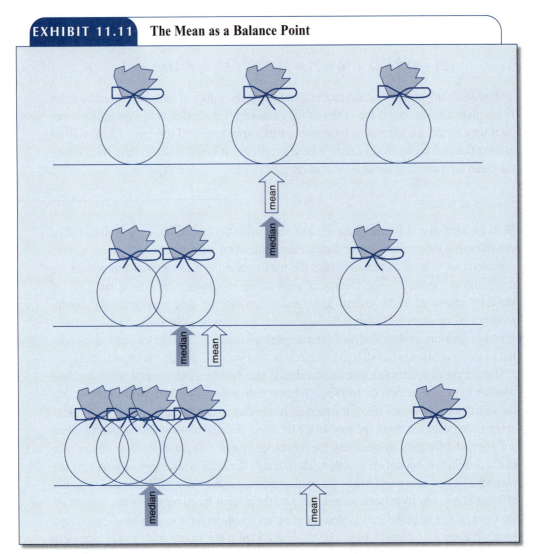

Source: Schutt (2005).

or more distributions, then the median is the appropriate statistic regardless of whether the distribution is skewed. For example, with respect to the age distribution from the General Social Survey you could report that half the American population is younger than 41 years old and half the population is older than that. But if the purpose is to show how likely different groups are to have age-related health problems, the measure of central tendency for these groups should take into account people's ages, and not just the number who are older and younger than a particular age. For this purpose, the median would be inappropriate because it would not distinguish the two distributions as shown in Exhibit 11.12. In the top distribution, everyone is between the ages of 35 and 45 years, with a median of 41. In the

| EXHIBIT 11.12 | **Insensitivity of Median to Variation at End of Distribution** |

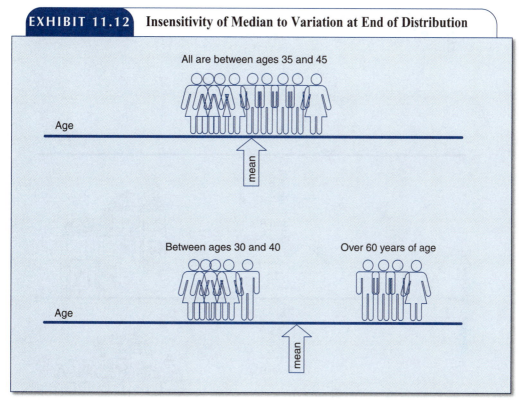

Source: Schutt (2005).

bottom distribution, the median is still 41 years but half the cases have ages above 60. The higher mean in the second distribution reflects the fact that it has more older people.

The lesson is that one should probably report both the mean and the median. In general, the mean is the most commonly used measure of central tendency for quantitative values, because it takes into account the values of all cases in the distribution and it is the foundation for many other more advanced statistics. However, the mean's popularity results in its use in situations for which it is inappropriate.

Measures of Variation

A summary of distributions based only on their central tendency can be incomplete and even misleading. For example, three towns might have the same mean and median income but still be different in their social character due to the shape of their income distributions. As illustrated in Exhibit 11.13, Town A is a homogeneous middle-class community, Town B is heterogeneous, and Town C has a polarized, bimodal income distribution, with mostly very poor and very rich people and few in between. However, all three towns have the same median income.

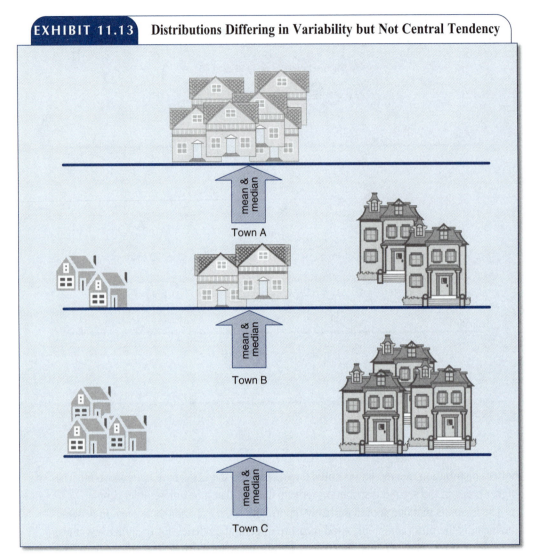

EXHIBIT 11.13 **Distributions Differing in Variability but Not Central Tendency**

Town A

mean & median

Town B

mean & median

Town C

mean & median

Source: Schutt (2005).

The way to capture these differences is with statistical measures of variation. Four popular measures of variation are the range, the interquartile range, the variance, and the standard deviation (which is the most popular measure of variability). To calculate these measures, the variable must be at the interval or ratio level. Statistical measures of variation are used infrequently with qualitative variables, so these measures are not presented here.

Range

The **range** is a simple measure of variation, calculated as the highest value in a distribution minus the lowest value:

$$\text{Range} = \text{Highest value} - \text{Lowest value.}$$

It often is important to report the whole range of actual values that might be encountered. However, because the range can be drastically altered by just one exceptionally high or low value termed an *outlier,* it is not a good summary measure of a variable's distribution for most purposes.

Interquartile Range

The **interquartile range** avoids the problem created by outliers. **Quartiles** are the points in a distribution corresponding to the first 25% of the cases, the first 50% of the cases (the median), and the first 75% of the cases. The second quartile corresponding to the first 50% of cases is simply the median. The first and third quartiles are determined by finding the points corresponding to 25% and 75% of the cases, just as you find the median. The interquartile range is the difference between the first quartile and the third quartile.

Variance

The **variance** provides a statistic that uses all the reported scores to determine the spread. The variance is the average squared deviation of each case from the mean. As you can see in Exhibit 11.14, you take each case, subtract it from the overall mean, and compute the square of the value. To get the *sample variance,* the result is summed across all cases and then divided by the number of cases minus 1. The formula for the *sample variance* is

$$s^2 = \frac{\Sigma(X_i - \bar{X})^2}{n-1},$$

where $\bar{X}$ is the sample mean, n is the sample size, Σ is the total for all cases, and X_i is the value of each case i on variable X. The *population variance* only differs by dividing by the total number of cases. You also should note that the use of squared deviations in the formula accentuates the impact of relatively large deviations, since squaring a large number makes that number count much more.

   The variance is used in many other statistics, although it is more conventional to measure variability with the closely related standard deviation than with the variance.

Standard Deviation

Because the variance provides a measure of the square of the deviations, it does not express the spread in the original units of the measure, so it is hard to interpret the variance. For example, what does a variance of 43.42 mean in relation to the actual reported scores in Exhibit 11.14? To correct this, variation is often expressed by the **standard deviation,**

EXHIBIT 11.14	Calculation of the Variance		

Case #	Score (X_i)	$X_i - \bar{X}$	$(X_i - \bar{X})^2$
1	21	−3.27	10.69
2	30	5.73	32.83
3	15	−9.27	85.93
4	18	−6.27	39.31
5	25	0.73	0.53
6	32	7.73	59.75
7	19	−5.27	27.77
8	21	−3.27	10.69
9	23	−1.27	1.61
10	37	12.73	162.05
11	26	1.73	2.99
	267		434.15

Mean = 267/11 = 24.27

Sum of squared deviations = 434.15

Variance: s_x^2 = 434.15/(11−1) = 43.42

Source: Schutt (2005).

which is simply the square root of the variance. By taking the square root, the sample standard deviation is expressed in the original units of the measure. It is the square root of the average squared deviation of each case from the mean:

$$s = \sqrt{\frac{\Sigma(X_i - \bar{X})^2}{n - 1}},$$

where $\sqrt{\ }$ is the square root. When the standard deviation is calculated from population data, the denominator is N, rather than $n - 1$, an adjustment that has no discernible effect when the number of cases is reasonably large.

The standard deviation has mathematical properties that make it the preferred measure of variability in many cases, particularly when a variable is normally distributed. A graph of a **normal distribution** looks like a bell, with one "hump" in the middle, centered on the population mean, and the number of cases tapering off on both sides of the mean (see Exhibit 11.15). A normal distribution is symmetric: If you folded it in half at its center (at the population mean), the two halves would match perfectly. If a variable is normally distributed, 68% of the cases will lie between plus and minus 1 standard deviation from the distribution's mean, and 95% of the cases will lie between 1.96 standard deviations above and below the mean. The correspondence of the standard deviation to the normal distribution enables us to infer how confident we can be that the mean (or some other statistic) of a population sampled randomly is within a certain range of the sample mean.

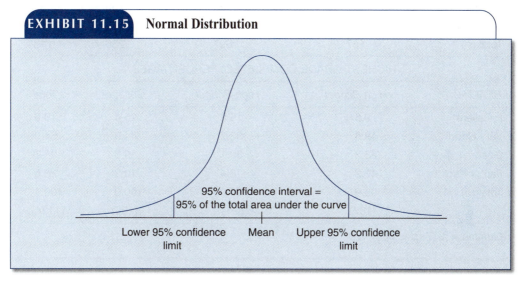

EXHIBIT 11.15	**Normal Distribution**

Source: Schutt (2005).

▣ DESCRIBING RELATIONS AMONG VARIABLES

Most data analyses focus on relationships among variables. The aim of many analyses is to test hypotheses about relationships among variables, while in some analyses the primary purpose is to describe or explore relationships. For each of these purposes, we must examine the association among two or more variables. **Crosstabulation** (crosstab) is one of the simplest methods for doing so. A crosstabulation displays the distribution of one variable for each category of another variable; it can also be termed a *bivariate distribution*. You can also display the association between two variables in a graph.

Exhibit 11.16 displays the crosstabulation of self-reported health by education (Jackson & Williams, 2004) so that we can test the hypothesis that perceived health increases with education (Franks, Gold, & Fiscella, 2003). The table is first presented with frequencies and then again with percentages. The cells of the table are defined by combinations of row and column values. Each cell represents cases with a unique combination of values of the two variables, corresponding to that particular row and column. The **marginal distributions** of

EXHIBIT 11.16	Crosstabulation of Health by Education			
HIGHEST GRADE COMPLETED: CELL COUNTS				
HEALTH	<High School	High School	College	Total
Excellent	18	109	65	192
Very Good	37	233	115	385
Good	53	222	50	325
Fair or Poor	79	127	26	232
Total (n)	187	691	256	1134
HIGHEST GRADE COMPLETED: PERCENTAGES				
HEALTH	<High School	High School	College	Total
Excellent	9.6	15.8	25.4	16.9
Very Good	19.8	33.7	44.9	34.0
Good	28.3	32.1	19.5	28.7
Fair or Poor	42.2	18.4	10.2	20.5
Total (n)	99.9	100.0	100.0	100.1
	(187)	(691)	(256)	(1134)

Gamma = .377 (p < .001)

Source: Jackson & Williams (2004).

Note: Percentages do not add to 100% due to rounding error.

the table are on the right (the row marginals) and underneath (the column marginals). These are just the frequency distributions for the two variables (in number of cases, percentages, or both), considered separately. In Exhibit 11.16, the column marginals are for the categories of education; the row marginals are for the distribution of health.

The first table in Exhibit 11.16 shows the number of cases with each combination of values of health and education. It is hard to look at the table in this form and determine whether there is a relationship between the two variables. We need to convert the cell frequencies into percentages, as in the second table in Exhibit 11.16. This table presents the data as percentages within the categories of the independent variable (the column variable, in this case). In other words, the cell frequencies have been converted into percentages of the column totals (the *n* in each column). For example, the number of people with less than a high school degree who felt in excellent health is 18 out of 187, or 9.6% (which rounds off to 10%). Because the cell frequencies have been converted to percentages of the column totals, the numbers add up to 100 in each column, but not across the rows.

To read the percentage table, compare the percentage distribution of health across the columns, starting with the lowest educational category (in the left column). As education increases, the percentage in excellent or very good health also rises, from about 30% of those with less than a high school degree (adding rounded-up values 10 + 20 in the first two cells in the first column), up to 70% of those with at least a college degree (adding rounded values 25 + 45 in the first two cells in the last column). This result is consistent with the hypothesis.

When the data in a table are percentages, usually just the percentages in each cell should be presented, not the number of cases in each cell. Include 100% at the bottom of each column (if the independent variable is the column variable) to indicate that the percentages add up to 100, as well as the base number (*n*) for each column (in parentheses). If the percentages add up to 99 or 101 due to rounding error, just indicate so in a footnote.

Graphing Association

Graphs provide an efficient tool for summarizing relationships among variables. Exhibit 11.17 displays the relationship between age and poverty in graphic form. It shows that the percentage of the population whose income is below the official poverty line is highest among the youngest age cohorts (0 to 17 years old and 18 to 24 years).

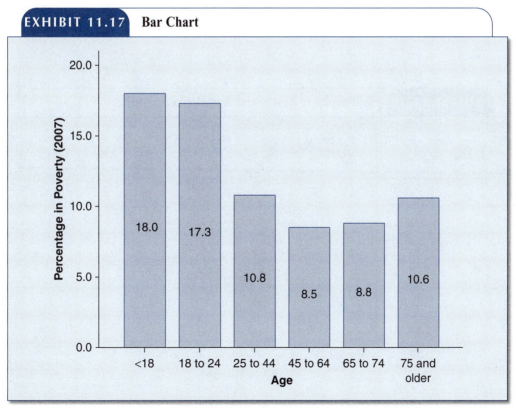

EXHIBIT 11.17   **Bar Chart**

Source: U.S. Census Bureau, Current Population Survey, Annual Social and Economic Supplement (2008).

A **scatterplot** is used to display the relationship between two continuous variables. Exhibit 11.18 displays the relationship between test scores and the number of hours studied. The dependent variable, test score, is placed on the *y*-axis while the independent variable, hours studied, is found on the *x*-axis. Visually, it appears that the distribution of responses confirms the expected relationship.

Describing Association

A crosstabulation table reveals four aspects of the association between two variables:

- *Existence.* Do the percentage distributions vary at all between categories of the independent variable?

- *Strength.* How much do the percentage distributions vary between categories of the independent variable?

- *Direction.* For quantitative variables, do values on the dependent variable tend to increase or decrease with an increase in value on the independent variable?

- *Pattern.* For quantitative variables, are changes in the percentage distribution of the dependent variable fairly regular (simply increasing or decreasing), or do they vary (perhaps increasing, then decreasing, or perhaps gradually increasing and then rapidly increasing)?

EXHIBIT 11.18   **Scatterplot of Test Scores and Hours Studied**

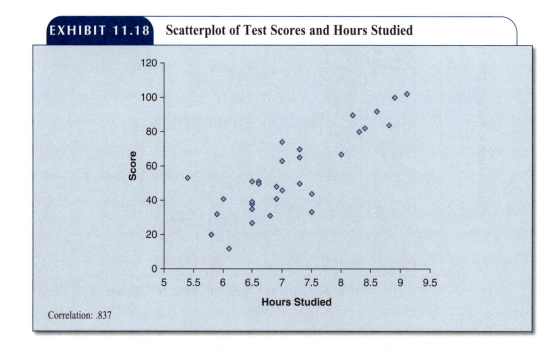

Correlation: .837

In Exhibit 11.16, an association exists; it is moderately strong (the difference in percentages between the first and last columns is about 15 percentage points), and the direction of association between perceived health and education is positive. The pattern in this table is close to what is termed **monotonic**. In a monotonic relationship, the value of cases consistently increases (or decreases) on one variable as the value of cases increases (or decreases) on the other variable. Monotonic is often defined a bit less strictly, with the idea being that as the value of cases on one variable increases (or decreases), the value of cases on the other variable tends to increase (or decrease) and at least does not change direction. This describes the relationship between health and education: Self-reported health increases as education increases, with shifts in the direction of better health in the columns after the first.

The relationship between race, another potential correlate (Franks et al., 2003), and health appears in Exhibit 11.19. There is a moderate association: 19% of Whites rate their health as excellent, compared with 15% of those who are members of a minority racial or ethnic group. Between the minority and White columns, the entire distribution of health shifts in the direction of better health. Note that we rounded off the percentages and, as a result, they no longer total 100 in each column. A table footnote makes this clear to the reader. Exhibit 11.20, by contrast, gives almost no evidence of an association between gender and health. There are no more than 5 percentage points separating the self-rated health of men and women in each health category.

Evaluating Association

When you read research reports and journal articles, you will find that social work researchers usually make decisions about the existence and strength of association on the basis of more statistics than just a single crosstabulation.

EXHIBIT 11.19	**Health by Race/Ethnicity**	
	RACIAL/ETHNIC GROUP	
HEALTH	*White*	*Minority*
Excellent	19%	15%
Very Good	39	29
Good	27	30
Fair or Poor	14	25
Total	99%*	99%*
(n)	(520)	(619)

Source: Jackson & Williams (2004).
*Percentages do not add to 100 due to rounding.

EXHIBIT 11.20	Health by Gender	

	GENDER	
HEALTH	Male	Female
Excellent	20%	15%
Very Good	37	32
Good	26	30
Fair or Poor	18	22
Total	101%*	99%*
(n)	(429)	(710)

Source: Jackson & Williams (2004).

*Percentages do not add to 100 due to rounding.

A **measure of association** is a type of descriptive statistic used to summarize the strength of an association. There are many measures of association, some of which are appropriate for variables measured at particular levels. One popular measure of association in crosstabular analyses with variables measured at the ordinal level is **gamma**. As with many measures of association, the possible values of gamma vary from –1, meaning the variables are perfectly associated in an inverse direction; to 0, meaning there is no association of the type that gamma measures; to +1, meaning there is a perfect positive association of the type that gamma measures. In Exhibit 11.16, the gamma is .377, suggesting there is a moderate positive relationship between education and perceived health.

The strength of a relationship for ratio variables can be determined using a **correlation coefficient** such as Pearson's *r*. The correlation coefficient can range from –1 to +1. Similar to gamma, the closer the correlation is to zero, the weaker the relationship; a correlation of +1 reflects a perfect positive relationship while –1 reflects a perfect inverse relationship. In Exhibit 11.18, the correlation coefficient is .837, suggesting that there is a strong positive relationship between test scores and hours studied.

Note that the appropriate measure depends on the level of measurement of each of the variables. You may remember these measures of association from a statistics course.

Statistic	*Minimum Level of Measurement*
Phi	Nominal, both dichotomous
Cramer's V	Nominal, one dichotomous

Gamma	Ordinal
Spearman's Rho	Ordinal
Pearson's *r*	Both interval
Eta	One interval, one nominal with three or more categories
Point biserial	One interval, one dichotomous

◲ IMPLICATIONS FOR EVIDENCE-BASED PRACTICE

The effectiveness of a particular intervention is usually tested with statistical methods beyond those we have described to this point. Even if it appears that there is a relationship between two variables that is consistent with the researcher's hypothesis, the association may have been just due to chance—such are the vagaries of sampling on a random basis (of course, the problem is even worse if the sample is not random). Therefore, researchers perform tests of their hypotheses using *inferential statistics* to determine whether it is likely that an association exists in the larger population from which the sample was drawn. Inferential statistics include many different bivariate statistical tests (tests of the relationship of two variables) and multivariate statistical tests (tests of the relationship of three or more variables), which we will not describe here. It is these tests that enable practitioners to conclude that the effectiveness of an intervention is not just a function of chance.

Statistical Significance

Quantitative findings that a practice method is effective rely on the analyst's ability to demonstrate that a relationship between two variables—an intervention and its effect or a comparison between two interventions and their effects on an outcome—is statistically significant; in other words, the relationship is not due to chance. **Statistical significance** means that an association is not likely to be due to chance, according to some criterion set by the analyst. The criterion is referred to as the *alpha* level (α) or *p* value—the probability level that will be used to evaluate statistical significance. The *alpha* level is usually set by the researcher prior to the analysis, while the *p* value is the probability level often computed by statistical software packages. It is conventional in statistics to use an *alpha* level of .05— that is, to avoid concluding that an association exists in the population from which the sample was drawn unless the probability that the association was due to chance is less than 5%. In other words, a statistician normally will not conclude that an association exists between two variables unless he or she can be at least 95% confident that the association was not due to chance.

Note that we have emphasized that the analyst "feels reasonably confident" that the association is "not likely to be due to chance" when there is a statistically significant relationship. There is still a degree of doubt since statistical testing is based on probability, which means that whatever we conclude, it is possible we could be wrong. As we described in Chapter 4, when we draw a sample from a population, we have no guarantee that the sample is truly representative; rather, we are confident it is representative within some degree of error. Because the conclusion made from statistical testing is based on probability, it is possible to make the wrong conclusion (see Exhibit 11.21). For example, we can test the relationship between the number of hours studied and student scores on examinations. One hypothesis, the *null hypothesis*, is that there is no relationship in the population, whereas the alternative hypothesis suggests that there is a relationship. With our sample of students, we find a statistically significant relationship, and so we are 95% sure that a relationship exists in the population. Yet note: There still remains a 5% possibility that we have reached the wrong conclusion. We have to consider the possibility that we have concluded that there is a relationship based on our one sample, but in fact there is no relationship between the two variables in the population we sampled. This type of error, called **Type I error**, threatens our ability to conclude that there is an association. Type I error is easy to calculate, as it is equal to the *alpha* level you chose as a criterion for statistical significance or the *p* value produced as part of an analysis computed by statistical software.

Type I error is influenced by the effect of the intervention or the strength of the relationship between an independent variable and a dependent variable. The greater the effect or impact of the intervention, the more likely the effect will be significant. Smaller effects or weaker relationships are less likely to provide statistically significant results.

Type I error is also influenced by sample size. A small sample is less likely to produce a statistically significant result for a relationship of any given strength. However, larger sample

---

EXHIBIT 11.21   **Type I and Type II Errors**

	In the Population	
In the Sample	The groups differ	The groups do not differ
The groups differ by a statistically significant amount, so the researcher *rejects the null hypothesis*	*The researcher's decision is* **CORRECT**	*The researcher has made a* **Type I Error (α)**
The groups do not differ by a statistically significant amount, so the researcher *fails to reject the null hypothesis*	*The researcher has made a* **Type II Error (β)**	*The researcher's decision is* **CORRECT**

sizes are likely to find statistically significant relationships even when the strength of the relationship is weak. You may remember from Chapter 4 that sampling error decreases as sample size increases. For this same reason, an association is less likely to appear on the basis of chance in a larger sample than in a smaller sample. In a table with more than 1,000 cases, the odds of a chance association are often low indeed. For example, with our table based on 1,134 cases, the probability that the association between education and health (Exhibit 11.16) was due to chance was less than 1 in 1,000 ($p < .001$). The association in that table was only moderate, as indicated by a gamma of .377. Even rather weak associations can be statistically significant with such a large random sample, which means that the analyst must be careful not to assume that just because a statistically significant association exists, it is therefore important. In other words, in a large sample an association may be statistically significant, but still be too weak to be substantively significant.

Type I error is not the only wrong conclusion that we can make. Let us return to the test of the relationship between the number of hours studied and examination scores. In our sample, we find that there is not a statistically significant relationship and conclude that the number of hours studied is unrelated to the examination scores. But we have to consider the possibility that we have concluded that there is no relationship based on our one sample, but in fact there is a relationship between the two variables in the population we sampled (see Exhibit 11.21). This is referred to as **Type II error** and is summarized by *beta* (β).

Type I and Type II errors are particularly important because finding an association between two variables is a necessary condition to establish causality. The problem that researchers encounter is that the risk of making Type I and Type II errors cannot be completely eliminated. When a researcher chooses an *alpha* level of .05, it means that the researcher is willing to accept a 5% chance of concluding that there is a relationship in a particular sample when there is no relationship in the population. The researcher could reduce Type I error by making it more difficult to find a statistically significant relationship: setting an *alpha* level of .01, for example, would mean that the researcher is willing to accept only a 1% chance of finding that there is a relationship when there is none in the population. By doing this, the likelihood of Type I error is reduced.

By minimizing Type I error, however, the researcher has increased the probability of Type II error. By making it less likely that we will falsely conclude that there is a relationship in the population, we have made it more likely that we will falsely conclude from sample data that there is no relationship when there is a relationship in the population.

Which type of error should be minimized? There is no easy answer. It depends on the level of risk associated with concluding there is a relationship when there is none (Type I error) or concluding there is no relationship when there is a relationship (Type II error). For example, you might need to assess the risk or consequence of using an intervention shown to be effective in a research study that is really not effective (Type I error) versus the consequence of not using an intervention found to be ineffective in a research study (Type II error), when it really is effective. Statisticians normally focus on the risk of Type I error, to minimize the risk when they say there is a relationship (that the favored hypothesis is supported), when there is not a relationship.

Statistical power analysis is a tool used by researchers to determine the sample size necessary to detect an effect of specific size for a particular *alpha* level. Statistical power analysis is also used to determine Type II error for a sample of specific size, effect size, and the level of statistical significance.

Therefore, it is important to keep Type I error and Type II error in mind as you weigh the evidence about the effectiveness of a particular intervention from the research articles you read or the research that you conduct. What is the probability that these errors may explain the findings? Is the sample size so big that even trivial effects are statistically significant? It is through replication that researchers try to reduce doubts generated by the potential for Type I and Type II errors.

Choosing a Statistical Test

There are many different statistical methods to test hypotheses. It is common for a researcher to start the analysis of an independent and a dependent variable with a **bivariate statistical test** such as the chi-square test mentioned earlier. Bivariate statistics test the relationship between two variables. A **multivariate statistical test** is used when the analyst tests the relation of several independent variables with a dependent variable; these tests allow the analyst to evaluate the effect of an independent variable while controlling for the effects of other independent variables on the dependent variable. For example, we could test separately the relationship of education and health and marital status and health using bivariate tests. But with a multivariate test, we could examine the relationship of education and health holding marital status constant. It is not unusual to find that a statistically significant relationship identified with a bivariate statistical test is no longer statistically significant when the effects of other variables are controlled in a multivariate statistical test.

Different statistical tests depend on the level of measurement of the variables. For example, the chi-square test requires the independent and dependent variable to be nominal measures. The commonly used Student *t*-test requires that the independent variable be nominal and dichotomous and the dependent variable be at least an interval measure. To conduct a bivariate regression analysis, both the independent and dependent variable must be at least interval measures. The level of measurement of independent and dependent variables also influences the choice of multivariate tests.

Discussing each of these tests is beyond the focus of this book, and many of you have already taken a class in statistics. For those of you interested in a review, we have placed the chapter *Reviewing Inferential Statistics* on the text's study Web site (http://www.sagepub.com/fswrstudy). To read most statistical reports and to conduct more sophisticated analyses of social data, you have to extend your statistical knowledge.

🔲 ETHICAL ISSUES: AVOIDING MISLEADING FINDINGS

Using statistics ethically means, first and foremost, being honest and open. Findings should be reported honestly, and researchers should be open about the thinking that guided the decision to use particular statistics. It is possible to distort social reality with statistics, and it is unethical to do so knowingly, even when the error is due more to carelessness than deceptive intent.

When we summarize a distribution in a single number, even in two numbers, we lose much information. Taken separately, neither measures of central tendency nor variation alone tell us about the other characteristic of the distribution. So, reports using measures of central tendency should also include measures of variation. Also, we should inspect the shape of any distribution for which we report summary statistics to ensure that the summary statistic does not mislead us (or anyone else) because of an unusual degree of skewness.

It is possible to mislead those who read statistical reports by choosing summary statistics that accentuate a particular feature of a distribution. Imagine an unscrupulous realtor trying to convince a prospective home buyer in community B that it is a community with high property values, when it actually has a positively skewed distribution of property values (see Exhibit 11.22). The realtor compares the mean price of homes in community B with

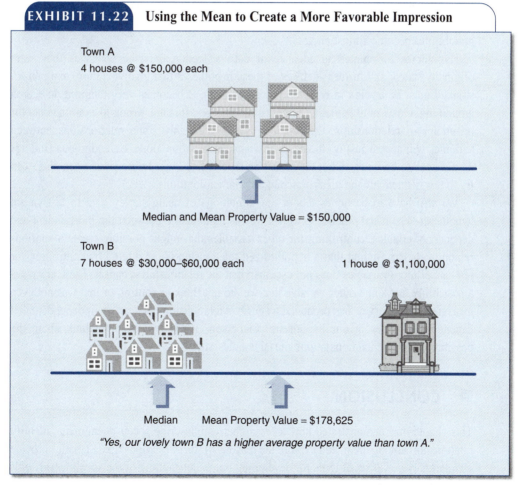

EXHIBIT 11.22   Using the Mean to Create a More Favorable Impression

Town A
4 houses @ $150,000 each

Median and Mean Property Value = $150,000

Town B
7 houses @ $30,000–$60,000 each   1 house @ $1,100,000

Median   Mean Property Value = $178,625

"Yes, our lovely town B has a higher average property value than town A."

Source: Schutt (2005).

that for community A (one with a homogeneous midpriced set of homes) and therefore makes community B look much better. In truth, the higher mean in community B reflects a skewed, lopsided distribution of property values; most residents own small, cheap homes. A median would provide a better basis for comparison.

It is possible to distort the shape of a distribution by ignoring some of the guidelines for constructing graphs and frequency distributions. Whenever you need to group data in a frequency distribution or graph, you can reduce the potential for problems by inspecting the ungrouped distributions and then using a grouping procedure that does not distort the distribution's basic shape. When you create graphs, be sure to consider how the axes you choose may change the distribution's apparent shape.

When the data analyst begins to examine relationships among variables in some real data, social science research becomes most exciting. The moment of truth, it would seem, has arrived. Either the hypotheses are supported or not. But, in fact, this is also a time to proceed with caution and to evaluate the analyses of others with even more caution. Once large data sets are entered into a computer, it becomes very easy to check out a great many relationships; when relationships are examined among three or more variables at a time, the possibilities become almost endless.

Hypotheses formulated in advance of data collection must be tested as they were originally stated; any further analyses of these hypotheses that involve a more exploratory strategy must be labeled in research reports as such. It becomes very tempting to search around in the data until something interesting emerges. It is not wrong to examine data for unanticipated relationships; the problem is that inevitably some relationships between variables will appear just on the basis of chance association alone. Serendipitous findings do not need to be ignored, but they must be reported as such. Subsequent researchers can try to test deductively the ideas generated by our explorations.

We also have to be honest about the limitations of using survey data to test causal hypotheses. The usual practice is to test for the relationship between the independent and dependent variables, controlling for other variables that might possibly create a spurious relationship. But finding that a hypothesized relationship is not altered by controlling for just one or more variables does not establish that the relationship is causal. There always is a possibility that some other variable that we did not think to control, or that was not even measured in the survey, has produced a spurious relationship between the independent and dependent variables in our hypothesis (Lieberson, 1985). We have to think about the possibilities and be cautious in our causal conclusions.

CONCLUSION

This chapter has demonstrated how a researcher can describe social phenomena, identify relationships among them, and explore the reasons for these relationships. Statistics provide a remarkably useful set of tools for developing our understanding of the social world, tools that we can use to both test our ideas and generate new ones.

Unfortunately, to the uninitiated, the use of statistics can seem to end debate right there—you cannot argue with the numbers. But you now know better than that. The numbers will be worthless if the methods used to generate the data are not valid, and the numbers will be misleading if they are not used appropriately, taking into account the type of data to which they are applied. Even assuming valid methods and proper use of statistics, there is one more critical step because the numbers do not speak for themselves. Ultimately, it is how we interpret and report the numbers that determines their usefulness.

KEY TERMS

Bar chart	Measure of association
Bivariate statistical test	Median
Central tendency	Mode
Check coding	Monotonic
Combined frequency display	Multivariate statistical tests
Compressed frequency display	Normal distribution
Correlation coefficient	Quartile
Crosstabulation	Range
Data cleaning	Scatterplot
Frequency distribution	Skewness
Frequency polygon	Standard deviation
Gamma	Statistical significance
Histograms	Type I error
Interquartile range	Type II error
Marginal distribution	Variability
Mean	Variance

HIGHLIGHTS

- Data must be prepared for analysis. This includes assigning unique identification numbers to each respondent, reviewing the forms for unclear responses, creating codes for open-ended questions, and developing a codebook.

- Data entry options include direct collection of data through a computer, use of scannable data entry forms, and use of data entry software. All data should be cleaned during the data entry process.

- Bar charts, histograms, and frequency polygons are useful for describing the shape of distributions. Care must be taken with graphic displays to avoid distorting a distribution's apparent shape.

- Frequency distributions display variation in a form that can be easily inspected and described. Values should be grouped in frequency distributions in a way that does not alter the shape of the distribution. Following several guidelines can reduce the risk of problems.

- Summary statistics are often used to describe the central tendency and variability of distributions. The appropriateness of the mode, mean, and median vary with a variable's level of measurement, the distribution's shape, and the purpose of the summary.

- The variance and standard deviation summarize variability around the mean. The interquartile range is usually preferable to the range to indicate the interval spanned by cases, due to the effect of outliers on the range. The degree of skewness of a distribution is usually described in words rather than with a summary statistic.

- Some of the data in many reports can be displayed more efficiently by using combined and compressed statistical displays.

- Crosstabulations should normally be percentaged within the categories of the independent variable. A crosstabulation can be used to determine the existence, strength, direction, and pattern of an association.

- Inferential statistics are used to test hypotheses. There is the potential for Type I and Type II errors.

- Honesty and openness are the key ethical principles that should guide data summaries.

DISCUSSION QUESTIONS

1. Using the data found at http://www.oas.samhsa.gov/statesList.cfm, locate the state in which you live (listed alphabetically). How did the researchers decide to group the data? Why do you believe they chose to do so in this manner? Would you have made the same choice? Why or why not?

2. Using the same table as referenced in Exercise 1, examine the distribution of substance use by age. Graph the results for the past month of cigarette use by age. What does the frequency distribution look like? What would you say with regard to skewness? Does the above referenced table give you enough information to make comparisons between variables? Why or why not?

CRITIQUING RESEARCH

1. Examine a quantitative study from a social work journal. Does the author provide you with summary statistics? Does the researcher provide you with information about the association among different variables? What statistics does the researcher use? Do the statistics he or she uses support the researcher's hypotheses?

MAKING RESEARCH ETHICAL

1. Review the frequency distributions and graphs in this chapter. Change one of these data displays so that you are "lying with statistics."

2. Consider the relationship between race and health that is presented in Exhibit 11.19. How might social work policies be affected by finding out that this relationship was due to differences in income rather than to racial differences in health?

DEVELOPING A RESEARCH PROPOSAL

1. Develop a plan to prepare your data for analysis. How will you assure the quality of the data?

2. Describe how you would analyze and present your data. What descriptive or inferential procedures would you use?

> To assist you in completing the Web exercises below and to gain a better under-standing of the chapter's contents, please access the study site at http://www.sagepub .com/fswrstudy where you will find the Web exercises reproduced with suggested links, along with self-quizzes, e-flash cards, interactive exercises, journal articles, and other valuable resources.

WEB EXERCISES

1. Go to the Henry J. Kaiser Family Foundation's Web site (http://www.kaisernetwork .org/health_poll/hpoll_index.cfm). After reviewing information about the Kaiser Network, select the link, Search by Topics. Choose a topic covered by the national poll, and compare the results for two different years. Based on poll data, create a brief report that includes the following for each year you chose: the topic and the years examined, the question asked in the polls, and bar charts showing years when polls were taken and total percentages in each response category, including the percentage who had no opinion on the issue, did not know, or refused to answer. Write a brief summary comparing and contrasting your two bar charts.

2. Do a Web search for information on a social work subject that interests you. How much of the information you find relies on statistics as tools for understanding the subject? How do statistics allow researchers to test their ideas about the subject and generate new ideas? Write your findings in a brief report, referring to the Web sites that you used.

CHAPTER 12

Reporting Research

Beginning With a Research Proposal

Reporting Results
  Writing Can Be Frustrating!
  Writing for Journals
  Applied Research Reports

Empirically Summarizing Reports: Meta-Analysis

Implications for Evidence-Based Practice

Social Work Research in a Diverse Society

Ethical Considerations

Conclusion

Key Terms

Highlights

Discussion Questions

Critiquing Research

Making Research Ethical

Developing a Research Proposal

Web Exercises

You learned in Chapter 2 that research is a circular process, so it is appropriate that we end this book where we began. The stage of reporting research results is also the point at which the need for new research is identified. It is the time when, so to speak, "the rubber hits the road"—when we have to make our research make sense to others. To whom will our research be addressed? How should we present our results to them? Will we seek to influence how our research report is used?

The primary goals of this chapter are to help you develop worthwhile reports for any research project you conduct and guide you in evaluating reports produced by others. We begin by teaching you how to write research proposals, as they also lay the groundwork for a final research report. We talk about the frustrations of writing and describe different approaches to writing for peer-reviewed journals and applied research reports. The next section introduces you to meta-analysis, a method used by researchers to combine the findings from several studies. We conclude with the implications of each of these sections for our diverse society and the ethical issues you should consider.

▣ BEGINNING WITH A RESEARCH PROPOSAL

If you have been completing the Developing a Research Proposal exercises at the end of each chapter, you are already familiar with the process of proposal writing. Nonetheless, we suggest that you read through this section carefully as an overview of the entire process.

Most research proposals will have at least six sections (Locke, Spirduso, & Silverman, 2000):

1. *An introductory statement of the research problem.* Clarify what it is that you are interested in studying and the significance of the research problem.

2. *A literature review.* Explain your issue in greater detail and how you plan to build on what has already been reported in the literature on your topic.

3. *A methodological plan.* Detail the methods you will use, including the design, sample, measures and variables, and data collection procedures.

4. *An ethics statement.* Identify human subjects' issues in the research, and establish how you will respond to them in an ethical fashion.

5. *A statement of limitations.* Review weaknesses of the proposed research and present plans for minimizing their consequences.

6. *A budget.* Present a careful listing of the anticipated costs.

If your research proposal will be reviewed competitively, it must present a compelling rationale for funding. It is not possible to overstate the importance of the research problem that you propose to study (see Chapter 2). If you propose to test a hypothesis, be sure that it is one for which there are plausible alternatives.

When you develop a research proposal, it helps to ask yourself the series of questions posed in Exhibit 12.1. It is easy to omit important details and to avoid being self-critical while rushing to put a proposal together. The items in Exhibit 12.1 can serve as a map to preceding chapters in this book and as a checklist of decisions that must be made throughout any research project. The questions are organized in five sections, each concluding with a *checkpoint* at which you should consider whether to proceed with the research as planned, modify the plans, or stop the project altogether. The sequential ordering of these questions obscures a bit the way in which they should be answered: not as single questions, one at a time, but as a unit—first as five separate stages, and then as a whole. You may change your answers to earlier questions on the basis of your answers to later questions.

EXHIBIT 12.1   **Decisions in Research**

PROBLEM FORMULATION (Chapters 1–2)

1. Developing a research question

2. Assessing researchability of the problem

3. Consulting prior research

4. Relating to social theory

5. Choosing an approach: Deductive? Inductive? Descriptive?

6. Reviewing research guidelines

> Checkpoint 1
> Alternatives: • Continue as planned.
> • Modify the plan.
> • STOP. Abandon the plan.

RESEARCH VALIDITY (Chapters 3–5)

7. Establishing measurement validity:
   - How are concepts defined?
   - Choose a measurement strategy.
   - Assess available measures or develop new measures.
   - What evidence of reliability and validity is available or can be collected?
   - Are the measures appropriate for use with the study population?

8. Establishing generalizability:
   - Was a representative sample used?
   - Are the findings applicable to particular subgroups?
   - Does the population sampled correspond to the population of interest?

9. Establishing causality:
   - What is the possibility of experimental or statistical controls?
   - How to assess the causal mechanism?
   - Consider the causal process

10. Data required: Longitudinal or cross-sectional?

11. Units of analysis: Individuals, families, groups, organizations, or communities?

12. What are the major possible sources of causal invalidity?

> Checkpoint 2
> Alternatives: • Continue as planned.
> • Modify the plan.
> • STOP. Abandon the plan.

Source: Engel & Schutt (2008).

RESEARCH DESIGN (Chapters 5–8, 10)

13. Choosing a research design and procedures:

    Experimental? Single-subject? Survey? Participant observation? Multiple methods?

14. Specifying the research plan: Type of surveys, observations, etc.

15. Secondary analysis? Availability of suitable data sets?

16. Causal approach: Idiographic or nomothetic?

17. Assessing ethical concerns

> Checkpoint 3
> Alternatives: • Continue as planned.
>   • Modify the plan.
>   • STOP. Abandon the plan.

DATA ANALYSIS (Chapters 9 and 11)

18. Choosing a statistical approach:
    • Statistics and graphs for describing data
    • Identifying relationships between variables
    • Deciding about statistical controls
    • Testing for interaction effects
    • Evaluating inferences from sample data to the population

> Checkpoint 4
> Alternatives: • Continue as planned.
>   • Modify the plan.
>   • STOP. Abandon the plan.

REVIEWING, PROPOSING, REPORTING RESEARCH (Chapters 2 and 12)

19. Clarifying research goals

20. Identifying the intended audience

21. Searching the literature and the Web

22. Organizing the text

23. Reviewing ethical and practical constraints

> Checkpoint 5
> Alternatives: • Continue as planned.
>   • Modify the plan.
>   • STOP. Abandon the plan.

⊡ REPORTING RESULTS

The goal of research is not just to discover something but to communicate that discovery to a larger audience: other social workers, consumer groups, government officials, your teachers, the general public—perhaps several of these audiences. Whatever the study's particular outcome, if the intended audience for the research comprehends the results and learns from them, the research can be judged a success. If the intended audience does not learn about the study's results, the research should be judged a failure—no matter how expensive the research or how sophisticated its design.

Writing Can Be Frustrating!

"Perfectionism is the voice of the oppressor; the enemy of the people. It will keep you cramped and insane your whole life and it is the main obstacle between you and a—first draft" (Lamott, 1994, p. 28). We often hear from students that "it is impossible to know where to begin," or "I have a hard time getting started." We have said it ourselves! To this we say, "Begin wherever you are most comfortable but begin early!" You do not have to start with the introduction; start in the methods section if you prefer. The main point is to begin somewhere and then keep typing, keep typing, and keep typing! It is easier to rewrite a paper than it is to write the first draft. The fine art of writing is really in the rewriting!

A successful report must be well organized and clearly written. Getting to such a product is a difficult but not impossible goal. Consider the following principles formulated by experienced writers (Booth, Colomb, & Williams, 1995):

- Start with an outline.

- Respect the complexity of the task and do not expect to write a polished draft in a linear fashion. Your thinking will develop as you write, causing you to reorganize and rewrite.

- Leave enough time for dead ends, restarts, revisions, and accept the fact that you will discard much of what you write.

- Write as fast as you comfortably can. Do not worry about spelling, grammar, and so on until you are polishing things up.

- Ask anyone whom you trust for their reactions to what you have written.

- Write as you go along, so you have notes and report segments drafted even before you focus on writing the report. (pp. 150–151)

It is important to remember that no version of a manuscript is ever final. As you write, you will get new ideas about how to organize the report. Try them out. As you review the first draft, you will see many ways to improve your writing. Focus particularly on how to shorten and clarify your statements. Make sure each paragraph concerns only one topic. Remember the golden rule of good writing: Writing is revising!

Another useful tip is called reverse outlining. After you have written a first complete draft, outline it on a paragraph-by-paragraph basis, ignoring the actual section headings you used. See if the paper you wrote actually fits the outline you planned.

If you began with a research proposal, you have a head start. Your proposal already has many of the components you will need for the final report. Use a word processing program on a computer to facilitate reorganizing and editing. And most important, leave yourself enough time so that you *can* revise, several times if possible, before turning in the final draft.

So begin to write. Different types of reports typically pose different problems. Writing for your professor will be guided, in part, by the expectations of your professor. Thesis and dissertation writers have to meet the requirements of different committee members but can benefit greatly from the areas of expertise represented on a typical committee. Journal articles and applied reports tend to follow a common pattern of content, which we describe in the next two sections.

Writing for Journals

Writing for academic journals is perhaps the toughest form of writing because articles are submitted to several other experts in your field for careful review—anonymously, with most journals—prior to acceptance for publication. This process is called **peer review**. Perhaps it would not be such an arduous process if so many academic journals did not have exceedingly high rejection rates and turnaround times for reviews that are, at best, several months. Even the articles that the reviewers judge initially to be the best are most often given a "revise and resubmit" after the first review and then are evaluated all over again after the revisions are concluded.

But there are some important benefits of journal article procedures. First and foremost is the identification of areas in need of improvement, as the author's eyes are replaced by those of previously uninvolved subject matter experts and methodologists. A good journal editor makes sure that he or she has a list of many different types of experts available for reviewing whatever types of articles the journal is likely to receive. There is a parallel benefit for the author(s): It is always beneficial to review criticisms of your own work by people who know the field well. It can be a painful and time-consuming process, but the entire field moves forward as researchers continually critique and suggest improvements in each other's research reports.

While there are slight variations in style across journals, there are typically seven standard sections within a journal article in addition to the title page:

1. *Abstract.* The abstract is a concise summary of the research report that describes the research problem, the sample, the method, and the findings.

2. *Introduction.* The body of a paper should open with an introduction that presents the specific problem under study, highlights why such a study is important, and describes the research strategy. A good introduction answers *what, why,* and *how* in a few paragraphs.

3. *Literature review.* Discuss the literature relevant to the topic, including what is known about the particular topic and what has been left unanswered. At the end of this section, you are ready to conceptually define your variables and formally state your hypotheses.

4. *Method.* Describe in detail how the study was carried out. This description enables the reader to evaluate the appropriateness of your methods and the reliability and validity of your results. It enables other researchers to replicate your study. In this section, you typically include subsections that describe the research design, the sample, the independent and dependent variables (measures), data collection procedures, and statistical or other analytic procedures.

5. *Results.* Summarize the results of the statistical or qualitative analyses performed on the data.

6. *Discussion.* Evaluate and interpret the findings, taking into account the purpose of the study. The findings may be discussed in light of the current state of knowledge as reflected in the literature review and the utility of the findings for social work practice or policy. Address the limitations of the study, the generalizability of the findings, and directions for future research.

7. *References.* All citations in the manuscript must appear in the reference list, and all references must be cited in the text.

Applied Research Reports

Applied research reports are written for a different audience than the professional social scientists and students who read academic journals. Typically, an applied report is written with a wide audience of potential users in mind and to serve multiple purposes. Often, both the audience and purpose are established by the agency or other organization that funded the research project on which the report is based. Sometimes the researcher may use the report to provide a broad descriptive overview of study findings that will be presented more succinctly in a subsequent journal article. In either case, an applied report typically provides much more information about a research project than does a journal article and relies primarily on descriptive statistics, rather than only those statistics useful for the specific hypothesis tests that are likely to be the primary focus of a journal article.

Exhibit 12.2 outlines the sections in one applied research report. This particular report was funded by a county agency responsible for services to children, youth, and families and was intended to comply with new state work standards. The goals of the report are to provide both description and evaluation. The body of the report presents findings on the actual time spent on different work-related activities in two different departments as well as a summary of focus group findings related to work activities. The discussion section highlights optimal caseloads for each department and the relation of the report's findings to other strategies to estimate caseloads. Five appendixes then provide details on the study methodology as well as detailed results.

EXHIBIT 12.2 **Sections in an Applied Report**

EXECUTIVE SUMMARY
Recently adopted . . . Standards for Child Welfare Practice (2000) include the expectation that agency management will conduct a workload study in order to determine staff levels necessary to perform the activities outlined in the Standards of Practice . . . (p. ii). This study examines the questions of how much time is required for workers to fulfill their responsibilities, and how many cases might reasonably comprise the workload of one trained person.

By analyzing the three streams of data, it was determined that the recommended maximum caseload per worker at a point in time is sixteen (16) in the Intake Department and seventeen (17) cases in Family Services. The results are noticeably compatible with national standards (e.g., the Child Welfare League of America) and studies completed in other states (e.g., California).

OVERVIEW OF RESEARCH ACTIVITIES AND PROCESS

SPECIFICATIONS OF RESEARCH QUESTION AND METHOD
     Research question
     Research approach
     Sample selection
     Data instrument

INTAKE DEPARTMENT ASSESSMENT
     Available work hours per month
     Average amount of time spent per case per month
     Time expended for family visits
     Total time needed per case during a month
     Estimated maximum caseload

FAMILY SERVICES DEPARTMENT ASSESSMENT
     Available work hours per month
     Average amount of time spent per case per month
     Time expended for family visits
     Total time needed per case during a month
     Estimated maximum caseload

OVERVIEW OF FOCUS GROUP FINDINGS
     Case-based focus group assessment
     Summary of focus group survey findings

DISCUSSION
Appendix

    A. Randomly selected caseworkers
    B. Distribution of task time spent on case per day – Intake Department
    C. Distribution of task time spent on case per day – Family Services
    D. Focus Group Participants
    E. Second Focus Group's Delineation of "good casework practice"

Consulted Literature and References

Source: Yamatani & Engel (2002).

One of the major differences between an applied research report and a journal article is that a journal article must focus on answering a particular research question, whereas an applied report is likely to have the broader purpose of describing a wide range of study findings and attempting to meet the needs of diverse audiences that have divergent purposes in mind for the research. But a research report that simply describes "findings" without some larger purpose in mind is unlikely to be effective in reaching any audience. Anticipating the needs of the audience (or audiences) for the report and identifying the ways in which the report can be useful to them will result in a product that is less likely to be ignored.

▣ EMPIRICALLY SUMMARIZING REPORTS: META-ANALYSIS

Meta-analysis is a quantitative method for identifying patterns in findings across multiple studies of the same research question (Cooper & Hedges, 1994). Unlike a traditional literature review, which describes previous research studies verbally, meta-analyses treat previous studies as cases whose features are measured as variables and are then analyzed statistically. It is like conducting a survey in which the respondents are previous studies. Meta-analysis shows how evidence about interventions varies across research studies. If the methods used in these studies varied, then meta-analysis can be used to describe how this variation affected study findings. If social contexts or demographic characteristics varied across the studies, then meta-analysis can indicate how social context or demographic characteristics affected study findings. Meta-analysis often accompanies systematic reviews that summarize what we know about the effectiveness of a particular intervention. By integrating different study samples and controlling for social context and demographic characteristics, meta-analysis enhances the generalizability of the findings.

Meta-analysis can be used when a number of studies have attempted to answer the same research question with similar quantitative methods. It is not typically used for evaluating results from multiple studies that used different methods or measured different dependent variables. It is also not very sensible to use meta-analysis to combine study results when the original case data from these studies are available and can actually be combined and analyzed together (Lipsey & Wilson, 2001). Rather, meta-analysis is a technique to combine and statistically analyze the statistical findings in published research reports.

After a research problem is formulated about prior research, the literature must be searched systematically to identify the entire population of relevant studies. Typically, multiple bibliographic databases are used; some researchers also search for related dissertations and conference papers. Eligibility criteria must be specified carefully to determine which studies to include and which to omit as too different. Lipsey and Wilson (2001) suggest that eligibility criteria include the following:

- *Distinguishing features.* This includes the specific intervention tested and perhaps the groups compared.

- *Research respondents.* These specify the population to which generalization is sought.

- *Key variables.* These must be sufficient to allow tests of the hypotheses of concern and controls for likely additional influences.

- *Research methods.* Apples and oranges cannot be directly compared, but some trade-off must be made between including the range of studies about a research question and excluding those that are so different in their methods as not to yield comparable data.

- *Cultural and linguistic range.* If the study population is going to be limited to English-language publications, or limited in some other way, this must be acknowledged, and the size of the population of relevant studies in other languages should be estimated.

- *Time frame.* Social processes relevant to the research question may have changed for such reasons as historical events or new technologies, so temporal boundaries around the study population must be considered.

- *Publication type.* Will the analysis focus only on published reports in professional journals, or will it include dissertations and unpublished reports? (pp. 16–21)

Once the studies are identified, their findings, methods, and other features are coded (e.g., sample size, location of sample, and strength of the association between the independent and dependent variables). Statistics are then calculated to identify the average effect of the independent variable on the dependent variable, as well as the effect of methodological and other features of the studies (Cooper & Hedges, 1994). The **effect size** statistic is the key to capturing the association between the independent and dependent variables across multiple studies. The effect size statistic is a standardized measure of association—often the difference between the mean of the experimental group and the mean of the control group on the dependent variable, adjusted for the average variability in the two groups (Lipsey & Wilson, 2001).

The meta-analytic approach to synthesizing research results can result in more generalizable findings than those obtained with just one study. Methodological weaknesses in the studies included in the meta-analysis are still a problem; only when other studies without particular methodological weaknesses are included can we estimate effects with some confidence. In addition, before we can place any confidence in the results of a meta-analysis, we must be confident that all (or almost all) relevant studies were included and that the information we need to analyze was included in all (or most) of the studies (Matt & Cook, 1994).

One of the challenges of meta-analysis is that the authors of the articles to be reviewed may not always report sufficient information. For example, the study reports (whether a journal article or unpublished report) may not contain information about participant characteristics, an especially important variable if we are to consider the generalizability of the results to different population groups. Littell (2005) noted that to conduct her meta-analysis of Multisystemic Therapy, she had to contact principal investigators to obtain more information about participant characteristics, interventions, and outcomes.

Meta-synthesis is a related method used to analyze and integrate findings from qualitative studies (Thorne, Jensen, Kearney, Noblit, & Sandelowski, 2004). This type of analysis requires not just aggregating findings from different qualitative studies but also reinterpreting the data once in aggregate.

Meta-analyses and meta-syntheses make us aware of how hazardous it is to base understandings of social processes on single studies that are limited in time, location, and measurement. Although one study may not support the hypothesis that we deduced from what seemed to be a compelling theory, this is not a sufficient basis for discarding the theory itself, nor even for assuming that the hypothesis is no longer worthy of consideration in future research. You can see that a meta-analysis combining the results of many studies may identify conditions for which the hypothesis is supported and others for which it is not.

Of course, we need to have our wits about us when we read reports of meta-analytic studies. It is not a good idea to assume that a meta-analysis is the definitive word on a research question just because it cumulates the results of multiple studies. Fink (2005) suggests evaluating meta-analytic studies in terms of the following seven criteria:

- *Clear statement of the analytic objectives.* The study's methods cannot be evaluated without knowledge of the objectives they were intended to achieve. Meta-analyses are most appropriate for summarizing research conducted to identify the effect of some type of treatment or other readily identifiable individual characteristic.

- *Explicit inclusion and exclusion criteria.* On what basis were research reports included in the analysis? Were high-quality studies distinguished from low-quality studies? If low-quality studies were included, were they analyzed separately, so that effects could be identified separately for the population of only high-quality studies?

- *Satisfactory search strategies.* Both electronic and written reference sources should be searched. Was some method used to find studies that were conducted but not published? It may be necessary to write directly to researchers in the field and to consult lists of papers presented at conferences.

- *A standardized protocol for screening the literature.* Screening involves rating the quality of the study and its relevance to the research question. This screening should be carried out with a simple rating form.

- *A standardized protocol for collecting data.* It is best to have two reviewers use a standard form for coding the characteristics of the reported research. The level of agreement between these reviewers should be assessed.

• *Complete explanation of the method of combining results.* Some checks should be conducted to determine where variable study features influenced the size of the treatment effect.

• *Report of results, conclusions, and limitations.* This seems obvious, but it is easy for a researcher to skirt over study limitations or some aspects of the findings.

Case Study

Do Parent Training Programs Prevent Child Abuse?

Lundahl, Nimer, and Parsons (2006) were interested in the effect of parent training and parent education programs on reducing risk factors associated with child abuse. They included only studies that met six eligibility criteria, such as that the training was conducted with families in which there were no developmental or cognitive delays in the parents or the children and that the training was directed to preventing physical abuse, child neglect, or emotional abuse only. Using three key words (child abuse, child neglect, and parent training), they searched three databases (ERIC, PsycInfo, and Social Work Abstracts) for any articles published between 1970 and 2004. Of 186 studies, they found 23 studies that met the eligibility criteria. They coded outcome measures, including parents' emotional adjustment, child-rearing attitudes, child-rearing behaviors, and documented abuse and moderating and independent variables, including participant characteristics, parent training program characteristics, and the methodological rigor of the studies.

Overall, the authors found that parent training was effective in changing attitudes and emotions as well as child-rearing behaviors and documented abuse. They also found that specific program characteristics, such as programs that included home visitors, had a greater impact in comparison with other program characteristics (Lundahl et al., 2006).

IMPLICATIONS FOR EVIDENCE-BASED PRACTICE

One of the primary ways in which social work practitioners learn about effective social work interventions is through the dissemination efforts of social work researchers and program evaluators. While journal articles and applied research reports differ in emphasis as well as in the degree of review and scrutiny they receive, both are vehicles to inform social work practice. It is likely that many of the readings used in your classes come from journal articles and applied research reports. By drawing on published articles, meta-analyses of the effectiveness of particular interventions are particularly valuable as the analysts test the effectiveness of a treatment across several research studies.

Just because research results are published does not mean that changes to practice come quickly. Therapeutic techniques for which there is a large body of evidence, such as cognitive-behavioral therapy, took time to be widely utilized by practitioners in some fields of practice (Dattilio & Epstein, 2005; Probst, 2008). In health care, it takes an average of 17 years for clinical research findings to be used in practice (Balas & Boren, 2000; Institute of Medicine, 2001). Even when the findings are applied, interventions may be less effective when tried in real-world settings as the clients are more diverse, with more diverse symptoms, and less compliant than participants in research studies, and are seen by clinicians with a range of expertise (U.S. Department of Health and Human Services, 1999).

Such findings have led to the emergence of *translational research,* or efforts both to speed the use of research findings into treatment settings and to make that research more relevant to these settings (Brekke, Ell, & Palinkas, 2009). The translational challenge is to figure out how to apply evidence-based findings to human service agencies with different community and organizational contexts than the setting for the research, with clients who may have different characteristics and motivations than the research participants and professionals whose incentive for following the intervention exactly is different than those testing the intervention (Probst, 2008). Therefore, there is a need for researchers to study how to best implement evidence-based findings in human service agencies (Brekke et al., 2009).

We do not mean to suggest that this challenge is so difficult that you should therefore ignore evidence-based findings. There are many examples of research findings applied to practice settings. The report summarized in Exhibit 12.2 led to caseload changes and the hiring of additional social workers (Yamatani & Engel, 2002). Carrilio (2001) described a process one agency used to digest all the best evidence regarding early childhood and family intervention programs. She and her team adapted research findings regarding home visiting and center-based interventions to create a program integrating both approaches. And their experiences led them to conclude that prepackaged parenting curricula required time to process and practice the skills within a coordinated group setting.

Of course, one necessary requirement is for social work graduates to be prepared to understand, assess, and interpret research findings. Another necessary requirement is to assess how these findings might be applied to your clients and in your agency. We hope that much of what you have read in the previous chapters has prepared you to do these tasks.

▣ SOCIAL WORK RESEARCH IN A DIVERSE SOCIETY

We return to our admonition from Chapter 1—social work research is being conducted in an increasingly diverse society. It places a responsibility on researchers to develop proposals and report findings that recognize this diversity if we are to adequately address questions about the impact of interventions or to understand the nature of social problems. The studies whose findings we read about in journals or reports most often begin with formal research proposals, and so writing the research proposal is part of the foundation for a successful research report. In turn, researchers are dependent on the quality of research reports when they synthesize studies to conduct meaningful meta-analyses in an attempt to clarify what works and for whom it works. So the decisions made in developing the proposal bear on reporting the findings in a single study and the synthesis of the findings of different studies.

Implications for research proposals. We hope you have now learned the kinds of issues that you must consider in carrying out research or evaluating research. The diversity of the populations that we study impacts all phases of the research process, whether it is the formulation of the research question, the meaning given to concepts and measurement of these concepts, the strategies used to recruit and retain participants, the kinds of categories used to classify participant characteristics, the analysis of the findings, or unique ethical concerns. These are all questions that must be addressed in the research proposal.

Implications for meta-analysis. We have suggested that meta-analysis is an important tool for summarizing the effect of different interventions and, therefore, helps social work practitioners assess the evidence about treatment outcomes. It can be used to help answer the questions, "Does it work?" and "For whom does it work?" We hope that you understand why it is so important that different population groups be included in research studies and that these studies reflect culturally competent research. In Chapter 5 we described how few intervention studies included different ethnic groups and the kinds of constraints this poses on conclusions from the research. Without the inclusion of different population subgroups, the "for whom" question becomes much more difficult to assess.

Implications for writing research. How the findings are reported is essential for reviewing individual studies and for conducting meta-analyses. It is not just enough to report the characteristics of the sample, such as the percentage who are female or the percentage who are African American, although this is certainly a good first step (Geller, Adams, & Carnes, 2006). To be meaningful, the analysis must account for group differences, whether by controlling for ethnicity or gender in a regression model or reporting group mean scores in intervention studies. Without these findings, it becomes more difficult for the meta-analyst to answer the "for whom" question.

⊡ ETHICAL CONSIDERATIONS

At the time of reporting research results, the researcher's ethical duty to be honest becomes paramount. Here are some guidelines:

• Provide an honest accounting of how the research was carried out and where the initial research design had to be changed. Readers do not have to know about every change you made in your plans and each new idea you had, but they should be informed about major changes in hypotheses or research design.

- Maintain a full record of the research project so that questions can be answered if they arise. Many details will have to be omitted from all but the most comprehensive reports, but these omissions should not make it impossible to track down answers to specific questions about research procedures that may arise in the course of data analysis or presentation.

- Avoid "lying with statistics" or using graphs to mislead.

- Acknowledge the sponsors of the research. This is important, in part, so that others can consider whether this sponsorship may have tempted you to bias your results in some way.

- Thank staff who made major contributions. This is an ethical as well as a political necessity. Let's maintain our social relations!

- Be sure that the order of authorship for coauthored reports is discussed in advance and reflects agreed-upon principles. Be sensitive to coauthors' needs and concerns.

Ethical research reporting should not mean ineffective reporting. You need to tell a coherent story in the report and avoid losing track of the story in a thicket of minuscule details. You do not need to report every twist and turn in the conceptualization of the research problem or the conduct of the research. But be suspicious of reports that do not seem to admit to the possibility of any room for improvement. Social science is an ongoing enterprise in which one research report makes its most valuable contribution by laying the groundwork for another, more sophisticated research project. Highlight important findings in the research report, but use the research report also to point out what are likely to be the most productive directions for future researchers.

▣ CONCLUSION

Too much research lacks one or more of the three legs of validity—measurement validity, causal validity, or generalizability—and contributes more confusion than understanding about the social world. Top journals generally maintain very high standards, partly because they have good critics in the review process and distinguished editors who make the final acceptance decisions. But some daily newspapers do a poor job of screening, and research reporting standards in many popular magazines, TV shows, and books are often abysmally poor. Keep your standards high and your view critical when reading research reports, but not so high or so critical that you turn away from studies that make tangible contributions—even if they do not provide definitive answers. And do not be so intimidated by the need to maintain high standards that you shrink from taking advantage of opportunities to conduct research yourself.

Good critical skills are essential when evaluating research reports, whether your own or those produced by others. There are *always* weak points in any research, even published research. It is an indication of strength, not weakness, to recognize areas where one's own research needs to be, or could have been, improved. You need to be able to weigh the strengths and weaknesses of particular research results and to evaluate a study in terms of its contribution to understanding social conditions and improving social work practice—but not in terms of whether it gives a definitive answer for all time.

Of course, social work research methods are no more useful than the commitment of researchers to their proper application. Research methods, like all knowledge, can be used poorly or well, for good purposes or bad, when appropriate or not. A claim that a belief is based on research provides no extra credibility. As you have learned throughout this book, we must first learn which methods were used, how they were applied, and whether interpretations square with the evidence. Having done all that, we can enhance our efforts to improve the well-being of our clients and our communities.

KEY TERMS

Effect size   Meta-synthesis
Meta-analysis   Peer review

HIGHLIGHTS

• Proposal writing should be a time for clarifying the research problem, reviewing the literature, considering the methods of implementation and data analysis, and thinking about the report that will be required. Trade-offs between different design elements should be considered and the potential for using multiple methods evaluated.

• Meta-analysis is a tool for summarizing research findings from different studies.

• Different types of reports typically pose different problems. Authors of student papers must be guided in part by the expectations of their professors. Thesis and dissertation writers have to meet the requirements of different committee members but can benefit greatly from the areas of expertise represented on a typical committee. Program evaluators and applied researchers are constrained by the expectations of the research sponsor. Journal articles must pass a peer review by other social scientists and often are much improved in the process.

• Research reports should include an introductory statement of the research problem, a literature review, a methodology section, a findings section with pertinent data displays, and a discussion/conclusions section that identifies the social work practice or policy implications of the findings, notes any weaknesses in the research methodology, and points out implications for future research. The report format should be modified according to the needs of a particular audience.

• All reports should be revised several times and critiqued by others before being presented in final form.

• To answer the "for whom" question, it is crucial to integrate diverse populations into research studies.

• The central ethical precept in research reporting is to be honest. This honesty should include providing a factual accounting of how the research was carried out, maintaining a full record about the project, using appropriate statistics and graphs, acknowledging the research sponsors, and being sensitive to the perspectives of coauthors.

DISCUSSION QUESTIONS

1. List and describe the sections included in research proposals. How are the research proposal and the research report similar? How do they differ?

2. Under what circumstances would a researcher choose to perform a meta-analysis? What are the strengths and weaknesses of this approach?

3. Describe the elements of successful research reporting. How does reverse outlining assist the writer? After the final draft of the article is written, how does the author find an appropriate audience?

4. Describe the similarities and differences between journal articles and applied research reports. Discuss the political and ethical considerations of research reporting in journals and in applied research.

5. Prepare an abstract of your research paper. Give the abstract to several students in your class and have them edit and evaluate your work. Give the same abstract to several friends who are not students in social work. Have them also edit and evaluate your work. Compare the critiques.

CRITIQUING RESEARCH

1. Read a journal article about a social issue that interests you. Read an applied research report (these can easily be obtained online) on the same social issue focusing on the same population. Compare and contrast these reports.

2. Reread the journal article you have chosen for Exercise 1. Was the research sponsored by any particular organization? If so, how might that sponsorship have influenced the reporting? How easy was the article to understand? Was the language simple and clear, or did the author use technical jargon? Did the author include practice or policy recommendations?

MAKING RESEARCH ETHICAL

1. Would you recommend legal regulations about the release of research data? What would those regulations be? Would they differ depending on the researcher's source of funding? Would you allow researchers exclusive access to their own data for some period of time after they have collected it?

2. Full disclosure of sources of research as well as of other medically related funding has become a major concern for medical journals. Should researchers publishing in social work journals also be required to fully disclose all sources of funding? Should full disclosure of all previous funds received by social work agencies be required in each published article? What about disclosure of any previous jobs or paid consultations with social work agencies? Write a short justification of the regulations you propose.

DEVELOPING A RESEARCH PROPOSAL

1. Organize the proposal material you wrote for previous chapters in a logical order. Based on your research question, select the most appropriate research method as your primary method.

2. Select another research method that could add knowledge about your research question.

3. Rewrite the entire proposal, adding an introduction. Add sections that outline a budget and state the limitations of your study.

4. Think about how the study findings can be used to inform policies, service design, or practice activities. What future research might you suggest given the study findings?

5. How will the results of the study be disseminated? How will you make your findings known to the professional community?

> To assist you in completing the Web exercises below and to gain a better understanding of the chapter's contents, please access the study site at http://www.sagepub .com/fswrstudy where you will find the Web exercises reproduced with suggested links, along with self-quizzes, e-flash cards, interactive exercises, journal articles, and other valuable resources.

WEB EXERCISES

1. The National Academy of Sciences wrote a lengthy report on ethics issues in scientific research. Visit the site and read the report (http://www.nap.edu/readingroom/books/obas). Summarize the information and guidelines in the report.

2. Using the Web, find five different examples of social science research projects that have been completed around the treatment of substance abuse or divorce and delinquency. Briefly describe each. How does each differ in its approach to reporting the research results? Who do you think the author(s) of each is (are) "reporting" to (i.e., who is the audience)? How do you think the predicted audience has helped to shape the authors' approach to reporting the results? Be sure to note the Web sites at which you located each of your five examples.

Finding Information and Conducting Literature Reviews

Elizabeth Schneider, MLS

How do we find prior research on a question of interest? You may already know some of the relevant material from prior coursework or your independent reading, but that will not be enough. You need to find reports of previous investigations that sought to answer the same research question that you wish to answer. If there have been no prior studies of exactly the same research question on which you wish to focus, you should seek to find reports from investigations of similar research questions. For example, you may be thinking about a study of the impact of cognitive-behavioral therapy on post-traumatic stress but you cannot find any specific studies; you might turn to available research on cognitive-behavioral therapy with persons suffering from anxiety. Once you have located reports from prior research similar to the research you wish to conduct, you may expand your search to include studies about related topics or studies that used similar methods.

Many journals publish literature reviews on a variety of topics. For example, Rizzo and Rowe (2006) reviewed studies of the cost-effectiveness of social work services in aging. Most research articles will include a literature review. These are helpful, but they are no substitute for reviewing the literature yourself. Only you can decide what is relevant for your research question, the setting for the study, the issues you confront, and your research methods. And you cannot depend on any published research review for information on the most recent studies.

Finding Information

Conducting a thorough search of the research literature and then critically reviewing what you have found is an essential foundation for any research project. Fortunately, most of this information can be identified online, without leaving your desk, and an increasing number of published journal articles can be downloaded directly to your own computer, depending on your particular access privileges. But just because there is a lot available does not mean that you need to find it all. Keep in mind that your goal is to find reports of prior research investigations; this means that you should focus on scholarly journals that choose articles for publication after they have been reviewed by other social scientists—that is, "refereed journals." Newspaper and magazine articles just will not do, although you may find some that raise important issues or even summarize social work research investigations.

Every year the World Wide Web offers more and more useful material, including indexes of the published research literature. You may find copies of particular rating scales, reports from research in progress, and papers that have been presented at professional conferences. Many well-respected research centers maintain papers on the Web. This section reviews the basic procedures for finding relevant research information both in the published literature and on the Web, but keep in mind that the primary goal is to identify articles published in refereed journals.

Searching the Literature

Social work and social science literature should be consulted at the beginning and end of an investigation. Even while an investigation is in progress, consultations with the literature may help to resolve methodological problems or facilitate supplementary explorations.

Specify your research question. Formulate a research question before you begin to search, even though the question may change later. Your question should be neither so broad that hundreds of articles are judged relevant nor so narrow that you miss important literature. "What is the relationship of informal support on the well-being of older adults?" is probably too broad, while "What is the relationship of informal support on somatic symptoms?" is probably too narrow. "What is the relationship of informal support to depressive symptoms experienced by older adults?" is probably about right.

Identify appropriate databases to search. Searching a computerized bibliographic database is by far the most efficient search strategy, although some libraries still carry paper indexes. The specifics of a database search will vary among libraries and according to your own computer resources. Check with your librarian for help. Most academic libraries provide access to online databases like *Social Work Abstracts, PsycINFO, EBSCO,* and the *Web of Science.* The search engine Google offers Google Scholar to anyone with Web access.

Start to identify a list of search terms. Identify the question's parts and list the authors of relevant studies. Specify the most important journals that deal with your topic. For example, if your research question involves the effect of informal support on depression in the elderly, you might consider searching the literature electronically for studies that mention *informal support* or just *support* as well as *depression* or *elderly depression.* You might include synonyms for the word *elderly*, such as *older adults*. You might plan to check journals like the *Journal of Gerontology, Journal of Gerontological Social Work, Gerontologist, Health and Social Work,* and *Psychology and Aging.*

Narrow your search. The sheer number of references you find can be a problem. For example, searching for *elderly* resulted in 2,372 citations in *Social Work Abstracts.* Depending on the database you are working with and the purposes of your search, you may want to limit your search to English-language publications, to journal articles rather than conference papers or dissertations (both of which are more difficult to acquire), and to materials published in recent years.

There are other methods to narrow your search. One method is to use Boolean search logic. You can narrow down your search by requiring that abstracts contain combinations of words or phases that include more specific details of your research question. Using the Boolean connector "and" allows you to do this. For example, entering *informal* in *Social Work Abstracts* resulted in 755 abstracts; entering *support* resulted in 7,310 abstracts; and entering *informal* and *support* resulted in 317 entries. Searching for a phrase will produce a shorter list. Entering the phrase *informal support* in *Social Work Abstracts* resulted in 112 English-language documents.

It is often a good idea to narrow down your search further by requiring that abstracts contain combinations of words or phrases. For example, searching for *elderly* and *informal support* in the same search reduced the number of documents to 40.

The choice of key words is also crucial in searching databases. If instead of *elderly,* we had searched for *older adults,* only 554 documents would have been retrieved in *Social Work Abstracts.* And some of these documents do not appear in the broader number of citations found in the search on *elderly.* The Boolean connector "or" can be used to find abstracts containing different words that mean the same thing. A search using *elderly* or *older adults* retrieves 2,821 documents.

Check the results. Read the titles and abstracts to identify articles that appear to be relevant. In some databases, you are able to click on these article titles and generate a list of their references, as well as links to other articles that quoted the original article. Once you have identified relevant articles, it is time to find the full text of articles of interest. If you are lucky, some of the journals you need will be available from your library in online versions, and you will be able to link to the full text of articles in those journals just by clicking on the "full text" link.

Take notes. You may be tempted to write up a review of the literature based on reading the abstracts or using only those articles available online, but you will be selling yourself short. Many crucial details about methods, findings, and theoretical implications will be found only in the body of the article, and many important articles will not be available online. To understand, critique, and really benefit from previous research studies, you must read the important articles, no matter how you have to retrieve them.

If you have done your job well, you will have more than enough literature as background for your own research, unless it is on a very obscure topic. Of course, your search will also be limited by library holdings you have access to and by the time required to order copies of conference papers and dissertations. At this point, your main concern is to construct a coherent framework in which to develop your research problem, drawing as many lessons as you can from previous research. You may use the literature to identify hypotheses to be reexamined, to find inadequately studied specific research questions, to explicate the disputes about your research question, to summarize the major findings of prior research, and to suggest appropriate methods of investigation.

Be sure to take notes on each article you read, organizing your notes into the standard sections: research questions, theory, methods, findings, and conclusions. In any case, write the literature review so that it contributes to your study in some concrete way; do not feel compelled to discuss an article just because you have read it. Be judicious. You are conducting only one study of one issue; it will only obscure the value of that study if you try to relate it to every tangential point in related research.

Do not think of searching the literature as a one-time-only venture—something that you leave behind as you move on to your *real* research. You may encounter new questions or unanticipated problems as you conduct your research or as you burrow deeper into the literature. Searching the literature again to determine what others have found in response to these questions or what steps they have taken to resolve these problems can yield substantial improvements in your own research. There is so much literature on so many topics that it often is not possible to figure out in advance every subject you should search the literature for or what type of search will be most beneficial.

Another reason to make searching the literature an ongoing project is that the literature is always growing. During the course of one research study, whether it takes only one semester or several years, new findings will be published and relevant questions will be debated. Staying attuned to the literature and checking it at least when you are writing up your findings may save your study from being outdated.

Searching the Web

The World Wide Web provides access to vast amounts of information of many different sorts (O'Dochartaigh, 2002). You can search the holdings of other libraries and download the complete text of government reports, some conference papers, and newspaper articles. You can find policies of local governments, descriptions of individual social scientists and particular research projects, and postings of advocacy groups. It is also hard to avoid finding a lot of information in which you have no interest, such as commercial advertisements, 3rd-grade homework assignments, or college course syllabi. Back in 1999, there were about 800 million publicly available pages of information on the Web (Davis, 1999). By 2003, there were as many as 15 billion pages on the Web (Novak, 2003). One newer search engine, Cuil, includes more than 124 billion Web pages (Cuil, 2009).

After you are connected to the Web with a browser like Microsoft Internet Explorer or Mozilla Firefox, you can use three basic strategies for finding information: direct addressing (typing in the address or URL of a specific site); browsing (reviewing online lists of Web sites); and searching. For some purposes, you will need to use only one strategy; for other purposes, you will want to use all three.

One problem that you may encounter when searching the Web is the sheer quantity of resources that are available. It is a much bigger problem when searching the Web than when searching bibliographic databases. For example, searching for *informal support* on Google (on November 18, 2007) produced 38.8 million sites, while putting quotation marks around *"informal support"* produced 60,100 sites. On the Web, less is usually more. Limit your inspection of Web sites to the first few pages that turn up in your list (they are ranked by relevance). See what those first pages contain and then try to narrow your search by including some additional terms.

Remember the following warnings when you conduct searches on the Web.

- *Clarify your goals.* Before you begin the search, jot down the terms that you think you need to search for and a statement of what you want to accomplish with your search. Then you will have a sense of what to look for and what to ignore.

- *Quality is not guaranteed.* Anyone can post almost anything, so the accuracy and adequacy of the information you find may be suspect. There is no journal editor or librarian to evaluate quality and relevance.

- *Anticipate change.* Web sites that are not maintained by stable organizations can come and go very quickly. Any search will result in attempts to link to some URLs that no longer exist.

- *One size does not fit all.* Different search engines use different procedures for identifying and indexing Web sites. Some attempt to be all-inclusive, while others aim to be selective. As a result, you can get different results from different search engines, even though you are searching for exactly the same terms.

- *Be concerned about generalizability.* You might be tempted to characterize elder abuse policies by summarizing the documents you find at a state Web site. But that state might not represent all states. And not all states may post their elder abuse policies.

- *Evaluate the sites.* There is a lot of material out there, so how do you know what is good? Some Web sites contain excellent advice and pointers on how to differentiate the good from the bad.

- *Avoid Web addiction.* Another danger of the extraordinary quantity of information available on the Web is that one search will lead to another and to another and so on. There are always more possibilities to explore and one more interesting source to check. Establish boundaries of time and effort to avoid the risk of losing all sense of proportion.

- *Cite your sources.* Using text or images from Web sources without attribution is plagiarism. It is the same as copying someone else's work from a book or article and pretending that it is your own. Use the referencing system required in your class. Instructions for the American Psychological Association's style can be found in the 5th edition of the *Publication Manual of the American Psychological Association*.

Reviewing Research

Effective review of the prior research you find is an essential step in building the foundation for new research. You must assess carefully the quality of each research study, consider the implications of each article for your own plans, and expand your thinking about your research question to take account of new perspectives and alternative arguments.

The research information you find at various Web sites comes in a wide range of formats and represents a variety of sources. *Caveat emptor* (buyer beware) is the watchword when you search the Web; following review guidelines like those we have listed will minimize, but not eliminate, the risk of being led astray. By contrast, the published scholarly journal literature that you find in databases like *Social Work Abstracts* and *PsycINFO* follows a standard format more closely and has been subjected to a careful review process. There is some variability in the content of these databases: some journals publish book reviews, comments on prior articles, dissertation abstracts, conference papers, and brief reports on innovative service programs. However, most literature you will find on a research topic in these databases represents peer-reviewed articles reporting analyses of data collected in a research project. These are the sources on which you should focus.

Reviewing the literature is really a two-stage process. In the first stage, you must assess each article separately. This assessment should follow a standard format like that represented by the "Questions to Ask About a Research Article" in Appendix B. However, you should keep in mind that you cannot adequately understand a research study if you just treat it as a series of discrete steps, involving a marriage of convenience among separate techniques. Any research project is an integrated whole, so you must be concerned with how each component to the research design influenced the others—for example, how the measurement approach might have affected the causal validity of the researcher's conclusions and how the sampling strategy might have altered the quality of measures.

The second stage of the review process is to assess the implications of the entire set of articles (and other materials) for the relevant aspects of your research question and procedures, and then to write an integrated review that highlights those implications. Although you can find literature reviews that consist simply of assessments of one published article after another—that never get beyond stage one in the review process— your understanding of the literature and the quality of your own work will be much improved if you make the effort to write an integrated review.

In the next two sections, we will show how you might answer many of the questions in Appendix B as we review a research article about domestic violence. We will then show

how the review of a single article can be used within an integrated review of the body of prior research on the research question. Because at this early point in the text you will not be familiar with all the terminology used in the article review, you might want to read through the more elaborate article review in Appendix C later in the course.

🔲 A SINGLE-ARTICLE REVIEW: PROGRAM COMPLETION AND RE-ARREST IN A BATTERER INTERVENTION SYSTEM

Bennett, Stoops, Call, and Flett (2007) designed a study to examine program participation factors and the subsequent re-arrest of male batterers. The study was supported by the Cook County Courts and the Illinois Criminal Justice Information Authority. In this section, we will examine the article that resulted from that study, which was published in *Research on Social Work Practice* in 2007. The numbers in brackets (below) refer to the article review questions in Appendix B.

Research question. Bennett et al. (2007) wanted to understand what characteristics and factors predicted completing batterer intervention programs (BIPs) and re-arrest as well as whether completing a BIP was related to re-arrest [1]. The study was both descriptive and explanatory, though the design did not allow for causality to be established [2]. The authors used an ecological framework and based the study on a typology of male batterers proposed by Holtzworth-Munroe and Stuart (1994) as well as Feder and Dugan's (2002) proposition that men who are more marginalized in society are more likely to be violent with their partners [4]. The literature review referred appropriately to research on other controlled intervention studies, studies of attrition, and research about factors related to re-arrest [3]. Finally, the authors describe how consent to participate in the study was obtained and how the strategy was approved by the university institutional review board [6].

Research design. The study was designed systematically with careful attention to specification of terms and clarification of assumptions; it focused on the possibility of different outcomes rather than certainty about one preferred outcome [5]. The major concepts in this study, generality of violence, severity of past violence, psychopathology, social factors, personal accountability, and program completion and re-arrests, were clearly defined [9]. The specific measurement procedures were discussed; the authors chose commonly used scales, and there is evidence of measurement reliability though less evidence for measurement validity [9, 10]. No specific hypotheses were stated, but throughout the literature review the authors pointed to variables that should be related to program completion and re-arrests [7]. The study design focused on the behavior of individuals [13]. Data were collected over time; the background data were collected at an initial assessment and the re-arrest records were reviewed slightly more than 2 years later

[14]. The authors used a quasi-experimental design by constructing a comparison group of men who did not complete BIPs and tried to enhance the adequacy of the comparison group through a series of estimations. By using a quasi-experimental design, the authors could not control for selection bias and, therefore, could not make causal assertions [15, 17]. The research project involved all cases for a specific period, but there were a number of eligibility criteria that narrowed the sample and, therefore, the ability to generalize these results [11]. The authors explain why certain cases were excluded from the assessment [15].

Research findings and conclusion. Bennett et al. (2007) were motivated by the opportunity to describe program completion and re-arrest for the entire network of BIP programs in one community, all of which were connected to the county criminal justice system [19]. Bennett et al. found that age, marital status, employment status, motivation to change, and being Latino predicted program completion, and that program completion reduces the likelihood of re-arrest [20]. Because the study is of a natural network of programs, the recommendations made can speak to the need for different types of programs to exist in the community and the specific content of batterers' programs [22, 23].

Overall, the Bennett et al. (2007) study represents an important contribution to understanding the effectiveness of BIPs in reducing domestic violence. While the lack of a control group precluded asserting causality, that the authors were able to include the entire network of programs in one community offers a model for further research in other communities.

An Integrated Literature Review: Female-Initiated Violence

The goal of the second stage of the literature review process is to integrate the results of your separate article reviews and develop an overall assessment of the implications of prior research. The integrated literature review should accomplish three goals: (1) summarize prior research; (2) critique prior research; and (3) present pertinent conclusions (Hart, 1998).

Summarize prior research. Your summary of prior research must focus on the particular research questions that you will address, but you may need to provide some more general background. Carney and Buttell (2006) began their research article thus: "Among the debates in the field of domestic violence none is more acrimonious than the debate around female initiated violence" (p. 571). They trace the background of this debate and the factors that have increased attention to female-initiated violence. They then discuss the differences between men and women arrested for domestic violence. Finally, they conclude with research about treatment programs and the lack of research on women in these programs. Their conclusions frame their research questions: "(a) Does the current standardized program for [female] batterers significantly alter psychological variables related to domestic violence? and (b) Does the current standardized treatment program for batterers differentially affect African American and White batterers?" (p. 573).

Ask yourself three questions about your summary of the literature:

1. *Have you been selective?* If there have been more than a few prior investigations of your research question, you will need to narrow your focus to the most relevant and highest-quality studies. Do not cite a large number of prior articles just because they are there or because you read them.

2. *Is the research up-to-date?* Be sure to include the most recent research, not just the "classic" studies.

3. *Have you used direct quotes sparingly?* To focus your literature review, you need to express the key points from prior research in your own words. Use direct quotes only when they are essential for making an important point (Pyrczak, 2005).

Critique prior research. Evaluate the strengths and weaknesses of the prior research. Consider the following questions as you decide how much weight to give to each article:

1. *How was the report reviewed prior to its publication or release?* Articles published in academic journals go through a rigorous review process, usually involving careful criticism and revision. Dissertations go through a lengthy process of criticism and revision by a few members of the dissertation writer's home institution. A report released directly by a research organization is likely to have had only a limited review, although some research organizations maintain a rigorous internal review process. Papers presented at professional meetings may have had little prior review. Needless to say, more confidence can be placed in research results that have been subject to a more rigorous review.

2. *What is the author's reputation?* Reports by an author or team of authors who have published other work on the research question may have greater credibility.

3. *Who funded and sponsored the research?* Major federal funding agencies and private foundations fund only research proposals that have been evaluated carefully and ranked highly by a panel of experts. They also often monitor closely the progress of the research. This does not guarantee that every such project report is good, but it goes a long way toward ensuring some worthwhile products. On the other hand, research that is funded by organizations that have a preference for a particular outcome should be given particularly close scrutiny (Locke, Silverman, & Spirduso, 1998).

Present pertinent conclusions. Do not leave the reader guessing about the implications of the prior research for your own investigation. Present the conclusions you draw from the research you have reviewed. As you do so, follow several simple guidelines:

- Distinguish clearly your own opinion of prior research from conclusions of the authors of the articles you have reviewed.

• Make it clear when your own approach is based on the theoretical framework you are using rather than on the results of prior research.

• Acknowledge the potential limitations of any empirical research project. Do not emphasize problems in prior research that you cannot avoid either (Pyrczak, 2005).

• Explain how the unanswered questions raised by prior research or the limitations of the methods used in those studies make it important for you to conduct you own investigation (Fink, 2005).

▣   SEARCHING THE WEB

To find useful information on the Web, you have to be even more vigilant than when you search the literature directly. With billions of Web pages on the Internet, there is no limit to the amount of time you can squander and the volume of useless junk you can find as you conduct your research on the Web. However, we can share with you some good ways to avoid the biggest pitfalls.

Direct Addressing

Knowing the exact address (uniform resource locator, or URL) of a useful Web site is the most efficient way to find a resource on the Web.

Professional Organizations

- American Evaluation Association (http://www.eval.org)
- Council on Social Work Education (http://www.cswe.org)
- National Association of Social Workers (http://naswdc.org)

Government Sites

- National Institute on Aging (http://www.nia.nih.gov)
- National Institutes of Health (http://www.nih.gov)
- U.S. Bureau of the Census (http://www.census.gov)

Bibliographic Formats for Citing Electronic Information

- Electronic reference formats suggested by the American Psychological Association (http://www.apastyle.org/elecref.html)
- Style sheets for citing resources (print & electronic) (http://www.lib .berkeley.edu/TeachingLib?guides/Internet/Style.html)

When you find Web sites that you expect you will return to often, you can save their addresses as "bookmarks" or "favorites" in your Web browser. However, since these can very quickly multiply, you should try to be very selective.

Browsing Subject Directories

Subject directories (also called guides, indexes, or clearing houses) contain links to other Web resources that are organized by subject. They vary in quality and authoritativeness, but a good one can be invaluable to your research and save you much time. The main advantage to using subject directories is that they contain links to resources that have been selected, evaluated, and organized by human beings, and thus present a much more manageable number of resources. If the person managing the guide is an expert in the field of concern, or just a careful and methodological evaluator of Web resources, the guide can help you to identify good sites that contain useful and trustworthy information, and you can avoid wading through thousands of "hits" and evaluating all the sites yourself.

There are general and specialized directories. The following are three examples of general directories:

- Yahoo! (http://www.yahoo.com) is often mistaken for a search engine, but it is actually a subject directory—and a monster one at that. It also functions as a portal or gateway for a collection of resources that can be customized by the user. Unlike when you use search engines, with Yahoo! you are not searching across the Web, but rather just within the Web pages that Yahoo! has cataloged. Yahoo! has a subject directory for the social sciences with more specific listings, including one for social work (http://dir.yahoo.com/social_science/social_work/). Yahoo! also links to versions of its site in about 20 countries, which would be good to go to when conducting extensive research on one of those countries (http://world.yahoo.com/).

- Open Directory (http://dmoz.org) is the largest Web directory with 4 million sites (Hock, 2004), and unlike Yahoo!, it is not a portal. In fact, other directories and search engines such as Yahoo! and Google use it. It has 16 top-level categories, including Social Sciences.

- Librarian's Index to the Internet (http://lii.org) is a small and highly selective Web directory produced by the Library of California.

The following are some examples of specialized subject directories:

- Argus Clearinghouse (http://www.clearinghouse.net/searchbrowse.html) is a guide to subject directories on the Internet, and it classifies them under subject headings.

- Social Sciences Virtual Library (http://www.vl-site.org/sciences/index.html) includes listings for anthropology, demographics, psychology, social policy and evaluation, sociology, women's studies, and other areas.

- BUBL INK (http://bubl.ac.uk/link) contains over 12,000 links covering all academic areas.

- INFOMINE: Scholarly Internet Resource Collections (http://infomine.ucr.edu) is produced by librarians across several campuses of the University of California system, and it includes a subject directory for the social sciences.

- SOSIG—Social Science Information Gateway (http://www.sosig.ac.uk) is a British site that aims to be comprehensive. It is classified according to the Dewey Decimal System—the classification system used by most public libraries.

Many other Internet subject directories are maintained by academic departments, professional organizations, and individuals. It is often hard to determine whether a particular subject directory like this is up-to-date and reasonably comprehensive, but you can have some confidence in subject directories published by universities or government agencies. *The Internet Research Handbook* is an excellent source for more information on subject directories (O'Dochartaigh, 2002).

Search Engines

Search engines are powerful Internet tools—it is already impossible to imagine life without them. The biggest problem is the huge number of results that come back to you. If the number of results is unmanageable, you can try searching using phrases such as informal support or a title search. This search will retrieve those pages that have that phrase in their title as opposed to anywhere on the page. This practice usually results in a dramatically smaller yield of results. If you are looking for graphical information, such as a graph or a chart, you can limit your search to those pages that contain an image. On Google, this just requires clicking on the Images link located above the search box.

There are many search engines, and none of them will give you identical results when you use them to search the Web. Different search engines use different strategies to find Web sites and offer somewhat different search options for users. Due to the enormous size of the Web and its constantly changing content, it simply is not possible to identify one search engine that will give you completely up-to-date and comprehensive results. Although there are many search engines, you may find the following to be particularly useful for general searching:

- Google (http://www.google.com) has become the leading search engine for many users in recent years. Its coverage is relatively comprehensive, and it does a good job of ranking search results by their relevancy (based on the terms in your search request). Google also allows you to focus your search just on images, discussions, or directories.

- AlltheWeb (http://www.alltheweb.com) is a more recent comprehensive search engine that also does a good job of relevancy ranking and allows searches restricted to images and so on.

• Microsoft's search engine (http://search.msn.com) adds a unique feature: Editors review and pick the most popular sites. As a result, your search request may result in a "popular topics" list that can help you to focus your search.

In conclusion, use the appropriate tool for your searches. Do not use a search engine in place of searching literature that is indexed in tools such as *Social Work Abstracts*. Bookmark the key sites that you find in your area of interest. Become familiar with subject directories that cover your areas of interest, and look there before going to a search engine. And when you do use a search engine, take a moment to learn about how it works and what steps you should take to get the best results in the least amount of time.

Questions to Ask About a Research Article

1. What is the social condition under study? What is the basic research question or problem? Try to state it in just one sentence. (Chapter 2)

2. Is the purpose of the study explanatory, evaluative, exploratory, or descriptive? Did the study have more than one purpose? (Chapter 1)

3. How did the author(s) explain the importance of the research question? Is the research question relevant to social work practice, social welfare policy, or both? (Chapter 2)

4. What prior literature was reviewed? Was it relevant to the research problem? To the theoretical framework? Does the literature review appear to be adequate? Are you aware of (or can you locate) any important omitted studies? Is the literature review up-to-date? (Chapter 2)

5. Was a theoretical framework presented? What was it? Did it seem appropriate for the research question addressed? Can you think of a different theoretical perspective that might have been used? (Chapter 2)

6. Were any hypotheses stated? Were these hypotheses justified adequately in terms of the theoretical framework? In terms of prior research? (Chapter 2)

7. What were the independent and dependent variables in the hypothesis or hypotheses? What direction of association was hypothesized? Were any other variables identified as potentially important? (Chapter 2)

8. What were the major concepts in the research? Did the author(s) provide clear and complete nominal definitions for each concept? What are the nominal definitions? Were some concepts treated as unidimensional that you think might best be thought of as multidimensional? (Chapter 3)

9. How are variables operationally defined by the author(s)? Are the operational definitions adequate? Did the instruments used and the measures of the variables seem valid and reliable? How did the author(s) attempt to establish measurement reliability and measurement validity? Could any more have been done in the study to establish measurement validity? Have the measures used in the study been evaluated in terms of reliability and validity with populations similar to the study sample? (Chapter 3)

10. Was a sample of the entire population of elements used in the study? Was a probability or nonprobability sampling method used? What specific type of sampling method was used? How was the sample recruited and selected? How large is the sample? Are women and people of color adequately represented in the sample? Did the authors think the sample was generally representative of the population from which it was drawn? Do you? How would you evaluate the likely generalizability of the findings to other populations? (Chapter 4)

11. Was the response rate or participation rate reported? Does it appear likely that those who did not respond or participate were markedly different from those who did participate? Why or why not? Did the author(s) adequately discuss this issue? (Chapters 4 and 7)

12. What were the units of analysis? Were they appropriate for the research question? If some groups were the units of analysis, were any statements made at any point that are open to the ecological fallacy? If individuals were the units of analysis, were any statements made at any point that suggest reductionist reasoning? (Chapter 4)

13. Was the study design cross-sectional or longitudinal, or did it use both types of data? If the design was longitudinal, what type of longitudinal design was it? Could the longitudinal design have been improved in any way, as by collecting panel data rather than trend data or by decreasing the drop-out rate in a panel design? If cross-sectional data were used, could the research question have been addressed more effectively with longitudinal data? (Chapter 2)

14. Were any causal assertions made or implied in the hypotheses or in subsequent discussion? What approach was used to demonstrate the existence of causal effects? Were all five issues in establishing causal relationships addressed? What, if any, variables were controlled in the analysis to reduce the risk of spurious relationships? Should any other variables have been measured and controlled? (Chapter 5)

15. Was an experimental, single-subject, survey, participant observation, or some other research design used? How does the author describe the design? How well was this design suited to the research question posed and the specific hypotheses tested, if any? Why do you suppose the author(s) chose this particular design? (Chapters 5, 6, 7, and 8)

16. Did the design eliminate potential alternative explanations, and how did the design do this? How satisfied (and why) are you with the internal validity of the conclusions? (Chapter 5)

17. What is the setting for the study? Does the setting limit the generalizability of the results to other similar settings or to the broader population? Is reactivity a problem? Are there other threats to external validity? (Chapter 5)

18. Was this an evaluation research project? If so, which type of evaluation was it? Which design alternatives did it use? (Chapter 10)

19. How were data collected? What were the advantages and disadvantages of the particular data collection method? (Chapter 7)

20. What did the author(s) find? Are the statistical techniques used appropriate for the level of measurement of the variables? How clearly were statistical or qualitative data presented and discussed? Were the results substantively important? (Chapters 9 and 11)

21. Did the author(s) adequately represent the findings in the discussion and conclusion sections? Were conclusions well grounded in the findings? Can you think of any other interpretations of the findings? (Chapter 12)

22. Compare the study with others addressing the same research question. Did the study yield additional insights? In what ways was the study design more or less adequate than the design of previous research? (Chapter 12)

23. What additional research questions and hypotheses are suggested by the study's results? What light did the study shed on the theoretical framework used? On social work practice questions? On social policy questions? (Chapters 2 and 12)

24. How well did the study live up to the guidelines for science? Do you need additional information in any areas to evaluate the study? To replicate it? (Chapter 2)

25. Did the study seem consistent with current ethical standards? Were any trade-offs made between different ethical guidelines? Was an appropriate balance struck between adherence to ethical standards and use of the most rigorous scientific practices? (Chapter 2)

How to Read a Research Article

In Chapter 1 you learned about evidence-based practice. Evidence-based practice assumes that social work practitioners base their practice on both their own experience and the best available research evidence. The discussions of research articles throughout the text may provide all the guidance you need to read and critique research on your own. But reading about an article in bits and pieces to learn about particular methodologies is not quite the same as reading an article in its entirety to learn what the researcher found out. The goal of this appendix is to walk you through an entire research article, answering the review questions introduced in Appendix B. Of course, this is only one article, and our "walk" will take different turns than a review of other articles might take, but after this review, you should feel more confident when reading other research articles on your own.

We use an article by Christopher Mitchell (1999) on the use of cognitive-behavioral therapy to treat panic disorders. This article, published in a leading journal, *Research on Social Work Practice,* has many strengths; yet, as you will see, there are gaps in the information reported by the author.

We have reproduced below each of the article review questions from Appendix B, followed by our answers to them. After each question, we indicate the chapter where the question was discussed and after each answer, we cite the article page or pages to which we refer. You can also follow our review by reading through the article itself and noting our comments.

1. *What is the social condition under study? What is the basic research question or problem? Try to state it in just one sentence.* (Chapter 2)

The specific concern in this study is the efficacy of short-term interventions to treat anxiety. The clearest statement of the research question is this: "Do cognitive-behavioral

Source: Christopher, M. (1999). Treating anxiety in a managed care setting: A controlled comparison of medication alone versus medication plus. *Research on Social Work Practice, 9,* 188–200. Copyright © Sage Publications.

interventions for panic disorder have an effect that goes beyond the effect of medication alone" (Mitchell, 1999, p. 192)?

2. *Is the purpose of the study explanatory, evaluative, exploratory, or descriptive? Did the study have more than one purpose?* (Chapter 1)

This study is evaluative in nature; the author describes it as an "outcome study" (Mitchell, 1999, p. 189).

3. *How did the author(s) explain the importance of the research question? Is the research question relevant to social work practice, social welfare policy, or both?* (Chapter 2)

The author connects the need to evaluate short-term treatment to changes in the mental health service delivery system and the advent of managed care. He notes that "insurers increasingly scrutinize and question the expenses associated with unlimited use of mental health services. . . . Open-ended therapies have given way to highly focused, time-limited treatments with specific and clearly defined objectives" (Mitchell, 1999, p. 188). Because social workers are primary providers of mental health services, the findings have implications for clinical social work practice and agencies that are reimbursed by third-party payers.

4. *What prior literature was reviewed? Was it relevant to the research problem? To the theoretical framework? Does the literature review appear to be adequate? Are you aware of (or can you locate) any important omitted studies? Is the literature review up-to-date?* (Chapter 2)

The literature review includes a discussion about panic disorders and their etiology, consequences, and prevalence (Mitchell, 1999, pp. 189–191). The second half of the literature review focuses on treatment within a managed care setting (pp. 191–192). One problem with the literature review is that there is only a passing reference to studies about the effectiveness of cognitive-behavioral therapy, and there is no description about the studies. Furthermore, the two studies referenced by the author date back to the 1980s. We leave it to you to find the more recent research.

5. *Was a theoretical framework presented? What was it? Did it seem appropriate for the research question addressed? Can you think of a different theoretical perspective that might have been used?* (Chapter 2)

The author does not present a theoretical perspective. Given the purpose of this study, it was not necessary to use a particular theoretical perspective.

6. *Were any hypotheses stated? Were these hypotheses justified adequately in terms of the theoretical framework? In terms of prior research?* (Chapter 2)

The one hypothesis in this study is, "People with panic disorder who participate in an 8-week program of cognitive-behavioral group therapy in addition to medication will have significantly lower levels of anxiety than people who receive medication alone" (Mitchell,

1999, pp. 192–193). The hypothesis is found in the Methods and Procedures section, which is unusual. Because the literature review describes so little research about cognitive-behavioral therapy and panic disorders, the hypothesis lacks empirical support. The lengthy description of cognitive-behavioral therapy suggests that the hypothesis rests on practice experience.

7. *What were the independent and dependent variables in the hypothesis or hypotheses? What direction of association was hypothesized? Were any other variables identified as potentially important?* (Chapter 2)

The independent variable is cognitive-behavioral intervention while the dependent variable is anxiety. It is hypothesized that the intervention will reduce anxiety level. No other variables were identified as important.

8. *What were the major concepts in the research? Did the author(s) provide clear and complete nominal definitions for each concept? What are the nominal definitions? Were some concepts treated as unidimensional that you think might best be thought of as multidimensional?* (Chapter 3)

There are several key concepts in this study: panic disorder, anxiety, and cognitive-behavioral group intervention. The author provides nominal definitions for each term. A "panic disorder is a subtype of anxiety that is characterized by discrete periods of intense apprehension or fear" (Mitchell, 1999, p. 189). The clinical criteria for a panic disorder are derived from the *Diagnostic and Statistical Manual of Mental Disorders*, 4th edition, and are provided in the literature review (pp. 189–190). Anxiety is defined as "inordinate worry and nervousness manifested in the cognitive, somatic, and behavioral domains" (p. 193). Cognitive-behavioral therapy is introduced as "techniques that include cognitive restructuring, breathing and relaxation techniques, and phobic desensitization" (p. 192).

9. *How are variables operationally defined by the author(s)? Are the operational definitions adequate? Did the instruments used and the measures of the variables seem valid and reliable? How did the author(s) attempt to establish measurement reliability and measurement validity? Could any more have been done in the study to establish measurement validity? Have the measures used in the study been evaluated in terms of reliability and validity with populations similar to the study sample?* (Chapter 3)

The author provides information about the group intervention and summarizes the content covered in each week of the intervention. Anxiety is measured using the Somatic, Cognitive, Behavioral Anxiety Inventory (SCBAI). The author reports the number of subscales, the number of items in the scale, scoring, and the interpretation of scores. Measurement reliability and validity are established by reporting split-half reliability coefficients for each of the subscales, and this suggests that it has strong concurrent validity (Mitchell, 1999, p. 194). The lack of detailed information about measurement reliability and validity is one of the weaknesses of this study. There is information from only one study and no data about the strength of the concurrent validity, so we are left to trust the author's conclusion. Because the author did not report the characteristics of the sample used to establish reliability and validity, we do not know whether the findings apply to the study sample.

10. *Was a sample of the entire population of elements used in the study? Was a probability or nonprobability sampling method used? What specific type of sampling method was used? How was the sample recruited and selected? How large is the sample? Are women and people of color adequately represented in the sample? Did the authors think the sample was generally representative of the population from which it was drawn? Do you? How would you evaluate the likely generalizability of the findings to other populations?* (Chapter 4)

The sample is described as a "convenience sample of 56 participants consist[ing] of adult men and women with panic disorder who voluntarily sought treatment in a large HMO in Washington, DC" (Mitchell, 1999, p. 193). We do not know how they were recruited for the study. Although the author recognizes that the sample lacks generalizability, he does note that the demographic composition of his participants is similar to the overall panic disorder population. The sample consists primarily of women (77%); 55% of the sample are African American, 11% are other people of color, and 34% are Caucasian (Table 1, p. 196).

11. *Was the response rate or participation rate reported? Does it appear likely that those who did not respond or participate were markedly different from those who did participate? Why or why not? Did the author(s) adequately discuss this issue?* (Chapters 4 and 7)

The participation rate is not reported by the author. Although we know that 56 people participated in the study, we do not know how many people refused to participate.

12. *What were the units of analysis? Were they appropriate for the research question? If some groups were the units of analysis, were any statements made at any point that are open to the ecological fallacy? If individuals were the units of analysis, were any statements made at any point that suggest reductionist reasoning?* (Chapter 4)

The unit of analysis is the individual. There are no statements suggesting reductionist reasoning.

13. *Was the study design cross-sectional or longitudinal, or did it use both types of data? If the design was longitudinal, what type of longitudinal design was it? Could the longitudinal design have been improved in any way, as by collecting panel data rather than trend data or by decreasing the drop-out rate in a panel design? If cross-sectional data were used, could the research question have been addressed more effectively with longitudinal data?* (Chapter 2)

Because of the experimental design used in this study, we are less concerned with this question. The findings and the clinical significance would have been strengthened had there been a follow-up several months after the conclusion of treatment.

14. *Were any causal assertions made or implied in the hypotheses or in subsequent discussion? What approach was used to demonstrate the existence of causal effects? Were*

all five issues in establishing causal relationships addressed? What, if any, variables were controlled in the analysis to reduce the risk of spurious relationships? Should any other variables have been measured and controlled? (Chapter 5)

The causal assertion is that changes in anxiety level will be due to the intervention, cognitive-behavioral therapy. The experimental design used in this study is sufficient to establish an association and time order but leaves open the issue of spuriousness as we describe in the next question. The literature review suggests that cognitive-behavioral therapy can trigger the desired change in anxiety. We do not know what effect contextual variables such as the setting (an HMO) or the community might have on the findings.

15. *Was an experimental, single-subject, survey, participant observation, or some other research design used? How does the author describe the design? How well was this design suited to the research question posed and the specific hypotheses tested, if any? Why do you suppose the author(s) chose this particular design?* (Chapters 5, 6, 7, and 8)

This quasi-experimental design is described by the author as "a comparative pretest-posttest design with nonequivalent groups" (Mitchell, 1999, p. 193). Four treatment groups of 8 to 10 participants were formed on a first-come basis. Each participant in the experimental condition received medication and cognitive-behavioral therapy. The comparison group received medication alone and consisted of clients on the wait list or those who had declined group therapy. The design does provide a plausible method to compare the effects of the intervention. This is a reasonable design given the practicalities of agency-based research and the need to serve clients as they come to the agency.

16. *Did the design eliminate potential alternative explanations, and how did the design do this? How satisfied (and why) are you with the internal validity of the conclusions?* (Chapter 5)

There are threats to internal validity because the author uses a quasi-experimental design. One problem is selection bias. To demonstrate the similarity of the two groups, the author compares the groups by age, gender, marital status, education, and race, as well as panic disorder history and frequency of attack. There are no statistically significant differences between groups on these variables, suggesting that selection might not be problematic. However, the author notes that the pretest scores on the subscales were greater for the experimental group. This suggests that those who went into the treatment group might have been more in need of help and more motivated to deal with their anxiety. The failure to statistically test whether the scores are comparable leaves doubt about the lack of a selection bias. Another threat is statistical regression. Because the experimental group starts with higher scores, the lower posttest scores might be due to regression to the mean. These explanations cannot be ruled out.

17. *What is the setting for the study? Does the setting limit the generalizability of the results to other similar settings or to the broader population? Is reactivity a problem? Are there other threats to external validity?* (Chapter 5)

The study is conducted in a large HMO in Washington, DC. It is possible that there are systematic differences between people who are and who are not HMO members. Reactivity to testing, selection, and treatment are not likely to be problems.

18. *Was this an evaluation research project? If so, which type of evaluation was it? Which design alternatives did it use?* (Chapter 10)

This is an agency-based outcome evaluation conducted by an external evaluator.

19. *How were data collected? What were the advantages and disadvantages of the particular data collection method?* (Chapter 7)

Data were collected using a four-page, self-administered questionnaire given at the beginning and end of the program. This method of data collection eliminates interviewer effects such as social desirability. There is a possibility of a response set because we do not know whether any of the scale items were worded in reverse.

20. *What did the author(s) find? Are the statistical techniques used appropriate for the level of measurement of the variables? How clearly were statistical or qualitative data presented and discussed? Were the results substantively important?* (Chapters 9 and 11)

The results supported the hypothesis "that those who participated in the therapy group in addition to medication experienced a greater reduction in anxiety than those who received medication alone" (Mitchell, 1999, pp. 195–196). Statistical data are presented clearly using tables to illustrate the differences. No qualitative data are presented. The choice of ANOVA to compare the groups on each of the subscales was a suitable analytic technique but not necessarily the best technique for this type of analysis. The author notes that although the group differences may be statistically significant, the findings may not be clinically significant.

21. *Did the author(s) adequately represent the findings in the discussion and conclusion sections? Were conclusions well grounded in the findings? Can you think of any other interpretations of the findings?* (Chapter 12)

The findings are briefly discussed in Discussion and Applications for Social Work Practice (Mitchell, 1999, p. 197) and are linked back to the literature review. The discussion does go beyond the data to talk about the unique contributions of social work practice when using cognitive-behavioral therapy. This information either should have been reported in the opening discussion about cognitive-behavioral therapy or should be linked to how the author used the treatment in this study.

22. *Compare the study with others addressing the same research question. Did the study yield additional insights? In what ways was the study design more or less adequate than the design of previous research?* (Chapter 12)

The study contributed to social work practice by investigating the application of cognitive-behavioral therapy to panic disorders. The findings complement what we know about cognitive-behavioral therapy when applied to other disorders such as depression. The design is commonly used in other studies conducted in agency settings.

23. *What additional research questions and hypotheses are suggested by the study's results? What light did the study shed on the theoretical framework used? On social work practice questions? On social policy questions?* (Chapters 2 and 12)

The article suggests that "cognitive-behavioral approaches need to draw more attention to the concept of the person-in-environment" (Mitchell, 1999, p. 198). The author suggests that more work needs to be done in integrating the effects of environmental factors into the therapy.

24. *How well did the study live up to the guidelines for science? Do you need additional information in any areas to evaluate the study? To replicate it?* (Chapter 2)

The study clearly involves a test of ideas against empirical reality, in this case a test of a clinical intervention and its impact on clients. The researcher carried out the investigation systematically and provided detail about the procedures used to carry out the study. The author does not clarify his own assumptions, but there is an assumption based on the literature that the treatment should be effective. Despite this, the author does note that "given these small proportions of explained variance, one may question how critical the therapy really was in effecting change" (Mitchell, 1999, pp. 196–197). The author specified the meaning of key terms, as required in scientific research. The author may be too accepting of current knowledge, and his conclusions may be stronger than what the findings suggest. In general, the study seems to exemplify adherence to basic scientific guidelines and to be very replicable.

25. *Did the study seem consistent with current ethical standards? Were any trade-offs made between different ethical guidelines? Was an appropriate balance struck between adherence to ethical standards and use of the most rigorous scientific practices?* (Chapter 2)

The author specifically states that "the entire research design and methodology was reviewed and approved for use by the Institutional Review Board (IRB) of the HMO" (Mitchell, 1999, p. 193). The author also notes that enrollment into a cognitive-behavioral therapy group occurred after giving informed consent. There was an appropriate balance between ethical standards and the use of rigorous scientific standards. For example, the researcher "could not [ethically and practically] monitor and enforce compliance with the medication regime" (p. 198).

References

Abel, David. 2008. "For the Homeless, Keys to a Home." *The Boston Globe,* February 24, pp. A1, A14.

Addison, Richard B. 1999. "A Grounded Hermeneutic Editing Approach." Pp. 145-161 in *Doing Qualitative Research,* edited by Benjamin E. Crabtree and William L. Miller. Thousand Oaks, CA: Sage.

Altheide, David L. and John M. Johnson. 1994. "Criteria for Assessing Interpretive Validity in Qualitative Research." Pp. 485–99 in *Handbook of Qualitative Research,* edited by Norman K. Denzin and Yvonna S. Lincoln. Thousand Oaks, CA: Sage.

American Psychiatric Association. 2004. *Diagnostic and Statistical Manual of Mental Disorders: DSM-IV-TR.* 4th ed. Arlington, VA: American Psychiatric Publishing.

American Psychological Association. 2006. "Evidence-Based Practice in Psychology." *American Psychologist* 61:271–85.

Anderson, Elijah. 1999. *Code of the Street: Decency, Violence, and the Moral Life of the Inner City.* New York: W. W. Norton.

Anderson, Elijah. 2007. "Jelly's Place: An Ethnographic Memoir." *International Journal of Politics, Culture and Society* 19:35–52.

Anderson-Butcher, Dawn, Angela Oliver Khairallah, and Janis Race-Bigelow. 2004. "Mutual Support Groups for Long-Term Recipients of TANF." *Social Work* 49:131–40.

Angell, Beth, Colleeen A. Mahoney, and Noriko Ishibashi Martinez. 2006. "Promoting Treatment Adherence in Assertive Community Treatment." *Social Service Review* 80:485–526.

Arbin, Afua Ottie and Eileen Cormier. 2005. "Racial Disparity in Nursing Research: Is Single Subject Experimental Design a Solution?" *The Journal of Theory Construction and Testing* 9:11–13.

Arean, Patricia A. and Dolores Gallagher-Thompson. 1996. "Issues and Recommendations for the Recruitment and Retention of Older Ethnic Minority Adults Into Clinical Research." *Journal of Consulting and Clinical Psychology* 64:875–80.

Aronson, Elliot and Judson Mills. 1959. "The Effect of Severity of Initiation on Liking for a Group." *Journal of Abnormal and Social Psychology* 59(9):177–81.

Axinn, William, Lisa Pearce, and Dirgha Ghimire. 1999. "Innovations in Life History Calendar Applications." *Social Science Research* 28:243–64.

Bachman, Ronet. 1992. *Death and Violence on the Reservation: Homicide, Family Violence, and Suicide in American Indian Populations.* New York: Auburn House.

Bae, Sung-Woo and John S. Brekke. 2003. "The Measurement of Self-Esteem Among Korean Americans: A Cross-Ethnic Study." *Cultural Diversity and Ethnic Minority Psychology* 9:16–33.

Baker, Tamara A. and Caroline C. Wang. 2006. "Photovoice: Use of a Participatory Action Research Method to Explore the Chronic Pain Experience in Older Adults." *Qualitative Health Research* 16:1405–13.

Balas, E. A. and S. A. Boren. 2000. "Managing Clinical Knowledge for Health Care Improvement." In *Yearbook of Medical Informatics.* Bethesda, MD: National Library of Medicine. Retrieved May 22, 2009 (http://www.ihi.org/NR/rdonlyres/A375C84E-AE83–422C-B2ED-E11BEE298DE2/0/BalasBorenManagingClinicalKnowledgeforHCImprovement_2000.pdf).

Balaswamy, Shantha and Holly I. Dabelko. 2002. "Using a Stakeholder Participatory Model in a Community-wide Service Needs Assessment of Elderly Residents: A Case Study." *Journal of Community Practice* 10:55–70.

Bangs, Ralph, Cheryl Z. Kerchis, and S. Laurel Weldon. 1997. *Basic Living Cost and Living Wage Estimates for Pittsburgh and Allegheny County.* Pittsburgh, PA: University of Pittsburgh and UCSUR.

Barlow, David H., Matthew K. Nock, and Michel Hersen. 2009. *Single Case Experimental Designs: Strategies for Studying Behavior Change.* 3rd ed. Boston: Allyn & Bacon.

Beals, Janette, Spero M. Manson, Christina M. Mitchell, Paul Spicer, and the AI-SUPERPFP Team. 2003. "Cultural Specificity and Comparison in Psychiatric Epidemiology: Walking the Tightrope in American Indian Research." *Culture, Medicine, and Psychiatry* 27:259–89.

Becker, Howard S. 1958. "Problems of Inference and Proof in Participant Observation." *American Sociological Review* 23:652–60.

Bellah, Robert N., Richard Madsen, William M. Sullivan, Ann Swidler, and Steven M. Tipton. 1985. *Habits of the Heart: Individualism and Commitment in American Life.* New York: Harper & Row.

Bennett, Larry W., Charles Stoops, Christine Call, and Heather Flett. 2007. "Program Completion and Re-arrest in a Batterer Intervention System." *Research on Social Work Practice* 17:42–54.

Beyer, William H., ed. 1968. *CRC Handbook of Tables for Probability and Statistics.* 2nd ed. Boca Raton, FL: CRC Press.

Bloom, Martin, Joel Fischer, and John Orme. 2009. *Evaluating Practice: Guidelines for the Accountable Professional.* 6th ed. Boston: Allyn & Bacon.

Bogdewic, Stephan P. 1999. "Participant Observation." Pp. 33–45 in *Doing Qualitative Research,* 2nd ed., edited by Benjamin F. Crabtree and William L. Miller. Thousand Oaks, CA: Sage.

Booth, Wayne C., Gregory G. Colomb, and Joseph M. Williams. 1995. *The Craft of Research.* Chicago: University of Chicago Press.

Borckardt, Jeffrey J., Martin D. Murphy, Michael R. Nash, and Darlene Shaw. 2004. "An Empirical Examination of Visual Analysis Procedures for Clinical Practice Evaluation." *Journal of Social Service Research* 30:55–73.

Borckardt, Jeffrey, Michael R. Nash, Martin D. Murphy, Mark Moore, Darlene Shaw, and Patrick O'Neil. 2008. "Clinical Practice as Natural Laboratory for Psychotherapy Research: A Guide to Case-Based Time-Series Analysis." *American Psychologist* 63:77–95.

Boruch, Robert F. 1997. *Randomized Experiments for Planning and Evaluation: A Practical Guide.* Thousand Oaks, CA: Sage.

Bradshaw, William. 1997. "Evaluating Cognitive-Behavioral Treatment of Schizophrenia: Four Single-Case Studies." *Research on Social Work Practice* 7:419–45.

Bradshaw, William. 2003. "Use of Single-System Research to Evaluate the Effectiveness of Cognitive-Behavioural Treatment of Schizophrenia." *British Journal of Social Work* 33:885–99.

Bradshaw, William and David Roseborough. 2004. "Evaluating the Effectiveness of Cognitive-Behavioral Treatment of Residual Symptoms and Impairment in Schizophrenia." *Research on Social Work Practice* 14:112–20.

Brekke, John S., Kathleen Ell, and Lawrence A. Palinkas. 2009. "Translational Science at the National Institute of Mental Health: Can Social Work Take Its Rightful Place?" *Research on Social Work Practice,* 17:123–33.

Brett, Pamela J., Kathryn Graham, and Cynthia Smythe. 1995. "An Analysis of Specialty Journals on Alcohol, Drugs, and Addictive Behaviors for Sex Bias in Research Methods and Reporting." *Journal of Studies on Alcohol* 56:24–34.

Brewer, John and Albert Hunter. 1989. *Multimethod Research: A Synthesis of Styles.* Thousand Oaks, CA: Sage.

Brown, Judith Belle. 1999. "The Use of Focus Groups in Clinical Research." Pp. 109–24 in *Doing Qualitative Research,* 2nd ed., edited by Benjamin F. Crabtree and William L. Miller. Thousand Oaks, CA: Sage.

Burt, Martha R. 1996. "Homelessness: Definitions and Counts." Pp. 15–23 in *Homelessness in America,* edited by Jim Baumohl. Phoenix, AZ: Oryx Press.

Burt, Martha R., Laudan Y. Aron, Toby Douglas, Jesse Valente, Edgar Lee, and Britta Iwen. 1999. *Homelessness: Programs and the People They Serve: Summary Report.* Urban Institute. Retrieved October 22, 2007 (http://www.urban.org/UploadedPDF/homelessness.pdf).

Cain, Leonard D., Jr. 1967. "The AMA and the Gerontologists: Uses and Abuses of 'A Profile of the Aging: USA.'" Pp. 78–114 in *Ethics, Politics, and Social Research,* edited by Gideon Sjoberg. Cambridge, MA: Schenkman.

Campbell, Donald. T. and Julian C. Stanley. 1966. *Experimental and Quasi-experimental Designs for Research.* Chicago: Rand McNally.

Carney, Michelle Mohr and Frederick P. Buttell. 2006. "An Evaluation of a Court-Mandated Batterer Intervention Program: Investigating Differential Program Effect for African American and White Women." *Research on Social Work Practice* 16:571–81.

Carrilio, Terry. 2001. "Family Support Program Development—Integrating Research, Practice and Policy." *Journal of Family Social Work* 6:53–78.

Cauce, Ann Mari, Kimberly D. Ryan, and Kwai Grove. 1998. "Children and Adolescents of Color, Where Are You? Participation, Selection, Recruitment, and Retention in Developmental Research." Pp. 147–66 in *Studying Minority Adolescents: Conceptual, Methodological, and Theoretical Issues,* edited by Vonnie C. McLoyd and Laurence Steinberg. Mahwah, NJ: Lawrence Erlbaum.

Chavez, Ligia, Leida Matías-Carrelo, Concepcion Barrio, and Glorisa Canino. 2007. "The Cultural Adaptation of the Youth Quality of Life Instrument–Research Version for Latino Children and Adolescents." *Journal of Child and Family Studies* 16:75–89.

Chen, Huey-Tsyh. 1990. *Theory-Driven Evaluations.* Thousand Oaks, CA: Sage.

Chen, Huey-Tsyh and Peter Rossi. 1987. "The Theory-Driven Approach to Validity." *Evaluation and Program Planning* 10:95–103.

Clark, H. Westley, A. Kathryn Power, Charlene E. Le Fauve, and Elizabeth I. Lopez. 2008. "Policy and Practice Implications of Epidemiological Surveys on Co-occurring Mental and Substance Use Disorders." *Journal of Substance Abuse Treatment* 34:3–13.

Coffey, Amanda and Paul Atkinson. 1996. *Making Sense of Qualitative Data: Complementary Research Strategies.* Thousand Oaks, CA: Sage.

Cohen, Gary and Barbara Kerr. 1998. "Computer-Mediated Counseling: An Empirical Study of a New Mental Health Treatment." *Computers in Human Services* 15:13–26.

Cole, Danny, Subadra Panchanadeswaran, and Clara Daining. 2004. "Predictors of Job Satisfaction of Licensed Social Workers: Perceived Efficacy as a Mediator of the Relationship Between Workload and Job Satisfaction." *Journal of Social Service Research* 31:1–12.

Converse, Jean M. 1984. "Attitude Measurement in Psychology and Sociology: The Early Years." Pp. 3–40 in *Surveying Subjective Phenomena,* Vol. 2, edited by Charles F. Turner and Elizabeth Martin. New York: Russell Sage Foundation.

Cook, Deborah, David L. Sackett, and Walter O. Spitzer. 1995. "Methodologic Guidelines for Systematic Reviews of Randomized Control Trials in Health Care From the Potsdam Consultation on Meta-Analysis." *Journal of Clinical Epidemiology* 48:167–71.

Cook, Thomas D. and Donald T. Campbell. 1979. *Quasi-experimentation: Design and Analysis Issues for Field Settings.* Chicago: Rand McNally.

Cooper, Harris and Larry V. Hedges. 1994. "Research Synthesis as a Scientific Enterprise." Pp. 3–14 in *The Handbook of Research Synthesis,* edited by Harris Cooper and Larry V. Hedges. New York: Russell Sage Foundation.

Costner, Herbert L. 1989. "The Validity of Conclusions in Evaluation Research: A Further Development of Chen and Rossi's Theory-Driven Approach." *Evaluation and Program Planning* 12:345–53.

Cotrell, Victoria and Rafael J. Engel. 1998. "Predictors of Respite Service Utilization." *Journal of Gerontological Social Work* 30:117–32.

Counts, Dorothy Ayers and David R. Counts. 1996. *Over the Next Hill: An Ethnography of RVing Seniors in North America.* Orchard Park, NY: Broadview Press.

Couper, Mick P., Reginald P. Baker, Jelke Bethlehem, Cynthia Z. F. Clark, Jean Martin, William L. Nicholls II, and James M. O'Reilly, eds. 1998. *Computer Assisted Survey Information Collection.* New York: Wiley.

Cress, Daniel M. and David A. Snow. 2000. "The Outcomes of Homeless Mobilization: The Influence of Modernity and Proto-modernity on Political and Civil Rights, 1965 to 1980. *American Journal of Sociology* 4:1063-1104.

Cuil. 2009. Retrieved May 22, 2009 (www.cuil.com).

Curtin, Richard, Stanley Presser, and Eleanor Singer. 2005. "Changes in Telephone Survey Nonresponse Over the Past Quarter Century." *Public Opinion Quarterly* 69:87–98.

Dattilio, Frank and Norman B. Epstein. 2005. "Introduction to the Special Section: The Role of Cognitive-Behavioral Interventions in Couple and Family Therapy." *Journal of Marital and Family Therapy* 31:7–13.

Davis, Ryan. 1999. "Study: Search Engines Can't Keep Up With Expanding Net." *The Boston Globe,* July 8, pp. C1, C3.

Decker, Scott H. and Barrik Van Winkle. 1996. *Life in the Gang: Family, Friends, and Violence.* Cambridge, UK: Cambridge University Press.

DeNavas-Walt, Carmen, Bernadette D. Proctor, and Jessica C. Smith. 2008. *Income, Poverty, and Health Insurance Coverage in the United States: 2007.* U.S. Census Bureau, Current Population Reports, P60-235. Washington, DC: U.S. Government Printing Office.

Dentler, Robert A. 2002. *Practicing Sociology: Selected Fields.* Westport, CT: Praeger.

Denzin, Norman K. 2002. "The Interpretative Process." Pp. 349–68 in *The Qualitative Researcher's Companion,* edited by A. Michael Huberman and Matthew B. Miles. Thousand Oaks, CA: Sage.

Denzin, Norman K. 2005. "The First International Congress of Qualitative Inquiry." *Qualitative Social Work* 4:105–11.

Denzin, Norman K. and Yvonna S. Lincoln. 1994. "Introduction: Entering the Field of Qualitative Research." Pp. 1–17 in *Handbook of Qualitative Research,* edited by Norman K. Denzin and Yvonna S. Lincoln. Thousand Oaks, CA: Sage.

Denzin, Norman K. and Yvonna S. Lincoln. 2000. *Handbook of Qualitative Research.* 2nd ed. Thousand Oaks, CA: Sage.

Diamond, Timothy. 1992. *Making Gray Gold: Narratives of Nursing Home Care.* Chicago: University of Chicago Press.

Dillman, Don A. 2000. *Mail and Internet Surveys: The Tailored Design Method.* 2nd ed. Hoboken, NJ: Wiley.

Dillman, Don A. 2007. *Mail and Internet Surveys: The Tailored Design Method. Update With New Internet, Visual, and Mixed-Mode Guide.* 2nd ed. Hoboken, NJ: Wiley.

Dillman, Don A. and Leah Melani Christian. 2005. "Survey Mode as a Source of Instability in Response Across Surveys." *Field Methods* 17:30–52.

Drake, Robert E., Gregory J. McHugo, Deborah R. Becker, William A. Anthony, and Robin E. Clark. 1996. "The New Hampshire Study of Supported Employment for People With Severe Mental Illness." *Journal of Consulting and Clinical Psychology* 64:391–99.

Edin, Kathryn and Laura Lein. 1997. *Making Ends Meet: How Single Mothers Survive Welfare and Low-Wage Work.* New York: Russell Sage Foundation.

Emerson, Robert M., Rachel I. Fretz, and Linda L. Shaw. 1995. *Writing Ethnographic Fieldnotes.* Chicago: University of Chicago Press.

Engel, Rafael J. 1993, December. *Evaluation of the Reach Out Program, Boys and Girls Clubs.* (Unpublished monograph.) Pittsburgh, PA: Pittsburgh Foundation.

Engel, Rafael J., Daniel Rosen, and Tracy Soska. 2008, January. *Raising the Stakes: Assessing Allegheny County's Human Service Response Capacity to the Social Impact of Casino Gambling.* Pittsburgh, PA: University of Pittsburgh School of Social Work.

English, Brian. 1997. "Conducting Ethical Evaluations With Disadvantaged and Minority Target Groups." *Evaluation Practice* 18:49–55.

Erikson, Kai T. 1967. "A Comment on Disguised Observation in Sociology." *Social Problems* 12:366–73.

Essock, Susan M., Linda K. Frisman, and Nina J. Kontos. 1998. "Cost-Effectiveness of Assertive Community Treatment Teams." *American Journal of Orthopsychiatry* 68:179–90.

Feder, Lynette and Laura Dugan. 2002. "A Test of the Efficacy of Court-Mandated Counseling for Domestic Violence Offenders: The Broward Experiment." *Justice Quarterly* 19:343–75.

Fink, Arlene. 2005. *Conducting Research Literature Reviews: From Internet to Paper.* 2nd ed. Thousand Oaks, CA: Sage.

Fischer, Joel and Kevin Corcoran. 2007. *Measures for Clinical Practice and Research.* 4th ed. Oxford, UK: Oxford University Press.

Flaherty, Joseph A., Moises Gaviria, Dev Pathak, Timothy Mitchell, Ronald Wintrob, Judith Richman, and Susan Birz. 1976. "Developing Instruments for Cross-Cultural Psychiatric Research." *The Journal of Nervous and Mental Disease* 176:257–63.

Fowler, Floyd J. 1988. *Survey Research Methods.* Rev. ed. Thousand Oaks, CA: Sage.

Fowler, Floyd J. 1995. *Improving Survey Questions: Design and Evaluation.* Thousand Oaks, CA: Sage.

Franklin, Ronald D., David B. Allison, and Bernard S. Gorman. 1997. *Design and Analysis of Single-Case Research.* Mahwah, NJ: Lawrence Erlbaum.

Franks, Peter, Marthe R. Gold, and Kevin Fiscella. 2003. "Sociodemographics, Self-Rated Health, and Mortality in the U.S." *Social Science and Medicine* 56:2505–514.

Gambrill, Eileen. 1999. "Evidence-Based Practice: An Alternative to Authority-Based Practice." *The Journal of Contemporary Human Services* 80:341–50.

Gambrill, Eileen. 2001. "Social Work: An Authority-Based Profession." *Research on Social Work Practice* 11:166–75.

Gambrill, Eileen. 2006. "Evidence-Based Practice and Policy: Choices Ahead." *Research on Social Work Practice* 16:338–57.

Garland, Diana, Robin Rogers, and Gaynor Yancey. 2001. "The Faith Factor in Effective Models of Multi-sector Collaboration." (Grant proposal to the Pew Charitable Trusts.) Waco, TX: Baylor University.

Geertz, Clifford. 1973. "Thick Description: Toward an Interpretive Theory of Culture." Pp. 3–30 in *The Interpretation of Cultures,* edited by Clifford Geertz. New York: Basic Books.

Geller, Stacie E., Marci Goldstein Adams, and Molly Carnes. 2006. "Adherence to Federal Guidelines for Reporting of Sex and Race/Ethnicity in Clinical Trials." *Journal of Women's Health* 15:1123–131.

Glaser, Barney G. and Anselm L. Strauss. 1967. *The Discovery of Grounded Theory: Strategies for Qualitative Research.* London: Weidenfeld and Nicholson.

Goffman, Erving. 1961. *Asylums: Essays on the Social Situation of Mental Patients and Other Inmates.* Garden City, NY: Doubleday.

Goldfinger, Stephen M., Russell K. Schutt, George S. Tolomiczenko, Winston M. Turner, Norma Ware, Walter E. Penk, Mark S. Abelman, et al. 1997. "Housing Persons Who Are Homeless and Mentally Ill: Independent Living or Evolving Consumer Households?" Pp. 29–49 in *Mentally Ill and Homeless: Special Programs for Special Needs,* edited by William R. Breakey and James W. Thompson. Amsterdam: Harwood.

Goleman, Daniel. 1993. "Placebo Effect Is Shown to Be Twice as Powerful as Expected." *The New York Times,* August 17, p. C3.

Gordon, Raymond. 1992. *Basic Interviewing Skills.* Itasca, IL: Peacock.

Graham, Sandra. 1992. "'Most of the Subjects Were White and Middle Class': Trends in Published Research on African Americans in Selected APA Journals, 1970–1989." *American Psychologist* 47:629–39.

Griffin, Christine and Ann Phoenix. 1994. "The Relationship Between Qualitative and Quantitative Research: Lessons From Feminist Psychology." *Journal of Community and Applied Social Psychology* 4:287–98.

Grinnell, Frederick. 1992. *The Scientific Attitude.* 2nd ed. New York: Guilford Press.

Grisso, Thomas and Paul S. Appelbaum. 1995. "Comparison of Standards for Assessing Patients' Capacities to Make Treatment Decisions." *American Journal of Psychiatry* 152:1033–37.

Groves, Robert M. 1989. *Survey Errors and Survey Costs.* New York: Wiley.

Groves, Robert M. and Mick P. Couper. 1998. *Nonresponse in Household Interview Surveys.* New York: Wiley.

Guba, Egon G. and Yvonna S. Lincoln. 1989. *Fourth Generation Evaluation.* Thousand Oaks, CA: Sage.

Guba, Egon G. and Yvonna S. Lincoln. 1994. "Competing Paradigms in Qualitative Research." Pp. 105–17 in *Handbook of Qualitative Research,* edited by Norman K. Denzin and Yvonna S. Lincoln. Thousand Oaks, CA: Sage.

Gubrium, Jaber F. and James A. Holstein. 1997. *The New Language of Qualitative Method.* New York: Oxford University Press.

Guterbock, Thomas M. 2008, May. *Strategies and Standards for Reaching Respondents in an Age of New Technology.* Presentation to the Harvard Program on Survey Research Spring Conference, New Technologies and Survey Research. Cambridge, MA: Institute of Quantitative Social Science, Harvard University.

Hage, Jerald and Barbara Foley Meeker. 1988. *Social Causality.* Boston, MA: Unwin Hyman.

Haney, C., C. Banks, and Philip G. Zimbardo. 1973. "Interpersonal Dynamics in a Simulated Prison." *International Journal of Criminology and Penology* 1:69–97.

Hann, Danette, Kristin Winter, and Paul Jacobsen. 1999. "Measurement of Depressive Symptoms in Cancer Patients: Evaluation of the Center for Epidemiological Studies Depression Scale (CES-D)." *Journal of Psychosomatic Research* 46:4387–443.

Harris, Mary Beth and Cynthia G. Franklin. 2003. "Effects of a Cognitive-Behavioral, School-Based, Group Intervention With Mexican American Pregnant and Parenting Adolescents." *Social Work Research* 27:71–83.

Harrison, R. Steven, Scott Boyle, and O. William Farley. 1999. "Evaluating the Outcomes of Family-Based Intervention for Troubled Children: A Pretest-Posttest Study." *Research on Social Work Practice* 9:640–55.

Hart, Chris. 1998. *Doing a Literature Review: Releasing the Social Science Research Imagination.* London: Sage.

Hartung, Cynthia M. and Thomas A. Widiger. 1998. "Gender Differences in the Diagnosis of Mental Disorders: Conclusions and Controversies of the DSM-IV." *Psychological Bulletin* 123:260–78.

Haynes, R. Brian, P. J. Devereaux, and Gordon H. Guyatt. 2002. "Clinical Expertise in the Era of Evidence-Based Medicine and Patient Choice." *Evidence Based Medicine* 7:36–38.

Herek, Gregory, Douglas C. Kimmel, Hortensia Amaro, and Gary B. Melton. 1991. "Avoiding Heterosexist Bias in Psychological Research." *American Psychologist* 46:957–63.

Hergenrather, Kenneth C., Scott D. Rhodes, and Glenn Clark. 2006. "Windows to Work: Exploring Employment-Seeking Behaviors of Persons With HIV/AIDS Through Photovoice." *AIDS Education and Prevention* 18:243–58.

Herrera, C. D. 2003. "A Clash of Methodology and Ethics in 'Undercover' Social Science." *Philosophy of the Social Sciences* 33:351–62.

Hicks-Coolick, Anne, Patricia Burnside-Eaton, and Ardith Peters. 2003. "Homeless Children: Needs and Services." *Child and Youth Care Forum* 32:197–210.

Hock, Randolph. 2004. *The Extreme Searcher's Internet Handbook: A Guide for the Serious Searcher.* Medford, NJ: CyberAge Books.

Holcombe, Ariane, Mark Wolery, and David L. Gast. 1994. "Comparative Single-Subject Research Designs Used to Make Comparisons Between Two or More Interventions." *Topics in Early Childhood Special Education* 14:119–45.

Holtzworth-Munroe, Amy and Gregory L. Stuart. 1994. "Typologies of Male Batterers: Three Subtypes and the Differences Among Them." *Psychological Bulletin* 11:476–97.

Huberman, A. Michael and Matthew B. Miles. 1994. "Data Management and Analysis Methods." Pp. 428–44 in *Handbook of Qualitative Research,* edited by Norman K. Denzin and Yvonna S. Lincoln. Thousand Oaks, CA: Sage.

Huddy, Leonie, Joshua Billig, John Gracciodieta, Lois Hoeffler, Patrick J. Moynihan, and Patricia Pugliani. 1997. "The Effect of Interviewer Gender on the Survey Response." *Political Behavior* 19:197–220.

Hui, Chi-chiu H. and Harry C. Triandis. 1985. "Measurement in Cross-Cultural Psychology: A Review and Comparison of Strategies." *Journal of Cross-Cultural Psychology* 16:131–52.

Humphrey, Nicholas. 1992. *A History of the Mind: Evolution and the Birth of Consciousness.* New York: Simon & Schuster.

Humphreys, Laud. 1970. *Tearoom Trade: Impersonal Sex in Public Places.* Chicago: Aldine.

Hunt, Morton. 1985. *Profiles of Social Research: The Scientific Study of Human Interactions.* New York: Russell Sage Foundation.

Ingersoll-Dayton, Berit, Margaret B. Neal, Jung-hwa Ha, and Leslie B. Hammer. 2003. "Collaboration Among Siblings Providing Care for Older Parents." *Journal of Gerontological Social Work* 40:51–66.

Institute of Medicine. 2001. *Crossing the Quality Chasm: A New Health System for the 21st Century—Brief Report.* Washington, DC: National Academy of Sciences. Retrieved May 22, 2009 (http://www.iom.edu/Object.File/Master/27/184/Chasm-8pager.pdf).

Irvine, Leslie. 1998. "Organizational Ethics and Fieldwork Realities: Negotiating Ethical Boundaries in Codependents Anonymous." Pp. 167–83 in *Doing Ethnographic Research: Fieldwork Settings,* edited by Scott Grills. Thousand Oaks, CA: Sage.

Jackson, James and David Williams. 2004. *Detroit Area Study: Social Influence on Health, Stress, Racism, and Health Protective Resources.* Ann Arbor, MI: Interuniversity Consortium for Political and Social Research, Study No. 3272. Retrieved August 29, 2004 (http://webapp.icpsr.umich.edu/cocoon/ICPSR-PRINT-STUDY/03272.xml).

Jensen, Carla. 1994. "Psychosocial Treatment of Depression in Women: Nine Single-Subject Evaluations." *Research on Social Work Practice* 4:267–82.

Jenson, William R., Elaine Clark, John C. Kircher, and Sean D. Kristjansson. 2007. "Statistical Reform: Evidence-Based Practice, Meta-Analyses, and Single Subject Designs." *Psychology in the Schools* 44:483–93.

Jesnadum, Anick. 2000. "Researchers Fear Privacy Breaches With Online Research." Retrieved September 15, 2000 (www.digitalmassmedia.com/news/daily/09/15/researchers.htm).

Johnson, Alice. 1999. "Working and Nonworking Women: Onset of Homelessness Within the Context of Their Lives." *Affilia* 14:42–77.

Johnston, Mark, Mark Sherer, and John Whyte. 2006. "Applying Evidence Standards to Rehabilitation Research." *American Journal of Physical Medicine and Rehabilitation* 85:292–309.

Kagawa-Singer, Marjorie. 2000. "Improving the Validity and Generalizability of Studies With Underserved U.S. Populations Expanding the Research Paradigm." *Annals of Epidemiology* 10:S92–S103.

Kahana, Eva, Boaz Kahana, and Kathryn P. Riley. 1988. "Contextual Issues in Quantitative Studies of Institutional Settings for the Aged." Pp. 197–216 in *Qualitative Gerontology,* edited by Shulamit Reinharz and Graham D. Rowles. New York: Springer.

Kaufman, Sharon R. 1986. *The Ageless Self: Sources of Meaning in Late Life.* Madison: University of Wisconsin Press.

Kaufman, Sharon R. 1994. "In-Depth Interviewing." Pp. 123–36 in *Qualitative Methods in Aging Research,* edited by Jaber F. Gubrium and Andrea Sankar. Thousand Oaks, CA: Sage.

Kayser-Jones, Jeanie and Barbara A. Koenig. 1994. "Ethical Issues." Pp. 15–32 in *Qualitative Methods in Aging Research,* edited by Jaber F. Gubrium and Andrea Sankar. Thousand Oaks, CA: Sage.

Kincaid, Harold. 1996. *Philosophical Foundations of the Social Sciences: Analyzing Controversies in Social Research.* Cambridge, UK: Cambridge University Press.

King, Gary, Robert O. Keohane, and Sidney Verba. 1994. *Scientific Inference in Qualitative Research.* Princeton, NJ: Princeton University Press.

Koegel, Paul. 1987. *Ethnographic Perspectives on Homeless and Homeless Mentally Ill Women.* Washington, DC: U.S. Department of Health and Human Services, Public Health Service, Alcohol, Drug Abuse, and Mental Health Administration.

Koeske, Gary. 1994. "Some Recommendations for Improving Measurement Validation in Social Work Research." *Journal of Social Service Research* 18:43–72.

Korr, Wynne S. and Antoine Joseph. 1996. "Effects of Local Conditions on Program Outcomes: Analysis of Contradictory Findings From Two Programs for Homeless Mentally Ill." *Journal of Health and Social Policy* 8:41–53.

Kotsopoulos, Sotiris, Selena Walker, Karyn Beggs, and Barbara Jones. 1996. "A Clinical and Academic Outcome Study of Children Attending a Day Treatment Program." *Canadian Journal of Psychiatry* 41:371–78.

Kuzel, Anton J. 1999. "Sampling in Qualitative Inquiry." Pp. 33–45 in *Doing Qualitative Research,* 2nd ed., edited by Benjamin F. Crabtree and William L. Miller. Thousand Oaks, CA: Sage.

Kvale, Steinar. 1996. *Interviews: An Introduction to Qualitative Research Interviewing.* Thousand Oaks, CA: Sage.

Lamott, Anne. 1994. *Bird by Bird: Some Instructions on Writing and Life.* New York: Anchor Books.

Larsen, Daniel L., C. Clifford Attkisson, William A. Hargreaves, and Tuan D. Nguyen. 1979. "Assessment of Client/Patient Satisfaction: Development of a General Scale." *Evaluation and Program Planning* 2:197–207.

Larson, Calvin J. 1993. *Pure and Applied Sociological Theory: Problems and Issues.* New York: Harcourt.

Leiter, Jeffrey. 2007. "School Performance Trajectories After the Advent of Reported Maltreatment." *Children and Youth Services Review* 29:363–82.

Levy, Paul S. and Stanley Lemeshow. 1999. *Sampling of Populations: Methods and Applications.* 3rd ed. New York: Wiley.

Lewis, Robert E., Elaine Walton, and Mark W. Fraser. 1995. "Examining Family Reunification Services: A Process Analysis of a Successful Experiment." *Research on Social Work Practice* 5:259–82.

Lieberson, Stanley. 1985. *Making It Count: The Improvement of Social Research and Theory.* Berkeley: University of California Press.

Lietz, Cynthia. 2006. "Uncovering Stories of Family Resilience: A Mixed Methods Study of Resilient Families, Part 1." *Families in Society: Journal of Contemporary Social Services* 87:575–81.

Lietz, Cynthia. 2007. "Uncovering Stories of Family Resilience: A Mixed Methods Study of Resilient Families, Part 2." *Families in Society: Journal of Contemporary Social Services* 88:147–55.

Lindsey, Michael A., Wynne S. Korr, Marina Broitman, Lee Bone, Alan Green, and Philip J. Leaf. 2006. "Help-Seeking Behaviors and Depression Among African American Adolescent Boys." *Social Work* 51:49–58.

Lipp, Allyson. 2007. "Using Systematic Reviews." *Nursing Management* 14:30–32.

Lipsey, Mark W. and David B. Wilson. 2001. *Practical Meta-Analysis.* Thousand Oaks, CA: Sage.

Littell, Julia H. 2005. "Lessons From a Systematic Review of Effects of Multisytemic Therapy." *Children and Youth Services Review* 27:445–63.

Littell, Julia, Melanie Popa, and Burnee Forsythe. 2005. *Multisystemic Therapy for Social, Emotional and Behavioral Problems in Children and Adolescents Aged 10–17.* (Review for the Campbell Collaboration.) Retrieved May 29, 2009 (http://www.campbellcollaboration.org/doc-pdf/Mst_Littell_Review.pdf/).

Litwin, Mark S. 1995. *How to Measure Survey Reliability and Validity.* Thousand Oaks, CA: Sage.

Locke, Lawrence F., Stephen J. Silverman, and Waneen Wyrick Spirduso. 1998. *Reading and Understanding Research.* Thousand Oaks, CA: Sage.

Locke, Lawrence F., Waneen Wyrick Spirduso, and Stephen J. Silverman. 2000. *Proposals That Work: A Guide for Planning Dissertations and Grant Proposals.* 4th ed. Thousand Oaks, CA: Sage.

Lofland, John and Lyn H. Lofland. 1984. *Analyzing Social Settings: A Guide to Qualitative Observations and Analysis.* 2nd ed. Belmont, CA: Wadsworth.

Luna, Isela, Esperanza Torres de Ardon, Young Mi Lim, Sandra Cromwell, Linda Phillips, and Cynthia Russell. 1996. "The Relevance of Familism in Cross-Cultural Studies of Family Caregiving." *Journal of Nursing Research* 18:267–83.

Lundahl, Brad, Janelle Nimer, and Bruce Parsons. 2006. "Preventing Child Abuse: A Meta-Analysis of Parent Training Programs." *Research on Social Work Practice* 16:251–62.

Lyman, Karen A. 1994. "Fieldwork in Groups and Institutions." Pp. 155–70 in *Qualitative Methods in Aging Research,* edited by Jaber F. Gubrium and Andrea Sankar. Thousand Oaks, CA: Sage.

Lynch, Michael and David Bogen. 1997. "Sociology's Asociological 'Core': An Examination of Textbook Sociology in Light of the Sociology of Scientific Knowledge." *American Sociological Review* 62:481–93.

Mak, Winnie W. S., Rita W. Law, Jennifer Alvidrez, and Eliseo J. Perez-Stable. 2007. "Gender and Ethnic Diversity in NIMH-Funded Clinical Trials: Review of a Decade of Published Research." *Administration and Policy in Mental Health and Mental Health Services Research* 34:497–503.

Mangione, Thomas W. 1995. *Mail Surveys: Improving the Quality.* Thousand Oaks, CA: Sage.

Marin, Gerardo and Barbara VanOss Marin. 1991. *Research With Hispanic Populations.* Thousand Oaks, CA: Sage.

Marini, Margaret Mooney and Burton Singer. 1988. "Causality in the Social Sciences." Pp. 347–409 in *Sociological Methodology,* Vol. 18, edited by Clifford C. Clogg. Washington, DC: American Sociological Association.

Marshall, Catherine and Gretchen B. Rossman. 1999. *Designing Qualitative Research.* 3rd ed. Thousand Oaks, CA: Sage.

Martin, James I. and Jo Knox. 2000. "Methodological and Ethical Issues in Research on Lesbians and Gay Men." *Social Work Research* 24:51–59.

Martin, James I. and William Meezan. 2003. "Applying Ethical Standards to Research and Evaluations Involving Lesbian, Gay, Bisexual, and Transgender Populations." *Journal of Gay and Lesbian Social Services* 15:181–201.

Martin, Lawrence L. and Peter M. Kettner. 1996. *Measuring the Performance of Human Service Programs.* Thousand Oaks, CA: Sage.

Matt, Georg E. and Thomas D. Cook. 1994. "Threats to the Validity of Research Syntheses." Pp. 503–20 in *The Handbook of Research Synthesis,* edited by Harris Cooper and Larry V. Hedges. New York: Russell Sage Foundation.

Maxwell, Joseph A. 1996. *Qualitative Research Design: An Interactive Approach.* Thousand Oaks, CA: Sage.

McKillip, Jack. 1987. *Need Analysis: Tools for the Human Services and Education.* Thousand Oaks, CA: Sage.

McNeill, Ted. 2006. "Evidence-Based Practice in an Age of Relativism: Toward a Model for Practice. *Social Work* 51:147–56.

Milburn, Norweeta G., Lawrence E. Gary, Jacqueline A. Booth, and Diane R. Brown. 1992. "Conducting Epidemiologic Research in a Minority Community: Methodological Considerations." *Journal of Community Psychology* 19:3–12.

Miles, Matthew B. and A. Michael Huberman. 1994. *Qualitative Data Analysis.* 2nd ed. Thousand Oaks, CA: Sage.

Miller, Cynthia, Aletha C. Huston, Greg J. Duncan, Vonnie C. McLoyd, and Thomas S. Weisner. 2008. *New Hope for the Working Poor: Effects After Eight Years for Families and Children.* New York: MDRC. Retrieved February 24, 2008 (http://www.mdrc.org/publications/488/full.pdf).

Miller, Delbert C. and Neil Salkind. 2002. *Handbook of Research Design and Social Measurement.* 6th ed. Thousand Oaks, CA: Sage.

Miller, Susan. 1999. *Gender and Community Policing: Walking the Talk.* Boston: Northeastern University Press.

Miller, William L. and Benjamin F. Crabtree. 1999. "The Dance of Interpretation." Pp. 127-143 in *Doing Qualitative Research,* 2nd ed., edited by Benjamin F. Crabtree and William L. Miller. Thousand Oaks, CA: Sage.

Miranda, Jeanne, Francisca Azocar, Kurt C. Organista, Ricardo F. Munoz, and Alicia Lieberman. 1996. "Recruiting and Retaining Low-Income Latinos in Psychotherapy Research." *Journal of Consulting and Clinical Psychology* 64:868–74.

Miranda, Jeanne, Richard Nakamura, and Guillermo Bernal. 2003. "Including Ethnic Minorities in Mental Health Intervention Research: A Practical Approach to a Long-Standing Problem." *Culture, Medicine, and Psychiatry* 27:467–86.

Mitchell, Christopher G. 1999. "Treating Anxiety in a Managed Care Setting: A Controlled Comparison of Medication Alone Versus Medication Plus." *Research on Social Work Practice* 9:188–200.

Mitchell, Richard G., Jr. 1993. *Secrecy and Fieldwork.* Thousand Oaks, CA: Sage.

Mohr, Lawrence B. 1992. *Impact Analysis for Program Evaluation.* Thousand Oaks, CA: Sage.

Molloy, Jennifer K. 2007. "Photovoice as a Tool for Social Justice Workers." *Journal of Progressive Human Services* 18:39–55.

Montgomery, Paul, Evan Mayo-Wilson, and Jane Dennis. 2008. *Personal Assistance for Older Adults (65+) Without Dementia.* (Review for the Campbell Collaboration.) Retrieved May 29, 2009 (http://www.campbellcollaboration .org/doc-pdf/Montgomery_PA_65+_review.pdf).

Moreno, Carmen L. 2003. "The Role of Appraisal and Expressive Support in Mediating Strain and Gain in Hispanic Alzheimer's Disease Caregivers." *Journal of Ethnic & Cultural Diversity in Social Work* 12:1–18.

Morrill, Calvin, Christine Yalda, Madeleine Adelman, Michael Musheno, and Cindy Bejarano. 2000. "Telling Tales in School: Youth Culture and Conflict Narratives." *Law and Society Review* 34:521–65.

Nápoles-Springer, Anna M., Jasmine Santoyo-Olsson, Helen O'Brien, and Anita L. Stewart. 2006. "Using Cognitive Interviews to Develop Surveys in Diverse Populations." *Medical Care* 44:S21–S30.

Nápoles-Springer, Anna M. and Anita L. Stewart. 2006. "Overview of Qualitative Methods in Research With Diverse Populations: Making Research Reflect the Population." *Medical Care* 44:S5–S9.

National Association of Social Workers. 1999. *Code of Ethics of the National Association of Social Workers.* Retrieved June 28, 2004 (http://www.naswdc.org/pubs/code/code.asp).

National Association of Social Workers. 2001. *NASW Standards for Cultural Competence in the Practice of Social Work.* Washington, DC: Author. Retrieved July 24, 2009 (www.socialworkers.org/practice/standards/NASWCultural Standards.pdf).

National Institutes of Health. 1994. *NIH Guidelines on the Inclusion of Women and Minorities as Subjects in Clinical Research.* Retrieved June 29, 2004 (http://grants.nih.gov/grants/guide/notice-files/not94–100.html).

National Opinion Reseach Center. 2000. *General Social Survey* Chicago, IL: Author.

Nelson, Judith C. 1994. "Ethics, Gender, and Ethnicity in Single-Case Research and Evaluation." *Journal of Social Service Research* 18:139–52.

Neuendorf, Kimberly A. 2002. *The Content Analysis Guidebook.* Thousand Oaks, CA: Sage.

Newmann, Joy Perkins. 1987. "Gender Differences in Vulnerability to Depression." *Social Service Review* 61:447–68.

Norton, Ilena M. and Spero M. Manson. 1996. "Research in American Indian and Alaska Native Communities: Navigating the Cultural Universe of Values and Process." *Journal of Consulting and Clinical Psychology* 64:856–60.

Novak, David. 2003. "The Evolution of Internet Research: Shifting Allegiances." *Online* 27:21.

Nugent, William. 2000. "Single Case Design Visual Analysis Procedures for Use in Practice Evaluation." *Journal of Social Service Research* 27:39–75.

O'Brien, Kerth. 1993. "Improving Survey Questionnaires Through Focus Groups." Pp. 105–17 in *Successful Focus Groups: Advancing the State of the Art,* edited by David L. Morgan. Thousand Oaks, CA: Sage.

O'Dochartaigh, Niall. 2002. *The Internet Research Handbook: A Practical Guide for Students and Researchers in the Social Sciences.* Thousand Oaks, CA: Sage.

Ortega, Debora M. and Cheryl A. Richey. 1998. "Methodological Issues in Social Work Research With Depressed Women of Color." *Journal of Social Service Research* 23:47–68.

Padgett, Deborah, Leyla Gulcur, and Sam Tsemberis. 2006. "Housing First Services for People Who Are Homeless With Co-occurring Serious Mental Illness and Substance Abuse." *Research on Social Work Practice* 16:74–83.

Papineau, David. 1978. *For Science in the Social Sciences.* London: Macmillan.

Parks, Kathleen A., Ann M. Pardi, and Clara M. Bradizza. 2006. "Collecting Data on Alcohol Use and Alcohol-Related Victimization: A Comparison of Telephone and Web-Based Survey Methods." *Journal of Studies on Alcohol* 67:318–23.

Parlett, Malcolm and David Hamilton. 1976. "Evaluation as Illumination: A New Approach to the Study of Innovative Programmes." Pp. 140–57 in *Evaluation Studies Review Annual,* Vol. 1, edited by G. Glass. Thousand Oaks, CA: Sage.

Pasick, Rena J., Susan L. Stewart, Joyce A. Bird, and Carol N. D'Onofrio. 2001. "Quality of Data in Multiethnic Health Surveys." *Public Health Reports* 116:223–44.

Patton, Michael Quinn. 2002. *Qualitative Research and Evaluation Methods.* 3rd ed. Thousand Oaks, CA: Sage.

Payne, Malcolm. 1997. *Modern Social Work Theory: A Critical Introduction.* 2nd ed. Chicago: Lyceum.

Perry, Robin E. 2006. "Do Social Workers Make Better Child Welfare Workers Than Non–Social Workers?" *Research on Social Work Practice* 16:392–405.

Peterson, Robert A. 2000. *Constructing Effective Questionnaires.* Thousand Oaks, CA: Sage.

Petrosino, Anthony, Robert F. Boruch, Cath Rounding, Steve McDonald, and Iain Chalmers. 2000. "The Campbell Collaboration Social, Psychological, Educational, and Criminological Trials Register (C2-SPECTR)." *Evaluation and Research in Education* 14:206–19. Retrieved May 10, 2008 (http://geb9101.gse.upenn.edu/RISIMAGES/c2spectrorigin.pdf).

Plath, Debbie. 2006. "Evidence-Based Practice: Current Issues and Future Directions." *Australian Social Work* 59:56–72.

Pollio, David. 2006. "The Art of Evidence-Based Practice." *Research on Social Work Practice* 16:224–32.

Posavac, Emil J. and Raymond G. Carey. 1997. *Program Evaluation: Methods and Case Studies.* 5th ed. Upper Saddle River, NJ: Prentice Hall.

Presser, Stanley and Johnny Blair. 1994. "Survey Pretesting: Do Different Methods Produce Different Results?" *Sociological Methodology* 24:74–104.

Probst, Barbara. 2008. "Issues in Portability of Evidence-Based Treatment for Adolescent Depression." *Child and Adolescent Social Work Journal* 25:111–23.

Pryor, Carolyn B. 1992. "Peer Helping Programs in School Settings: Social Workers Report." *School Social Work Journal* 16:16–26.

Pyrczak, Fred. 2005. *Evaluating Research in Academic Journals: A Practical Guide to Realistic Evaluation.* 3rd ed. Glendale, CA: Pyrczak Publishing.

Radloff, Lenore. 1977. "The CES-D Scale: A Self-Report Depression Scale for Research in the General Population." *Applied Psychological Measurement* 1:385–401.

Ragin, Charles C. 1987. *The Comparative Method: Moving Beyond Qualitative and Quantitative Strategies.* Berkeley: University of California Press.

Ragin, Charles C. 1994. *Constructing Social Research.* Thousand Oaks, CA: Pine Forge Press.

Reynolds, Paul Davidson. 1979. *Ethical Dilemmas and Social Science Research.* San Francisco: Jossey-Bass.

Richards, Thomas J. and Lyn Richards. 1994. "Using Computers in Qualitative Research." Pp. 445–62 in *Handbook of Qualitative Research,* edited by Norman K. Denzin and Yvonna S. Lincoln. Thousand Oaks, CA: Sage.

Richardson, Laurel. 1995. "Narrative and Sociology." Pp. 198–221 in *Representation in Ethnography,* edited by John Van Maanen. Thousand Oaks, CA: Sage.

Riedel, Marc. 2000. *Research Strategies for Secondary Data: A Perspective for Criminology and Criminal Justice.* Thousand Oaks, CA: Sage.

Riessman, Catherine Kohler. 2002. "Narrative Analysis." Pp. 217–70 in *The Qualitative Researcher's Companion,* edited by A. Michael Huberman and Matthew B. Miles. Thousand Oaks, CA: Sage.

Rivard, Jeanne C. and Joseph P. Morrissey. 2003. "Factors Associated With Interagency Coordination in a Child Mental Health Service System Demonstration." *Administration and Policy in Mental Health* 30:397–414.

Rizzo, Victoria M. and Jeannine M. Rowe. 2006. "Studies of the Cost-Effectiveness of Social Work Services in Aging: A Review of the Literature." *Research on Social Work Practice* 16:67–73.

Roffman, Roger, Lois Downey, Blair Beadnell, Judith Gordon, Jay Craver, and Robert Stephens. 1997. "Cognitive-Behavioral Group Counseling to Prevent HIV Transmission in Gay and Bisexual Men: Factors Contributing to Successful Risk Reduction." *Research on Social Work Practice* 7:165–86.

Rosen, Aaron. 2003. "Evidence-Based Social Work Practice: Challenges and Promises." *Social Work* 27:197–208.

Rosen, Daniel, Mary Lindsey Smith, Sara Goodkind, and Latika Davis-Jones. 2006. "Using Photovoice to Identify Service Needs of Older African American Methadone Clients." Presented at the annual meeting of the Society for Social Work Research, January, San Antonio, Texas.

Rossi, Peter H. 1989. *Down and Out in America: The Origins of Homelessness.* Chicago: University of Chicago Press.

Rossi, Peter H. and Howard E. Freeman. 1989. *Evaluation: A Systematic Approach.* 4th ed. Thousand Oaks, CA: Sage.

Rossman, Gretchen B. and Sharon F. Rallis. 1998. *Learning in the Field: An Introduction to Qualitative Research.* Thousand Oaks, CA: Sage.

Royse, David, Bruce Thyer, Deborah K. Padgett, and T. K. Logan. 2006. *Program Evaluation: An Introduction.* 4th ed. Belmont, CA: Thomson Brooks/Cole.

Rubin, Herbert J. and Irene S. Rubin. 1995. *Qualitative Interviewing: The Art of Hearing Data.* Thousand Oaks, CA: Sage.

Sacks, Stanley, Karen McKendrick, George DeLeon, Michael T. French, and Kathryn E. McCollister. 2002. "Benefit-Cost Analysis of a Modified Therapeutic Community for Mentally Ill Chemical Abusers." *Evaluation and Program Planning* 25:137–48.

Sampson, Robert J. and Janet L. Lauritsen. 1994. "Violent Victimization and Offending: Individual, Situational, and Community-Level Risk Factors." Pp. 1–114 in *Understanding and Preventing Violence.* Vol. 3, *Social Influences,* edited by Albert J. Reiss, Jr., and Jeffrey A. Roth. Washington, DC: National Academy Press.

Sands, Robert G. and Robin S. Goldberg-Glen. 2000. "Factors Associated With Stress Among Grandparents Raising Their Grandchildren." *Family Relations: Interdisciplinary Journal of Applied Family Studies* 49:97–105.

Schaie, K. Warner. 1993. "Ageist Language in Psychological Research." *American Psychologist* 48:49–51.

Schein, Rebecca L. and Harold G. Koenig. 1997. "The Center for Epidemiological Studies–Depression (CES-D) Scale: Assessment of Depression in the Medically Ill Elderly." *International Journal of Geriatric Psychiatry* 12:436–46.

Scher, Lauren Sue, Rebecca A. Maynard, and Matthew Stagner. 2006. *Interventions Intended to Reduce Pregnancy-Related Outcomes Among Teenagers.* (Review for the Campbell Collaboration.) Retrieved May 29, 2009 (http://www.campbellcollaboration.org).

Schober, Michael F. 1999. "Making Sense of Survey Questions." Pp. 77–94 in *Cognition and Survey Research,* edited by Monroe G. Sirken, Douglas J. Herrmann, Susan Schechter, Norbert Schwartz, Judith M. Tanur, and Roger Tourangeau. New York: Wiley.

Schulberg, Herbert C., M. Saul, Maureen McClelland, M. Ganguli, W. Christy, and R. Frank. 1985. "Assessing Depression in Primary Medical and Psychiatric Practices." *Archives of General Psychiatry* 42:1164–70.

Schuman, Howard and Stanley Presser. 1981. *Questions and Answers in Attitude Surveys: Experiments on Question Form, Wording, and Context.* New York: Academic Press.

Schutt, Russell K. 2009. *Investigating the Social World.* 6th ed. Thousand Oaks, CA: Sage.

Schutt, Russell K., Tatjana Meschede, and Jill Rierdan. 1994. "Distress, Suicidality, and Social Support Among Homeless Adults." *Journal of Health and Social Behavior* 35(June):134–42.

Seefeldt, Kristen S. and Sean M. Orzol. 2005. "Watching the Clock Tick: Factors Associated With TANF Accumulation." *Social Work Research* 29:215–29.

Selm, Martine Van and Nicholas W. Jankowski. 2006. "Conducting Online Surveys." *Quality and Quantity* 40:435–56.

Selzer, Melvin L. 1997. "The Michigan Alcoholism Screening Test: The Quest for a New *Diagnostic* Instrument." *American Journal of Psychiatry* 127:165–58.

Shadish, William R., Thomas D. Cook, and Laura C. Leviton, eds. 1991. *Foundations of Program Evaluation: Theories of Practice.* Thousand Oaks, CA: Sage.

Shapiro, Janet R. and Sarah C. Mangelsdorf. 1994. "The Determinants of Parenting Competence in Adolescent Mothers." *Journal of Youth and Adolescence* 23:621–41.

Shepherd, Jane, David Hill, Joel Bristor, and Pat Montalvan. 1996. "Converting an Ongoing Health Study to CAPI: Findings From the National Health and Nutrition Study." Pp. 159–64 in *Health Survey Research Methods Conference Proceedings,* edited by Richard B. Warnecke. Hyattsville, MD: U.S. Department of Health and Human Services.

Sieber, Joan E. 1992. *Planning Ethically Responsible Research: A Guide for Students and Internal Review Boards.* Thousand Oaks, CA: Sage.

Silvestre, Anthony J. 1994. "Brokering: A Process for Establishing Long-Term and Stable Links With Gay Male Communities for Research and Public Health Education." *AIDS Education and Prevention* 6:65–73.

Singer, Muriel. 2005. "A Twice-Told Tale: A Phenomenological Inquiry Into Clients' Perceptions of Therapy." *Journal of Marital and Family Therapy* 31:269–81.

Smith, Tom W. 1984. "Nonattitudes: A Review and Evaluation." Pp. 215–55 in *Surveying Subjective Phenomena,* Vol. 22, edited by Charles F. Turner and Elizabeth Martin. New York: Russell Sage Foundation.

Smyth, Jolene D., Don A. Dillman, Leah Melani Christian, and Michael J. Stern. 2004, May. "How Visual Grouping Influences Answers to Internet Surveys." Extended version of paper presented at the Annual Meeting of the American Association for Public Opinion Research, Phoenix, AZ. Retrieved July 5, 2005 (http://survey.sesrc.wsu.edu/dillman/papers.htm).

Snider, D. E. 1999. *Guidelines for Defining Public Health Research and Public Health Non-research* (Centers for Disease Control, Associate Director for Science). Retrieved June 28, 2004 (http://www.cdc.gov/od/ads/opsp0111.htm).

Sobeck, Joanne L., Elizabeth E. Chapleski, and Charles Fisher. 2003. "Conducting Research With American Indians: A Case Study of Motives, Methods, and Results." *Journal of Ethnic and Cultural Diversity* 12:69–84.

Stake, Robert E. 1995. *The Art of Case Study Research.* Thousand Oaks, CA: Sage.

Stanfield, John H. 1999. "Slipping Through the Front Door: Relevant Social Scientific Evaluation in the People of Color Century." *American Journal of Evaluation* 20:415–31.

Starin, Amy. 2006. "Clients Role Choices: Unexplored Factors in Intervention Decisions." *Clinical Social Work Journal* 34:101–19.

Steng, J. Matt, Scott D. Rhodes, Guadalupe X. Rhodes, Eugenia Eng, Ramiro Arceo, and Selena Phipps. 2004. "Realidad Latina: Latino Adolescents, Their School, and a University Use Photovoice to Examine and Address the Influence of Immigration." *Journal of Interprofessional Care* 18:403–15.

Stevens, Christine A. 2006. "Being Healthy: Voices of Adolescent Women Who Are Parenting." *Journal for Specialists in Pediatric Nursing* 11:28–40.

Stewart, Anita L. and Anna Nápoles-Springer. 2000. "Health-Related Quality of Life Assessments in Diverse Population Groups in the United States." *Medical Care* 38:II102–24.

Stewart, David W. 1984. *Secondary Research: Information Sources and Methods.* Thousand Oaks, CA: Sage.

Straus, Sharon, W. Scott Richardson, Paul Glasziou, and R. Brian Haynes. 2005. *Evidence-Based Medicine: How to Practice and Teach EBM.* 3rd ed. New York: Churchill Livingstone.

Sudman, Seymour. 1976. *Applied Sampling.* New York: Academic Press.

Sullivan, Michael K., Christopher R. Larrison, Larry Nackerud, Ed Risler, and Laura Bodenschatz. 2004. "Examining the Relationship Between Psychological Well-Being and the Need for Continued Public Assistance Benefits." *The Journal of Contemporary Social Services* 85:425–29.

Thompson, Estina E., Harold W. Neighbors, Cheryl Munday, and James S. Jackson. 1996. "Recruitment and Retention of African American Patients for Clinical Research: An Exploration of Response Rates in an Urban Psychiatric Hospital." *Journal of Consulting and Clinical Psychology* 64:861–67.

Thompson, Noreen C., Edward E. Hunter, Lorraine Murray, Lisa Ninci, Elaine M. Rolfs, and Leonie Pallikkathayil. 2008. "The Experience of Living With Chronic Mental Illness: A Photovoice Study." *Perspectives in Psychiatric Care* 44:14–24.

Thorne, Sally, Louise Jensen, Margaret H. Kearney, George Noblit, and Margarete Sandelowski. 2004. "Qualitative Metasynthesis: Reflections on Methodological Orientation and Ideological Agenda." *Qualitative Health Research* 14:1342–65.

Thyer, Bruce A. 2001. "What Is the Role of Theory in Research on Social Work Practice?" *Journal of Social Work Education* 37:9–21.

Tichon, Jennifer G. and Margaret Shapiro. 2003. "The Process of Sharing Social Support in Cyberspace." *CyberPsychology and Behavior* 6:161–70.

Tourangeau, Roger. 2004. "Survey Research and Societal Change." *Annual Review of Psychology* 55:775–801.

Tran, Thanh V., G. Khatutsky, K. Aroian, A. Balsam, and K. Conway. 2000. "Living Arrangements, Depression, and Health Status Among Elderly Russian-Speaking Immigrants." *Journal of Gerontological Social Work* 33:63–77.

Tripodi, Tony. 1994. *A Primer on Single-Subject Design for Clinical Social Workers.* Washington, DC: National Association of Social Workers.

Turner, Charles F. and Elizabeth Martin, eds. 1984. *Surveying Subjective Phenomena,* Vols. I and II. New York: Russell Sage Foundation.

U.S. Bureau of the Census. 1996. *Current Population Survey. Annual Social and Economic Supplement.* Washington, DC: Author.

U.S. Bureau of the Census. 2003. *Survey Abstracts.* Retrieved July 12, 2004 (http://www.census.gov/main/www/dsabstract_Jan03.pdf).

U.S. Bureau of the Census. 2008. *Current Population Survey. Annual Social and Economic Supplement.* Washington, DC: Author.

U.S. Department of Health and Human Services. 1999. *Mental Health: A Report of the Surgeon General—Executive Summary.* Retrieved May 22, 2009 (http://www.surgeongeneral.gov/library/mentalhealth/pdfs/ExSummary-Final.pdf). Rockville, MD: U.S. Department of Health and Human Services.

U.S. Department of Health and Human Services. 2001. *Mental Health: Culture, Race, and Ethnicity—A Supplement to Mental Health: A Report of the Surgeon General.* Rockville, MD: U.S. Department of Health and Human Services, Office of the Surgeon General. Retrieved April 8, 2008 (http://mentalhealth.samhsa.gov/cre/toc.asp).

Van den Berg, Nan and Catherine Crisp. 2004. "Defining Culturally Competent Practice With Sexual Minorities: Implications for Social Work Education and Practice." *Journal of Social Work Education* 40:221–38.

Van Maanen, John. 1995. "An End to Innocence: The Ethnography of Ethnography." Pp. 1–35 in *Representation in Ethnography,* edited by John Van Maanen. Thousand Oaks, CA: Sage.

Van Maanen, John. 2002. "The Fact of Fiction in Organizational Ethnography." Pp. 101–17 in *The Qualitative Researcher's Companion,* edited by A. Michael Huberman and Matthew B. Miles. Thousand Oaks, CA: Sage.

Vega, William A., Bohdan Kolody, Sergio Aguilar-Gaxiola, Ethel Alderete, Ralph Catalano, and Jorge Caraveo-Anduaga. 1998. "Lifetime Prevalence of DSM-III-R Psychiatric Disorders Among Urban and Rural Mexican Americans in California." *Archives of General Psychiatry* 55:771–78.

Wallace, J. Brandon. 1994. "Life Stories." Pp. 137–54 in *Qualitative Methods in Aging Research,* edited by Jaber F. Gubrium and Andrea Sankar. Thousand Oaks, CA: Sage.

Wallace, Walter L. 1983. *Principles of Scientific Sociology.* New York: Aldine.

Walton, Elaine. 2001. "Combining Abuse and Neglect Interventions With Intensive Family Preservation Services: An Innovative Approach to Protecting Children." *Research on Social Work Practice* 11:627–44.

Walton, Elaine, Mark W. Fraser, Robert E. Lewis, Peter J. Pecora, and Wendel K. Walton. 1993. "In-Home Family-Focused Reunification: An Experimental Study." *Child Welfare* 72:473–87.

Wang, Caroline and Mary Ann Burris. 1997. "Photovoice: Concept, Methodology, and Use for Participatory Need Assessment." *Health Education and Behavior* 24:369–87.

Weber, Robert Philip. 1985. *Basic Content Analysis.* Thousand Oaks, CA: Sage.

Weiss, Carol H. 1972. *Evaluation Research.* Englewood Cliffs, NJ: Prentice Hall.

Weiss, Carol H. 1998. *Evaluation.* 2nd ed. Upper Saddle River, NJ: Prentice Hall.

Whitelaw, Carolyn and Edgardo L. Perez. 1987. "Partial Hospitalization Programs: A Current Perspective." *Administration in Mental Health* 15:62–72.

Whittaker, James K., Kari Greene, Derenda Schubert, Rich Blum, Keith Cheng, Kerry Blum, Norman Reed, Kim Scott, and Robert Roy. 2006. "Integrating Evidence-Based Practice in the Child Mental Health Agency: A Template for Clinical and Organizational Change." *American Journal of Orthopsychiatry* 76:194–201.

Whyte, William Foote. 1955. *Street Corner Society.* Chicago: University of Chicago Press.

Witkin, Belle Ruth and James W. Altschuld. 1995. *Planning and Conducting Needs Assessments: A Practical Guide.* Thousand Oaks, CA: Sage.

Witkin, Stanley L. 2001. "The Measure of Things." *Social Work* 46:101–104.

W. K. Kellogg Foundation. 2004. *Using Logic Models to Bring Together Planning, Evaluation, and Action: Logic Model Development Guide.* Battle Creek, MI: Author. Retrieved May 15, 2009 (http://www.wkkf.org/Pubs/Tools/Evaluation/Pub3669.pdf).

Wolcott, Harry F. 1995. *The Art of Fieldwork.* Walnut Creek, CA: AltaMira Press.

Yamatani, Hidenori and Rafael J. Engel. 2002. *Workload Assessment Study.* Pittsburgh, PA: University of Pittsburgh.

Yamatani, Hidenori, Aaron Mann, and Patricia Wright. 2000. *Garfield Community Needs Assessment.* Pittsburgh, PA: University of Pittsburgh.

Zayas, Luis H., Leopoldo Cabassa, and M. Carmela Perez. 2005. "Capacity to Consent in Psychiatric Research: Development and Preliminary Testing of a Screening Tool." *Research on Social Work Practice* 15:545–56.

Zimet, Gregory D., Nancy W. Dahlem, Sara G. Zimet, and Gordon K. Farley. 1988. "The Multidimensional Scale of Perceived Social Support." *Journal of Personality Assessment* 52:30–41.

Glossary/Index

A-B design, 158–159, 167

A-B-A design, 159–161

A-B-A-B design, 159–161, 171

A-B-C-D design, 164–167

Abel, David, 2

Absolute zero point, 64

Acquiescence bias The tendency for people to agree with a statement just to avoid seeming disagreeable, 66, 186–187

Adherence to authority Unquestioning acceptance of statements by authority figures such as parents, teachers, and professionals, 5

Advocacy and research, 41, 259

African American participation, 101

After-Only Design, 125

Aggregate matching Two or more groups, such as classes, are matched and then randomly assigned to the experimental and control conditions, 117

Agreement bias, 186–187

Aid to Families with Dependent Children (AFDC), 127

Alpha level (α), 313, 315

Alternate-forms reliability A procedure for testing the reliability of responses to survey questions in which subjects' answers are compared after the subjects have been asked slightly different versions of the questions or when randomly selected halves of the sample have been administered slightly different versions of the questions, 68

American Medical Association (AMA), 41

American Psychological Association (APA) style, 345, 349

Anderson, Elijah, 242, 246, 249, 250–251

Anomalous findings Unexpected findings in data analysis that are inconsistent with most other findings with those data, 31

Anonymity Provided by research in which no identifying information is recorded that could be used to link respondents to their responses, 45, 207, 259

Anthony, William A., 272

Applied research reports, 328–330

Arean, Patricia A., 101

Assertive Community Treatment (ACT), 232–233

Assessment, 51. *See also* Evaluation research; Measurement

Association A criterion for establishing a causal relationship between two variables; variation in one variable is related to variation in another variable, 111

describing relations among variables, 307–313

direction of, 33–34

effect size, 331

experimental designs and, 118

measures of, 312

monotonic, 311

time series designs and, 123

Type I and Type II errors, 314–316

Attrition effects, 126, 131

Authority, adherence to, 5

Availability sampling A sampling method in which elements are selected on the basis of convenience, 94

Average. *See* Mean

B-A design, 167

Banks, C., 43

Bar chart A graphic for categorical variables in which the variable's distribution is displayed with solid bars separated by spaces, 293, 309

Barlow, David H., 169

Baseline phase (A) The initial phase of a single-subject design, typically abbreviated by the letter *A*; it represents the period in which the intervention to be evaluated is not offered to the subject. During the baseline phase, repeated measurements of the dependent variable are taken or constructed, 141–146

A-B design, 158–159

multiple baseline designs, 161–164, 171

visual analysis, 152–157

Batterer intervention programs, 346–347

B design, 167

Becker, Deborah R., 272

Behavioral measures, 147

Behavior coding Observation in which the researcher categorizes, according to strict rules, the number of times certain behaviors occur, 190, 203

Behavior theory, 30

Bellah, Robert N., 228

Bennett, Larry W., 346–347

Best current evidence, 7

Bias errors in measurement (systematic error), 66

Bimodal distribution, 299

Bivariate distributions, 307

Bivariate statistical tests Statistical tests of the relationship between two variables, 316

Black box Occurs when an evaluation of program outcomes ignores, and does not identify, the process by which the program produced the effect, 275

Block matching A form of matching that groups individuals by their characteristics. Within each group, members are randomly assigned to the experimental and control groups, 117

Boolean search, 342

Bradshaw, William, 29–30, 159, 164

Burnside-Eaton, Patricia, 13

Burris, Mary Ann, 230

Burt, Martha, 9

C2-SPECTR Archive of over 11,000 intervention experiments, 280

Call, Christine, 346–347

Campbell Collaboration Group producing systematic reviews of interventions in education, criminal justice, social welfare, and research methods, 26, 280

Carey, Raymond G., 120–121

Carryover effect The impact of an intervention persists after the end of the treatment process, 160

Causal effect The finding that change in one variable leads to change in another variable, ceteris paribus (other things being equal), 110

association criterion, 111

context, 113

nonspuriousness, 112

time order criterion, 112

time series designs, 123

Causal mechanism A discernable process that creates the connection between variation in an independent variable and the variation in the dependent variable, 112–113

Causal network model, 247

Causal validity Exists when a conclusion that A leads to or results in B is correct. Also called *internal validity,* 17–18, 111

Census Bureau resources, 202

Center for Epidemiologic Studies Depression Scale (CES-D), 56–57, 70–74, 76

Central tendency The most common value (for variables measured at the nominal level) or the value on which cases tend to center (for a quantitative variable), 292

measures of, 299–303

Check coding A check of the accuracy of coding information; it is estimated by comparing the coding completed by one person with the coding completed by a second person, 291

Child abuse risk factors, 333

Chi-square test, 316

Clark, Robin E., 272

Client context and evidence-based practice, 7–8

Client monitoring, 158–159, 167

Client preferences and evidence-based practice, 7

Client satisfaction measures, 61–63, 271

Clinical expertise, 8

Clinical replication Used to enhance generalizability of single-subject designs; clinical replication involves combining different interventions into a clinical package to treat multiple problems, 169

Clinical screening tools, 72–74

Clinical significance, 152

Closed-ended question A survey question that provides preformatted response choices for the respondent to check or circle, 185–186

Cluster A naturally occurring, mixed aggregate of elements of the population, 93

Cluster sampling A sampling method in which elements are selected in two or more stages, with the first stage being the random selection of naturally occurring clusters and the last stage being the random selection of elements within clusters, 93

Codebook, 290

Code of the Streets (Anderson), 250–251

Coding open-ended questions, 290

Coercion, 44, 232–233

Cognition theory, 30

Cognitive-behavioral theory, 29–30

Cognitive-behavioral therapy (CBT), 159, 164, 356

Cognitive interview   A technique for evaluating questions in which researchers ask people test questions, then probe with follow-up questions to learn how they understood the question and what their answers mean, 190, 203

Cohen, Gary, 17

Cohort study   A type of longitudinal study in which data are collected at two or more points in time from individuals or groups with a common starting point, for example, from people who were born in the 1940s and the 1950s (the "baby boom generation"), 38–39

Colloquialisms, 205

Combined frequency display   A table that presents together the distributions for a set of conceptually similar variables having the same response categories; common headings are used for the responses, 296

Comparison group   In an experiment, a group that has been exposed to a different treatment (or value of the independent variable) than the experimental group, 113, 114

Pretest-Posttest Comparison Group Design, 272

threats to internal validity, 126

See also Control group

Compensatory equalization of treatment   A threat to internal validity. When staff providing a treatment to a comparison group feel it is unfair that the group is not getting the experimental treatment, the staff may work harder or do more than if there were no experiment, 128

Compensatory rivalry   A type of contamination in true experimental and quasi-experimental designs that occurs when control group members are aware that they are being denied some advantage and so increase their efforts by way of compensation, 128

Complete observation   A role in participant observation in which the researcher does not participate in group activities and is publicly identified as a researcher, 216–218

Compressed frequency display   A table that presents cross-classification data efficiently by eliminating unnecessary percentages, such as the percentage corresponding to the second value of a dichotomous variable, 296–297

Computer-assisted personal interviewing (CAPI), 197

Computer-assisted qualitative data analysis   Use of computer software to assist qualitative analyses through creation, application, and refinement of categories, tracing linkages between concepts, and making comparisons between cases and events, 254–257

Computer-assisted telephone interview (CATI), 195, 290

Computerized bibliographic databases, 341

Computer-mediated counseling, 17

Concept   A mental image that summarizes a set of similar observations, feelings, or ideas, 51–53

nominal definition, 52

Conceptual equivalence, 74, 204

Conceptualization   The process of specifying what we mean by a term. In deductive research, conceptualization helps to translate portions of an abstract theory into specific variables that can be used to test hypotheses. In inductive research, conceptualization is part of the process to make sense of related observations, 52, 245–246

Concurrent multiple baseline design, 161

Concurrent validity   The type of validity that exists when scores on a measure are closely related to scores on a criterion measured at the same time, 70

Confidence interval   The range of values within which the true population value will fall. Often a 95% confidence interval is used; this means that the researcher is 95% certain that the true population value falls within the range, 99

Confidence limits, 99

Confidentiality   Provided by research in which identifying information that could be used to link respondents to their responses is available only to designated research personnel for specific research needs, 20, 44–45, 207, 234

legal disclosure requirements, 283

qualitative research and, 234–235, 259

Constructivist paradigm Methodology based on questioning belief in an external reality. Emphasizes the importance of exploring the way in which different stakeholders in a social setting construct their beliefs, 35–36

Construct validity The type of validity that is established by showing that a measure is related to other measures as specified in a theory, 70, 71

Contamination effects, 128

Content analysis A research method for systematically analyzing and making inferences from text.

Content analysis, 257–259

Content equivalence, 204

Content validity The type of validity that exists when the full range of a concept's meaning is covered by the measure, 69–70

Context A focus of idiographic causal explanation; a particular outcome is understood as part of a larger set of interrelated circumstances, 113

Context effect Occurs in a survey when one or more questions influence how subsequent questions are interpreted, 181

Contingency question A question that is asked of only a subset of survey respondents, 187–188, 291

Continuous variable A variable for which the number represents a quantity that can be described in terms of order, spread between the numbers, and relative amounts, 58

Control group A comparison group that receives no treatment, 114
  contamination effects, 128
  quasi-experimental designs, 121–122
  true experimental designs, 117–119
  See also Comparison groups

Convenience sampling, 94

Convergent validity The type of validity achieved when one measure of a concept is associated with different types of measures of the same concept, 71

Correlation, 111

Correlation coefficient A statistic summarizing the strength of a relationship between two continuous variables, 312

Cost-benefit analysis A type of evaluation that compares program costs with the economic value of program benefits, 273–274

Cost considerations, survey design alternatives, 192

Cost-effectiveness analysis A type of evaluation that compares program costs with program outcomes, 274

Counts, Dorothy, 220

Cover letter The letter sent with a mail questionnaire. It explains the survey's purpose and auspices and encourages the respondent to participate, 192–193

Covert participation A role in field research in which the researcher does not reveal his or her identity as a researcher to those who are observed, 219, 233–234

Crabtree, Benjamin F., 242–243

Cress, Daniel M., 251–253

Criterion equivalence, 204

Criterion validity The type of validity established by comparing the scores obtained on the measure being validated with scores obtained with a more direct or already validated measure of the same phenomenon (the criterion), 70, 71

Cronbach's alpha coefficient A statistic commonly used to measure interitem reliability, 68

Cross-population generalizability Exists when findings about one group, population, or setting hold true for other groups, populations, or settings. Also called *external validity,* 16–17, 74, 84, 103, 178

Cross-sectional research design A study in which the data are collected at only one point in time, 36, 206
  trend studies, 37–38

Crosstabulation In the simplest case, a bivariate (two-variable) distribution, showing the distribution of one variable for each category of another variable, 307
  table, 310–311

Cultural barriers, 102

Cultural diversity. *See* Diversity issues

Culturally competent practice, 19.
  See also Diversity issues

Current Population Survey (CPS), 37–38

Cut-off score A score used in a scale to distinguish between respondents with a particular status and respondents who do not have that status, 73–74, 75, 76

Cycle A baseline phase pattern reflecting ups and downs depending on the time of measurement, 142

Data analysis:
   diversity issues, 19–20
   qualitative, 240–262
   quantitative, 287–319
   single-subject designs, 148–157
   See also Qualitative data analysis;
      Quantitative data analysis
Database search, 341–342, 345
Data cleaning   The process of checking data for
   errors after the data have been entered in a
   computer file, 291
Data entry, 290–291
Data preparation, 288–292
Davis-Jones, Latika, 230
Debriefing   A researcher's informing subjects
   after an experiment about the experiment's
   purposes and methods and evaluating
   subjects' personal reactions to the
   experiment, 44, 133
Decentering   A method of making equivalent
   different language versions of an instrument;
   it involves modifying both the original
   instrument and the translated instrument to
   increase their equivalence, 204
Descriptive research   Research in which social
   phenomena are defined and described, 133
Decker, Scott H., 256–257
Deductive research, 30–34, 36
DeLeon, George, 273
Dependent variable   A variable that is
   hypothesized to vary depending on or under
   the influence of another variable, 33–34, 111
   identifying in research articles, 358
   in single-subject designs, 147
Depression measures, 56–57, 70–74, 75, 76
Descriptive research   Research in which social
   phenomena are defined and described, 9, 35
Diagnostic and Statistical Manual of Mental Disorders,
   4th ed., text revision *(DSM-IV-TR),* 52
Diamond, Timothy, 212, 214–216, 218, 219,
   221, 223–224, 245
Dichotomous variables, 64
Differential attrition, 126
Diffusion of treatment   A type of contamination
   in experimental and quasi-experimental
   designs that occurs when treatment and
   comparison groups interact and the nature of
   the treatment becomes known to the
   comparison group, 128
Direction of association   A pattern in a
   relationship between two variables; the values
of one variable tend to change consistently in
   relation to change in the value of the second
   variable, 33–34
Direct replication   Used to enhance the
   generalizability of a single-subject design; the
   single-subject design is repeated using the
   same procedures by the same researchers and
   the same providers, in the same setting, and in
   the same situation with different clients, 169
Discrete variable   A type of variable for which
   the number assigned to each category is
   arbitrary. The variable categories do not
   represent an order, 58
Discriminant validity   An approach to construct
   validity; the scores on the measure to be
   validated are compared with scores on
   another measure of the same variable and
   with scores on variables that measure
   different but related concepts. Discriminant
   validity is achieved if the measure to be
   validated is related most strongly to its
   comparison measure and less so to the
   measures of other concepts, 70
Disproportionate stratified sampling   Sampling
   in which elements are selected from strata in
   different proportions from those that appear
   in the population, 91
Diversity issues, 18–20
   client categorization, 281
   cultural barriers to research participation, 102
   culturally competent practice, 19
   data analysis, 19–20
   equivalence, 74, 203, 204
   evaluation research, 281
   instrument translation, 204–205
   interviewer-respondent characteristics, 205
   measurement, 74–76
   minority sampling, 19
   participation enhancement, 101–103
   qualitative research, 231–232
   relevance validity, 281
   reporting research results, 334–335
   research designs and, 131–132
   research external validity, 132
   research questions and, 27
   research validity, 19
   single-subject designs, 170
   survey research, 203–205
   systematic measurement errors, 66
Domestic violence research, 346–349
"Don't know" responses, 187

Double-barreled question A survey question that actually asks two questions but allows only one answer, 183

Double-blind procedure An experimental method in which neither the subjects nor the staff delivering the experimental treatments know which subjects are getting the treatment and which are receiving a placebo, 128

Double negatives, 183

Drake, Robert E., 272

Duration The length of time an event or some symptom lasts; it usually is measured for each occurrence of the event or symptom, 147

Ecological fallacy, 99–100

Edin, Kathryn, 39

Effect size A standardized measure of association; the difference between the mean of the experimental group and the mean of the comparison group on the dependent variable, adjusted for the average variability in the two groups, 331

Efficiency analysis A type of evaluation that compares program costs with program effects. It can be either a cost-benefit analysis or a cost-effectiveness analysis, 273–274

Elderly, 212, 214–221, 229

Electronic reference formats, 349

Electronic surveys, 191, 198–199, 200–201

Elements The individual members of the population whose characteristics are to be measured, 82

Endogenous change A source of causal invalidity that occurs when natural developments or changes in the subjects (independent of the experimental treatment itself) account for some or all of the observed change from pretest to posttest, 127

Engel, Rafael J., 281, 389

English, Brian, 283

Enumeration units Units that contain one or more elements and that are listed in a sampling frame, 83

Equal probability of selection method (EPSM), 89

Equivalence issues, 74, 203, 204

Erikson, Kai T., 233–234

Errors
  causal conclusions, 99–100
  measurement. *See* Measurement error
  nonobservation, 178
  observation, 178
  reasoning, 2–6
  sampling. *See* Sampling error
  survey research, 178–180

Essock, Susan M., 273

Ethical issues, 8
  deception, 133
  evaluating research articles, 362
  evaluation research, 282–283
  honesty and openness, 41
  human subjects, 42–45
  participant observation, 218–219, 233–234
  program evaluation, 133
  qualitative research, 233–234, 259–260
  reporting research results, 335–336
  research designs and, 132–134
  research guidelines, 40–45
  selective distribution of benefits, 133–134
  single-subject designs, 170–171
  statistics, 316–318
  subject well-being, 234
  survey research and, 206–207, 318
  uses of science, 41–42
  See also Confidentiality; Informed consent

Ethnic diversity. *See* Diversity issues

Ethnography The study of a culture shared by some group of people, using participant observation over an extended period of time, 250–251

Evaluation research Research that describes or identifies the impact of social programs and policies, 11–12, 34, 158, 264–266
  black box approach, 275
  Campbell Collaboration, 26, 280
  design considerations, 274–279
  diversity issues, 281
  efficiency analysis, 273–274
  ethical issues, 133, 282–283
  evidence-based practice and, 279–280
  experimental designs and, 272–273
  formative evaluation, 271
  government-supported resources, 27
  informed consent, 171
  integrative approach, 277
  logic models, 266–270, 279–280
  needs assessment, 270–271
  nonexperimental designs, 123–125
  nonprobability sampling methods, 93
  obstacles, 284
  outcome complexity, 278–279

outcome evaluation, 272–273

process evaluation, 271–272

qualitative methods and, 232–233, 272, 277–278

social science approaches, 276–277

stakeholders, 266, 275–277

systems model, 265

theory-driven, 275

Evidence-based practice Social work practice that integrates the best research evidence, client values, client circumstances, and clinical expertise, 7–8

client contexts and, 7–8

clinical expertise and, 8

evaluation research and, 279–280

finding literature for, 26–27

government-supported resources, 27

measurement implications, 75–76

qualitative research and, 232–233

reading research articles, 356

research design implications, 130–131

research result reports and, 333–334

sampling method implications, 103–104

single-subject design implications, 167–170

statistical methods implications, 313–316

survey research implications, 205–206

Exhaustive Every case can be classified as having at least one attribute (or one value) for the variable, 59

Expectancies of experimental staff, 128

Experimental designs, 109, 113–121

agency-based research issues, 120–121

ethical issues, 132–134

evidence-based practice and, 131

features of true experiments, 113–114

goal of, 158

groups, 114

matching, 116–117, 121

outcome evaluation, 272–273

posttest and pretest, 117

Posttest-Only Control Group Design, 119

Pretest-Posttest Comparison Group Design, 272

Pretest-Posttest Control Group Design, 117–119

random assignment, 113, 114–116

Solomon Four Group Design, 119–120

threats to internal validity, 125–128

See also Quasi-experimental designs

Experimental group In an experiment, the group of subjects that receives the treatment or experimental manipulation, 114

Explanatory research Seeks to identify causes and effects of social phenomena and to predict how one phenomenon will change or vary in response to variation in some other phenomenon, 10–11, 34

Exploratory research Seeks to find out how people get along in the setting under question, what meanings they give to their actions, and what issues concern them, 9–10

External events, 127

External validity, 84, 129, 131, 132, 169. *See also* Generalizability.

Face validity The type of validity that exists when an inspection of items used to measure a concept suggests that they are appropriate in the opinion of the user or researcher, 69

False negative The participant does not have a particular problem according to a screening instrument, but the participant really does have the problem based on a clinical evaluation, 73

False positive A respondent has a particular problem according to a screening instrument, but in reality does not have the problem based on a clinical evaluation, 73

Family resilience, 253

Feedback Information about service delivery system outputs, outcomes, or operations that is available to stakeholders.

Feedback process, 266

Female-initiated violence, 347–349

Fence-sitters Survey respondents who see themselves as being neutral on an issue and choose a middle (neutral) response, 187

Field notes, 224, 225 (exh), 242, 245, 259

Filter question A survey question used to identify a subset of respondents who are then asked other questions, 187–188

Flett, Heather, 346–347

Floaters Survey respondents who provide an opinion on a topic in response to a closed-ended question that does not include a *"don't know"* option, but who will choose *"don't know"* if it is available, 187

Focus groups A qualitative method that involves unstructured group interviews in which the focus group leader encourages discussion among participants on the topics of interest, 190, 203, 213, 214, 229–230

Formative evaluation Process evaluation that is used to shape and refine program operations, 271

Franklin, Cynthia G., 118

French, Michael T., 273

Frequency In a single subject design, counting the number of times a behavior occurs or the number of times people experience different feelings within a particular time period, 147

Frequency distribution A numerical display showing the number of cases, and usually the percentage of cases (the relative frequencies), corresponding to each value or group of values of a variable, 292, 294–298
combined frequency display, 296
compressed frequency display, 296–297
distortion, 318

Frequency polygon A graphic for quantitative variables in which a continuous line connects data points representing the variable's distribution, 294

Frisman, Linda K., 273

Gallagher-Thompson, Dolores, 101

Gambrill, Eileen, 7

Gamma A measure of association that is sometimes used in crosstabular analysis, 312

Garland, Diana, 34

Gay, lesbian, and bisexual recruitment, 102–103

Generalizability Exists when a conclusion holds true for the population, group, setting, or event, 15–17
cross-population, 16–17, 74, 84, 103, 178
diversity issues, 132
external validity, 84, 129, 131, 169
sample, 15–16, 84, 129, 178
sampling, 82, 84–85
single-subject designs, 169
survey research and, 178

Generalization errors, 3

General Social survey (GSS), 202

Goal attainment scales, 61

Goldberg-Glen, Robin S., 28–29

Goodkind, Sara, 230

Government-supported registries, 27

Graphing, 146, 292–294
ethical issues, 318
relationships between variables, 309–310
single-subject data analysis, 149–157

Grounded theory Systematic theory developed inductively, based on observations that are summarized into conceptual categories, reevaluated in the research setting, and gradually refined and linked to other conceptual categories, 253

Group-administered survey A survey that is completed by individual respondents who are assembled in a group, 191, 194, 207

Group research designs, 109. *See also* Experimental designs

Guidelines for social work research
ethical, 40–45
scientific, 39–40

Guide to Community Preventive Services, 27

Gulcur, Leyla, 12

Ha, Jung-hwa, 229

Hammer, Leslie B., 229

Haney, C., 43

Harris, Mary Beth, 118

Hawthorne effect, 130

Hermeneutic perspective, 241

Heterosexist bias, 27

Hicks-Coolick, Anne, 13

Hispanic participation, 101

Histogram A graphic for quantitative variables in which the variable's distribution is displayed with adjacent bars, 293–294

History A source of causal invalidity that occurs when something other than the treatment influences outcome scores; also called an effect of *external events,* 127, 146, 161

Homelessness research, 2, 9–10, 11–12, 13, 15, 17, 34, 84

Homeless social movement organizations (SMOs), 251–253

Huberman, A. Michael, 259

Human capital theory, 30

Human subjects issues, 42–45, 234. *See also* Ethical issues; Informed consent

HyperRESEARCH, 254–255

Hypothesis A tentative statement about empirical reality involving a relationship between two or more variables, 32–34, 318, 357

Identification numbers, 288

Illogical reasoning Occurs when we prematurely jump to conclusions or argue on the basis of invalid assumptions, 4

Inaccurate observation Observations based on faulty perceptions of empirical reality, 3

Incomplete questionnaires, 290

Independent variable A variable that is hypothesized to cause, or lead to, variation in another variable, 32–34, 111
  identifying in research articles, 358

Inductive research The type of research in which general conclusions are drawn from specific data; compare with *deductive research,* 30, 34–36

Inferential statistics Mathematical tools for estimating how likely it is that a statistical result based on data from a random sample is representative of the population from which the sample is assumed to have been selected, 98, 313

Informed consent Exists when potential research study participants are given sufficient information about the costs and benefits of participating in the study, what their participation involves, and their rights as participants in the study, and they then make an "informed" decision to participate, 8, 43–44, 133, 170
  diversity issues, 283
  evaluation research and, 171, 283
  qualitative research and, 234

Ingersoll-Dayton, Berit, 229

In-person interview A survey in which an interviewer questions respondents face-to-face and records their answers, 191, 197–198, 200–201

Inputs The resources, raw materials, and staff that go into a program, 266

Institutional review board (IRB) A group of organizational and community representatives required by federal law to review the ethical issues in all proposed research that is federally funded, involves human subjects, or has any potential for harm to subjects, 42, 362

Instrumentation A problem that occurs in experimental designs when the measurement methods are not stable or equivalent, 127–128

Integrated literature review, 347–349

Integrative approach An orientation to evaluation research that expects researchers to respond to the concerns of people involved with the program as well as to the standards and goals of the social scientific community, 277

Intensive interviewing A qualitative method that involves open-ended, relatively unstructured questioning in which the interviewer seeks in-depth information on the respondent's feelings, experiences, and perceptions, 213, 214, 226–228

Interactive voice response (IVR), 195–196

Intermediate outcomes, 269

Internal consistency An approach to reliability based on the correlation among multiple items used to measure a single concept, 68

Internal validity A criterion necessary to demonstrate causality; it is the ability to rule out all other alternative explanations, 112, 118
  evaluating in research articles, 360
  random assignment and, 115–116
  single-subject designs, 143, 146
  threats to, 125–128, 360

Internet-based surveys, 191, 198–199, 200–201

Internet search. *See* Web search

Interpretivism Methodology based on the belief that reality is socially constructed and that the goal of social scientists is to understand the meanings people give to reality, 35

Interquartile range The range in a distribution between the end of the first quartile and the beginning of the third quartile, 305

Interrater reliability The degree of agreement when similar measurements are obtained by different observers rating the same people, events, or places, 69

Interrupted Time-Series Design, 122–123

Inter-University Consortium for Political and Social Research, 202

Interval Used in single-subject design, a measure of the length of time between events, behaviors, or symptoms, 147

Interval level of measurement A measurement of a variable in which the numbers indicating a variable's values represent fixed measurement units but have no absolute, or fixed, zero point, 61–63, 292

Intervention, as variable, 56–58

Interview:
  cognitive, 190
  intensive interviewing,
      213, 214, 226–228
  schedule, 180
Interview-based survey design, 191, 197–198, 200–201
Interview schedule   The survey instrument
  containing the questions asked by the
  interviewer in an in-person or phone survey.
Interviewer-respondent characteristics, 205
Interviewer training, 102
Intrarater reliability   Consistency of ratings by
  an observer of an unchanging phenomenon at
  two or more points in time, 69
Item equivalence, 74

Jargon, 183
Johnson, Alice, 10, 34
Journals, writing for, 327–328

Kagawa-Singer, Marjorie, 231
Kaufman, Sharon R., 226
Kerr, Barbara, 17
Key informant survey, 96
Key word search, 342
Known-groups validity   Demonstrating the
  validity of a measure using two groups with
  already identified characteristics, 71
Kontos, Nina J., 273

Language translation, 204–205
Leading questions, 66, 184
Level   Flat lines reflecting the amount or
  magnitude of the target variable; used in a
  single-subject design, 149
Level of measurement   The mathematical
  precision with which the values of a variable
  can be expressed, 59–65, 292
  choosing a statistical test, 316
  dichotomies, 64
  interval, 61–63, 292
  mathematical comparisons, 64–65
  measures of central tendency and, 301
  nominal, 59–60, 292
  ordinal, 60–61, 292
  ratio, 64, 292
Lewis, Robert E., 112–113
Lietz, Cynthia, 253
Likert-type response categories, 188
Lindsey, Michael A., 233

Literature review, 340–346
  APA style, 345, 349
  electronic reference formats, 349
  evaluating in research articles, 357
  how to read articles, 356–362
  integrated review example, 347–349
  literature for evidence-based practice, 26–27
  questions to ask about articles, 353–355
  research question development, 25
  reviewing research, 345–346
  searching the literature, 341–344
  searching the Web, 343–345, 349–352
  single-article review example, 346–347
  summarizing prior research, 347–349
  systematic review of findings, 26
Literature search, 341–344. *See also* Literature review
Logical errors, 2–6
Logic model   A schematic representation of the
  various components that make up a social
  service program, including the assumptions
  underlying the program, inputs, activities,
  outputs, and outcomes, 266–270, 279–280
Longitudinal research design   A study in which
  data are collected that can be ordered in time;
  research in which data are collected at two or
  more points in time, 36–39, 206
  cohort studies, 38–39
  panel studies, 38
  trend studies, 37–38
Lundahl, Brad, 333
Lyman, Karen, 217–218

Madsen, Richard, 228
Magnitude   In a single-subject design, measuring
  the extent to which people experience
  different feelings or symptoms at a particular
  time, 147
Mail survey   A survey involving a mailed
  questionnaire to be completed by the
  respondent, 191, 192–194, 200–201, 207
Mangelsdorf, Sarah C., 226
Manson, Spero M., 101
Marginal distributions   The summary
  distributions in the margins of a
  crosstabulation that correspond to the
  frequency distribution of the row variable and
  the column variable, 307–308
Matching   A procedure for equating the
  characteristics of individuals in different
  comparison groups in an experiment, 121

Matrix A form on which to systematically record particular features of multiple cases or instances that a qualitative data analyst needs to examine, 246–247

Matrix questions A series of questions that concern a common theme and have the same response choices, 188–189

Maturation effects, 127

McCollister, Kathryn E., 273

McHugo, Gregory J., 272

McKendrick, Karen, 273

Mean The arithmetic or weighted average computed by adding up the value of all the cases and dividing by the number of cases, 97, 149, 300–303
   sampling distribution of, 97

Measurement, 51
   behavioral measures, 147
   concepts and, 51–53
   diversity issues, 74–76, 203, 204
   equivalence, 74, 203, 204
   evidence-based practice and, 75–76
   operationalization, 53–59
   precision, 54
   reactivity effects, 148
   scales, 55–57, 72–74
   sensitivity and specificity, 73–74
   single-subject designs, 146–148
   triangulation, 58
   See also Levels of measurement

Measurement error, 65–67
   random error, 66–67
   survey research and, 178, 179
   systematic error, 66

Measurement reliability, 67–69
   instrumentation effects, 127–128
   See also Reliability

Measurement validity Exists when a measure measures what we think it measures, 15, 69–71
   evaluating in research articles, 358
   of existing measures, 71–72
   See also Validity

Measure of association A type of descriptive statistic that summarizes the strength of an association, 312. *See also* Association

Median The point that divides a distribution in half (the 50th percentile), 149, 300–303

Memory questions, 184–185

Meta-analysis The quantitative analysis of findings from multiple studies, 330–333, 335

Meta-synthesis The qualitative analysis of findings from multiple studies, 332

Miles, Matthew B., 259

Miller, Susan, 244–245, 248–249

Miller, William L., 242–243

Mitchell, Christopher G., 122, 356

Mixed-methods research, 13

Mixed-mode surveys Surveys that are conducted by more than one method, allowing the strengths of one survey design to compensate for the weaknesses of another and maximizing the likelihood of securing data from different respondents, 199

Mode The most frequent value in a distribution, 299–300

Model Program Guide, 27, 299–300

Molloy, Jennifer K., 231

Monitoring designs, 158–159, 167

Monitoring goals, 158

Monotonic A pattern of association in which the value of cases on one variable increases or decreases fairly regularly across the categories of another variable.

Monotonic relationship, 311

Morrissey, Joseph P., 30

Mortality effects (differential attrition), 126

Multidimensional scale A scale containing subsets of questions that measure different aspects of the same concept, 56

Multiple baseline designs, 161–164, 171

Multiple treatment designs, 164–167

Multiple treatment interference, 130

Multivariate statistical tests Statistical tests involving two or more independent variables, 316

Mutually exclusive A variable's attributes or values are mutually exclusive when every case can be classified as having only one attribute or value, 59

Nápoles-Springer, Anna M., 231

Narrative analysis A form of qualitative analysis in which the analyst focuses on how respondents impose order on their experiences and make sense of events and actions in which they have participated, 253

National Association of Social Workers (NASW), *Code of Ethics*, 8, 42, 171

National Institutes of Health (NIH), 42
National Registry of Evidence-Based Programs and
    Practices (NREPP), 27
Native American participation, 101
Neal, Margaret B., 229
Needs assessment   A type of evaluation research
    that is used to determine the needs of some
    population, 270–271
Neighborhood police officer study, 244, 248–249
NIH Revitalization Act of 1993, 131
Nimer, Janelle, 333
Nominal definition   Defining a concept using
    other concepts, 52
Nominal level of measurement   Variables whose
    values have no mathematical interpretation;
    they vary in kind or quality, but not in
    amount, 59–60, 292
Noncomparable groups, 126
Nonconcurrent multiple baseline design, 164
Nonequivalent Control Group Design, 121–122
Nonexperimental designs   Weakest form of
    research designs in attributing causality,
    123–125
    After-Only, 125
    evidence-based practice and, 131
    One Group Pretest-Posttest, 123–124
    Static-Group Design, 125
    threats to internal validity, 125–128
Nonprobability sampling methods   Sampling
    methods in which the probability of selection
    of population elements is unknown, 87, 93–97
    availability sampling, 94
    purposive, 96
    quota, 94–95
    snowball sampling, 96–97, 221, 251
    See also Sampling methods
Nonresponse rate, 88, 103, 178–179
Nonspuriousness   A criterion for establishing a
    causal relation between two variables; when a
    relationship between two variables is not due
    to variation in a third variable, 112
Normal distribution   A graph with a shape that
    looks like a bell, with one bump in the
    middle, centered on the population mean, and
    the number of cases tapering off on both sides
    of the mean. This shape is important for
    sampling and statistical analysis,
    97–99, 306–307
Norton, Ilena M., 101
Note taking, 222–224, 245

Nugent, William, 149
Null hypothesis, 314
Nursing home assistant study, 212, 214–216, 219–221,
    223–224
NVivo, 254–256

Office of Protection from Research Risks, 42
One Group Pretest-Posttest Design, 123–124
Online databases, 341
Online search. *See* Web search
Online survey, 191, 198–199, 200–201
Open directory, 350
Open-ended question   A survey question to
    which the respondent replies in his or her own
    words, either by writing or talking, 185–186,
    226, 290
Operational definition   The set of rules and
    operations used to find the value of cases on
    a variable, 53–54
Operational equivalence, 74
Operationalization   The process of specifying the
    operations that will indicate the value of cases
    on a variable, 53–59
Optical scan sheet, 290
Ordinal level of measurement   A measurement
    of a variable in which the numbers indicating
    the variable's values specify only the order of
    the cases, permitting *greater than* and *less
    than* distinctions, 60–61, 292
Ordinary Least Squares (OLS) regression, 149
Organizational behavior theory, 30
Orzol, Sean M., 30
Outcome   The impact of the program process on
    the cases processed, 266, 269
Outcome evaluation   A program evaluation
    designed to measure client or participant
    outcomes, 272–273
    simple or complex outcomes, 278–279
    See also Evaluation research
Outliers, 305
Output   Measures of the services delivered by the
    program process, 265, 266, 268
Overgeneralization   Occurs when we
    unjustifiably conclude that what is true for
    some cases is true for *all* cases, 3

Padgett, Deborah, 12
Panel study   A longitudinal study of the same
    individuals, 38
Parallel forms reliability, 68

Parent training programs, 333

Parsons, Bruce, 333

Participant observation   A qualitative method for gathering data that involves developing a sustained relationship with people while they go about their normal activities, 213, 214, 216–226

complete observation, 216–218

covert participation, 219, 233–234

entering the field, 219–220

ethical issues, 218–219, 233–234

ethnography, 250–251

managing relationships, 220–221

personal dimension management, 223–224

sampling, 221–222

systematic observation, 226

taking notes, 222–224

Participation enhancement for diverse populations, 101–103

Pearson's *r*, 312

Peer review   Journal review involving other researchers or knowledgeable experts to assess the quality of a manuscript, 25, 327

Periodicity, 91

Peters, Ardith, 13

Phone survey   A survey in which interviewers question respondents over the phone and then record their answers, 191, 195–196, 207

advantages and disadvantages, 200–201

computer-assisted, 195, 290

random digit dialing, 89, 195

Photovoice   A qualitative method in which participants both photograph meaningful scenes and interpret the photographs, 230–231, 235

Pilot study   A small initial study to determine the quality of the data collection procedures that will be used in a larger study, 190–191

Placebo effect   A source of treatment misidentification that can occur when subjects who receive a treatment that they consider likely to be beneficial improve because of that expectation rather than because of the treatment itself, 128

Population   The entire set of individuals or other entities to which study findings are to be generalized, 82

defining, 84, 103

homogeneity and sampling error, 88

homogeneity assessment, 85

target, 85, 268

Population parameter   The value of a statistic, such as a mean, computed using the data for the entire population; a sample statistic is an estimate of a population parameter, 98

Population variance, 305

Posavac, Emil J., 120–121

Positivist   The philosophical view that an external objective reality exists apart from human perceptions of it.

Positivist paradigm, 35, 231–232

Postpositivism   A philosophical view that modifies the positivist premise of an external reality by recognizing its complexity, the limitations of human observers, and therefore, the impossibility of developing more than a partial understanding of reality, 35

Posttest   In experimental research, the measurement of an outcome (dependent variable) after an experimental intervention or after a presumed independent variable has changed for some other reason, 117

Posttest-Only Control Group Design, 119

Posttest-Only Design, 125

Practical significance   In an evaluation of the impact of an intervention in a single-subject design, the determination that the intervention has made a meaningful difference in the well-being of the subject, 152

Precision, 54

Predictive validity   The type of validity that exists when a measure predicts scores on a criterion measured in the future, 70

Pretest   In experimental research, the measurement of an outcome (dependent) variable prior to an experimental intervention or change in a presumed independent variable, 117, 190

threats to internal validity, 127, 130

See also Pilot study

Pretest-Posttest Comparison Group Design, 272

Pretest-Posttest Control Group Design, 117–119

Primary sampling units, 83

Privacy, 259

Probability average, 299

Probability of selection   The likelihood that an element will be selected from the population for inclusion in the sample, 87

Probability sampling methods   Sampling methods that rely on a random or chance selection method so that the probability of selection of population elements is known, 87–93. *See also* Random sampling; Sampling methods

Process analysis   A research design in which periodic measures are taken to determine whether a treatment is being delivered as planned, usually in a field experiment, 128, 277

Process evaluation   Evaluation research that investigates the process of service delivery, 271–272

Professional judgment issues, 120

Program evaluation. *See* Evaluation research

Program process   The complete treatment of service delivered by the program, 265

Progressive focusing   The process by which a qualitative analyst interacts with the data and gradually refines his or her focus, 242

Project New Hope, 278

Proportionate stratified sampling   A sampling method in which elements are selected from strata in exact proportion to their representation in the population, 91

Proposal writing, 323–325

Purposive sampling   A nonprobability sampling method in which elements are selected for a purpose, usually because of their unique position, 96, 221

p value, 313

Qualitative comparative analysis   A systematic type of qualitative analysis that identifies the combination of factors that had to be present across multiple cases to produce a particular outcome, 251–253

Qualitative data analysis, 240–242
  as an art, 242–243
  authenticating conclusions, 247–249
  computer-assisted, 254–257
  conceptualization, coding, and categorizing, 245
  content analysis, 257–259
  documentation, 245
  ethical issues, 259–260
  ethnography, 250–251
  examining relationships, 246–247
  grounded theory, 253
  hermeneutic perspective, 241
  narrative analysis, 253
  progressive focusing, 242

  qualitative comparative analysis, 251–253
  quantitative data analysis versus, 241, 243–244
  reflexivity, 249
  techniques of, 244–249

Qualitative methods   Methods such as participant observation, intensive interviewing, and focus groups that are designed to capture social life as participants experience it, rather than in categories predetermined by the researcher. These methods typically involve exploratory research questions, inductive reasoning, an orientation to social context, human objectivity, and the meanings attached by participants to events, 7, 12–13, 212–214
  diversity issues, 231–232
  enhancing quantitative research, 231
  ethical issues, 233–234, 259–260
  ethnography, 250–251
  evaluation research, 232–233, 272, 277–278
  evidence-based practice and, 232–233
  focus groups, 213, 214, 229–230
  intensive interviewing, 213, 214
  mixed-methods, 13
  note taking, 222–224, 245
  nursing home assistant study, 212, 214–216
  participant observation, 213, 214, 216–226
  photovoice, 230–231, 235
  reflexive design, 214
  sampling in, 221–222
  thick description, 215–216

Quantitative data analysis, 287–319
  data preparation, 288–292
  describing relations among variables, 307–313
  displaying univariate distributions, 292–298
  evidence-based practice and, 313–316
  frequency distributions, 292, 294–298
  measures of central tendency, 299–303
  measures of variation, 303–307
  meta-analysis, 330–333, 335
  qualitative data analysis versus, 241
  summarizing univariate distributions, 299–307
  See also Statistical methods

Quantitative methods   Methods such as surveys and experiments that record variation in social life in terms of categories that vary in amount. Data that are treated as quantitative are either numbers or attributes that can be ordered in terms of magnitude, 7, 12–13
  content analysis, 258
  mixed-methods, 13

positivist philosophy, 231–232
qualitative data analysis versus, 243–244
qualitative research and, 231
See also Experimental designs
Quartile The point in a distribution corresponding to the first 25% of the cases, the first 50% of the cases, and the last 25% of the cases, 305
Quasi-experimental design A research design in which at least some of the threats to internal validity are controlled, 121–123
article review example, 347
evaluating in research articles, 360
evidence-based practice and, 131
Nonequivalent Control Group Design, 121–122
threats to internal validity, 125–128
time series, 122–123
Questionnaire The survey instrument containing the questions in a self-administered survey, 180
Questionnaire design and construction, 180–181
avoiding agreement bias, 186–187
closed-ended and open-ended questions, 185–186
existing instruments, 180–181
filter questions and skip patterns, 187–188
Likert-type response categories, 188
matrix questions, 188–189
memory questions, 184–185
minimizing fence-sitting and floating, 187
pretest and pilot study, 190–191
question clarity, 181–184
question order, 181
reducing bias risk, 184
scales, 189
sensitive questions, 189–190, 197
social desirability, 187
writing response categories, 186–188
See also Survey research
Quota sampling A nonprobability sampling method in which elements are selected to ensure that the sample represents certain characteristics in proportion to their prevalence in the population, 94–95, 221

Racial/ethnic diversity. *See* Diversity issues
Random assignment A procedure by which each experimental subject is randomly placed in a group, 113–116
ethical issues, 282
random sampling versus, 115

Random digit dialing The random dialing by a machine of numbers within designated phone prefixes, which creates a random sample for phone surveys, 89, 195
Random error Errors in measurement that are due to chance and are not systematic in any way, 66–67
sample size and, 67
Randomization, 114, 131
Randomized clinical trials, 113. *See also* Experimental designs
Random numbers table A table containing lists of numbers that are ordered solely on the basis of chance; it is used for drawing a random sample, 89, 90
Random sampling A method of sampling that relies on a random or chance selection method so that every element of the sampling frame has a known probability of being selected, 87
cluster, 93
random assignment versus, 115
simple, 89
stratified, 91–92
systematic, 89–91
threats to professional judgment, 120
Random sampling error Differences between the population and the sample that are due only to chance factors (random error), not to systematic sampling error. Random sampling error may or may not result in an unrepresentative sample. This can be estimated statistically, 98
Random selection, 87, 129
Randomization The random assignment of cases, such as by the toss of a coin.
Range The true upper limit in a distribution minus the true lower limit (or the highest rounded value minus the lowest rounded value), 304–305
Ratio level of measurement A variable in which the numbers indicating the variable's values represent fixed measuring units *and* an absolute zero point, 64, 292
Reactive effects The changes in an individual or group behavior due to being observed or otherwise studied, 217
Reactivity Changes in an individual or group behavior due to the process of measurement or the impact of the research design, 130, 148

Recall loss, 184
Reductionist fallacy, 100
Reflexive research design, 214
Reflexivity, 249
Regression to the mean, 66
Relationship analysis, 246–247
Relevance validity, 281
Reliability   A criterion to assess the quality of
    scales based on whether the procedure yields
    consistent scores when the phenomenon being
    measured is not changing, 67–69
  alternate-forms, 68
  instrumentation effects, 127–128
  internal consistency, 68
  interrater, 69
  intrarater, 69
  of existing measures, 71–72
  split-half, 68
  test-retest, 67–68
Repeated measurement, single-subject design, 141
  replication strategies, 169–170
Repeated Measures Panel Designs, 122
Replication strategies, 169–170
Report writing, 322–323
  applied research reports, 328–330
  diversity issues, 334–335
  ethical issues, 335–336
  evidence-based practice and, 333–334
  general writing guidelines, 323–325
  meta-analysis, 330–333, 335
  research proposal, 323–325
  writing for journals, 327–328
Representative sample   A sample that "looks
    like" the population from which it was
    selected in all respects potentially relevant to
    the study. The distribution of characteristics
    among the elements of a representative
    sample is the same as the distribution of those
    characteristics among the total population. In
    an unrepresentative sample, some
    characteristics are overrepresented or
    underrepresented, 85
Research circle   A diagram of the elements of the
    research process, including theories, hypotheses,
    data collection, and data analysis, 31, 34
Research designs:
  cross-sectional, 36, 206
  deductive, 30–34, 36
  descriptive research, 9, 35
  diversity issues, 131–132

ethical issues, 132–134
evaluation research, 11–12, 34
evidence-based practice and, 130–131
explanatory research, 10–11, 34
exploratory research, 9–10
goals of, 158
inductive, 30, 34–36
longitudinal, 36–39, 206
nonexperimental, 123–125
single-article review example, 346–347
threats to internal validity, 125–128
See also Experimental designs; Qualitative methods;
    Quantitative methods; Quasi-experimental
    designs; Survey research
Research literature review. *See* Literature review
Research paradigms, 35–36
Research proposals, 323–325, 335
Research question:
  development of, 24–28
  diversity issues, 27
  evidence-based practice, 26–27
  feasibility, importance, and relevance, 24–25
  identifying in research articles, 341, 356–357
  single-article review example, 346
Resentful demoralization   This problem for
    experimental designs occurs when comparison
    group members perform worse than they
    otherwise might have because they feel they
    have been left out of a valuable treatment, 128
Resistance to change   The reluctance to change
    our ideas in light of new information, 5
Resource dependency theory, 30
Response ambiguities, 288–290
Response rate, 88, 103
  strategies for increasing, 192, 194, 195–196, 198
Response set   Occurs when a respondent, asked a
    series of questions that have the same set of
    response categories, provides the same
    response for each question, 189
Reverse outlining, 327
Rivard, Jeanne C., 30
Rizzo, Victoria M., 340
Rogers, Robin, 34
Rosen, Daniel, 230
Rowe, Jeannine M., 340

Sacks, Stanley, 273
Sample   A subset of a population that is used to
    study the population as a whole, 82
  representative, 85

Sample generalizability   Exists when a conclusion based on a sample, or subset, of a larger population holds true for that population, 15–16, 84, 129, 178

Sample size:
  random error effects and, 67
  sampling error and, 88–89, 315
  statistical power and, 103–104, 131

Sample statistic   The value of a statistic, such as a mean, computed from sample data, 98

Sample variance, 305

Sampling, 81
  defining the population, 84, 103
  diversity issues, 19
  elements and units, 82–83
  evaluating in research articles, 359
  in field research, 221
  population homogeneity assessment, 85
  purposive, 221
  qualitative methods, 221–222
  quota, 221
  random selection, 87
  stratified, 91–92
  theoretical, 221
  units of analysis, 99–100

Sampling distribution   The hypothetical distribution of a statistic across all the random samples that could be drawn from a population, 97–99

Sampling distribution of the mean, 97

Sampling error   Any difference between the characteristics of a sample and the characteristics of a population. The larger the sample error, the less representative the sample, 84–85, 88
  cluster samples and, 93
  population homogeneity and, 88
  random, 98
  sample size and, 88–89, 315
  sampling distributions and, 97
  systematic, 98

Sampling frame   A list of all elements or other units containing the elements in a population, 87–88

Sampling interval   The number of cases from one sampled case to another in a systematic random sample, 90

Sampling methods, 86–87
  cluster, 93
  convenience or availability, 94

ethical issues, 97
evidence-based practice and, 103–104
nonprobability, 87, 93–97
probability, 87–93
purposive, 96
quota, 94–95
snowball, 96–97, 221, 251
See also Random sampling

Sampling units   Units listed at each stage of a multistage sampling design, 83

Sands, Robert G., 28–29

Saturation point   The point at which subject selection is ended in intensive interviewing, when new interviews seem to yield little additional information, 227

Scaler equivalence, 74

Scale   A composite measure based on combining the responses to multiple questions pertaining to a common concept, 55–56, 189
  clinical screening tools, 72–74
  diversity issues, 74–75
  multidimensional, 56
  response sets, 189

Scatterplot   A graph of individual responses to two continuous variables, 310

Schneider, Elizabeth, 340

Schutt, Russell K., 389

Science   A set of logical, systematic, documented methods for investigating nature and natural processes; the knowledge produced by these investigations, 6
  uses of, 41–42

Scientific relevance of research, 25

Search engines, 351–352

Searching the literature. *See* Literature review

Secondary data   Previously collected data that are used in a new analysis, 201–202

Secondary sampling units, 83

Secular drift   A type of contamination in true experimental and quasi-experimental designs that occurs when broader social or economic trends influence the findings of a study, 127

Seefeldt, Kristen, 30

Selection bias   A source of internal (causal) invalidity that occurs when characteristics of experimental and comparison groups differ in any way that influences the outcome, 126

Selective observation   Choosing to look only at things that are in line with our preferences or beliefs, 3

Self-esteem measures, 74

Semantic equivalence, 204

Sensitive questions, 189–190, 197

Sensitivity The proportion of true positives, which is based on the number of people assessed as having a diagnosis by a screening instrument, to the number of people who actually have the condition, 73–74

Sequential replication strategies, 169–170

Serendipitous findings Unexpected patterns in data that stimulate new ideas or theoretical approaches, 31

Service completions, 268–269

Shapiro, Janet R., 226

Shapiro, Margaret, 258

Significance of single-subject research results, 152

Simple random sampling A method of sampling in which every sample element is selected only on the basis of chance through a random process, 89

Singer, Muriel, 233

Single-subject design, 7, 139–146
  baseline phase (A), 141–146
  basic design (A-B), 158–159, 167
  clinical significance of findings, 152
  data analysis and interpretation, 148–157
  diversity issues, 170
  ethical issues, 170–171
  evidence-based practice and, 167–170
  generalizability, 169
  goals of, 158
  graphical data representation, 146
  internal validity, 143, 146
  measurement, 146–148
  monitoring, 158–159, 167
  multiple baseline designs, 161–164
  multiple treatment designs, 164–167
  repeated measurement, 141
  replication strategies, 169–170
  treatment phase, 146
  types of, 158
  withdrawal, 159–161

Skewness The extent to which cases are clustered more at one or the other end of the distribution of a quantitative variable, rather than in a symmetric pattern around its center. Skew can be positive (a right skew), with the number of cases tapering off in the positive direction, or negative (a left skew), with the number of cases tapering off in the negative direction, 292, 301

Skip patterns The unique combination of questions created in a survey by filter questions and contingency questions, 187–188

Smith, Mary Lindsey, 230

Snow, David A., 251–253

Snowball sampling A method of sampling in which sample elements are selected as they are identified by successive informants or interviewees, 96–97, 221, 251
  ethical issues, 97

Social desirability The tendency for individuals to respond in ways that make them appear in the best light to the interviewer, 66, 187

Social science The use of scientific methods to investigate individuals, societies, and social processes; the knowledge produced by these investigations, 2, 6

Social scientific approach, 276–277

Social theory. *See* Theory

Social work research:
  ethical guidelines for, 40–45
  evidence-based practice, 7–8
  need for, 6–7
  research question development, 24–28
  scientific guidelines for, 39–40
  strengths and limitations of, 13–14
  See also Research designs

Solomon Four Group Design, 119–120

Spanish language instruments, 204–205

Specificity The proportion of true negatives based on the number of people assessed as not having a diagnosis by a screening instrument relative to the number who really do not have the diagnosis, 73–74

Split-half reliability Reliability achieved when responses to the same questions by two randomly selected halves of a sample are about the same, 68

Spurious relationship, 112, 318

Stable line A line in the baseline phase that is relatively flat, with little variability in the scores so that the scores fall in a narrow band, 142

Staff expectancy effects, 128

Stake, Robert E., 245

Stakeholder approach An orientation to evaluation research that expects researchers to be responsive primarily to the people involved with the program, 276

Stakeholder participatory research, 276

Stakeholders Individuals and groups who have some basis of concern with the program, 266

Standard deviation The square root of the average squared deviation of each case from the mean, 305–307

Stanfield, John H., 281

Statistical methods, 287–288
  central tendency measures, 299–303
  choosing a statistical test, 316
  confidence interval, 99
  ethical issues, 316–318
  evaluating in research articles, 361
  evidence-based practice and, 313–316
  graphical data representation, 292–294
  inferential, 98
  measures of association, 312
  meta-analysis, 330–333, 335
  sampling distribution, 97–99
  single-subject data analysis, 148–149
  Type I and Type II errors, 314–316
  variable relationships, 307–313
  variation measures, 303–307
  See also Quantitative data analysis

Statistical power, 103–104, 131

Statistical power analysis, 316

Statistical programs, 291

Statistical regression, 127, 146, 360

Statistical significance The mathematical likelihood that an association is not due to chance, judged by a criterion set by the analyst (often that the probability is less than 5 out of 100, or $p < .05$), 313–316

Stewart, Anita L., 231

Stoops, Charles, 346–347

Stratified random sampling A method of sampling in which sample elements are selected separately from population strata that are identified in advance by the researcher, 91–92

Stress theory, 28–29

Structured interview, 39

Student *t*-test, 316

Subject directories, 350–351

Substance abuse, 52

Sullivan, William M., 228

Summary statistics, 299. *See also* Statistical methods

Survey of Income and Program Participation, 38

Survey research A research method in which information is obtained from a sample of individuals through their responses to questions about themselves or others, 176–177
  cognitive interview, 190
  cost considerations, 192
  design advantages and disadvantages, 199–201
  design alternatives, 191–192
  diversity issues, 19, 203–205
  errors in, 178–180
  ethical issues, 206–207, 318
  evidence-based practice and, 205–206
  focus groups, 190
  generalizability, 178
  group-administered, 191, 194, 207
  in-person interview, 191, 197–198, 200–201
  instrument translation, 204–205
  mail, 191, 192–194, 200–201, 207
  mixed-mode, 199
  online, 191, 198–199, 200–201
  phone, 89, 191, 195–196, 200–201, 207, 290
  pilot study, 190–191
  secondary data, 201–202
  versatility and efficiency of, 177
  See also Questionnaire design and construction

Swidler, Ann, 228

Systematic bias, 87
  random sampling and, 88–89

Systematic error Error due to a specific process that biases the results, 66

Systematic observation A strategy that increases the reliability of observational data by using explicit rules that standardize coding practices across observers, 226

Systematic random sampling A method of sampling in which sample elements are selected from a list or from sequential files, with every *n*th element being selected after the first element is selected randomly within the first interval, 89–91

Systematic replication Repeating a single-subject design in different settings, using different providers, and other related behaviors to increase generalizability, 169

Systematic review A summary review of the impact of an intervention in which the analyst tries to account, for example, for differences in design and participant characteristics, often using statistical techniques such as meta-analysis, 26

Systematic sampling error   Overrepresentation or underrepresentation of some population characteristics in a sample due to the method used to select the sample. A sample shaped by systematic sampling error is a biased sample, 98

Systematic scientific approach, 39

Tacit knowledge   In field research, a credible sense of understanding of social processes that reflects the researcher's awareness of participants' actions as well as their words, and of what they fail to state, feel deeply, and take for granted, 248

Tape recording, 228

Target   The focus of an intervention; it is the dependent variable in a single-subject design, 141, 147–148, 158

Target population   A set of elements larger than or different from the population sampled and to which the researcher would like to generalize study findings, 85, 268

Technical equivalence, 204

Telephone surveys. *See* Phone surveys

Telescoping effect   Remembering an event as happening more recently than when it really occurred, 184

Temporary Assistance for Needy Families (TANF), 87, 127, 134

Testing effects, 68, 130, 146
    regression to the mean, 66
    Solomon Four Group Design and, 119–120
    threats to internal validity, 127

Test-retest reliability   A type of reliability that is demonstrated by showing that the same measure of a phenomenon at two points in time is highly correlated, assuming that the phenomenon has not changed, 67–68

Testing effect   Measurement error related to how a test is given, the conditions of the testing including environmental conditions, and acclimation to the test itself.

Text analysis. *See* Qualitative data analysis

Theoretical construct validity, 70

Theoretical sampling   A sampling method recommended for field research; the sample is drawn in a sequential fashion, with settings or individuals selected for study as earlier observations or interviews indicate that these settings or individuals are influential.

Theoretical sampling, 221

Theory   A logically interrelated set of propositions about reality, 28–30, 40
    deductive research and, 30
    grounded, qualitative data analysis, 253
    logic models, 266
    research circle, 31, 34

Theory-driven evaluation   A program evaluation that is guided by a theory that specifies the process by which the program has an effect, 275

Therapeutic communities, 274

Thick description   A rich description that conveys a sense of what a phenomenon or situation is like from the standpoint of the actors in that setting, 215–216

Tichon, Jennifer G., 258

Time order   A criterion for establishing a causal relation between two variables. The variation in the presumed cause (the independent variable) must occur before the variation in the presumed effect (the dependent variable), 112, 118

Time series designs, 122–123

Tipton, Steven M., 228

Training interviewers, 102

Translational research, 334

Translation of instruments, 204–205

Treatment, as variable, 56–58

Treatment misidentification, 128

Treatment phase (B)   The intervention phase of a single-subject design, 146

Trend   Repeated measurement scores which are ascending or descending in magnitude; used in single-subject design, , 142, 149

Trend lines, single-subject data, 142, 149, 151

Trend studies   Longitudinal studies in which data are collected at two or more points in time from different samples of the same population, 37–38

Triangulation   The use of multiple methods to study one research question, 58

True experimental research designs   Group designs that are used to test the causal relationship between the independent and dependent variables. When these designs are used, the researcher can show that the independent variable occurs prior to the change in the dependent variable, that there is a statistical association, and that other explanations (internal validity) can be ruled out, 113–121. *See also* Experimental designs

True negative When it is determined from a screening instrument score that the participant does not have a particular status, and the participant really does not have the status based on a clinical evaluation, 73

True positive When it is determined from a screening instrument score that the participant has a particular status, and the participant really does have the status based on a clinical evaluation, 73

True score, 65–66

Tsemberis, Sam, 12

Type I error Error that occurs when there is evidence of a statistical relationship between two variables based on the sample, but in fact, there is no relationship between the two variables, 314–316

Type II error Error that occurs when there is no evidence of a statistical relationship between two variables based on the sample, but in fact, the two variables are related, 315–316

Ultimate outcome, 269

Underclass, 100

Unimodal distribution, 299

Unit of analysis The level of social life on which a research question is focused, 99–100, 359

Units of observation, 99

Univariate distributions
    displaying, 292–298
    summarizing, 299–307

Urban Institute, 9

U.S. Bureau of the Census, 202

Uses of science, 41–42

Vagueness, in survey questions, 182, 183

Validity The state that exists when statements or conclusions about empirical reality are correct, 14
    causal, 17–18, 111
    concurrent, 70
    construct, 70, 71
    content, 69–70
    convergent, 71
    criterion, 70, 71
    discriminant, 70
    diversity issues, 19
    evaluating in research articles, 358
    external, 84, 129, 131, 132, 169

face, 69
    internal, 112, 115–116, 118, 125–128, 143, 146, 360
    known-groups, 71
    measurement, 15, 69–71
    of existing measures, 71–72
    predictive, 70
    relevance, 281
    threats to internal validity, 125–128
    See also Generalizability; Internal validity

Van Winkle, Barrik, 256–257

Variability The extent to which cases are spread out through the distribution or clustered in just one location, 150, 292, 299
    measures of variation, 305

Variables Characteristics or properties that can take on different values or attributes, 32–34, 55–56, 59–65
    association between, 33–34, 111
    concepts and, 52–53
    describing relations between, 307–313
    dichotomies, 64
    discrete and continuous, 58
    intervention as, 56–58
    operationalization of, 53–59
    See also Dependent variable; Independent variable; Levels of measurement

Variance A statistic that measures the variability of a distribution as the average squared deviation of each case from the mean, 305

Visual analysis, 149-157

Walton, Elaine, 110, 111, 112, 113, 119

Wang, Caroline, 230

Ware, Norma, 224

Web search, 343–345, 349–352
    electronic reference formats, 349
    search engines, 351–352
    subject directories, 350–351

Web survey, 191, 198–199, 200–201

Weiss, Carol H., 266

Welfare reform, 127

Withdrawal designs, 159–161

Women, Infants, and Children (WIC) program, 206

Writing reports. *See* Report writing

Yahoo!, 350

Yancey, Gaynor, 34

Youth Quality of Life scale, 204

Zimbardo, Philip G., 43

About the Authors

Rafael J. Engel, PhD, is an Associate Professor at the University of Pittsburgh (Pennsylvania). He received his PhD (1988) from the University of Wisconsin, his MSW (1979) from the University of Michigan, and his BA (1978) from the University of Pennsylvania. He coordinates the graduate certificate program in aging and is the Principal Investigator for the Hartford Partnership Program for Aging Education. He has authored journal articles on such topics as poverty in later life, welfare benefits, and depressive symptomatology, and he has written a variety of monographs reporting agency-based evaluations. His research experience includes funded research studies on faith-based organizations and employment in late life as well as funded evaluation research studies on welfare-to-work programs and drug and alcohol prevention programs. His most recent research involves human service capacity to treat gambling-related problems.

Russell K. Schutt, PhD, is a Professor of Sociology at the University of Massachusetts, Boston, and a Lecturer on Sociology in the Department of Psychiatry (Beth Israel–Deaconess Medical Center) at the Harvard Medical School. He completed his BA, MA, and PhD (1977) degrees at the University of Illinois at Chicago and was a Postdoctoral Fellow in the Sociology of Social Control Training Program at Yale University (1977–1979). In addition to *Investigating the Social World: The Process and Practice of Research* (now in its 6th edition), *Making Sense of the Social World* (with Dan Chambliss), and adaptations for the fields of social work (with Ray Engel) and criminology/criminal justice (with Ronet Bachman), he is the author of *Organization in a Changing Environment,* coeditor of *The Organizational Response to Social Problems,* and coauthor of *Responding to the Homeless: Policy and Practice.* He has authored and coauthored numerous journal articles, book chapters, and research reports on homelessness, service preferences and satisfaction, mental health, organizations, law, and teaching research methods. His recently funded research experience includes a National Cancer Institute–funded study of community health workers and recruitment for cancer clinical trials, a large translational research project for the Massachusetts Department of Public Health's Women's Health Network, a National Institute of Mental Health–funded study of housing alternatives for homeless persons diagnosed with severe mental illness, and evaluations of case management programs in the Massachusetts Department of Public Health and the Massachusetts Department of Mental Health. His publications in peer-reviewed journals range in focus from the effect of social context on cognition, satisfaction, and functioning to the service preferences of homeless persons and service personnel, the admission practices of craft unions, and the social factors in legal decisions.

Supporting researchers for more than 40 years

Research methods have always been at the core of SAGE's publishing program. Founder Sara Miller McCune published SAGE's first methods book, *Public Policy Evaluation*, in 1970. Soon after, she launched the *Quantitative Applications in the Social Sciences* series—affectionately known as the "little green books."

Always at the forefront of developing and supporting new approaches in methods, SAGE published early groundbreaking texts and journals in the fields of qualitative methods and evaluation.

Today, more than 40 years and two million little green books later, SAGE continues to push the boundaries with a growing list of more than 1,200 research methods books, journals, and reference works across the social, behavioral, and health sciences. Its imprints—Pine Forge Press, home of innovative textbooks in sociology, and Corwin, publisher of PreK–12 resources for teachers and administrators—broaden SAGE's range of offerings in methods. SAGE further extended its impact in 2008 when it acquired CQ Press and its best-selling and highly respected political science research methods list.

From qualitative, quantitative, and mixed methods to evaluation, SAGE is the essential resource for academics and practitioners looking for the latest methods by leading scholars.

For more information, visit **www.sagepub.com**.